THE UNITED NATIONS SYSTEM

THE UNITED NATIONS SYSTEM

Toward International Justice

Nigel D. White

LYNNE
RIENNER
PUBLISHERS

BOULDER
LONDON

Published in the United States of America in 2002 by
Lynne Rienner Publishers, Inc.
1800 30th Street, Boulder, Colorado 80301
www.rienner.com

and in the United Kingdom by
Lynne Rienner Publishers, Inc.
3 Henrietta Street, Covent Garden, London WC2E 8LU

Library of Congress Cataloging-in-Publication Data
White, N. D., 1961–
    The United Nations system : toward international justice / Nigel White.
        p. cm.
    Includes bibliographical references and index.
    ISBN 1-58826-065-8 (alk. paper) — ISBN 1-58826-070-4 (pbk. : alk. paper)
    1. United Nations. I. Title.
JZ4984.5. W48   2002
341.23—dc21   2002017808

British Cataloguing in Publication Data
A Cataloguing in Publication record for this book
is available from the British Library.

Printed and bound in the United States of America

        The paper used in this publication meets the requirements
  ∞   of the American National Standard for Permanence of
        Paper for Printed Library Materials Z39.48-1984.

    5 4 3 2 1

Contents

Preface

In this book I critically evaluate the goals, purposes, and values of the United Nations system, analyze the institutional machinery created to fulfill those purposes, and examine the implementation of those goals—largely from a legal perspective. First, I develop a legal and conceptual analysis of values; I then move to a legal and political analysis of the structure and powers of the various UN bodies, and to an evaluation of its activities in light of its values.

The book is divided into three parts. Part 1 contains a discussion of the legal character of the UN family and system, addressing the existence of a UN system, its legal parameters, and the legal order produced by it. I also look at the legal evolution of the UN system, considering the living nature of the UN Charter and how it has been reshaped over the years. The limit of what I call "subsequent practice" is a critical aspect of this analysis. Finally, I consider the values of the UN system as found in the treaties and as developed by its organizations, judicial bodies, and other bodies. Peace and security, justice and law, human rights, self-determination, the environment, and economic and social well-being are the values I consider; their interrelationships are fully explored.

Part 2 contains an institutional examination of the United Nations and reflects a somewhat abstract analysis. The major issues examined include power, democracy, legitimacy, and accountability. Where does the power lie within the UN? What is the legal nature of this power? Is it democratic? Is it accountable politically and/or legally? How are non-state actors involved in the system? Should they be involved and, if so, should it be restricted to nongovernmental organizations? Should it also include civil society organizations? The role of the International Court of Justice—in particular its constitutional role—is also considered. I also examine how the system is coordinated, including an analysis of how mechanisms like the Administrative Committee on Coordination currently operate.

Part 3 contains an examination of UN mechanisms, procedures, and activities in the areas of security, democracy, justice, human rights, the environment, and development in order to reflect the current practical focus of UN activities. Again the intention is not to be comprehensive, with no independent analysis of the UN technical organizations. My aim is not to add flesh to the norms and mechanisms operating within the UN system, but to consider the delivery of the values identified in Part 1 via the machinery outlined in Part 2. Is the United Nations upholding and protecting its own values, or do aspects of it deviate from its constitutional parameters?

Of course UN values and constitutional law are not the only benchmarks against which to consider UN practice. In Part 3 I also comment on effectiveness, a subjective concept. To use P. Alston's critique of the UN human rights system—some may be "satisfied with a focused discussion in an international forum," but "others might insist upon a formal condemnation or at least the establishment of a fact-finding and reporting mechanism," and "still others might be unsatisfied with anything less than the imposition of sanctions or even the mounting of a military exercise designed to restore respect for human rights."[1] Evaluations of the effectiveness of the UN system in protecting UN values vary according to different assumptions about what is considered to be effective protection of human rights. This is compounded, as Alston states, by the difficult issue of "causality," meaning the problem of identifying whether it was the United Nations, or other factors, or a combination thereof, that helped alleviate an abusive situation.[2] Given the relative nature of the concept of effectiveness, as well as the problematic nature of causation, Part 3 evaluates UN actions against the standards outlined in Part 1 at two levels: first, the implementation of those standards by various mechanisms and techniques; and second, the effect of those actions on the ground, considered in general terms. The reader can then judge the effectiveness (or ineffectiveness) of the United Nations. It is not my intent to enter into a facile debate about whether the United Nations is good or bad, something that unfortunately dominates political debate at the moment.

This book is being published in the midst of dramatic world events that are redefining not only relationships among states but also the role that nonstate actors play. My analysis is intended to provide a useful basis from which we may consider the longer-term effects of these events, as well as the responses of the international community.

* * *

I would like to thank Angus Todd, the research assistant for Chapters 10 and 11, and Alexander Beck, the research assistant for Chapter 7.

I would like to express deep gratitude to my wife, Gillian (particularly for reading the manuscript), and my sons, Daniel and Hugh (particularly for taking my mind off it). I would also like to thank my parents, David and Barbara, for their support over the years.

Notes

1. Alston, "Appraising the United Nations," 1.
2. Ibid., 13.

PART 1

The Legal Nature
of the United Nations

1

A UN System

Is There a UN System?

The United Nations is not merely the monolithic intergovernmental organization (IGO) based in New York that consists of headline-grabbing political organs—the Security Council, the General Assembly, and the Secretariat headed by the UN Secretary-General. Additionally there are lesser known organs—the Economic and Social Council (ECOSOC), the Trusteeship Council, and the ICJ, which is headquartered in The Hague. Although article 7 of the UN Charter of 1945 lists them as the "principal organs of the United Nations," there are many specialized UN agencies that are intergovernmental organizations in their own right, possessing separate councils, assemblies, secretariats, and budgets, with headquarters around the globe. The main agencies are the International Labour Organization (ILO) based in Geneva; the Food and Agriculture Organization of the United Nations (FAO) based in Rome; the United Nations Educational, Scientific, and Cultural Organization (UNESCO) based in Paris; the World Health Organization (WHO) based in Geneva; the International Civil Aviation Organization (ICAO) based in Montreal; the International Maritime Organization (IMO) based in London; the World Meteorological Organization (WMO) based in Geneva; the Universal Postal Union (UPU) based in Berne; the International Telecommunications Union (ITU) based in Geneva; the International Monetary Fund (IMF) based in Washington, D.C.; the World Bank (the Bank) based in Washington, D.C.; the World Intellectual Property Organization (WIPO) based in Geneva; the International Fund for

3

Agricultural Development (IFAD) based in Rome; and the United Nations Industrial Development Organization (UNIDO) based in Vienna.

In addition, other IGOs, though not recognized as specialized UN agencies, do have a relationship with the United Nations, either with the General Assembly—like the International Atomic Energy Agency (IAEA) based in Vienna—or ECOSOC—like the World Tourism Organization based in Madrid. All the specialized UN agencies named above, plus the other two organizations, are recognized as having an international legal personality separate from that of the UN organization in New York (see Chapter 2). Put simply, this means they are independent legal persons, possessing legal rights and being subject to legal duties; along with similar IGOs outside the UN grouping, they are the subjects of international law along with states—the traditional actors in the international arena.

There are additional entities—powerful subsidiary organs of the United Nations—established by the main political organs such as the General Assembly under article 22 of the charter. Although not separate IGOs, they have a large degree of autonomy in their activities. The main bodies are the United Nations Development Programme (UNDP) based in New York; the United Nations Children's Fund (UNICEF) based in New York; the United Nations High Commissioner for Refugees (UNHCR) based in Geneva; the United Nations Institute for Training and Research (UNITAR) based in Geneva; the United Nations Relief and Works Agency for Palestine Refugees in the Near East (UNRWA) based in Amman; the United Nations Conference on Trade and Development (UNCTAD) based in Geneva; the World Food Programme (WFP) based in Rome; the United Nations Environment Programme (UNEP) based in Nairobi; the United Nations Fund for Population Activities (UNFPA) based in New York; and the United Nations High Commissioner for Human Rights based in Geneva.

ECOSOC itself has established subsidiary bodies pursuant to article 68 of the UN Charter (e.g., the Human Rights Commission established in 1946) and the five regional economic commissions (e.g., the Economic Commission for Africa [ECA] established in 1958). In addition, the Security Council has established subsidiary bodies under article 29 of the UN Charter. Examples include fact-finding bodies; committees established to oversee the implementation of economic sanctions ordered by the council using its powers contained in article 41 of the charter; a compensation commission in relation to Iraq's invasion of Kuwait; and international criminal tribunals to try war crimes or other international crimes in the former Yugoslavia and Rwanda. In addition to the International Criminal Tribunal for the Former Yugoslavia (ICTY) and the International Criminal Tribunal for Rwanda (ICTR) sitting in The Hague and Arusha, respectively, the Security Council and the General Assembly have established a plethora of observation, peacekeeping, human rights, and election monitoring bodies in countries around the world.

In addition to this incomplete list of bodies directly established by the constitutive treaties of the United Nations and its specialized agencies or established as subsidiary organs by those bodies, there is an increasing number of bodies established under treaties sponsored by the United Nations. For example, the Third UN Conference of the Law of the Sea produced the codificatory and legislative Law of the Sea Convention of 1982, which entered into force in 1994.[1] This treaty established several bodies, principally the International Tribunal for the Law of the Sea and the International Sea-Bed Authority. Another example is the Human Rights Committee (HRC) established under the International Covenant on Civil and Political Rights (ICCPR) signed in 1966 after negotiations and drafting by the UN Human Rights Commission.[2] Regarding the environment the UN Earth Summit held in Rio in 1992 produced, inter alia, the Framework Convention on Climate Change, which provides for the creation of a subsidiary body for the implementation of the treaty.[3] The UN-sponsored conference in Rome in June 1998 that led to the signing of a treaty to establish the International Criminal Court (ICC) is just the latest that can be included within the UN family.[4]

A cursory examination of the organizations, organs, committees, and individuals operating under the UN umbrella raises the question of whether they are part of a complex whole or are unconnected, disparate entities. Alternatively, these entities may form various, possibly changing, groupings but do not form part of a UN system or UN family. In other words, there are at least three alternative conceptions of the United Nations: First, it is a collection of autonomous groupings of states, each grouping having its own agenda; second, the UN umbrella enables those entities operating under it to form systems that address different goals; and finally, one can view the United Nations as a complete, functioning system.

For example, the first conception would see the Human Rights Commission (established by ECOSOC in 1946) as having its own agenda that is not being coordinated with the UN's other goals or bodies, even those dealing with human rights. The second conception would view the United Nations bodies grouping together under various goals and functions such as human rights with some degree of coordination, so that there will be a UN human rights system of which the UN Human Rights Commission is but a part. The final conception would see the United Nations as a system aiming to achieve goals and perform functions in a coordinated way. For instance, the protection of human rights by the Human Rights Commission would be seen as one facet of the United Nations compatible with and integral to its other goals and functions, such as the prevention of war, the improvement of the environment, and the like that are furthered and protected by other UN entities.

From this preliminary analysis, the three conceptions can be defined more precisely.

The Conference Model

The United Nations provides an umbrella—a label—under which all the bodies mentioned above act in an uncoordinated, almost anarchic way. These bodies are convenient forums or conference venues for states to meet on sundry issues. There is no sense that they are acting within the context of a wider system with integrated and coordinated functions and goals. In many ways this picture of the United Nations is based on the premise that international organizations and other forms of cooperation are created, dominated, and controlled by states. States are the original and complete actors on the international plane, whereas organizations are derivative and reflective of the state-based system. The portrayal of the self-interested state as the dominant actor results in a "pessimistic analysis of the prospects for international co-operation and the capabilities of international institutions."[5] Although there appears to be some cooperation by states, coming together in varying combinations in the various entities acting under the UN umbrella, the lack of coordinated direction to these bodies gives them the appearance of convenient conference venues for states to meet and formalize the balance of power among them in different contexts.[6] The derivative nature of those bodies signifies that they do not have any controlling effect on the states themselves through the enactment and enforcement of rules and principles. The organizations, organs, and bodies acting under the UN umbrella are reflections of states; they do not control state behavior.[7] States "function in [an] . . . environment that is defined by their own interests, power, and interaction. These orientations are resistant to the contention that principles, norms, rules, and decision making procedures have a significant impact on outcomes and behaviour."[8]

The weakness of the conference model is that it ignores the sheer number of entities operating under the UN umbrella. States would not create so many costly bodies out of self-interest unless an extreme view is taken that such bodies do help cement the status quo in international relations, perpetuating dominance by nation-states.[9] Nevertheless, the inherent hierarchy and inequity of this vision does not really explain why disadvantaged states meet powerful states—the sole beneficiaries of such a conception—in these forums. To contend that international organizations perpetuate, indeed legitimate, Eurocentric dominance is to deny smaller, developing, and even enlightened states any free will, any ability to change the world.[10] International bodies are potentially concrete mechanisms for checking the ambitions of powerful states. The plethora of bodies acting under the UN umbrella, some of which are dominated by powerful states, cannot be explained as maintaining the status quo. This leaves the possibility that the conference model still holds but that the uncoordinated entities acting under it do affect state behavior—each is a basic regime or "an intervening variable" that "stands between basic causal factors on the one hand and outcomes and behaviour on the other."[11] However, this ignores the fact that there does appear to be some coordination under the umbrella. Indeed there appears to be a hierarchy, which would suggest that there is not a jumble of bodies in which states meet and possibly regulate state behavior; rather there are systems or networks, no matter how weak, within that mass of bodies. Put simply, the conference model is too unrealistic despite its realist underpinnings.

The Systems Model

If the United Nations cannot be explained as a collection of entities acting in uncoordinated ways, then there must be UN systems although not necessarily a UN system. One way of explaining the systems that operate under the rubric of the United Nations is to ask whether there are regimes that consist of "persistent sets of rules that constrain activity, shape expectations, and prescribe roles" operating within UN bodies.[12] This analysis could be applied to each individual entity acting under the aegis of the United Nations. However, a more subtle approach is to state that a regime is a "set of implicit or explicit principles, norms, rules and decision-making procedures around which actors' expectations converge *in a given area of international relations*."[13] Thus there could be systems that cut across bodies and institutions such as human rights, collective security, environmental matters, and labor conditions. Some of these may be addressed within only one of the UN entities identified above. For example, the ILO has the main competence in regard to labor conditions. Others are more likely to be addressed across those bodies. Likewise, human rights are addressed by organs within the United Nations (the Security Council, the General Assembly, and the ICJ), several specialized agencies (UNESCO, ILO), several subsidiary organs (the Human Rights Commission), as well as bodies created under UN-sponsored treaties (the HRC). There is some coordination of these regimes, so it can be said that there are least weak systems within the United Nations. The question then arises as to whether these are systems per se or are subsystems within an overall UN system.

The System Model

Whereas the portrait of the United Nations as an umbrella for the grouping of states reflects a state-dominated international system, viewing the United Nations as having systems within it is indicative of levels of cooperation and coordination that cannot purely be explained in terms of the rational self-interest of states. As A. Hurrell states:

> As regimes become increasingly global, as the hard shell of the state is increasingly eroded, and as the scope of co-operation is expanded, the picture changes. As co-operation comes increasingly to involve the creation of rules that affect very deeply the domestic structures and organization of states, that invest individuals and groups within states with rights and duties, and seek to embody some notion of a common good (human rights, democratization, the environment, the construction of more elaborate and intrusive inter-state security orders), then these questions of society and community re-emerge and the validity of these models of co-operation that exclude them needs at least to be questioned.[14]

Applying such a vision to the United Nations, it is possible to see it developing, evolving toward an integrated whole, not a series of meeting places or networks of forums. Although the institutional framework of the United Nations is still grounded on the 1945 model, the powers of those institutions have developed just as UN goals and values have changed over the years (see Chapters 2 and 3). There is organic and systemic development to the extent that there is a UN system, though not necessarily a strong one. There are mechanisms for coordinating the diverse activities of the system (the ACC being a good example; see Chapter 7), though the weakness of these mechanisms is well known. One criticism goes so far as to contend that mechanisms like the ACC do not provide for any coordination, serving "principally as occasions for long and generally inconclusive arguments over territory—unless common interests are perceived to be threatened." The end result, according to this view, is that there is no UN system as such; instead each agency "is primarily concerned to assert" its "unique competence," leading "to the sort of territorial and bureaucratic infighting that impels fifteen different UN organizations to involve themselves in ocean management."[15]

Nevertheless, mechanisms for coordination and direction are present. Furthermore, and perhaps more important, there is a recognition within the United Nations—organization, body, individual—that everyone is part of a system; the elements of a system are present. Unless these elements fail to function at all, it is correct to assert that there is a weak system. Assuming the possibility of total breakdown (i.e., nonfunctioning), it would be realistic to at least presume that there *is* a UN system, albeit one that is fragmented and chaotic. This presumption is a useful starting point because, first, the question of whether the system is working can be considered; second, assuming it exists and works at a basic level, then its weaknesses can be eliminated and the protection and enforcement of its fundamental values can be improved.

The contention that there is a UN system is not to be confused with an idealistic view "of the organic unity of space ship earth."[16] The contention is not one of world government—which has not been achieved by the United Nations—but that the United Nations is a system, or has evolved into one, that has elements of global governance[17] and may evolve further into a form of government;[18] then again, it may not. In some ways this approach is similar to the "middle way" Hugo Grotius depicted between a Hobbesian vision of nation-states unrestrained in a state of nature and the rationalist conception of a "central authority." Although Grotius's "international society" of the early seventeenth century did not include within it international organizations, it did recognize that states "are bound by rules and form a society and community with one another."[19] The focus of this work is not the international community in general but one of the international community's most ambitious projects for strengthening regulation and management of interstate relations and global problems—the UN system. To cite M. Bertrand:

That endeavour which consists in attempting to establish "perpetual peace" among the peoples of the world is not, as the "realists" would have us think, an altogether ridiculous one. It is, on the other hand, highly revolutionary, in that it would involve changing the very model

of society; changing it, in fact, from a society divided into rival nation
states—for which, in accordance with Clausewitz's formula, "war is
the continuation of politics by other means"—into a society in which
a "world order" would reign supreme. Now, such an order involves the
acceptance of both a common ideology and a common culture, the establishment of a completely new system which, while still capable of
satisfying people's need for a sense of identity, would allow the formation of political units which no longer enjoy absolute sovereignty,
and the establishment of a political system for humanity amounting to
a world constitution.[20]

One serious weakness in the UN system recognized by Bertrand is
that it is a curious combination of centralization (e.g., in collective security, at least on paper) and decentralization (economic and social matters) through the establishment of specialized agencies.[21] Although these
agencies—namely, ECOSOC—have links with the UN center, they
enjoy autonomy. To have created in 1945 "one central organization em-
bracing all activities"[22] would have been too revolutionary, so under the
influence of functionalism the United Nations was built upon the basis
of decentralization.[23] Indeed, the prematurity of centralization is shown
by the fact that in the area of collective security, which, according to the
UN Charter, should be centralized under the control of the UN Security
Council, the practice has been one of decentralization (see Chapter 6).
A decentralized system may have weaknesses, especially in the overlap
and coordination of the activities of the agencies, but it is a system
nonetheless, the aim of which is to fulfill UN goals and values as formulated by the center—the United Nations itself through its political
organs. However, if that decentralized system collapses into "poly-
centrism" with no real coordination or central management, then (but
only then) is it possible to state that the UN system is a "myth."[24]

Of course, the 1945 design of the UN system can be viewed as consisting of the United Nations at the center, with the specialized agencies
as satellite bodies, each covering a fairly narrow area of common concern to the international community. This seems to have been the view
of the ICJ when considering the competence of the WHO in an advisory
opinion of 1996:

> The Charter of the United Nations laid down the basis of a "system"
> designed to organize international co-operation in a coherent fashion
> by bringing the United Nations, invested with powers of general
> scope, into relationship with various autonomous and complementary
> organizations, invested with sectorial powers.[25]

The court's vision of the system is very much framed in the immediate postwar period. However, it seems to ignore the impact of the proliferation of additional funds, programs, and commissions within the UN system. This proliferation was the result of "new tasks appearing which had not simply been anticipated when the specialized agencies were set up . . . to cover, however imperfectly, some of the functional gaps between the specialized agencies."[26] Though directly concerned with the international governmental organizations making up the UN system, the court fails to see that the system has evolved in ways beyond the 1945 model. This model unrealistically saw the United Nations dealing with general and security matters, the agencies with other, functionally defined areas such as health, labor, education, and agriculture, each agency having a narrow field of competence. Today the issues define the system rather than the entities that make it up. Thus, even though health matters are the major concern of the WHO, they are also of concern to other bodies established by the United Nations, such as the FAO, UNEP, and joint initiatives such as the United Nations Programme on Human Immunodeficiency Virus/Acquired Immunodeficiency Syndrome (UNAIDS).[27]

A political system has been defined as existing "wherever and whenever a group of actors are caught up in a nexus of relationships, both conflictual and co-operative, generated by common problems and the need to deal with them."[28] The UN system is a product of the international community's desire to address common problems, from the prevention of war to coordinating the use of radio frequencies. Furthermore, despite deficiencies in coordinating such disparate aims, the purpose of the system is to address problems in a coordinated way. This means that there should be no contradiction between the UN's actions—whether preventing war, coordinating radio frequencies, promoting the development of civil aviation, or protecting the environment. Clearly, the diversity in UN goals makes it an unwieldy system, and there is a gap not only in consistent coordination but also among the goals and achievements of the organization.

The Purposes and Principles of the UN System

Having established at least a presumption that there is a UN system, it is necessary to consider the purposes of that system. Why have states created such an elaborate and expensive system?[29] The purposes of the system will be detailed in Chapter 3, and the aim of this section is to ascertain the source of the purposes of the United Nations. "It is usually possible to ascertain the purposes for which an international organization has been created or for which it is being used by reading the constitutional documents and annotating them by a perusal of the organizations' record."[30] The combination of looking at the constitutive treaty alongside subsequent practice will be considered in more detail in Chapter 2. However, it is no simple task. The UN Charter must be examined alongside treaties establishing specialized agencies and documents establishing subsidiary organs. Furthermore, we must consider the practice of the entities operating within the UN system. Whether this involves looking at every resolution of the UN's plethora of bodies and organizations to see if they shed any light on the development of the purposes of the United Nations, or whether there are certain general resolutions of the United Nations that provide direct interpretation and development of general principles, is considered in greater detail below.

There does appear to be a hierarchy of instruments emerging with the UN Charter as the supreme treaty in the UN legal order. Article 103 of the charter states that "in the event of a conflict between the obligations of the Members of the United Nations under the present Charter and their obligations under any other international agreement, their obligations under the present Charter shall prevail." Although article 103 applies to obligations, not purposes, the obligations imposed by the subsidiary treaties in the UN order—those establishing the specialized agencies—are done so in pursuance of the goals of those agencies. The hierarchy established by article 103 is applicable to all the treaties in the system, but the obligation contained in article 103 is imposed on states and not (at least directly) on the organizations in the UN system. Within each organization, in addition to the treaty-based goals, there are what can be called the "general resolutions" of the main organs, the aim of which is to elaborate on those goals. After this comes the specific practice by the organization and its organs dealing with specific problems and issues in pursuance of these goals.

A distinction must also be drawn between the UN purposes and principles. The UN Charter makes a distinction between them in articles 1 and 2. The fundamental importance of these provisions necessitates citing them in full. Article 1 states:

> The Purposes of the United Nations are:
>   1. To maintain international peace and security, and to that end: to take effective collective measures for the prevention and removal of

threats to the peace, and for the suppression of acts of aggression or other breaches of the peace, and to bring about by peaceful means, and in conformity with the principles of justice and international law, adjustment or settlement of international disputes or situations which might lead to a breach of the peace;

2. To develop friendly relations among nations based on respect for the principle of equal rights and self-determination of peoples, and to take other appropriate measures to strengthen universal peace;

3. To achieve international co-operation in solving international problems of an economic, social, cultural, or humanitarian character, and in promoting and encouraging respect for human rights and for fundamental freedoms for all without distinction as to race, sex, language, or religion; and

4. To be a centre for harmonizing the actions of nations in the attainment of these common ends.

As shall be seen in Chapters 2 and 3, the treaties of the specialized agencies develop these purposes, especially the second and third, in each of their fields of operation. Article 2 of the UN Charter states:

The Organization and its Members, in pursuit of the Purposes stated in Article 1, shall act in accordance with the following Principles.

1. The Organization is based on the principle of sovereign equality of all its Members.

2. All Members, in order to ensure to all of them the rights and benefits resulting from membership, shall fulfill in good faith the obligations assumed by them in accordance with the present Charter.

3. All Members shall settle their disputes by peaceful means in such a manner that international peace and security, and justice, are not endangered.

4. All Members shall refrain in their international relations from the threat or use of force against the territorial integrity or political independence of any state, or in any other manner inconsistent with the Purposes of the United Nations.

5. All Members shall give the United Nations every assistance in any action it takes in accordance with the present Charter, and shall refrain from giving assistance to any state against which the United Nations is taking preventive or enforcement action.

6. The Organization shall ensure that states which are not Members of the United Nations act in accordance with these Principles so far as may be necessary for the maintenance of international peace and security.

7. Nothing contained in the present Charter shall authorize the United Nations to intervene in matters which are essentially within the

domestic jurisdiction of any state or shall require Members to submit
such matters to settlement under the present Charter; but this principle
shall not prejudice the application of enforcement measures under
Chapter VII.

By viewing the charter as "a legal framework determining certain
common values," purposes as well as principles can be collectively seen
as the values of the United Nations, but there is a qualitative difference.[31] The purposes are the collective goals of the UN community as
a whole, whereas the principles respect or secure the rights and duties
of member states as well as the organization.[32] Purposes and principles
establish the general legal framework within which the United Nations
and its member states can operate. However, whereas purposes set the
political agenda, principles establish legal rights and duties.

I now touch upon the duties placed on the United Nations (and
therefore the rights given to the states vis-à-vis the United Nations). At
least according to the text of the charter (disregarding any development
of the text in practice), the United Nations cannot, for instance, attempt
to secure the goal of collective security in violation of the principle of
nonintervention. The United Nations cannot promote economic prosperity at the expense of the principle of sovereign equality. It will be
shown in Chapter 2 that these basic values—purposes and principles—
of the UN system have been developed by the practice of the organization.[33] However, it remains true to say these values as developed by
practice remain the cornerstone of the organization and act as a brake
on the political ambitions of the United Nations and its member states.[34]

Constitutionalism and the United Nations

In outlining the values of the UN system, the identification of goal values and rights values suggests that the UN system is not only governed
by a series of constitutive treaties with the UN Charter at the apex but
also has at its heart a constitution.

> Constitutions almost always present a complex of fundamental norms
> governing the organization and performance of governmental func-
> tions in a given state ("frame of government") and the relationship
> between state authorities and citizens. More recently, statements of
> policy goals (regarding, for example, economic development, culture,

* What is the difference between a constitutional
document and an international treaty?

A UN SYSTEM   15

international peace, and conservation) feature prominently in constitutional texts.[35]

Transposing these comments on to the UN system, even at the outset the UN Charter was constructed as a constitutional document and
not as an international treaty. This is indicated by the opening words of
the UN Charter—"We the Peoples of the United Nations." Again this is
not to be viewed as an argument for world government, because a constitution at a basic level is not necessarily an instrument or reflection
of government. All a constitution "strives for is the establishment and
preservation of an international order in which basic rights and interests
. . . are acknowledged and conflicting claims settled peacefully."[36]
Nevertheless, "it is the minimum quality of any constitutional instrument that it provides for the performance of the basic functions of *governance,* that is to say, making and applying the law and adjudicating
legal claims."[37]

The UN General Assembly acts as a legislative body in a weak sense.
Although not accepted as a formal source of law, General Assembly resolutions create

> a presumption of legality in favor of conduct which is in accordance
> with its tenets. A State acting in accordance with the recommendations
> . . . will enjoy the benefit of the doubt should the legality of its con-
> duct be called into question. On the other hand, action contrary to the
> provisions of a recommendation can result in the shifting of the bur-
> den of proof against the person violating it.[38]

Unlike the mainly recommendatory character of General Assembly resolutions, the UN Security Council has mandatory legislative powers
regarding collective security.[39] As well as being a legislative body, the
Security Council acts as an executive body in enforcing those decisions.[40] Although no true separation of powers exists in the United Nations, there is the presence of legislative, executive, and judicial functions distributed unevenly among the principal organs. "Legislative
power is concerned with making general rules of conduct; executive
power carries out the laws; but only the judicial power determines how
the laws affect particular [legal] persons in particular circumstances."[41]

Yet the Security Council also possesses limited quasijudicial powers in that it has the power to recommend terms of settlement and to
determine whether there exists a threat to the peace, breach of the peace,

or act of aggression.[42] Furthermore, there is the ICJ's adjudicatory role, weak when compared to most national jurisdictions. Its jurisdiction over legal disputes between states is based on consent, and apart from rendering advisory opinions at the request of UN organs and agencies,[43] it has no express right to review the legality of actions taken by UN organs. Its position as a constitutional court is thus open to question (see Chapter 5).

The separation of powers in the United Nations is imperfect. One of the benefits of this constitutional tenet is the promotion of the rule of law in that it prevents one person or body from enacting, applying, and executing laws. Still, the lack of institutionalized judicial review undermines the principle of the rule of law, as does the concentration of power in the Security Council.[44] Indeed, possessing all three functions, the Security Council can act as legislator, judge, and executioner, at least in the area of collective security; this represents a recipe for abuse of power. More starkly, the combination of all three powers is the "very definition of tyranny."[45]

Although the charter and the constitutive documents of the specialized agencies form a complex constitutional hierarchy, it is not necessarily the case that they compose a constitution in anything more than a limited sense. The distinction is made clear by J. Crawford:

> There are layers of meaning to the idea of a "constitution." In a general sense, a constitution is that which constitutes an entity, of whatever kind—that which initiates and defines a body with a continuing existence and activity distinct from that of its instigators and participants. In other words, it may simply mean the constituent instrument of an organisation—of whatever kind. I will call this a constitution in a weak sense. But there is also the idea of a "constitution" in a stronger sense—a constitution which constitutes a society and not just an organisation—a constitution which is basal and not only bureaucratic.[46]

The question whether the constitutive documents of the United Nations are the constitution of the international community, as well as of the United Nations itself, will be revisited as activities performed in pursuance of the texts are examined. The issue is debated, with the assertion that "the Charter has become the constitution of the international community,"[47] as opposed to the assertion that the charter is a "mere interstate compact."[48] Others tread a more cautious path, pointing to the deficiencies in the constitutional structure of the United Nations, with a real lack of accountability to the international community. In addition, the successes of the United Nations in securing compliance with its decisions, "essential for a constitution in a strong sense," must be contrasted with its numerous failures.[49] For example, the "unprecedented image of a world community placed under the centralised authority" of the United Nations in successfully combating Iraq's aggression against Kuwait in 1990–1991 must be contrasted with its divisive and failed attempts to bring peace to Somalia in 1992–1993 and the former Yugoslavia in 1992–1995, as well as its abject failure to prevent the genocide in Rwanda in 1994.[50]

This preliminary discussion indicates that the UN's constitutive treaties create more than a constitution in a limited sense. However, it is probably correct to state that they have not yet developed to the point of becoming an "effective and stable constitution of the international community."[51]

The UN Legal Order

Nevertheless, all the above is indicative that the UN system is governed by the rule of law, though one not fully protected by separation of powers. A further benefit of a true separation of powers is that "power will check power," for example, by the judiciary reviewing the actions of the executive and legislature.[52] Though there is an insufficiency of constitutional checks and balances in the treaty makeup of the UN system to prevent abuses of power by the organs and agencies within it, the system has the potential to develop them. For instance, the ICJ should seize the opportunity to review the legality of the actions of UN organs, bodies, and agencies whenever the chance arises. The UN General Assembly, embodying the membership, has shown that it can act as the conscience of the Security Council during its Cold War paralysis[53] and has the power, through ECOSOC, to exert more control over specialized agencies.[54] Ensuring that the agencies are achieving their purposes, as set by the constitutive treaties of those agencies, is by its nature a review, both legal and political, of the activities of those agencies. Similarly, the assembly should ensure that the subsidiary bodies it has established are performing their tasks in accordance with their mandates. The development of greater constitutional checks and balances within the UN system will undoubtedly enhance the legitimacy of the organization and its ability to "pull the [international] community to compliance."[55] Decisions adopted in accordance with "the procedural and institutional framework" of the United Nations will also ensure enhanced compliance, as will greater consistency in treating like cases alike.[56] UN legitimacy has suffered due to its selective actions.

Although there is value in debating whether there is a UN legal *system* as such,[57] there can be no doubt that there is a UN legal *order* given the presence of "structures and processes for creating and applying law by and within the United Nations system of organizations."[58] Indeed, despite the inherent weaknesses of UN organs, bodies, and agencies, whose main form of resolution is the recommendation, the system does produce vast amounts of law. The phrase "UN law" is used throughout here to signify the corpus of rules produced by the UN system; in addition, the term can refer to the constitutional principles that frame the activities of UN organizations.

UN legislative capacity has increased over the years as the world moves away from a purely positivist horizontal system dependent upon state consent toward a more hierarchical system.[59] The seminal resolutions of the General Assembly, for example, on decolonization, are not the only examples.[60] Many of the resolutions of other agencies, though not always technically binding in a treaty sense, are accepted and acted upon as pieces of legislation for the world community because they consist of "good and technical rules."[61]

The production of laws, as well as their enforcement by the UN system, are of paramount importance as a significant, and perhaps the only viable, method of ensuring that the goals and values of the UN system are achieved.

O. Schachter, in his overview of the UN legal order, looks at the legal process in three stages: "law making in the UN system," "interpreting and applying law," and "compliance and enforcement."[62] On the lawmaking aspect, "neither the United Nations nor any of its specialized agencies was conceived of as a legislative body"; rather they were seen as "coordinating" or "harmonizing" the actions of member states through recommendations. However, the desire of member governments and international officials to produce "solutions to the world's problems through new law and legal regimes" has led the United Nations and its agencies to develop a legislative role. This has occurred either through sponsoring law-creating treaties, such as the ICCPR, and in a weaker sense through its recommendatory capacity. A UN General Assembly recommendation, though not binding in an institutional law or treaty sense, will nevertheless be law if it is "an authentic interpretation of the

UN Charter agreed to by all the parties" or if it affirms "recognized customary law." Further, a recommendation will become law if it is an "expression of general principles of law accepted by states." Custom, treaties, and general principles are recognized sources of international law.[63] Even if the resolution does not meet those requirements, it does create a presumption of illegality for states acting contrary to it. To this extent, then, the UN General Assembly creates and codifies law.

Indeed, it has been stated that "a predominant share of international law is being created under the aegis of IGOs of the UN System"—a system that "is by any standard a productive and useful creator of the ever greater number and ever more complex norms required by the world community."[64] Furthermore, the norms created by the UN system "have the capacity to channel the conduct of members in ways that are designed to advance, or at least not impede, an organization's attempts to achieve its stated goals." The norms are "promulgated or established by bodies recognized as legitimate by the members, and as a result they command the respect, even if not always the strict obedience, of decision-makers in national governments."[65]

Furthermore, the specialized agencies crystallize existing law but more often create new law in "an impressive variety of ways," going "far beyond the traditional sources of international law."[66] This is due to the necessity of having international regulation of matters such as disease prevention, radio frequencies, postal systems, and air safety. It is useful to cite the excellent summary provided by F. L. Kirgis:

> [They] include such normative instruments as "super-treaties" (treaties with strings attached such as a duty to submit them to a ratification process and a duty to report periodically to the promulgating agency on compliance); provisional application of some treaties before they formally enter into force; treaty-implementing standards that enter into force upon tacit consent, subject to a limited opt-out privilege; formally binding regulations, sometimes linked to an opt-out privilege; authoritative findings of legislative facts, to be implemented by regulatory regimes within or outside the agency; recommendations, often in the form of codes or guidelines, that have more than hortatory design and effect; pronouncements developing a "common law" for members, including formal pronouncements as part of dispute settlement proceedings or as reasoned interpretations by agency organs; and informal interpretations during contacts with individual members.[67]

The next step in the UN legal order—interpreting and applying the law—will be considered in more detail in Chapter 2. It is important to note, as Schachter does, that "applying and interpreting law take place continually throughout the UN system" by the organs, bodies, and agencies themselves often in accordance with the "principle of effectiveness." This principle "gives priority to achieving the major purposes of the organization."[68] This may lead to an overextension of power among the various bodies, which raises the question of developing checks and balances in the system to prevent that from occurring. The role of the ICJ is examined in Chapter 5.

On the final step in any legal system—compliance and enforcement—Schachter accurately notes that "for a long time" these "were on the margins of UN concern." The "busy world of UN law-making and law-applying carried on pretty much without serious consideration of the means of ensuring compliance."[69] Although relying on members' goodwill actually did work for much of the legislation produced by the technical agencies, for the more "political" matters[70] "it is far from evident that this was generally the case." However, the end of the Cold War unleashed techniques to "induce and even compel states to carry out their legal obligations."[71] These techniques will be the subject of more intensive treatment in Part 3.

Conclusion

Far from being a collection of interstate arenas, UN organizations and their bodies appear to form a complex political system that contains a legal order. The legal norms produced by the system flow from the basic principles contained in the constitutional documents, primarily the UN Charter, followed by the constitutive treaties of the specialized agencies, and are designed to fulfill the values of the UN system. There is preliminary evidence that such norms are generally efficacious in producing compliance; the extent to which the UN lawmaking process is effective in facilitating UN goals will be examined in Part 3. Only by examining the reality of UN action can we ascertain the issue of whether the UN system is successful in protecting its values. Of equal importance is whether states recognize that they are part of an international community controlled, or even governed in a limited sense, by the United Nations. If such is the case, then the constitutive documents of the United Nations form a constitution in a stronger sense. Despite the absence of separation of powers as well as legal and political accountability within the system, the United Nations has become something far more fundamental than a collection of IGOs. Neither an elaborate international conference nor a contractually based entity, the UN system has the potential to become an instrument for world governance.

Notes

1. (1982) 21 ILM 1261.
2. 999 UNTS 171. The treaty entered into force in 1976.
3. (1992) 31 ILM 848, Art. 10.
4. (1998) 38 ILM 999.
5. Grieco, "Anarchy and the Limits of Cooperation," 485.
6. Waltz, *Theory of International Politics,* 118.
7. Goodwin, "World Institutions," 63.
8. Krasner, "Structural Causes and Regime Consequences," 190.
9. Kennedy, "The Move to Institutions," 980.
10. Koskenniemi, *International Law,* xi.
11. Krasner, "Structural Causes and Regime Consequences," 189.
12. Keohane, "International Institutions," 384.
13. Krasner, "Structural Causes and Regime Consequences," 186.
14. Hurell, "International Society," 63.
15. Righter, *Utopia Lost,* 47, 53.
16. Taylor, *International Organizations,* 7.
17. Lister, *The European Union,* 162–163.
18. Goodwin, "World Institutions," 55–57.
19. Bull, "The Importance of Grotius," 71–72.
20. Bertrand, *The United Nations,* 7.
21. Ibid., 28.
22. Schermers and Blokker, *International Institutional Law,* 1056.
23. Mitrany, *A Working Peace System.*
24. Righter, *Utopia Lost,* 43–46.
25. *Legality of the Use by a State of Nuclear Weapons in Armed Conflict,* ICJ Rep. 1996, 66 at 80.
26. Taylor, *International Organizations,* 16.
27. Established in 1993 as a joint program of six UN organs and organizations. See Blokker, "Proliferation of International Organizations," 6–7.
28. Gregg and Barkun, *The United Nations System,* 4.
29. But see Harrod, "United Nations Specialized Agencies," 132, for figures that illustrate the relative inexpensiveness of the United Nations.
30. Gregg and Barkun, *The United Nations System,* 5–6.
31. Tomuschat, "Obligations Arising for States," 236.
32. Dworkin, *Taking Rights Seriously,* 82.
33. But see Fassbender, "The United Nations Charter," 602, 605.
34. Dworkin, *Law's Empire,* 211.
35. Fassbender, "United Nations Charter," 536.

36. Ibid., 555.

37. Ibid., 574.

38. Schreuer, "Recommendations and the Traditional Sources of International Law," 118.

39. Art. 25 of the UN Charter.

40. Arts. 41 and 42 of the UN Charter.

41. Gwynn, *The Meaning of the Separation of Powers,* 103.

42. Arts. 36(1) and 39 of the UN Charter.

43. Arts. 36 and 65 of the ICJ Statute.

44. Franck, "The United Nations as Guarantor," 37.

45. Gwynn, *The Meaning of the Separation of Powers,* 1.

46. Crawford, "The Charter of the UN," 8.

47. B. Simma, *The Charter,* 1117. See also Tomuschat, *The United Nations,* ix.

48. Arangio-Ruiz, "The 'Federal Analogy,'" 9.

49. Crawford, "The UN Charter as a Constitution," 11.

50. P-M. Dupuy, "The Constitutional Dimension of the Charter," 20.

51. Ibid., 32.

52. Gwynn, *The Meaning of the Separation of Powers,* 101.

53. White, *Keeping the Peace,* 161–178.

54. Arts. 60, 63, and 64 of the UN Charter.

55. Franck, "The *Bona Fides* of Power," 190.

56. Franck, *Fairness in International Law,* 41, 219, 221.

57. See, for example, Hart, *The Concept of Law,* 208–231, on the issue of an international legal system. See also Raz, *The Concept of a Legal System,* 205–208, who suggests two tests for the existence of a legal system—the test of efficacy and the test of exclusion.

58. Schachter, "The UN Legal Order," 1.

59. Kirgis, *International Organizations,* 274.

60. Declaration on the Granting of Independence to Colonial Territories and Peoples, GA Res. 1514, 14 Dec. 1960.

61. Schermers, "We the Peoples," 117.

62. Schachter, "United Nations Legal Order," 1–23.

63. Ibid., 4. See Art. 38 of the ICJ Statute. See also Higgins, *The Development of International Law.*

64. Szasz, "General Law-Making Processes," 37.

65. Kirgis, "Specialized Law-Making Processes," 109.

66. Ibid., 156.

67. Ibid., 157.

68. Schachter, "United Nations Legal Order," 8–12.

69. Ibid., 15.

70. Kartashkin, "The Marxist-Leninist Approach," 84.

71. Schachter, "United Nations Legal Order," 15.

2

Evolutionary Elements
of the Legal Order

Much of the basic machinery of the UN system remains as it was built in 1945. However, it has been supplemented by the creation of subsidiary organs and programs, as well as bodies created under UN-sponsored treaties. More important, the powers of the primary organs and specialized agencies have developed in combination with an evolution in the agendas of the various entities composing the UN system. Developments have occurred on three interlinked fronts: the institutional structure; the legal powers of UN entities; and the values pursued by the United Nations.

In this chapter I elucidate the legal methods by which the UN system has developed. Contrary to the view that law is slow to change and inflexible, producing a static system, my analysis will show that the UN legal order is dynamic and flexible. This enables its machinery to adapt to changing world conditions, to produce laws to help regulate the international community, and, potentially, to improve the world order.

Although all the constituent treaties within the UN system have formal amendment procedures, their usage has not been sufficient to adapt treaties to constantly changing world conditions. The concept of a treaty here is as a living instrument, considered along with the more juridical and abstract concept of international legal personality. It will be shown that the UN Charter and the constituent treaties of the specialized agencies are by nature living instruments, and that all the IGOs in the UN system are international legal persons in an original, not derivative, sense. From these important findings, I discuss the development of the legal powers of the organs of the system's IGOs, as well as how the practical interpretation of the system's treaties has moved them a significant distance from the original text. The constitutional nature of the system dictates that the developments in powers and practice cannot be purely arbitrary; there must be legal parameters within which they evolve. I conclude with an evaluation of these limits.

Formal Amendment of UN Treaties

There is considerable scope for development in the UN Charter and the treaties of the specialized agencies, over and above their formal amendment mechanisms. The formal methods of treaty modification are, by themselves, cumbersome, inadequate to keep up with changing world conditions.

The amendment provisions of the UN Charter are found in articles 108 and 109, the conditions for formal amendment being identical in both. Amendment can occur by the adoption of a vote by two-thirds of the UN member states followed by ratification "in accordance with their respective constitutional procedures by two thirds of the Members of the United Nations, including all the permanent members of the Security Council."[1] Article 108 envisages individual amendments, whereas article 109 foresees more general review and comprehensive amendments following a UN General Conference. The latter would be a more suitable method for a thorough revision of the UN's constitutional structure.

Although the machinery of formal amendment is the only viable method for instituting radical change to the system, incremental change can be achieved in practice. An obvious example is the acceptance of the People's Republic of China since 1971 and the Russian Federation since 1992; those countries occupy two permanent seats on the UN Security Council despite the fact that the text of article 23 continues to refer to "the Republic of China" and "the Union of Soviet Socialist Republics."

Another example of dramatic structural change relates to the division of competence among UN organs, with, for example, the UN General Assembly and Secretary-General taking a much more active role in collective security matters than envisaged in the charter text. There is also the possibility of the ICJ claiming greater powers of judicial review (see Chapter 5), despite the fact that neither the charter nor the statute of the court expressly recognizes this.

Although the UN Charter has evolved in practice, some changes, primarily increases in the number of members in certain organs, have by necessity been achieved through formal amendment procedures. Even relatively minor modifications were not achieved without some difficulty.

The increase in membership of the UN Security Council from eleven to fifteen (with the voting majority increased from seven to nine) and ECOSOC from eighteen to twenty-seven, which occurred in 1965, looked doubtful in the initial General Assembly vote, where it was opposed by two permanent members (France and the USSR) with abstentions by the United States and United Kingdom (plus China in the case of ECOSOC). However, opposition evaporated at the ratification stage. Another increase in ECOSOC's membership in 1973, from twenty-seven to fifty-four, again was initially opposed in the General Assembly by the United Kingdom and France, with the USSR abstaining and China not participating in the vote, though again these hurdles were removed by ratification by the five permanent members of the council (P5).[2]

Although by no means the only type of formal amendment to the constituent treaties of the specialized agencies, increasing the membership of certain nonplenary organs to reflect the growth of the international community (and therefore the membership of the IGOs in the UN system) accounts for many of the amendments that have occurred.[3] The more numerous amendments to these treaties are partly explained by the less politicized atmosphere in these organizations, as well as the lack of veto power over the amendment process. Some of the agencies' treaties do assign greater weight to certain members. For instance, article 36 of the ILO constitution requires that at least five out of ten members recognized as "members of chief industrial importance" in the governing body must form part of at least a two-thirds majority accepting an amendment. The treaties establishing the IMF and the International Bank for Reconstruction and Development (IBRD) require a proposal to be approved by their respective boards of governors, where weighted voting is the norm, before being put before the membership.[4] Other treaties in the system require a qualified majority for acceptance (normally two-thirds).[5]

In several UN IGOs, amendments adopted by a qualified majority bind the whole membership;[6] others, principally the ICAO, bind only those member states that ratify them.[7] The latter process is less satisfactory. When amendment is binding on all the membership, even those opposing it, the integrity of the treaty is maintained. When it is binding only on those ratifying or accepting the amendment, different provisions of the treaty bind different members.[8] This protects each member state from duties deemed undesirable, but it does undermine the integrity of the legal order produced by the system. Most treaties within the system maintain their integrity by providing that amendments are binding on the whole membership.[9] The dominance of the legislative method of amending treaties in the UN system, as opposed to the consensual method, is indicative of the general constitutional character of the UN system.

UN Treaties as Living Instruments

Constitutions of IGOs need to evolve in order to keep pace with changes in their areas of competence. It would be impractical and too legalistic to restrict the United Nations to the exact wording of the charter given that the treaty was formulated in 1945 and was designed to function in the world at that time. The same argument applies to the constitutions of the specialized agencies. In the words of Judge A. Alvarez, constitutions "can be compared to ships which leave the yards in which they have been built, and sail away independently, no longer attached to the dockyard."[10]

At a basic level, the issue of whether UN treaties are "living instruments" is a matter of interpretation, where there are three schools of thought: the "textual or ordinary meaning of the words school"; "the intention of the parties or founding fathers school"; and the "teleological or aims and objects school."[11]

In this context, there has been a general move away from the formalist position, dominant during the eighteenth and nineteenth centuries,[12] that the text is the sole source of information. Within the provisions of the Vienna Convention on the Law of Treaties 1969,[13] there is virtual parity among the different approaches, with the caveat that preparatory work is of supplemental value.[14] Subsequent practice, in contrast, is elevated to a primary method of interpretation, along with the text and the object and purposes.[15] The move has been away from the *intent* of the founding states toward more observable means of interpretation, namely, the purposes of the treaties and subsequent practice, concerned with the *current* intent of the members and thus subjective. However, the practice of the United Nations in interpreting and developing treaties is not the practice of all member states but rather that of the organs, where majorities prevail. This heightens the autonomy of the United Nations and reduces the control of the membership as a whole. As stated by Judge Alvarez, a "treaty . . . acquires a life of its own. Consequently in interpreting it we must have regard to the exigencies of contemporary life, rather than the intentions of those who framed it."[16]

Subsequent practice is therefore a significant means of interpreting and developing the charter. Nevertheless, sole reliance on practice as the test of legality is not acceptable, although, as S. Rosenne notes, it has become increasingly common.[17] The primary limit on the practice of the organs, agencies, and bodies of the UN family is the constitution. In the area of UN powers, constitutional limits are defined by the purposes as well as any express prohibitions contained in the treaties.

Thus the object and purposes of the UN Charter, as well as the constitutions of the agencies, can be said to define the framework of those constituent treaties. Such a framework is filled in by the express powers, implied powers, and even inherent powers of the United Nations as developed in the practice of the organization. Pollux recognized this in 1946:

> The charter, like every written Constitution, will be a living instrument. It will be applied daily; and every application of the Charter, every use of an Article, implies an interpretation; on each occasion a decision is involved which may change the existing law and start a new constitutional development. A constitutional customary law will grow up and the Charter itself will merely form the framework of the Organization which will be filled in by the practice of the different organs.[18]

The teleological, or purposive, approach to treaty interpretation, which relies on the objects and purposes of the treaty, must not be confused with the policy approach.[19] The latter school uses the language of goals and policies to be achieved but defines them by the wider needs of the international community rather than the objects as defined by the treaty.[20] The policy approach, taken to its extreme, advocates a much wider purposive interpretation and would allow the UN organizations to act beyond the four corners of their treaties, that is, beyond the face of the written instrument.

Nevertheless, the flexibility and adaptability accorded to the UN Charter and the UN system's primary treaties by purposes and practice must not be underestimated. C. Tomuschat describes the United Nations as "an entire system which is in constant movement, not unlike a national constitution whose original texture will be unavoidably modified by thick layers of political practice and jurisprudence."[21] Commenting on the UN Charter, R. Higgins states that "the Charter is an extraordinary instrument, and a huge variety of possibilities are possible under it."[22] The potential of the United Nations and other IGOs to assert their personality and use their powers on the international stage is expressed by M. McDougal, W. Reisman, and A. Willard, who state that "the United Nations, together with its affiliate bodies, [will] provide a set of institutional arrangements capable of mobilizing, over time, a sufficiently potent network of common interests in global order to transform the organization into a universal system of authoritative and controlling public order."[23]

The International Legal Personality of the United Nations

The question of whether the United Nations has international legal personality no longer vexes international lawyers. International law recognizes that the United Nations (established by the UN Charter) and all the specialized agencies (created by treaties) are separate legal persons on the international stage. However, it is necessary to trace the nature and meaning of this attribute in order to understand the legal nature of the United Nations and the consequences for rights, duties, and powers. Personality is a complex issue and, in many ways, unnecessarily legalistic, irrelevant to the real world. Yet the attribution of legal personality and its consequences reflect a profound battle for the soul of the United Nations.[24] It raises the issue of whether the United Nations is an actor on the international stage with the equivalent status of states, or whether it has an inferior status as a vehicle for states to meet and resolve differences. The distinction is important. On one hand, the United Nations is an international actor acting independently of its membership, pursuing collective goals and regulating the behavior of states.[25] On the other, it is not much more than elaborate standing conference machinery, based on nineteenth-century thought, and is controlled by states.[26]

However, recognizing that the United Nations and its specialized agencies possess international legal personality is a significant legal development. The United Nations is, like any state, an international legal person. As C. Amerasinghe states, "Having international personality for an international organization means possessing rights, duties, powers and liabilities etc. as distinct from its members or its creators on the international plane."[27] The significance is clear, for it is doubtful whether the United Nations or its specialized agencies would be able to regulate the behavior of states unless they possessed legal personality. It would be difficult, if not impossible, to create a UN legal order if the primary UN organizations were not legal persons under the law. How, for instance, would the ILO exercise legal powers to regulate working conditions if it were not a legal person?[28]

However, there are different approaches to personality.[29] There are at least two subjective approaches that base personality on member states' intent. In these approaches the United Nations is subservient to the state; whereas the legal personality of a state is original and complete, the personality of the United Nations is derivative and incomplete, perhaps nonexistent if taken to the extreme.

The first subjective approach can be called the "strict" or "express" approach, in that the only way an IGO can possess international legal personality is to be recognized as such in the constituent document. An IGO obtains personality only if member states express it in the original document. This view places states in absolute control over granting legal personality to an IGO. The rarity of express grants is indicative of how this extreme statist approach would reduce most IGOs—assuming there is no express recognition of personality—to mere diplomatic contrivances with little or no autonomy in legal and practical terms respectively.[30] An IGO without legal personality has no independent right to act; its only means of doing so is to "borrow" the personality of states or another IGO possessing personality. The absence of an unambiguous express grant of personality in the charter[31] or in most of the constitutive treaties of the agencies[32] would deny the attribution of legal personality to the United Nations.

The post-1945 emergence of numerous IGOs, including the United Nations and specialized agencies having apparent legal autonomy, has led to a reappraisal of the concept of international legal personality. This concession by states is recognized in the second school of thought (identified as "the currently prevailing view") whereby "organizations are international persons not *ipso facto*, but because the status is given to them, either explicitly or, if there is no constitutional attribution of this quality, *implicitly*." The pragmatism of this modified subjective approach is recognized: "If organizations are empowered to conclude treaties, to exchange diplomats, and to mobilize international forces . . . how can such powers be exercised without having the status of international legal person?"[33]

Conceding under implied intent that IGOs are more likely to have personality than under the express intent approach, the former view still satisfies the dogma that states are the supreme actors. States have original personality; organizations are given personality, express or implicit.

Although the United Nations and its agencies would have personality under the implied intent approach, the derivative nature of personality reduces its significance. Although it is stated to be the view generally favored by international lawyers as representing international law, most will favor the objective approach, discussed immediately below.[34]

The third view—the objective approach—requires that IGOs meet the requirements of legal personality under international law, just like any state.[35] Under the objective approach, personality for IGOs, as well as for states, is original, in theory placing IGOs on the same playing field as states. Although IGOs may *appear* to have more limited capacity than states, in theoretical terms they are equals. Indeed, IGOs may seem to have less competence than states, but once they obtain original personality they can actually possess greater rights and duties than member states. The consequences for the international order are huge.

Contrarily, some writers accept the concept of objective legal personality, although tentatively. Amerasinghe states that "in principle an organization should have objective personality, unless for some reason it is proved that there is . . . a vitiating factor," which amounts to a presumption of objective personality.[36] I. Brownlie's criteria for personality (a permanent association of states, with lawful objects, equipped with organs; a distinction, in terms of legal powers and purposes, between the organization and its member states; and the existence of legal powers exercisable on the international plane)[37] differs very little from that of Amerasinghe[38] and Higgins;[39] all point to an objective approach.

The issue of the UN's international personality was scrutinized by the ICJ in the *Reparation* case.[40] The UN General Assembly sought the advice of the court on the issue of whether the United Nations could bring an international claim to obtain reparations against a state responsible for injuries to a UN agent suffered in the course of performing his duties. The court saw this as directly raising the issue of personality. The functionalist approach of the court was established at the outset of the opinion, which stated that "the subjects of law in any legal system are not necessarily identical in their nature or in the extent of their rights, and their nature depends on the needs of the Community." The needs of the international community have led, according to the court, to an increasing amount of collective action and the creation of "certain entities which are not States," culminating in the creation of the United Nations in 1945, "whose purposes and functions are specified in the Charter." The court then emphasized that for the United Nations "to achieve these ends the attribution of international personality is indispensable."[41]

The court noted that the UN Charter "has not been content to make the Organization . . . merely a centre 'for harmonising the actions of nations in the attainment of those common ends'" as stated in article 1(4). In other words, the organization is not a forum or a meeting place for states to air differences but an autonomous actor that "occupies a position in certain respects in detachment from its Members," identifiable by the presence of separate organs. Other identifying features included the grant of "legal capacity and privileges and immunities in the territory of each of its Members," as well as provision "for the conclusion of agreements between the Organization and its Members."[42]

The court's approach was not clear-cut and was not expressly based on implied intent or the objective approach.[43] It did mention the criteria of personality but also referred to the intention of the founding members as reflected in the passage below, which contains the court's general pronouncement on the personality of the United Nations:

> In the opinion of the Court, the Organization was intended to exercise and enjoy, and is in fact exercising and enjoying, functions and rights which can only be explained on the basis of a large measure of international personality and the capacity to operate upon an international plane. It is at present the supreme type of international organization, and it could not carry out the intentions of its founders if it was devoid of international personality. It must be acknowledged that its Members, by entrusting certain functions to it, with the attendant duties and responsibilities, have clothed it with the competence required to enable those functions to be effectively discharged.

The court emphasized that this did not amount to claiming that the United Nations was the same thing as a state, or that it possessed the same rights and duties as a state: "But what it does mean is that it is a subject of international law and capable of possessing international rights and duties, and that it has the capacity to maintain its rights by bringing international claims."[44] The court thus hesitated to apply a purely objective approach. Furthermore, the court suggested that in terms of the hierarchy of international actors nation-state supremacy remains unchallenged: "Whereas a State possesses the totality of international rights and duties recognised by international law, the rights and duties of an entity such as the Organization must depend upon its purposes and functions as specified or implied in its constituent documents and developed in practice."[45]

Although it recognizes the functional or, perhaps more accurately, constitutional limit to the UN's personality, this statement seems too traditional, especially in light of developments since the opinion was handed down in 1949. At that time the UN was blocked by the Cold War superpowers from fully developing its potential. Since then the United Nations has evolved and asserted its rights and enforced the duties of its members in ways never envisaged by the court. The end of the Cold War freed the United Nations to develop and expand its powers in a much more dynamic way than envisaged by the ICJ.

The Powers of the United Nations

A common view among international jurists is that the issue of whether an IGO has international legal personality is a "'black and white' or yes or no issue."[46] Generally, only when the IGO has recognized personality can the issue of its legal rights, duties, and powers be examined. Accordingly, the extent of the powers of an IGO like the United Nations is dependent upon the unique terms of the constitution. "To be an international legal person means only *to be capable* of bearing rights and duties."[47] The supremacy of the state is preserved: although personality is more readily conceded to the United Nations, the extent of its real legal powers is still subject to the grant by member states.

However, there does appear to be common agreement on the core of rights and duties shared by organizations that possess personality.[48] These include: treaty-making capacity; privileges and immunities; standing to bring claims; and responsibility for illegal acts, irrespective of whether an IGO claims them in its constituent instrument. A recognition that personality carries with it certain powers and responsibilities signifies that personality is not merely an empty concept but that it has consequences as to legal rights and duties. Nevertheless, few writers go so far as to recognize inherent powers, namely, those that enable the United Nations to fulfill its purposes, concentrating instead on the common core powers and implied powers, the latter being based on the presumed intent of the founding members.[49] As with personality, the use of intent as the basis of power is stretched beyond credibility because most writers accept a wide view of implied powers. This is done by focusing on the functions of the organization as opposed to those powers that are necessary to make the express powers work.[50]

Thus the approach favored by international lawyers, despite some vagueness and confusion, readily accepts personality. This is achieved by using objective criteria or by presuming that the intent was to imbue the United Nations with personality. This approach is supported by the doctrine of implied powers, which allows an organization to pursue its goals by focusing on its functions rather than being held to the letter of its constituent document.[51]

The ICJ in the *Reparation* case was not averse in 1949 to recognizing a right that cannot be readily implied from any express provision in the charter. In so doing it recognized that the United Nations had rights of protection over individuals overlapping or in "competition" with those customarily belonging to states.[52]

The court paid respect to the implied intent approach in regard to the issue of powers when it stated that "under international law, the Organization must be deemed to have those powers which, though not expressly provided in the Charter, are conferred upon it by necessary implication as being essential to the performance of its duties."[53] However, it is apparent that the court's lenient approach permits the United Nations to possess a range of rights and duties. Such a range will not necessarily be static but will develop with time in accordance with the needs of the international community, perhaps to the extent of rivaling, or indeed overthrowing, the supremacy of the nation-state.

The court stated it was necessary for the United Nations to be able to bring a claim on behalf of its employees, though it did not state the express power from which such an implied power derived. It appeared to be the general nature and purposes of the United Nations as a body aimed at securing international peace and security, an aim requiring the extensive use of personnel in dangerous situations. Judge G. Hackworth, in his dissenting opinion, pointed to the majority's unacceptable extension of the doctrine of implied powers given that the doctrine is based on the intent of the founding members and is therefore restricted: "It is to be presumed that such powers as the Member States desired to confer upon it are stated either in the Charter or in complementary agreements concluded by them. Powers not expressed cannot freely be implied. Implied powers flow from a grant of expressed powers, and are limited to those that are 'necessary' to the exercise of powers expressly granted. No necessity for the exercise of power here in question has been shown to exist."[54]

The weaker the tie between implied and express powers, the weaker the justification if based on intent. Although the implication of powers from express functions may appear to be based on intent (i.e., the founders *intended* the United Nations to have those functions), in fact it is far removed. When formulating the functions of the United Nations, the founding states intended to create functions via the express powers in the treaty. Recognizing unexpressed powers that further UN functions divorces powers from the intent of member states.[55] In effect, UN powers are developed by the United Nations itself: its organs, bodies, and even employees, not by the membership.

As seen in the *Reparation* case, the ICJ has adopted an expansive doctrine of implied powers. And in the *Namibia* case the court reinforced its view when it found that the General Assembly's termination of South Africa's mandate was within its competence. The court pointed to no specific charter provision but made the more general proposition that "the United Nations as a successor to the League, acting through its competent organs, must be seen above all as the supervisory institution, competent to pronounce, in that capacity, on the conduct of the mandatory with respect to its international obligation, and competent to act accordingly." The action of the assembly in terminating the mandate was viewed by the court "as the exercise of the right to terminate a relationship in the case of a deliberate and persistent violation of obligations which destroys the very object and purpose of that relationship," in accordance with the general principles of international law governing termination of a treaty based on breach.[56] This recognizes that the United Nations has the same powers of termination as any state.[57] The court's approach is liberal and functionalist "so that powers *relating* to the purposes and functions specified in the constitution can be implied," rather than narrow and formalist, whereby "one can imply only such powers as arise by necessary intendment from the constitutional provisions."[58]

The ICJ in the *Expenses* case seemed to adopt the principle of "functional limitation."[59] There it considered whether expenditures authorized by the UN General Assembly relating to the UN Operation in the Congo (ONUC) and the UN Emergency Force in the Middle East (UNEF) constituted "expenses of the Organization" within the meaning of article 17(2) of the UN Charter. The ICJ stated that the issue of expenses "must be tested by their relationship to the purposes of the United Nations." The court recognized the width of the UN's purposes and stated "the primary place ascribed to international peace and security is natural, since the fulfilment of the other purposes will be dependent upon the attainment of that basic condition. The purposes are broad indeed, but neither they nor the powers conferred to effectuate them are unlimited."[60]

Furthermore, in considering the General Assembly's ability to create a peacekeeping force, the court was eager to assume that such action was within the powers of the organization and within the functions of that organ (as well as the Security Council). This was based on the fact that the General Assembly possesses wide subsidiary powers for peace and security.[61] Thus the court had little problem in finding that the United Nations had the capacity to create a peacekeeping force, even though there is no express grant of that power in the charter.

The liberal approach to implied powers is exemplified in the *Expenses* case, where the court considered whether the development of a power to create and mandate peacekeeping forces by the General Assembly was *necessary* for the fulfillment of the express provisions of the charter.[62] On the issue of the assembly's power, the court stated that "the provisions of the Charter which distribute functions and powers to the Security Council and to the General Assembly give no support to the view that such distribution excludes from the powers of the General Assembly the power" to adopt measures designed to maintain peace and security. The emphasis is not on the implication of powers necessary to make an express provision effective but on the absence of any provision in the charter *prohibiting* the exercise of a power. The only limitation on the General Assembly regarding peace and security is that only the Security Council can "order coercive action."[63] Thus the assembly's powers are limited only by charter provisions that prohibit acts; in this case the restriction was that only the Security Council could order enforcement action under chapter VII.

The court accepted the British view on the creation of UNEF, contained in a minister's response in the House of Commons on the question of which charter article the force had been created under. The minister's response was that UNEF was not being created under any express provisions but under a resolution of the General Assembly that was not prohibited by the charter.[64] By emphasizing that UN organs have the power to undertake any action within the UN's purposes as long as the charter does not expressly prohibit it, the court moved away from the doctrine of implied powers to that of inherent powers. Indeed, in all three judgments discussed above, the ICJ paid lip service to the traditional approach to personality and powers, which respects state sovereignty, yet realized that the United Nations is an IGO that is not a derivative entity in terms of personality or power. The discourse may sound like implied powers, but the reality is that IGOs have inherent powers. Implied powers are a "fiction."[65]

However, the ICJ did not follow its liberal approach to powers in the *Nuclear Weapons* advisory opinion of 1996 (the WHO opinion).

This was in part due to a misconstruction of the purposes of the WHO. The court opined that this UN IGO did not have the power to request an advisory opinion on the legality of the use of nuclear weapons but only as to the effects of those weapons on health.[66]

Contrary to the court's opinion, the prevention of acts damaging the health of individuals is within the purposes of the WHO and, further, is a policy that can be pursued by the development of legal structures to control the use of nuclear weapons.[67] It was therefore within the powers of the WHO to seek guidance from the court on the current legal position in regard to nuclear weapons.[68] The court incorrectly refused to recognize a power that would have helped the WHO fulfill its purposes and that did not violate any express provision in the WHO constitution. The court though did seem to want to alter precedent by adopting a narrower view of implied powers despite favorable citations to the *Reparation* and *Expenses* cases.[69] Its conservative view of implied powers here was the product of viewing the UN system as a series of closed organizations with little or no overlap. To recognize that the specialized agencies had wide-ranging implied powers would break down this division, undermining the court's concept of the UN system.

The court's view of the UN system was inaccurate (see Chapter 1), a nostalgic attempt to return to the blueprint of the immediate postwar era. The fact that the original system was so rapidly outdated shows that it was flawed upon inception, and so the court's opinion cannot be defended as an attempt to return to some sort of ideal. Unfortunately, in attempting to turn the clock back on the system the ICJ did the same thing to interpretation—adopting a narrow textual approach to a constituent treaty—and in terms of powers—regressing to a subjective approach. Although its views on the UN system, treaty interpretation, and powers may be internally consistent, they are externally inconsistent with its own jurisprudence and with the nature of the UN system.[70]

Despite the *Nuclear Weapons* decision, the United Nations is increasingly recognized as an international legal person equal to states, capable of performing sovereign acts. Its powers as well as its personality are not dependent on intent but exist under international law. Legal personality is accorded when certain objective criteria are met by an IGO; powers are accorded under a principle recognized by international law that an IGO, possessing personality, has powers that enable it to fulfill functions and are not expressly prohibited by its constitutive document. Under these principles the United Nations has achieved objective legal existence. This allows it to pursue its goals by a variety of means and to regulate states. The extent of this power remains to be seen.

The United Nations can and does take international action in a way similar to states. Furthermore, these international acts cannot often be matched to the express or implied powers found in the constituent document.[71] F. Seyersted analyzes the powers of the United Nations in terms entirely divorced from intent:

> It appears that while intergovernmental organizations, unlike States, are restricted by specific provisions in their constitutions as to the aims for which they shall work, such Organizations are, like States, in principle free to perform any sovereign act, or any act under international law, which they are in a factual position to perform to attain these aims, provided that their constitutions do not preclude such acts.

Furthermore,

> it is not necessary to look for specific provisions in the constitution, or to resort to strained interpretations of texts and intentions, or to look for precedents or constructions to justify legally the performance by an intergovernmental organization of a sovereign or international act not specifically authorized in its constitution. As an intergovernmental organization it has an *inherent power* to perform such acts.[72]

The doctrine of inherent powers has two clear advantages over the doctrine of implied powers. First, it satisfies the functionalist agenda by allowing the United Nations to fulfill its aims and not be bound by the legal niceties of its individual, and often obscurely drafted, compromise provisions. Second, it enables courts and commentators to review the actions of the organizations quickly and accurately as there are only two real legal controls. The action (1) must be aimed at achieving one of the purposes of the United Nations, and (2) must not be expressly prohibited by the constitution. If one of these legal thresholds is crossed, then an international court, jurist, or member state can maintain that the action is ultra vires (beyond the scope of its powers).

This reveals that the objective approach is based on a constitutional model; IGOs like the United Nations are governed by their constitutions and cannot exercise powers that do not fulfill the purposes of the IGO or violate express provisions. Thus they are different, legally and factually, than states, at least in the traditional positivist sense. Yet it cannot be denied that IGOs are the creation of states. States can limit IGOs when formulating their goals and, when establishing powers, by expressly prohibiting certain actions.

Once created by states, however, there is no denying that an IGO meeting the criteria of legal personality can take action that fulfills the purposes of the organization. States control the founding of the organization, not its development, though the significance of founding must not be underestimated. Although states make up the membership of the organization, they do not control it thereafter. A member state in the minority in the plenary body (e.g., the UN General Assembly) or one not represented in the executive organ (e.g., the UN Security Council) cannot object to resolutions that are contrary to its interests. Furthermore, many of the more technical specialized agencies that have increasing legislative capacity are run by individual experts rather than state representatives. UN employees in the various agencies, programs, and secretariats have an increasing influence on the work of the organization. Even in the more politicized organs of the United Nations—the Security Council and the General Assembly—due to the vagueness of the politically compromised mandates produced by the state representatives, there is considerable scope for individual development of those mandates.

The Value of Subsequent Practice

Recognizing inherent powers reduces the significance of subsequent practice as a method of developing UN powers, for UN powers are defined by the purposes of the constitution. However, the form those powers take is a product of practice (i.e., of the various UN organs). Furthermore, subsequent practice is the most dynamic form of interpreting and developing many other charter provisions—for instance, those that define the duties of the United Nations and its member states.

Although article 31(3) of the 1969 Vienna Convention on the Law of Treaties mentions subsequent agreement and subsequent practice as methods of interpretation, subsequent practice plays a dominant role in the United Nations and other organizations. It may be possible to view some practice as subsequent agreement—for instance, UN General Assembly resolutions adopted by consensus—but there appears to be no need for it, as the Vienna Convention views subsequent agreement and subsequent practice as equally valid.

Subsequent practice, as a means of interpreting, modifying, and possibly amending a treaty, is a gray area in the law. Although it is an issue of fundamental importance, especially for the constituent documents of international organizations or any other treaty that is a living instrument, there is considerable disagreement as to the role of subsequent practice in treaty interpretation.[73] Judge P. Spender in the *Expenses* case, although not an advocate of the narrow textual approach, came down against subsequent practice, as it operated against the sovereign will of a minority of states; he instead gave greater weight to the purposive approach.[74] Other writers follow the textual approach, a view adopted by Marxist writers during the Cold War. This derived partly from a desire not to be subject to a United Nations with greater powers than those originally agreed, partly from a doctrinaire position that the United Nations was a meeting place for states. In terms of treaty interpretation, this approach sticks to the original text. It does not cater to implied or inherent powers, which would allow the organization to extend beyond its treaty base. Neither does it allow for any significant interpretation by subsequent practice, which would allow the organization to act in a way differently than that allowed by its original constitution.[75]

Nevertheless, despite some formalist dissent, the principle of subsequent practice is accepted as a method of interpreting, developing, and even modifying original texts.[76] In regard to the type and level of practice required within a constituent treaty, Amerasinghe provides useful criteria. First, he is rightly careful to identify that a practical interpretation of a treaty must be based on a consistent line of conduct by an organ and be regarded as normative by that organ. Care must be taken not to fall into the trap of accepting, and thereby legitimating, the patterns of behavior.

What is important is that the conduct has been pursued by the organ in the belief that it was acting lawfully under the constitutive instrument. The practice usually does not reflect a sense of obligation but a sense that the practice or conduct is lawful or not unlawful under the governing provisions of the constitution.[77]

Second, where a practice does not amend a text but fills in lacunae or removes ambiguities, practice unanimously supported by the membership is sufficient. Amerasinghe states the following propositions in relation to the support within the particular organ in question: "Where there is a *large* majority in favour of the practice . . . it is arguable that a small obstinate minority, whether it is always the same minority or not, cannot obstruct an interpretation given by the membership of the organ."[78]

However, when there is a substantial minority opposing the interpretation, such practice has limited effect. "This position may change with time and repetition, as members adjust themselves to a new practice but the mere fact of a majority vote, irrespective of its size, cannot be sufficient to establish a practice."[79] The justification for these reasonably practical guidelines seems to be the achievement of a compromise between the two extremes identified at the outset of this chapter. The narrow view subjected any development to the express consent of all members—that is, the state was firmly in charge.[80] The wider view saw the organization as an autonomous international actor, and so emphasis is placed on the powers of the organization and its ability to reinvent itself, thereby reducing the role of state consent. Amerasinghe relies on implied consent:

> While a practice may not "change" a constitutional provision in the sense of amending it, a substantial minority may be entitled to maintain that it did not implicitly agree to "development" of the text against its will. The same argument may not be applied to a small minority. There is an element of implied agreement in the case of the latter, to the extent that it cannot obstruct the functioning of the organization.[81]

Implied consent also explains why the practice of the executive body can bind the whole membership.[82] Yet this use of implied consent has been criticized. A consistent line of conduct adopted by the requisite majority within an organ of the United Nations, accompanied by evidence that the majority views the behavior as normative, is evidence that the development of the charter is in the hands of those organs, not in the hands of the membership.

Subsequent practice can also amend a treaty. Here, however, a much greater evidence of practice must be present for amendment to occur. According to Amerasinghe, "Even if every party might not itself have actively participated in the practice, [the practice] must be such as to establish the agreement of the parties as a whole to the modification in question."[83] Thus when practice has allegedly modified the text, express consent, though still not in an absolute sense, prevails. This must be correct in regard to amendments that are directly contrary to the text. However, amendments that clarify or modify the meaning of the text will occur under the lower threshold identified by Amerasinghe.

The ICJ recognized an amendment to the UN Charter by practice in the *Namibia* case. There it considered South Africa's arguments that the Security Council resolution requesting the court's advisory opinion was invalid because two of the permanent members had abstained. According to South Africa, this did not comply with the requirements of article 27(3) that such decisions "shall be made by an affirmative vote of nine members including the concurring votes of the permanent members."

The court, by looking at "the proceedings of the Security Council, extending over a long period of time," concluded that the "practice of voluntary abstention by a permanent member" did not prevent the adoption of a valid resolution; only a negative vote by a permanent member constituted a veto. Although relying on the practice of the council, the court also noted that there was general support for this among the membership of the United Nations.[84] Although the practice did not result in an amendment that was directly contrary to the text, it did move the text a considerable way from its literal meaning.

Furthermore, despite some equivocation in the *Namibia* case, within the UN system it is not the practice of the membership that is to be examined but rather the practice of the organs.[85] This was recognized in an earlier decision of the ICJ when it stated that "the organs to which Article 4 entrusts the judgment of the Organization . . . have consistently interpreted the text."[86] The independence of the organization from the will of the membership is as apparent in the area of practice as it is in the areas of legal personality and powers.

Evolution Within the UN System

Thus a liberal approach to the charter favors flexibility and supports the living instrument ideal. This in turn encourages the development of the treaty by subsequent practice, as well as the fulfillment of the object and purpose, which in the case of constituent documents is in part achieved through the doctrines of implied and inherent powers. Although practice and the teleological approach encourage expansion from the express words, they do not necessarily encourage parallel expansion. What if practice is contrary to the object and purpose? Does this constitute a limitation on the development of the treaty by subsequent practice? Similarly, if practice indicates an interpretation that is directly contrary to the text, then is such practice valid? As in the analysis of powers, the text—in the form of the purposes and any express prohibitions—provides the framework within which practice can expand. The ICJ recognized that the main limitation on the practice of the United Nations was the purposes of the organization when it stated in the *Expenses* case that "when the Organization takes action which warrants the assertion that it was appropriate for the fulfilment of one of the stated purposes of the United Nations, the presumption is that such an action is not *ultra vires* the Organization."[87]

Although practice can amend certain provisions of the charter, the case against permitting amendments by consistent and overwhelming practice that violate the basic constitutional "values and principles most of which are set out in the Preamble and Articles 1 and 2" is overwhelming. To allow such amendments would be to undermine the basic constitutional order of the United Nations design to enhance peace, protect human rights, and promote development. "Constitutional change of a legal system" committed to these basic values "is inherently limited by the responsibility for maintaining" and furthering these values. "Such 'amendments' would result in a legal order so different from the constitution associated with the name of the United Nations to such an extent that the latter would have to be regarded as discontinued."[88] It will be seen, however, in Chapter 3 that development of these values as well as changes in the perceived hierarchy in these values are possible. A strengthening of these goals and values is enhancing the constitutional order of the United Nations.

Although practice cannot violate the purposes of the United Nations, it can amend other provisions, even those imposing duties on the United Nations itself, subject to the limitations outlined in the above section.[89] In particular, a very high threshold of practice must be achieved if the amendment is directly contrary to the wording of the treaty.

Modification of the UN Charter by subsequent practice can occur to develop the text, to fill in lacunae, and to provide concrete definitions of ambiguous terms, but it can also amend or revise the text and the plain meaning. However, if such a revision produces a result that is directly contrary to the text of the treaty, then the presumption must be that it is unlawful unless there is overwhelming and consistent support (at least to a level required for a formal amendment of the charter) for that revision among the membership. The line between interpretation and revision is inevitably blurred, and thus it is impossible in normal cases to apply separate rules about levels of support to each, except in the case of a clear violation of the core meaning of an express term. This requires the higher level of support required for amendment.

Thus the major limiting factors on the development of the powers and practice by UN organs and bodies are the purposes of the organization as contained in the charter and the constituent documents of the specialized agencies. Other limitations derived from general principles of international law must be that practice by UN organs cannot violate the peremptory rules of international law—*jus cogens* (fundamental laws).[90] The high degree of correlation between the purposes and principles of the UN Charter and the recognized rules of *jus cogens*[91] signify that such violations will be rare and, if they do occur, will in all likelihood violate the purposes of the charter as well. A final limitation is that the practice of the UN's organs and bodies cannot be undertaken in manifest bad faith.[92]

Conclusion

Although there is considerable flexibility and scope for development within the UN system, it is governed by the rule of law. Laws take shape in the fundamental values of the UN system as contained in the constitutional documents, as well as the fundamental values of the international legal order as a whole—the rules of *jus cogens*. The constitutional order based on the rule of law would be strengthened if the ICJ had the power to review the legality of UN action (see Chapter 5).

Yet despite this deficiency in the constitutional structure, the treaties of the UN system are living instruments. They are kept relevant by the practice of the organs created by those treaties, practice that to be intra vires (within the scope of their powers) should occur within the confines of the four corners of each treaty. The conduct of the organs in enumerating and applying the inherent powers of the United Nations makes for a dynamic and flexible mechanism that should allow the United Nations to take concerted action to achieve its values.

International law recognizes the significance of IGOs in general, and the United Nations in particular, by accepting UN autonomy in three fundamental ways: first, by accepting the original international legal personality of the IGOs operating in the UN system; second, by recognizing the existence of powers that further the purposes of the United Nations; and third, by accepting the ability of the organs of UN IGOs to develop their treaties by conduct. Each factor strengthens the independence of the United Nations and reduces the membership's control over the whole. Thus the basis of the UN system is not the intent of the members but the *will of the organization*. This will is directed toward the establishment of a UN legal order that aims to fulfill the values of the United Nations by directing and regulating state behavior. I now turn to the UN's values.

Notes

1. Art. 108 of the UN Charter.
2. Simma, *The Charter,* 1176–1178.

3. See, for example, Art. 7 ILO Constitution; Art. 5 FAO Constitution; Art. 5 UNESCO Constitution.

4. Art. 8 IBRD Agreement; Art. 28 IMF Agreement.

5. Art. 20 FAO Constitution; Art. 13 UNESCO Constitution; Art. 73 WHO Constitution; Art. 94 ICAO Convention; Art. 62 IMO Constitution.

6. Art. 108 UN Charter; Art. 28(c) IMF Agreement; Art. 8(c) IBRD Agreement; Art. 73 WHO Constitution.

7. Art. 94 ICAO Convention.

8. See, for example, Art. 3 *bis*, ICAO Convention (not yet in force).

9. See also Schermers and Blokker, *International Institutional Law,* 734–737.

10. *Reservations to the Genocide Convention,* ICJ Rep. 1951, 53.

11. Fitzmaurice, "Law and Procedure," 1.

12. McDougal, Lasswell, and Miller, *Interpretation of International Agreements,* 78–79.

13. Art. 31.

14. Art. 32.

15. Art. 31(3)(b).

16. *Second Admissions* case, ICJ Rep. 1950, 18.

17. Rosenne, *Developments in the Law of Treaties,* 244.

18. Pollux, "The Interpretation of the Charter," 54.

19. See Art. 31(1) of the Vienna Convention of the Law of Treaties, 1969.

20. McDougal, "The International Law Commission's," 992.

21. Tomuschat, "Obligations Arising," 251–252.

22. Higgins, *Problems and Process,* 184.

23. McDougal, Reisman, and Willard, "The World Process of Effective Power," 357.

24. But see Bedermen, "The Souls of International Organizations," 277.

25. Higgins, "Western Interpretations," 194.

26. Brezhnev cited in Morozov, "The Socialist Conception," 179. See also Tunkin, "The Legal Nature of the United Nations," 15; Goodwin, "World Institutions," 63.

27. Amerasinghe, *Principles,* 78.

28. Ibid., citing several PCIJ judgments on the powers of the ILO at n. 30.

29. Schermers and Blokker, *International Institutional Law,* 978–979.

30. Few IGOs expressly claim personality—see, for example, Art. 31 of the Statute establishing the World Tourism Organization, 985 UNTS 339; Art. 210 of the Treaty of Rome, 298 UNTS 11.

31. Art. 104 of the UN Charter is insufficient in this respect in that it only states that the United Nations "shall enjoy in the territory of each of its Members such legal capacity as may be necessary for the exercise of its functions and the fulfilment of its purposes." This only recognizes the UN capacity in domestic law, not in international law; Simma, *The Charter,* 1126.

32. See Art. 16 FAO Constitution, UKTS 47 (1946); Art. 12 UNESCO Constitution, 4 UNTS 275; Art. 66 WHO Constitution, 14 UNTS 185; Art. 47 ICAO Convention on Civil Aviation, 15 UNTS 295; Art. 60 IMO Convention,

289 UNTS 48. For slightly stronger, but still insufficient, wording, see Art. 39 ILO Constitution, UKTS 47 (1948); Art. 7(2) IBRD Agreement, 2 UNTS 134; Art. 9(2) IMF Agreement, 1 UNTS 39. See Schermers and Blokker, *International Institutional Law,* 995.

33. Schermers and Blokker, *International Institutional Law,* 979.

34. See also Bowett, *Institutions,* 337.

35. On the requirements of statehood, see Harris, *Cases and Materials,* 102–104.

36. Amerasinghe, *Principles,* 89–90.

37. Brownlie, *Principles,* 679–680.

38. Amerasinghe, *Principles,* 83.

39. Higgins, *Problems and Process,* 46–47.

40. *Reparation for Injuries* case, ICJ Rep. 1949, 174.

41. Ibid., 178.

42. Ibid., 178–179.

43. Amerasinghe, *Principles,* 80–81. But see Schermers and Blokker, *Institutional Law,* 979.

44. *Reparation* case, 179.

45. Ibid., 180. See also *WHO Agreement* case, ICJ Rep. 1980, 89.

46. Schermers and Blokker, *International Institutional Law,* 981; Amerasinghe, *Principles,* 99.

47. Schermers and Blokker, *International Institutional Law,* 981.

48. Bowett, *Institutions,* 341–345, 362–363; Bekker, *Legal Position,* 96; Rama-Montaldo, "International Legal Personality," 155. But see Brownlie, *Principles,* 681–687.

49. Amerasinghe, *Principles,* 97–100; Brownlie, *Principles,* 687–689.

50. Amerasinghe, *Principles,* 97.

51. Rama-Montaldo, "International Legal Personality," 143.

52. The court attempted to distinguish "functional" protection offered by IGOs from "diplomatic" protection offered by states; *Reparation* case, 182–186.

53. Ibid., 182–183.

54. Ibid., 198.

55. But see *Effect of Awards* case, ICJ Rep. 1954, 57.

56. *Namibia* case, ICJ Rep. 1971, 46–47, 49–50.

57. See also the ICJ's view on SC Res. 276, *Namibia* case, 52.

58. Bowett, *Institutions,* 337–338.

59. Rama-Montaldo, "International Legal Personality," 122.

60. *Expenses* case, ICJ Rep. 1962, 167–168.

61. Ibid., 163.

62. Bowett, *Institutions,* 338.

63. *Expenses* case, 163–164.

64. Seyersted, *United Nations Forces,* 133–134.

65. Seyersted, "Basic Distinctions in the Law," 691.

66. *Legality of the Use by a State of Nuclear Weapons in Armed Conflict,* ICJ Rep. 1996, 76.

67. See Arts. 1 and 2 of the WHO Constitution.

68. Akande, "The Competence of International Organizations," 443–450.

69. *Legality of Nuclear Weapons,* 78–79.

70. See also White, "The World Court, the WHO."

71. Seyersted, "International Personality," 6, 19.

72. Seyersted, *United Nations,* 155.

73. Waldock, "Third Report," 59–60; Sato, *Evolving Constitutions,* 232.

74. ICJ Rep. 1962, 184–185.

75. Haraszti, *Fundamental Problems,* 63–64.

76. Jacobs, "Varieties of Approach to Treaty Interpretation," 332; McNair, *Law of Treaties,* 424–431; Fitzmaurice, "Law and Procedure," 223–225; Sinclair, *The Vienna Convention,* 136–138.

77. Amerasinghe, *Principles,* 50.

78. Ibid., 51.

79. Ibid., 52.

80. Sinclair, *The Vienna Convention,* 138.

81. Amerasinghe, *Principles,* 53. See also Sato, *Evolving Constitutions,* 32; ILC (1966) 2 *YearBook of the ILC,* 222, at para. 15; Lauterpacht, "The Development of the Law," 460.

82. Amerasinghe, *Principles,* 55.

83. Ibid., 419, citing the ILC (1966) 2 *YearBook of the ILC,* 236.

84. *Namibia* case, para. 22.

85. Fassbender, "The United Nations Charter," 598.

86. *Competence of the Assembly,* ICJ Rep. 1950, 15.

87. ICJ Rep. 1962, 168.

88. Fassbender, "The United Nations Charter," 605.

89. See for example article 2(7) of the charter—White, *Keeping the Peace,* 55–59, 155–157.

90. *Application of the Genocide Convention,* ICJ Rep. 1993, 439–482 (Judge Lauterpacht).

91. Fassbender, "The United Nations Charter," 589–593.

92. Franck, "The *Bona Fides* of Power," 191.

3

The UN's Values

In Chapter 1, I established at least a strong presumption that there is a UN system with an integral UN legal order based on constitutional foundations. In Chapter 2, I explained the legal mechanisms by which that system and order are continually and dynamically able to evolve to meet the needs of the international community. In this chapter, I delineate the core values of the UN system. Many of these values—peace, human rights, self-determination—marked new departures for the international community in 1945. They provide the goals to which the system aspires, as well as the benchmarks against which the success and failure of the system can be measured. The values to be identified here are, in essence, the raison d'être of the entire system.

Many of these values are found in the preambles and opening articles of the principal treaties. Core values have been elaborated upon by the practice of the various IGOs in the United Nations. However, resolutions produced by organs of IGOs should not be treated the same as treaty texts given their usage of rhetorical language. Nevertheless, other values have been added to the core laid down in the immediate postwar period.

The first new value reflects the emergence of a serious problem facing the international community: protecting the *environment*.[1] This has been thrust into the list of values since the UN Conference on the Human Environment held in Stockholm in 1972. The rapid development of mechanisms and bodies to prevent further deterioration of the global environment is testament to the need to embed environmental protection as a core value, although there is still controversy surrounding the methods and principles.

The promotion of *democracy* also is established as a core value, deriving from the principle of self-determination. A more detailed analysis of this value will follow; suffice it to say for the moment that the promotion of democracy does not only reflect a change in ideology corresponding with the end of the Cold War in the 1980s.

The consistency of these new values with the established order needs to be examined. Protecting the environment and promoting democracy can be firmly tied to the UN's core value of protecting and promoting *human rights*. They are in the nature of third-generation (i.e., people's) human rights rather than first- and second-generation (i.e., individual) rights with which the United Nations had traditionally concerned itself.[2] However, the principle of *self-determination,* a third-generation right, is a value that the United Nations recognized in 1945 and has developed since. Although it is possible to see these UN values and others as human rights, progress on this front is hard to achieve.

Other established UN values to be examined in the course of this chapter are *peace and security, justice and law,* and *economic and social well-being.*[3] Whereas peace and security are largely the concern of the principal organs established by the UN Charter, many of the other values are pursued by the specialized agencies and subsidiary bodies and programs. This has in part led to a perceived hierarchy with peace and security being at the top, whereas others are of secondary value (discussed further below).

Peace and Security

The values of peace and security are listed in the preamble and article 1 of the UN Charter. The preamble speaks of saving "succeeding generations from the scourge of war," as well as of uniting "our strength to maintain international peace and security." Article 1(1) states that one of the purposes of the United Nations is to take effective collective measures to combat "acts of aggression or other breaches of the peace," as well as the removal of "threats to the peace." Article 2(3) then obliges member states to settle disputes by peaceful means, and article 2(4) places them under a duty not to use or threaten force in their international relations, thereby reinforcing the commitment of the United Nations to eradicate armed force as an instrument of state policy.

Although there are no definitions of "peace" or "security" in the charter, it can be gleaned from the above provisions that fairly restrictive (or negative) interpretations can be given to these values.[4] Peace can be viewed as the absence of war, probably only international and not civil wars. Security can be seen as safety from international uses of armed force. However, these are flexible terms. For instance, the concept of threat to the peace does not, by itself, appear limited to international uses of force. Article 1(1) also mentions the settlement of international disputes by peaceful means "in conformity with the principles of justice and international law." The introduction of the values of justice and law alongside peace and security has the potential to allow for cross-fertilization of values. These caveats to the negative definitions of peace and security have enabled the United Nations to develop the concept of peace to include the absence of civil conflicts and the concept of security to include, for example, safety from human rights abuses.[5]

Here the focus will be on the concept of peace, as security involves a separate analysis of the UN collective security system designed to protect the value of peace. Nevertheless, looking at the UN Security Council and General Assembly in practice, there has been a movement away from defining peace as the absence of war.[6] In fact, as early as 1949 the UN General Assembly gave an expansive definition. It included not only noninternational use of force but also any outside fomentation of civil war, the effective regulation of weaponry, respect for human rights, and the promotion of higher standards of living.[7] The absence of war is one component in positive or just peace recognized by the assembly. Although other resolutions have occasionally veered toward negative peace, these seemed to be more a case of the assembly focusing on different aspects of peace in different resolutions. For instance, the 1984 Declaration on the Right of Peoples to Peace focused more on negative peace.[8] The declaration emphasized that

> the exercise of the right of peoples to peace demands that the policies of States be directed towards the elimination of the threat of war, particularly nuclear war, the renunciation of the use of force in international relations and the settlement of disputes by peaceful means.

This can be contrasted to the assembly's 1991 Promotion of Peace resolution, which stated that

> peace is not merely the absence of war, but that interdependence and cooperation to foster human rights, social and economic development, disarmament, protection of the environment and ecosystems and the improvement of the quality of life for all are indispensable elements for the establishment of peaceful societies.[9]

In 1996 the General Assembly developed the concept of positive peace further to include respect for democracy.[10]

In addition to developing the aspects of positive peace, the assembly has also kept the notion of negative peace up to date, recognizing in 1996 that the violent disintegration of states can threaten international peace and that the absence of force should include the elimination of terrorist violence.[11] In the 1994 Declaration on Measures to Eliminate International Terrorism, the assembly stated:

> Acts, methods and practices of terrorism constitute a grave violation of the purposes and principles of the United Nations, which may pose a threat to international peace and security, jeopardize friendly relations among States, hinder international cooperation [aspects of negative peace] and aim at the destruction of human rights, fundamental freedoms and the democratic bases of society [aspects of positive peace].[12]

Although the assembly has radically developed the concept of peace, it has been wary of advocating intervention in purely civil conflicts to protect negative peace. However, it has been forthright in advocating the promotion of human rights, self-determination, and democracy in these situations. Resolutions on Non-Intervention in 1965[13] and Friendly Relations in 1970[14] emphasize the principle of nonintervention in the internal or external affairs of states. However, this principle, contained in article 2(7), has an exception built into it allowing the Security Council to intervene in the domestic jurisdiction of a state using enforcement measures under chapter VII.

I now turn to the Security Council, looking at how it has developed the concept of threat to the peace in article 39 of the UN Charter to include civil conflicts. The focus here is on threat to the peace, as breaches of the peace and acts of aggression are more applicable to traditional interstate violence.[15]

In its early existence, and faced with the Arab-Israeli conflict in 1948, the Security Council adopted a very restrictive approach to peace. It did this by placing the concept of threat to the peace solely in the context of interstate conflict as prelude to a determination of a breach of the peace.[16] The number of internal conflicts in the post-1945 world order led to a refashioning of the notion of a threat to the peace, although the council still required there to be international repercussions before it determined a civil war to be a threat to the peace. The condition of a threat to *international* peace was made explicit in the council's determination that the civil war in the Congo was a threat to the peace in 1961 due to the presence of international elements (Belgian troops and mercenaries) and the potential of the conflict to drag in outside states.[17] More obvious was the determination that the situation in Cyprus, where civil strife had been in evidence for a decade, constituted a threat to international peace in 1974 following the Turkish intervention in northern Cyprus.[18] Both of these cases are indicative of a partial move toward a more complete concept of negative peace, to include absence of war, whether international or civil.

Furthermore, positive aspects of peace could be secured only if there was an internal conflict that had international repercussions. The southern Rhodesia question met these requirements. There was not just an internal conflict, in that the guerrilla campaign to oust the white minority regime operated in part from surrounding frontline states. The denial of self-determination, which was at the heart of the Rhodesian question, was the target of Security Council action from 1966. However, the action followed a finding of a threat to the peace primarily because there was a civil war with international repercussions.[19] The council was not prepared to recognize that a denial of self-determination could by itself constitute a threat to the peace. It came close to this in its dealings with the apartheid regime in South Africa, although its determination in 1977 that there was a threat to the peace was linked to the acquisition of arms by South Africa, as well as its attacks on frontline states. However, the resolution also made reference to the "policies" of the racist regime.[20]

Nevertheless, the post–Cold War practice of the Security Council indicates it is adopting a more complete concept of negative peace to include purely internal situations involving "extreme violence."[21] In addition, there is an increasing recognition of the importance of positive peace, though this aspect is still dependent on the existence of an armed conflict, whether international or civil. The determination that the internal conflicts in Iraq in 1991,[22] Yugoslavia in 1991,[23] and Somalia in 1992[24] constituted threats to the peace were followed by findings of threats in relation to civil conflicts in Liberia[25] and Angola in 1992–1993.[26] The Security Council extended the concept to cover widespread violations of humanitarian law in Bosnia in 1993,[27] as well as massive humanitarian crises caused by conflict in Rwanda, Burundi, Zaire, Albania, Kosovo, East Timor, and Sierra Leone in 1994–1999.[28] Further moves toward a complete conception of negative peace are reflected in the council's designation of terrorism, especially when state-sponsored, as constituting a threat to the peace. This occurred in the case of Libya in 1992 (as evidenced by the Lockerbie bombing in 1988),[29] Sudan in 1996 (as evidenced by the attempted assassination attempt on President Hosni Mubarek in 1995),[30] as well as the Taliban regime in Afghanistan in 1999 (as evidenced by its support for Osama bin Laden).[31]

The council strengthened and developed this line of resolutions in September 2001 when it recognized that the acts of hijacking in the United States that led to the destruction of the World Trade Center and damage to the Pentagon constituted a threat to international peace and security. The council made it clear than any act of international terrorism was a threat to the peace.[32] Although the council condemned states harboring or sponsoring terrorism, the resolution was not solely directed against those states but also the individuals responsible. The council's approach to terrorism has thus moved beyond the state-sponsored variety. This is illustrated by the follow-up measures, binding on states, that were directed against *all* states, not certain rogue ones. The measures were directed at terrorists, especially their finances, which can be found in any state.[33]

The practice of the Security Council shows that it has developed the concept of threat to the peace to cover the absence of conflict whatever its modern form.[34] Its moves toward promoting positive peace are tangential to the existence of such a conflict. Although the initial finding of a threat to the peace in Somalia was based on the civil conflict raging there since 1992, later resolutions determined that "the magnitude of the human tragedy caused by the conflict in Somalia, further exacerbated by the obstacles being created to the distribution of humanitarian assistance, constituted a threat to international peace and security."[35]

The council does not determine that famine in and of itself can constitute a threat to the peace. However, in the case of Haiti the council stretched the link between internal conflict and the denial of a positive aspect of peace to the breaking point. In 1993, the Security Council determined that the humanitarian crisis and the problems of refugees in Haiti—and then the failure by the military regime to restore the democratically elected leaders of Haiti—constituted a threat to the peace.[36] Although there was clear evidence of brutal repression by the military regime, the emphasis was on the denial of democracy in Haiti, and it can be argued that this was what the Security Council decided was the threat to the peace. Other indications that the Security Council is moving toward extending the concept of threat to cover aspects of positive peace can be found in the statement made by heads of state and government at the special meeting of the Security Council held in January 1992, when environmental disasters were mentioned as potential threats to the peace.[37]

Although the concept of peace in both assembly and council practice has developed beyond the absence of war, most practice has centered on prevention or removal of armed conflicts and the use of military force. Positive aspects, such as the protection of human rights, have occurred only in the wake of international or civil conflict. Of course, the General Assembly, the Security Council, and many other UN bodies promote and protect human rights and other positive aspects of peace. Indeed, these are reviewed below as UN values in their own right. However, it will be seen that the most powerful body in the UN system—the UN Security Council—reserves its most coercive powers almost exclusively for dealing with ruptures of peace caused by the occurrence of armed conflict. The Security Council has imposed economic sanctions and taken military measures in those situations it has deemed to be a threat to the peace as defined in practice, as well as breaches of international peace (see Chapter 6).

The Security Council's possession and use of supranational powers to prevent and control war explain the paramountcy often accorded to the value of peace, as do the circumstances in which the United Nations was created—at the end of a devastating interstate conflict.[38] The ICJ in the *Expenses* case, for instance, examined the purposes of the United Nations and stated that the maintenance of international peace and security had "primary place."[39] The General Assembly has recognized that the protection of peace "is one of the foremost" purposes of the United Nations.[40] Although the ICJ characterized this primacy as a prerequisite to the fulfillment of the other UN purposes, it remains an unproven assumption. Requiring that peace be established before other values are protected is dangerous, placing the need to assert order over justice and other positive aspects of peace.[41] The primacy argument is refuted by the functionalist school of thought, which sees the protection of security as one of many common problems that can lead to international cooperation.[42] As M. Bedjaoui has stated, there can be "no development without peace, no peace without development."[43] Thus rather than prioritizing the UN's values, all the UN's values should carry equal status and be protected and upheld as such. Take one example involving only two of the UN's values: peace and humanitarian assistance. People can differ as to whether a famine is caused by a war or whether the war results from the desperate fight for limited resources. The dual aims of the United Nations should be to stop the war and to prevent starvation. Priority can be given to one over the other given practical exigencies, but there is no reason in law or logic why peace should be given priority over other values in every situation.

Yet peace as a value dominates the UN system, and the only way to reconcile this apparent contradiction is to recognize that negative peace is a value alongside all others. Positive peace, however, is an overarching value that draws on all the others, including negative peace. The only exception to this is the value of law and justice. Many of the UN's constituent treaties reflect the status of positive peace as the fundamental value. The ICAO treaty, the so-called Chicago Convention of 1944, states in the preamble that the "future development of international civil aviation can greatly help to create and preserve friendship and understanding among the nations and peoples of the world, yet its abuse can become a threat to general security." This is demonstrated by the horrific events in the United States on 11 September 2001, when hijacked civilian airliners toppled the World Trade Center and damaged the Pentagon, killing thousands of innocents.

The preamble of the 1946 UNESCO constitution is even more forthright in proclaiming that the furtherance of educational, scientific, and cultural goals is a means of securing peace. It boldly states that "since wars begin in the minds of men, it is in the minds of men that the defences to peace must be constructed." Of course the conception is a just and lasting peace, rather than the absence of war. This is clear in the preamble, which also states that "the great and terrible war which has now ended was a war made possible by the denial of the democratic principles of the dignity, equality and mutual respect of men." Peace "based exclusively upon the political and economic arrangements of governments" would not last, so peace must be founded "upon the intellectual and moral solidarity of mankind." The preamble then goes on to declare that UNESCO was created for the "purpose of advancing, through the educational and scientific and cultural relations of the peoples of the world, the objectives of international peace and the common welfare of mankind for which the United Nations Organization was established and which its Charter proclaims." The preamble of the 1946 WHO constitution declares that the "health of all peoples is fundamental to the attainment of peace and security." Finally, the preamble of the 1919 ILO constitution declares that "universal and lasting peace can be established only if based upon social justice." The integrity of the system is apparent with the value of peace, perhaps more in the negative sense, being pursued by the United Nations while positive aspects are pursued by the specialized agencies.

Justice and Law

In light of the thriving UN legal order, law and justice are core values within the system, perhaps the primary values. All the other values and mechanisms attached to them are based on the legal foundation of the UN Charter; for that reason they are legal as well as political values. Law and justice underpin these other values—especially human rights. Thus positive peace, which has been shown to overarch the other values, and all the other values of the system are ultimately based on law and justice, thereby establishing a hierarchy of values. However, it is argued that the Security Council is not always limited by international law regarding protecting peace.[44] This argument is supported by charter article 1(1), which states that the "principles of justice and international law" relate only to the peaceful settlement of disputes, not to collective measures to address threats to or breaches of the peace. The Security Council has latitude to take coercive action under chapter VII, but this does not mean that it can ignore fundamental principles of international (such as *jus cogens*) or charter law (namely, the basic values of the system).

Furthermore, notions of law and justice[45] are infusing all other values. This is shown by the fact that it is possible to see most of the core values as human rights and therefore legal rights belonging to people either individually or collectively—the right to peace, the right to a clean environment, the right to health, the right to democracy, and the like. There is evidence that the orientation of the core values is toward individuals and away from states. However, progress toward this has been variable, so in some areas, especially peace, the environment, and development, protection of these values has not always occurred in a human rights context. This signifies that the existence of a right to peace, a right to a clean environment, and a right to development remains largely theoretical. Indeed, it can be argued that the effective protection of these values is not dependent on them being recognized in practice as human rights.

Nevertheless, in many of its recent dealings with armed conflicts, the Security Council has recognized that the achievement of justice in a situation is just as important as securing peace and actually an integral part of that peace. By establishing the ICTY in 1993 for the prosecution of individuals responsible for violations of international humanitarian law in the former Yugoslavia,[46] and the ICTR in 1994 for prosecuting individuals responsible for breaches of international humanitarian law and genocide in Rwanda, the Security Council recognized that the implementation of justice would "contribute to the process of national reconciliation and to the restoration and maintenance of peace."[47]

The core values of justice and law are also recognized in the preamble to the charter, which states that the United Nations is determined to "establish the conditions under which justice and respect for the obligations arising from treaties and other sources of international law can be maintained." There is debate over the difference, if any, between justice and law, with some suggestions that the former introduces notions of natural law into the charter.[48] Another possibility is that justice refers to equity—a notion that has more precise legal content and is meant to remedy the injustices that can arise by the formalistic application of law to the facts.[49] The notion of justice appears to be introduced to emphasize that the strict application of positive law might not always produce fairness, so that the law should be applied in a way to produce justice.[50] Within the UN context, justice is achieved by the application of law if it furthers rather than denudes one or more UN values.

The UN system is governed by charter law, makes and develops international law, and encourages the development of municipal systems based on the rule of law.[51] Law is central to the system, though there are still defects—for example, lack of legal accountability and deficiencies in enforcement. Here I outline the contribution of the United Nations to the development of law by sponsoring treaties and formulating lawmaking/codifying resolutions on matters such as space law and the law of the sea.[52] The basic mandate for these activities comes from article 13(1)(a) of the charter, which empowers the UN General Assembly to initiate studies and make recommendations for the purpose of "encouraging the progressive development of international law and its codification." In its resolutions on the UN Decade of International Law (1990–1999), this mandate was extended to include the promotion of the acceptance of international law, greater use of the ICJ (see Chapter 5), and the encouragement of the teaching, study, and dissemination of international law.[53]

Much of the work on developing and codifying international law comes through the Sixth Committee of the UN General Assembly, which inter alia, receives and acts upon reports of the International Law Commission (ILC)—a subsidiary organ of the UN General Assembly established in 1947.[54] The impact of the ILC on the development of international law has fallen short, although it has made significant contributions to the drafting of fundamental treaties.[55] In addition, it has made progress on the Draft Code of Crimes Against the Peace and Security of Mankind (including aggression, genocide, crimes against humanity, and crimes against UN personnel). It submitted draft articles[56] in December 1996 to the General Assembly, which sent them out for comments from states.[57] The ILC first had this item on its agenda in 1947. An adequate explanation of the extreme slowness of the project is that it is unlike most of the other projects for which the ILC prepared drafts: "The great majority of projects prepared by the ILC dealt with questions that did not involve profound political differences among states; they were mainly technical matters of international law."[58]

The end of the Cold War has meant that some measure of agreement has been possible on matters fundamental to establishing peaceful international relations based on respect for principles of law and justice. The establishment of the code, either as a treaty or a declaration by the General Assembly, alongside the closely related statute for an International Criminal Court (derived from an ILC draft)[59] agreed at Rome in 1998,[60] will at last lay the basic foundations for a truly international system of criminal justice. However, it may be that the advent of the statute on the International Criminal Court will have a negative effect on the development of the draft code, whose terms are somewhat more radical than the statute of the court, certainly as to the crimes covered. Yet the progress made in the ILC demonstrates that the values of the UN system are increasingly focused not only on the rights of the individual but also on individuals' responsibilities.

The value is being advanced in formulating basic principles of international law. Furthermore, lawmaking occurs in far greater detail and depth in technical matters, where agreement is more readily achieved. This occurs in several of the specialized agencies—the ICAO in regard to regulation of air services; the IMO in regard to the regulation of shipping; the ITU in regard to the allocation of radio frequencies and increasingly orbital slots for satellites; the UPU in regard to the regulation of postal services; and the WIPO in regard to the protection of intellectual property. In addition, the IAEA, which has a close relationship with the United Nations, shares the same lawmaking features as the agencies mentioned above, with its standards on the use of nuclear energy and power, though not always binding in a treaty sense, being treated as law by states.[61] Many of the other agencies contribute to the development in law (see below).

Human Rights

Human rights is a core value of the UN system featured in the UN Charter, in the preamble, and in articles 1(3), 13(1)(b), 55, 56, and 62. These provisions are repetitious. The basic value is stated in the preamble, where there is affirmation of "faith in fundamental human rights, in the dignity and worth of the human person, in the equal rights of men and women and of nations large and small." Article 13 charges the General Assembly with promoting the realization of human rights, and article 62 enables ECOSOC to make recommendations or prepare draft conventions on the issue. Article 55 requires the United Nations as a whole to "promote . . . universal respect for, and observance of, human rights and fundamental freedoms for all without distinction as to race, sex, language, or religion." Article 56 places an obligation on members to cooperate with the United Nations for the achievement of the purposes stated in article 55.

Although human rights receives many mentions, there is no development of its content or any significant machinery to ensure adequate compliance by members. Indeed, there is no express obligation for states to protect human rights. Though the UN Charter is woefully lacking in substance, many of the UN specialized agencies, including the ILO, FAO, WHO, and UNESCO, were charged with promoting and protecting human rights. This has been achieved by setting standards, in the form of recommendations, regulations, and treaties, in specific areas such as rights in the workplace, freedom from hunger, the right to health, and education.[62] The United Nations itself was quick to fill the gaps in the UN Charter, with ECOSOC establishing the UN Commission on Human Rights in 1946.[63] That body produced the Universal Declaration of Human Rights (UDHR) adopted by the General Assembly in 1948 as a "common standard of achievement for all peoples and nations."[64]

The declaration contains twenty-seven rights and freedoms, protecting civil as well as political rights and freedoms: rights to life, privacy, fair trial, free movement, freedom of thought and religion, freedom of expression and assembly, and the right to take part in government; and freedoms from slavery, torture, discrimination, and arbitrary arrest. The

UDHR also promotes economic, social, and cultural rights: rights to social security, work, rest, and leisure, adequate standard of living, education, and to participate in the cultural life of the community.

Although formally a nonbinding resolution of the General Assembly, the UDHR has become the yardstick against which state behavior is
measured. This was recognized as early as 1966 at the first World Conference on Human Rights in Tehran[65] and was reaffirmed by the Vienna
Conference on Human Rights in 1993.[66] Further declarations by the assembly to mark the fiftieth anniversary of the declaration affirm its status as the core[67]—universal, not merely international[68]—human rights
document. "The standards contained in the [UDHR] are, in practice, applicable to every state, whatever its formal attitude to their status."[69]

Along with a proliferation in human rights machinery (see Chapter
9) designed to supervise compliance with the standards first recognized
in the UDHR, the United Nations has developed those standards through
a combination of declarations and treaties. The principal declarations
are the 1959 Declaration on the Rights of the Child, the 1963 Declaration on the Elimination of All Forms of Racial Discrimination, the 1967
Declaration on the Elimination of Discrimination Against Women, the
1981 Declaration on the Elimination of All Forms of Intolerance and of
Discrimination Based on Religion or Belief, and the 1992 Declaration
on the Rights of Persons Belonging to National or Ethnic, Religious and
Linguistic Minorities. Recent sessions of the General Assembly show
that its current concerns are in relation to the rights of female children,[70]
the right of women and girls to be free from sexual violence and sexual
trafficking,[71] and the freedom of women and girls from genital muti-
lation.[72] None of these latest issues have yet fully entered into UN law
in the form of a universally accepted declaration or treaty.

Further development in the entrenchment of human rights standards
is even more evident in the number of UN-sponsored human rights
treaties, with many of the more recent ones establishing machinery for
the supervision of the treaty obligations contained therein. Although
binding only on state parties, several treaties provide more intrusive
mechanisms than those contained in UN declarations. The several treaty
bodies such as the Committee Against Torture and the HRC, though
technically separate treaty-based bodies, have factual and formal links
to the UN system and therefore are treated as part of it here. The treaties
together with the declarations form an impressive body of UN human
rights law, which is a tremendous statement about human rights as a UN
value. The principal treaties are the 1948 Convention on the Prevention

and Punishment of the Crime of Genocide, the 1966 Convention on the Elimination of All Forms of Racial Discrimination, the 1973 Convention on the Suppression and Punishment of the Crime of Apartheid, the 1979 Convention on the Elimination of All Forms of Discrimination Against Women, the 1984 Convention Against Torture and Other Cruel, Inhuman, or Degrading Treatment or Punishment, and the 1989 Convention on the Rights of the Child. Many of these were drafted in the Human Rights Commission, in particular the 1966 Covenants on Civil and Political Rights and Economic and Cultural Rights, which together with the UDHR constitute an international bill of rights.

Furthermore, the United Nations has developed the value of human rights to cover three generations of rights without hierarchy. Although first-generation (civil and political) rights are more firmly embedded in Western philosophy, "the premise underlying all human rights texts is that civil and political rights and economic, social and cultural rights [second-generation rights] are of equal priority, with the realisation of the two groups of rights being interdependent."[73] This is reflected in the presence of both in the UDHR and the emergence of a foundational international covenant for each type. Whereas first- and second-generation rights belong to the individual, third-generation rights, which have emerged since the 1970s, are group, or collective, rights. Some of these have already been depicted—a peoples' right to peace and a group's right to freedom from genocide. Others will be discussed below (e.g., peoples' rights to self-determination, to democracy, to the environment, to development, and to humanitarian assistance). Although some are less firmly embedded in UN law, third-generation rights are undoubtedly human rights of equal value to first- and second-generation rights, though not necessarily equally protected.[74] The Vienna Declaration on Human Rights of 1993 states that "all human rights are universal, indivisible and interdependent and interrelated. The international community must treat human rights globally in a fair and equal manner, on the same footing, and with the same emphasis."[75]

Self-Determination and Democracy

The values of self-determination and democracy are analyzed together because democracy develops from self-determination. Self-determination is found in article 1(2), which states that one UN purpose is the development of friendly relations among nations "based on respect for the principle of equal rights and self-determination of peoples." The principle of self-determination is also found in article 55. The UN Charter lacks any elaboration of this principle, though it can be argued that the declaration regarding non–self-governing territories contained in articles 73 and 74, creating certain obligations for administering powers, is the only concrete charter application of the principle.[76] Again practice has elevated this value into a general legal right[77] recognized by the ICJ.[78]

The development of the right of self-determination has occurred through the Declaration on the Granting of Independence to Colonial Countries and Peoples of 1960[79] and the Declaration on Principles of International Law Concerning Friendly Relations and Cooperation Among States in Accordance with the Charter of the United Nations (the Declaration on Friendly Relations) of 1970.[80] In addition, the two UN-sponsored International Covenants on Human Rights of 1966 both guarantee in article 1 the right of peoples to self-determination. The protection of this right by the committees that are empowered to uphold the two covenants has provided content to the right (see Chapter 9).

The core meaning of the right of self-determination can be gleaned from the two principal assembly resolutions. The 1960 declaration states that "the subjection of peoples to alien subjugation, domination and exploitation constitutes a denial of fundamental human rights, is contrary to the Charter of the United Nations." The declaration then states that "all peoples have the right to self-determination, by virtue of their right they freely determine their political status and freely pursue their economic, social and cultural development." Those peoples entitled to self-determination are those subject peoples, not only those in colonies or non–self-governing territories. UN practice "suggests that the peoples the United Nations had in mind were categories of subjugated peoples: those non-self-governing, those occupied, those under foreign rule and those deprived of a previous independent condition."[81]

However, self-determination does not permit secession from an established state as recognized by the 1960 declaration, which stated that "any attempt aimed at the partial or total disruption of the national unity and the territorial integrity of a country is incompatible with the purposes and principles of the Charter." This is repeated in the 1970 declaration with the caveat that this does not apply to states not complying with the principle of self-determination by not possessing "a government representing the whole people belonging to the territory without distinction as to race, creed or colour." Minorities within states, though not having the right of external self-determination, have some right of internal self-determination, such as representation or autonomy.[82] The democratic entitlement of minorities within a state was recognized in 1992 in the General Assembly's Declaration on the Rights of Persons Belonging to National or Ethnic, Religious and Linguistic Minorities. This resolution recognizes that the protection of such rights is "an integral part of the development of society as a whole and within a democratic framework based on the rule of law." Furthermore, article 2(2) of the 1992 declaration states that "persons belonging to minorities have the right to participate effectively in cultural, religious, social, economic and public life."[83]

The current status of UN law on self-determination is accurately summarized by D. Harris:

> The evidence . . . suggests that the point has been reached where the principle has generated a rule of international law by which the political future of a colonial or similar non-independent territory should be determined in accordance with the wishes of its inhabitants, within the limits of the principle of *uti possidetis* [colonial boundaries should be maintained on independence]. It does not extend to claims for independence by minority groups in a non-colonial context. The principle may, however, have an internal, as well as an external aspect: it may require that government generally have a democratic base, and that minorities be allowed political autonomy.[84]

It is from the internal aspect of self-determination that the value of democracy has grown apace, especially but not solely with the end of the Cold War. "Self-determination is the historic root from which the democratic entitlement grew,"[85] a view supported by the jurisprudence of the HRC operating under the ICCPR.[86] That covenant provides further support to the value, indeed the right of, democracy in article 25, which builds on article 21 of the assembly's 1948 UDHR. Article 21 states that "everyone has the right to take part in the government of his country, directly or through freely chosen representatives." It goes on to provide a core definition of democracy, stating that "the will of the people shall be the basis of the authority of government," that will being "expressed in periodic and genuine elections which shall be by universal and equal suffrage." Thus democracy is not a group right but can be seen as an individual right. Furthermore, its embodiment in the UDHR reveals it as a core value and that the recent focus is due to changed political circumstances at the United Nations.

The assembly has supported the practical application of democracy outside the colonial and non–self-governing contexts in the form of genuine periodic elections. In a series of resolutions since 1991, the assembly's support for democracy has grown, reflecting the increase of democratic states throughout the world. In 1991 the assembly made a tentative move toward supporting the provision of UN verification of elections by stressing that such an activity was "exceptional," only to be carried out in certain circumstances, "primarily those having an international character." Despite this caveat, the assembly stressed its conviction that

> periodic and genuine elections are a necessary and indispensable element of sustained efforts to protect the rights and interests of the governed and that . . . the rights of everyone to take part in the government of his or her country is a crucial factor in the effective enjoyment of all of a wide range of other human rights and fundamental freedoms, embracing political, economic, social and cultural rights.[87]

However, later resolutions on periodic and genuine elections have moved away from the notion that UN help is exceptional "while recognizing that the fundamental responsibility for ensuring free and fair elections lies with Governments."[88] These later resolutions, which stress the strengthening of democratic pluralism in society, were widely supported, with only fifteen states abstaining on the vote.[89]

The value of democracy reinforces other core values of the UN system. First, democracy is recognized as "the political framework in which human rights can best be safeguarded."[90] Second, there is increasing recognition that democracy promotes the value of peace; "the right to democracy can readily be shown to be an important subsidiary of the community's most important norm: the right to peace"[91] by the fact that democracies rarely wage war on each other (see Chapter 7).[92]

The Environment

The ascension of the environment as a core value is the best evidence of the dynamism and adaptability of the UN system. The environment is not mentioned in the UN Charter, but its protection can be seen as a significant development by practice of the UN's inherent powers in relation to social and humanitarian problems identified in article 1(3) of the UN Charter. Stronger links between this value and the original charter can be made, at least theoretically, by viewing the issue as the right to a clean environment. The different types and generations of rights that have been recognized include a third-generation right to a clean environment (but see Chapter 10). The protection of this value occurs primarily at the state level. It is not true to say that the postwar UN system entirely neglected the environment. Part of the FAO's mandate, for instance, is "the conservation of natural resources and the adoption of improved methods of agricultural production."[93] Other specialized agencies that can claim environmental protection within their competence include UNESCO, IMO, WHO, the World Bank, as well as the IAEA.[94]

The catalyst was the declaration adopted at the 1972 UN Stockholm Conference on the Human Environment.[95] Although a nonbinding resolution, certain aspects of it were quickly accepted as international legal principles. This was especially so in the case of principle 21, which outlined the "no-harm" principle, namely, that states have "the responsibility to ensure that activities within their jurisdiction or control do not cause damage to the environment of other states or of areas beyond the limits of national jurisdiction."[96]

The conference also led to the establishment of UN mechanisms to facilitate protecting the environment, principally UNEP, with a UN General Assembly mandate to promote international cooperation, provide policy guidance, and review implementation of its programs as well as the "world environment situation."[97] UNEP has promoted the development of "soft" and "hard" law,[98] the former being in the form of declarations (e.g., the 1982 World Charter for Nature),[99] the latter in the form of treaties (e.g., the 1985 Vienna Convention for the Protection of the Ozone Layer).[100]

Nevertheless, it "was not until the occurrence of the environmental disasters in Bhopal, Chernobyl, and Basel in the mid 1980s, and the 1987 discovery of the ozone hole over the Antarctic, that the world community was brought face to face with global environmental challenges."[101] Both UNEP and ECOSOC called on the UN General Assembly to convene the UN Conference on Environment and Development in 1989.[102] The content of the General Assembly's resolution, which was adopted without a vote, reveals the major difficulty of agreeing on environmental controls. The assembly recognized a "continuing deterioration of the state of the environment and the serious degradation of the global life support systems," which if allowed to continue "could disrupt the ecological balance, jeopardize the life-sustaining qualities of the earth and lead to an ecological catastrophe." The assembly also recognized the "global character of environmental problems, including climate change, depletion of the ozone layer, transboundary air and water pollution, the contamination of the oceans and the seas and degradation of land resources." As well as attempting to direct the conference toward the adoption of measures for protecting the environment, the assembly condemned economic development and its accompanying pollution in industrialized countries while encouraging development, alongside environmental protection, in developing countries. The overall aim of the conference, according to the assembly, should have been to "elaborate strategies and measures to halt and reverse the effects of environmental degradation in the context of strengthened national and international efforts to promote sustainable and environmentally sound development in all countries."[103]

The UN's June 1992 Rio Conference, also known as the Earth Summit, produced two treaties for formal ratification: the Framework Convention on Climate Change,[104] which contains guiding principles and commitments regarding the stabilization of greenhouse gases; and the Convention on Biological Diversity,[105] which is another framework treaty to create general obligations for the conservation of ecosystems, species, and diversity of species. Although both treaties contain compromise and ambiguity, they do create institutions to promote compliance and contain financial mechanisms to ease the burden on developing states (see Chapter 10).

In addition, the Rio Conference produced two nonbinding declarations and a program of action known as Agenda 21. One of the declarations was a statement of principles on the management, conservation, and sustainable development of all types of forest. The Statement of Principles on Forests restates principle 21 of the Stockholm declaration, which might suggest that states that deplete forests within their jurisdiction may be responsible for the consequent deterioration in the climates of other countries. However, the statement then makes it clear that "states have the sovereign and inalienable right to utilize, manage and develop their forests in accordance with the development needs and level of socio-economic development and on the basis of national policies consistent with sustainable development."[106] The more significant Rio Declaration on Environment and Development encapsulates a greater emphasis on development than found twenty years earlier at Stockholm.[107] For example, principle 4 states that "in order to achieve sustainable development, environmental protection shall constitute an integral part of the development process and cannot be considered in isolation from it."

Turning to Agenda 21, a similar emphasis on economic issues is found, namely, making environmental standards relative to socioeconomic factors.[108] As well as urging UNEP and the UNDP to develop and expand activities in the environmental and developmental fields, Agenda 21 urges the creation of another institution within the UN framework. The aim of such a body would be to "rationalize the intergovernmental decision-making capacity for the integration of environment and development and to examine the progress in the implementation of Agenda 21 at the national, regional and international levels." The Commission on Sustainable Development was established by the UN General Assembly in 1993 pursuant to this aim.[109] It monitored progress in the implementation of Agenda 21 by examining reports from organizations and bodies concerned with environment and development; considered "information provided by Governments . . . in the form of . . . national reports regarding the activities they undertake to implement Agenda 21"; reviewed Agenda 21 commitments such as the transfer of technology; reviewed the progress toward the UN target of 0.7 percent of gross national product (GNP) of the developed countries for development assistance; and received and analyzed reports from NGOs. The commission's mandate contains a breakthrough in the monitoring and supervision of standards by providing for a state reporting system. Its record of achievement, along with UNEP, which is working toward an international legal framework for the implementation of Agenda 21, is reviewed in Chapter 10.

Overall the United Nations has made progress in making protecting the environment one of the fundamental UN purposes. It has contributed to many of the principles of environmental law that have developed since Stockholm in 1972. Principally these are the polluter-pays principle, the notion of common but differentiated responsibility, with industrialized countries having more responsibility for environmental protection, the concept of intergenerational equity, the sharing of research, and the precautionary principle, which dictates that action should not be deferred until there is sufficient scientific evidence.[110] Overarching all is sustainable development, that is, environmental protection should not prevent development, and development should not occur at the expense of protecting the environment (see Chapters 10 and 11). The concept of sustainable development adopts the proposition "that continued economic growth and development, as well as population growth, can take place in a manner that will bring the global population to an acceptable overall standard of living, without damaging the life support system so much that it prevents this goal from ever being attained."[111] The United Nations has attempted to integrate the two values at the conceptual level.[112]

Economic and Social Well-Being

The significance of economic and social well-being is evident from the plethora of organizations, agencies, and programs with competence in the field: the IMF, the World Bank, UNIDO, UNDP, UNCTAD, ILO, UNESCO, FAO, WHO, WFP, and UNHCR. The aim of this section is to identify the value in treaty provisions and its development through subsequent practice. However, development has been through the creation of organs and programs with specific tasks in the economic and social fields (see Chapter 11).

Social and economic well-being are given some prominence in the preamble and article 1 of the UN Charter. The preamble lists the promotion of "social progress and better standards of life in larger freedom," after collective security and human rights, and then talks about the employment of "international machinery for the promotion of the economic and social advancement of all peoples." Article 1 states that one of the purposes of the United Nations is "to achieve international cooperation in solving international problems of an economic, social, cultural, or humanitarian character." Article 55 elaborates upon this by placing emphasis on the promotion of "higher standards of living, full employment, and conditions of economic and social progress and development." Through article 13(1)(b) the General Assembly has competence, inter alia, in "the economic, social, and cultural, educational, and health fields"; under charter chapter X ECOSOC is established with competence solely in these areas. Through articles 63 and 64 ECOSOC is responsible for supervising the activities of the specialized agencies, many of whose competencies lie in this area. The WHO, for instance, has the sole objective of the "attainment by all peoples of the highest possible levels of health";[113] UNESCO's mandate covers the vital area of developing education systems in member states.

Although ECOSOC has been criticized for failure to coordinate the activities of agencies, it has contributed to the development of this value, for example through its draft code on the conduct of transnational corporations.[114] The General Assembly has made more impact by promoting in 1962 the right of peoples to permanent sovereignty over their natural wealth and resources (economic self-determination), allowing expropriation of foreign investment and assets for a public purpose subject to the payment of appropriate compensation.[115] This principle has been accepted as customary international law despite the initial lack of consensus in the General Assembly.[116] Later attempts in the early 1970s by UNCTAD, an organ of the assembly with a mandate "to promote international trade . . . particularly trade between countries at different stages of development,"[117] and the General Assembly, to create a New International Economic Order (NIEO) aimed at redressing the imbalance between North and South by, inter alia, allowing for nationalization without regulation by international law, were less successful, being opposed by Western states.[118] The same problem confronted UNESCO in its drive to combat the uncontrolled flow of information from West to East by the creation of a New World Information and Communication Order.[119]

More success was achieved by the General Assembly in promoting the concept of the common heritage of mankind, whereby certain areas beyond national jurisdiction—the moon and the deep sea-bed—were proclaimed as not being capable of acquisition by states or private investors.[120] The creation of an international regime for the regulation of these areas was partially embodied in the Outer Space Treaty of 1967 and in the 1979 Moon Treaty, sponsored by the UN Committee on the Peaceful Uses of Outer Space. It was more firmly entrenched in the UN-sponsored Law of the Sea Convention of 1982 in relation to the deep sea-bed.[121] The influence of the concept of common heritage has been felt in other UN forums such as the ITU. Here the allocation of slots in geostationary orbit is no longer made on the basis of first-come, first-served (which obviously favored the developed states) but has moved toward a system of predetermining remaining slots and reserving some for latecomers.[122]

It can be seen that the value of economic and social well-being in the General Assembly and ECOSOC moves toward the ideal of redistributing wealth from North to South. Indeed, the concept of development seems to be the increase in the economic and social well-being of individuals and peoples in developing countries. With the demise of the NIEO in the 1970s, the General Assembly, with its majority of developing states, turned to this concept. In 1986 it adopted the controversial and ambiguous Declaration on the Right to Development,[123] which stated that "the right to development is an inalienable human right by virtue of which every human person and all peoples are entitled to participate in, contribute to and enjoy economic, social, cultural and political development." A very imprecise duty is placed on states "to take steps, individually and collectively, to formulate international development policies with a view to facilitating the full realisation of the right to development." The attempt by the General Assembly to establish a clear, new third-generation human right was prevented by developed states, leading to a compromise text with little substance. Despite the compromise, the resolution was still not adopted by consensus.[124]

Nevertheless, the drive toward creating such a right with a concomitant obligation to provide development aid has continued in other UN forums. UNDP was founded by the General Assembly in 1965 with the aim of promoting development through "consideration and approval of projects and programmes and the allocation of funds."[125] In 1994–1995 UNDP's executive board interpreted its general mandate to be the promotion of sustainable human development, in particular to include not only poverty eradication and sustainable livelihoods but also good governance, the advancement of women, and the sustainable management of environmental resources.[126] In addition, UNIDO, which was constituted as a specialized agency in 1979 after previously being an organ of the General Assembly, had the broad objective of the "promotion and acceleration of industrial development in the developing countries with a view to assist in the establishment of a New International Economic Order. The Organization shall also promote development and cooperation on global, regional and national, as well as sectoral levels."[127]

Although the evolution of the value of economic and social wellbeing has focused on the issue of development, at least in those UN bodies dominated by the developing states, the reality is that a much less ambitious goal has been developed (see Chapter 11). At the Vienna Conference on Human Rights in June 1993, UN Secretary-General Boutros Boutros-Ghali spoke of a right to humanitarian assistance to "victims of natural disasters and similar emergency assistance." In these cases, the antithesis of development has occurred, through floods, earthquakes, drought, or man-made famine, which often set back the development of a country by decades.

It is premature to claim that a right to humanitarian assistance has developed, just as the right to development has yet to be made more concrete in UN practice. In 1988 the General Assembly adopted a resolution that, due to the objections of many developing states, paid respect to the sovereignty of states by "recognizing that it is up to each State first and foremost to take care of the victims" of disasters. The resolution also upheld the objections of developed states by not obliging them to provide humanitarian assistance, stating that "the international community should respond speedily and effectively to appeals for emergency humanitarian assistance." However, the resolution does place considerable pressure on donor countries by "considering that the abandonment of the victims of natural disasters and similar emergency situations without humanitarian assistance constitutes a threat to human life and an offence to human dignity."[128]

Further development of humanitarian assistance occurred in 1991 with the adoption of guiding principles, which link assistance and development by urging that assistance is not short-term aid to cope with the disaster but should support recovery and long-term development.[129] Such assistance is delivered not only by states but through UN mechanisms such as the UNHCR and WFP, which first became operational in 1963 under a General Assembly mandate arising out of an FAO initiative.[130] The WFP is now the world's largest food aid organization.

Although the NIEO has been blocked by Western states due to a belief in free enterprise,[131] the rights to development and humanitarian assistance have taken on a consensual base, though it is difficult to assess the duty actually imposed on rich states.[132] The majority-dominated bodies of the UN system have concentrated on the redistribution of wealth and technology from North to South. Other elements of the UN system with weighted voting mechanisms dominated by developed states are founded on the notion "that liberal rules of free trade, free payments, monetary stability and capital mobility would best promote international economic welfare."[133] Whether the aims and activities of the UN financial institutions—the IMF and the World Bank—are compatible with the interpretation of economic and social well-being pursued by the other elements of the UN system remains a debate (see Chapter 11). It is not conceptually impossible to have an economic system based on the liberal principles of free trade alongside concepts of social justice. To argue for one extreme or another may by ideologically pure, but they are two ends of a spectrum of choice for the UN system.

The components of the UN system arguing for wealth redistribution, combined with obligations on richer states to donate to poorer states, have developed the value under one-state, one-vote, which naturally favors developing states. The two UN financial institutions have upheld the value more in accordance with classical liberal notions of finance, of borrowing and repayment, due in part to the weighted voting system under which they operate.[134] The different voting mechanism is explained on the basis that "insufficient money would have been made available had the donating States not obtained a preponderant influence in decision making."[135]

The purposes of the IBRD (known, together with the International Development Association [IDA] and the International Finance Corporation [IFC], as the World Bank), are "to assist in the . . . development of . . . members by facilitating the investment of capital for productive purposes"; "to promote private foreign investment by means of guarantees or participation in loans . . . made by private investors; and when private capital is not available on reasonable terms, to supplement private investment by providing, on suitable conditions, finance for productive purposes out of its own capital"; and "to arrange loans . . . so that the more useful and urgent projects . . . will be dealt with first."[136] At this level development is compatible with the General Assembly's and UNDP's promotion of the right to development. However, in the case of the IBRD, loans made to countries must be repaid within fifteen to twenty years, and interest is charged at three-quarters of a percent above what was paid for the funds, although the IDA has the ability to provide for interest-free loans.[137]

Whereas the World Bank acts as a development bank for poorer countries, the IMF can lend to any member country lacking sufficient foreign currency to cover short-term obligations to creditors in other countries. The purposes of the IMF are to promote international monetary cooperation by means of exchange-rate stability and orderly exchange arrangements, especially

> to give confidence to members by making the general resources of the Fund temporarily available to them under adequate safeguards, thus providing them with the opportunity to correct maladjustments in their balance of payments without resorting to measures destructive of national or international prosperity.[138]

The IMF and World Bank operate under classic liberal financial principles. Loans to a country with balance-of-payment difficulties above 25 percent of its IMF quota are usually to be repaid within five years at interest rates of about 4.5 percent; the borrower must also show how it will solve payment difficulties. To satisfy the IMF, the borrower usually undertakes reforms—such as a reduction in government expenditures and perhaps a recognition of the need to privatize inefficient public enterprises. Sometimes IMF-mandated reforms cut deeper into a country's economic and political structure and can include the development of health, education, and good governance.[139]

The conditions of IMF and, since 1989, World Bank loans can be linked to the furtherance of other values in the UN system: democracy and social values such as health and education. In the case of the World Bank, the environment is now included, especially with the establishment, jointly with UNDP and UNEP, of the Global Environmental

Facility (GEF) in 1991. Whether it is possible to assist the development of countries through the creation of debt is open to debate, as is the question of whether the IMF and World Bank have promoted economic and social well-being, as well as other UN values (see Chapter 11).

Conclusion

The values of the United Nations have taken on complex and concrete forms via the treaties of the specialized agencies and the practice of the UN system. The value of peace and security is given predominance for historical reasons. The main reason for this perceived hierarchy is that the international community vested the UN Security Council with coercive power not possessed by other components. The development of the concept of positive peace by the council and the assembly has brought many of the other values within the remit of the Security Council when dealing with conflict. However, all the elements of the UN system are concerned with promoting positive peace, the overarching value of the system; it encompasses all others, including negative peace.

However, with the infusion of justice into the concept of peace, it could be argued that the cornerstone value of the UN system is not peace but justice and law. This contention is strengthened by the fact that all the values are entrenched in the constitutional order of the system. Furthermore, many values can be seen as legal rights, either individual or group. This reinforces the constitutional nature of the UN system, buttressing the ideal that the United Nations is based on the rule of law; it is governed by legal provisions and pursues its values by means of creating and developing international norms. Thus what starts out as a political goal—self-determination of peoples—becomes a constitutional value through embodiment in the UN Charter, then a legal right through UN practice—the right to self-determination.

Law, being principled and consistent, is preferred to a purely pragmatic political approach, which would be inconsistent and unfair. Nevertheless, progress toward the human rights ideal has not been uniform, with the protection of several of the UN's values, principally the environment, development, and peace, occurring at the interstate level rather than the individual or group level. Of course, effective protection can occur at all levels (see Part 3). Furthermore, this lack of evolution in values does not undermine law's fundamental role in the system, for law is the basis of all the values in the legal system and the methods pursued to protect them. Law underpins the whole system.

The values developed by the UN system cannot be completely separated. Democracy derives from self-determination yet is an aspect of civil and political rights and is being tied to the effective promotion of economic and social well-being. The notion of economic and social well-being becomes reinforced by economic, social, and cultural human rights. The concept of development—central to economic and social well-being—cannot be separated from the protection of the environment, which is also supported by second-generation human rights. A just peace cannot be achieved without protection and promotion of all the other values in the UN system.

The interlocking nature of UN values demonstrates the need for a coherent and coordinated system. Attempts at coordination are seen in the GEF of the World Bank, UNDP, and UNEP, as well as the Commission on Sustainable Development. Furthermore, integrity and compatibility of all the values can be seen, yet their promotion and application needs to be examined in practice (see Part 3). Potential problems include the pressing issue of whether the World Bank's and IMF's promotion of development through debt is compatible with the idea that development assistance is an obligation of richer states and thus a right for poorer states. These questions are explored further in Part 3.

Notes

1. Falk, Kim, and Mendlovitz, *The United Nations,* 212.
2. See also Kim, "Global Rights," 356.
3. Falk, Kim, and Mendlovitz, *The United Nations,* 208.
4. Simma, *The Charter,* 50.
5. Report of the Commission on Global Governance, *Our Global Neighbourhood,* 79.
6. Bertrand, *Third Generation,* 8.
7. GA Res. 290(IV), 1 Dec. 1949.
8. GA Res. 39/11, 12 Nov. 1984.
9. GA Res. 46/14, 31 Oct. 1991.
10. GA Res. 51/101, 12 Dec. 1996.
11. GA Res. 51/55, 10 Dec. 1996.
12. GA Res. 49/60, 9 Dec. 1994.
13. GA Res. 2131 (XX), 21 Dec. 1965.
14. GA Res. 2625 (XXV), 24 Oct. 1970.
15. White, *Keeping the Peace,* 47–52.
16. SC Res. 54, 15 July 1948.
17. SC Res. 161, 21 Feb. 1961.
18. SC Res. 353, 20 July 1974.

19. SC Res. 232, 16 Dec. 1966.

20. SC Res. 418, 4 Nov. 1977.

21. Simma, *The Charter,* 611. See also Arend, "The United Nations," 529.

22. SC Res. 688, 5 April 1991.

23. SC Res. 713, 25 Sept. 1991.

24. SC Res. 733, 23 Jan. 1992.

25. SC Res. 788, 19 Nov. 1992.

26. SC Res. 864, 15 Sept. 1993.

27. SC Res. 827, 25 May 1993.

28. SC Res. 929, 22 June 1994 (Rwanda); 1049, 5 March 1996 (Burundi); 1078, 9 Nov. 1996 (Zaire); 1101, 28 March 1997 (Albania); SC Res. 1199, 23 Sept. 1998 (Kosovo); 1264, 15 Sept. 1999 (East Timor); 1270, 22 Oct. 1999 (Sierra Leone).

29. SC Res. 748, 31 March 1992.

30. SC Res. 1054, 26 April 1996.

31. SC Res. 1267, 15 Oct. 1999.

32. SC Res. 1368, 12 Sept. 2001.

33. SC Res. 1371, 28 Sept. 2001.

34. Gordon, "United Nations Intervention," 522.

35. SC Res. 794, 3 Dec. 1992.

36. SC Res. 841, 16 June 1993; 873, 13 Oct. 1993.

37. SC 3046 mtg., 1992.

38. Falk, Kim, and Mendlovitz, *The United Nations,* 213.

39. ICJ Rep. 1962, 167.

40. GA Res. 503 (VI), 12 Jan. 1952.

41. Bertrand, *Third Generation,* 11.

42. Mitrany, *Working Peace,* 38.

43. Cited in Falk, Kim, and Mendlovitz, *The United Nations,* 178.

44. Kelsen, *Law of the United Nations,* 727.

45. GA Res. 44/55, 8 Dec. 1989.

46. SC Res. 827, 25 May 1993.

47. SC Res. 955, 8 Nov. 1994.

48. Simma, *The Charter,* 48.

49. Franck, *Fairness,* 48.

50. Kelsen, *Law of the United Nations,* 366.

51. GA Res. 48/132, 20 Dec. 1993.

52. Schachter and Joyner, *United Nations Legal Order,* chs. 14 and 16. Tomuschat, "International Law," 281.

53. GA Res. 44/23, 17 Nov. 1989; GA Res. 49/50, 9 Dec. 1994.

54. GA Res. 174(III), 21 Nov. 1947.

55. Harris, *Cases and Materials,* 66.

56. UN doc. A/51/332/Corr.1 (1996).

57. GA Res. 51/160, 16 Dec. 1996.

58. Ortega, "The ILC Adopts the Draft Code of Crimes," 284.

59. (1994) 33 ILM 253.

60. (1998) 38 ILM 999.

61. Schermers and Blokker, *Institutional Law,* 765 (re IAEA), 781 (re ICAO).

62. Gibson, *International Organizations,* 44.

63. ECOSOC Res. 9(II), 1946.

64. GA Res. 217A(III), 1948.

65. UN doc. A/CONF.32/41.

66. (1994) 1(1) IHRR 240.

67. GA Res. 52/117, 12 Dec. 1997.

68. Boutros-Ghali, "Human Rights: The Common Language of Humanity," opening statement made at the 1993 Vienna Conference.

69. P. Alston, "The UN's Human Rights Record," 356. See also Eide et al., *The Universal Declaration.*

70. GA Res. 50/154, 21 Dec. 1995.

71. GA Res. 50/167, 22 Dec. 1995.

72. GA Res. 52/99, 12 Dec. 1997.

73. Harris, *Cases and Materials,* 625.

74. Crawford, *The Rights of Peoples,* 159–166.

75. (1994) 1(1) IHRR 240.

76. But see Simma, *The Charter,* 60.

77. Higgins, *The Development,* 104. But see Wright, "Recognition and Self-Determination," 29.

78. *Namibia* case, ICJ Rep. 1971, 31. *Western Sahara* case, ICJ Rep. 1975, 31–33.

79. GA Res. 1514 (XV), 14 Dec. 1960.

80. GA Res. 2625, 24 Oct. 1970.

81. Ofuatey-Kodjoe, "Self-Determination," 375.

82. Ibid., 385.

83. GA Res. 47/135, 18 Dec. 1992. See also Art. 27 of the International Covenant on Civil and Political Rights.

84. Harris, *Cases and Materials,* 113.

85. Franck, "The Emerging Right," 52.

86. Crawford, "Democracy and International Law," 116.

87. GA Res. 46/137, 17 Dec. 1991.

88. GA Res. 49/190, 23 Dec. 1994.

89. GA Res. 50/185, 22 Dec. 1995; GA Res. 52/129, 12 Dec. 1997.

90. Boutros-Ghali, "Human Rights: The Common Language of Humanity," 17.

91. Franck, "The Emerging Right," 87.

92. Crawford, "Democracy and International Law," 113.

93. Art. 1(2)(c), FAO Constitution.

94. Nanda, "Environment," 646.

95. UN doc. A/CONF 48/14 (1972).

96. Detter de Lupis, "The Human Environment"; Kiss and Shelton, *International Environmental Law,* 129; Sohn, "The Stockholm Declaration," 423.

97. GA Res. 2997, 15 Dec. 1972.

98. Birnie and Boyle, *Environment,* 47–52.

99. GA Res. 37/7, 28 Oct. 1982.

100. (1987) 26 ILM 1529.

101. Nanda, "Environment," 636.

102. UNEP Res. 15/3, 1989; ECOSOC Res. 1989/87.

103. GA Res. 44/228, 22 Dec. 1989.

104. (1992) 31 ILM 848.

105. (1992) 31 ILM 818.

106. (1992) 31 ILM 882.

107. (1992) 31 ILM 876.

108. UN doc. A/CONF.151/26 (1992).

109. GA Res. 47/191, 22 Dec. 1992.

110. Adede, "International Protection," 207–209.

111. McCluney, "Sustainable Values," 16.

112. Pallemaerts, "International Environmental Law," 17.

113. Art. 1 of the WHO Constitution.

114. Zamora, "Economic Relations," 544–545.

115. GA Res. 1803, 14 Dec. 1962.

116. *Texaco v. Libya* (1977) 53 ILR, 389 at para. 87.

117. GA Res. 1995, 30 Dec. 1964.

118. See, for example, GA Res. 3281, 12 Dec. 1974.

119. Marks, "Education, Science," 618–620.

120. GA Res. 1721 (XVI), 20 Dec. 1961; 1884 (XVIII), 17 Oct. 1963; 1962 (XVIII), 13 Dec. 1963 (outer space); GA Res. 2749 (XXV), 17 Dec. 1970 (deep sea-bed).

121. See Arts. 135–153 of the Law of the Sea Convention.

122. Lyall, "Posts and Telecommunications," 815–817. Seidl-Hohenveldern, "The International Economic Order," 221.

123. GA Res. 41/128, 4 Dec. 1986.

124. Harris, *Cases and Materials,* 724–725.

125. GA Res. 2029 (XX), 22 Nov. 1965.

126. UNDP Executive Board Decisions 94/14, 1994; 95/22, 1995.

127. Art. 1 UNIDO Constitution (1979) 18 ILM 667.

128. GA Res. 43/131, 8 Dec. 1988.

129. GA Res. 46/182, 19 Dec. 1991.

130. GA Res. 1714, 19 Dec. 1961.

131. Seidl-Hohenveldern, "The International Economic Order," 224.

132. Zomora, "Economic Relations," 550.

133. Ibid., 514.

134. Seidl-Hohenveldern, "The International Economic Order," 226.

135. Schermers and Blokker, *Institutional Law,* 521.

136. Art. 1 of the Articles of Agreement of the IBRD.

137. <http://www.worldbank.int/html/extdr/wheremoney.htm>.

138. Art. 1 of the Articles of Agreement of the IMF.

139. <http://www.imf.int/external/pubs/ft/exrp/what.htm>.

PART 2
Institutional Framework

4

The Political Organs:
Power and Accountability

Before considering the role of judicial bodies, my institutional analysis considers the political organs within the UN system. The purpose is not to merely list the organs and their mandates but to consider their structural makeup, division of competence, and interrelationships. I focus on the hierarchies within the organizations to consider issues of power and accountability, including relationships between executive and plenary UN bodies, those within the specialized agencies, and between the specialized agencies and ECOSOC. Furthermore, it is essential to assess the "fit" as well as the mandates of the various subsidiary organs and how they relate to the activities of the agencies. The UN system is huge and unwieldy; thus I also consider efforts to coordinate and reform the system.

The main themes are power and accountability. Where does power—legal and political—lie within the organization? Is the exercise of power legitimate, in the sense not only of complying with the constitutional order but also of inducing member states into voluntary compliance?[1] Transparency is part of that question. If an organ's decisions are regarded as legitimate, the greater the likelihood that the membership will accept and implement them. This goes to the heart of the effectiveness of the UN system.

The extent to which powerful organs are regarded as legitimate raises the issue of whether they are democratic. Other issues include representation (i.e., of the will of the membership); whether the organ is accountable; and whether the organization represents the views of individuals. In a global system based on states there is inevitably a democracy deficit. And the UN's increasing promotion of democracy within states is undermined if it is itself undemocratic. However, practical limitations abound. Are state representatives the best way to ensure the views of citizens are accorded proper attention? The problem may be the lack of connection between state representatives at the United Nations and their citizens, even in the case of democratic governments. A practical assessment of the democratic credentials of the UN system must therefore be undertaken.

Membership

The starting point is the membership, almost exclusively reserved for states. Article 3 of the UN Charter states that the "original Members of the United Nations shall be the States which, having participated in [the San Francisco Conference], or having previously signed the Declaration by United Nations of 1 January 1942, sign the present Charter and ratify it in accordance with Article 110."[2] Article 4 outlines the procedure for the admission of new states to the United Nations, stating that membership is "open to all other peace-loving states which accept the obligations contained in the present Charter and, in the judgment of the Organization, are able and willing to carry out these obligations." This judgment is to be effected "by a decision of the General Assembly upon the recommendation of the Security Council."

In 1945 UN membership numbered fifty-one and was, with the exception of the Soviet Union and its allies, Western-dominated; by the end of the Cold War in 1989 the membership had increased to 159. The bulk of the increase consisted of newly independent states (loosely known as the Non-Aligned Group or the Group of 77), dramatically altering the balance of voting power in the General Assembly. The fallout from the Cold War also meant a dramatic increase in membership, to 189, with new states emerging from the former Soviet Union and former Yugoslavia. In addition, post–Cold War shifts led to membership for Namibia, the two Koreas, Eritrea, the Czech Republic, and Slovakia. The remainder of the post–Cold War membership increase consists of so-called microstates, for example, Micronesia and Andorra.

On the question of admission of new members, article 4(1) lays down the criteria. However, it was obvious during the Cold War that member states, especially the superpowers in the Security Council, judged new applicants according to wider geopolitical criteria in contradiction to the legal requirements of article 4(1), a position made clear by the General Assembly of the United Nations, which requested an advisory opinion of the ICJ in 1948. The court declared that no member state is "juridically entitled to make its consent to the admission dependent on conditions not expressly provided for" in article 4(1).[3] However,

> the major powers in the Security Council did not accept this view. . . .
> The Soviet Union ha[d] rejected it from the beginning; the United
> States implicitly rejected it in 1975 when it blocked the admission of
> the Democratic Republic of Vietnam and the Republic of Vietnam for
> reasons other than those mentioned in Article 4 of the UN Charter.[4]

Furthermore, the same political machinations that prevented membership of certain *states,* even though eligible, led to certain *governments* not being able to occupy their country's seat at the United Nations, with certain states subverting the formal process of accepting the effective government's credentials. This was the case for the Chinese seat, which until 1971 was occupied by the Nationalist representative, thereby denying the communist regime. The misuse of the credentials process was also evident in the exclusion of the Vietnamese-installed government in Cambodia in 1979 in favor of the ousted and notorious Pol Pot regime; the apartheid regime in South Africa from 1974 to 1994; and in the late 1990s the Taliban regime in Afghanistan. In contrast, the process of transfer is very smooth when there is political will, as in 1992 when the Soviet Union was replaced by the Russian Federation.[5]

It is possible to argue that some of the excluded regimes did not uphold the basic principles of the United Nations, by extending the requirements for state membership in article 4. However, the failure to treat like cases alike undermines the credibility of the UN's composition, as well as its claims to universality. However, many of these issues have been laid to rest (with the burning exception of Taiwan and, until recently, the suspension and exclusion of the Federal Republic of Yugoslavia [FRY]);[6] the United Nations can now claim to be a universal organization representing the international community. On 3 March 2002, the Swiss people voted to join the United Nations. Significant states that are not members do so of their own volition and would not claim to be able to operate against the basic values of the system. "It is therefore correct to conclude that in UN practice the conception of membership has evolved from conditional to unconditional universality."[7]

The specialized UN agencies also aspire to universal membership subject to functional limitations inherent in the purposes of those organizations. For instance, the WMO, established as an IGO in 1947 with 185 members in September 2001, has the purposes of facilitating "world-wide cooperation in the establishment of networks of stations for the making of meteorological observations," as well as information exchange, standardization, and research in meteorology. With these purposes in mind, the constitution limits membership to states possessing a meteorological service, as well as the founding states.[8] Other UN specialized agencies do not limit membership by reference to functions.

The IMO was established in 1948 and had a membership of 158 states in September 2001. It facilitates cooperation among members on matters affecting international merchant shipping and encourages the highest practicable standards of maritime safety and efficiency of navigation, the prevention and control of marine pollution, and the removal of governmental discriminatory action affecting shipping. Membership is open to all states.[9] Other agencies' membership restrictions reflect their wartime origins and the fact that they were set up before the United Nations existed. For instance, article 92(a) of the Convention on International Civil Aviation of 1944, which inter alia established the ICAO, states "this Convention shall be open for adherence by members of the United Nations and States associated with them, and States which remained neutral during the present world conflict." This is a reference not to the United Nations of 1945 but to those parties adhering to the declaration by United Nations (principally the Allies) of 1942. In regard to new members, article 93 provides that admittance of states that were enemies of the World War II Allies is subject to a four-fifths majority vote "provided that in each case the assent of any State invaded or attacked during the present war by the State seeking admission shall be necessary." Despite these potentially divisive origins, the ICAO, as with the United Nations itself, has developed into a universal organization of 187 members in September 2001.

Of course, the United Nations and its agencies may have achieved near universal membership, but states are not necessarily representative of individuals and other actors. As will be seen in the following section, even purportedly democratic states are not necessarily an adequate vehicle for representing the views of citizens on the international stage. In addition, repressed peoples (e.g., Tibetans), stateless peoples (Palestinians and Kurds), as well as established minorities (Australian aborigines) are worthy of representation on the international stage. In addition, nonstate ideologies balance the domination of a state-based view of international relations. This is especially necessary in the areas of the environment, human rights, and development, where NGOs such as Greenpeace and Amnesty International should play an important role in the UN system.

However, the treatment of nonstate actors within the UN system is selective. Nonstate actors very rarely enjoy the same rights as state members. Even in the case of groups supported within the UN system, such as Palestinians, the normal procedure has been to grant observer status, allowing one to speak at meetings and to submit documents but not the right to vote. The Palestine Liberation Organization (PLO) was invited by the General Assembly in 1974 to participate as an observer.[10] However, following the Palestine National Council's declaration of independence in 1988,[11] the PLO applied for full membership in the WHO in May 1989. The WHO constitution provides in article 3 that "membership in the Organization is open to all States." The United States successfully objected on the grounds that the PLO was neither a state nor the government of one and that it should remain as an observer at the United Nations and within the specialized agencies.[12]

Other countries have been permitted to become members of a UN organization before they have achieved independence. Burma, Indonesia, and Tunisia all became members of the FAO before independence, and in 1977 the UN General Assembly requested all specialized agencies to grant full membership to the UN Council for Namibia, even though Namibia did not achieve independence until March 1990.[13] Furthermore, the UN's membership in 1945 included parts of the Soviet Union, namely, Byelorussia and Ukraine, to attempt to redress the imbalance in voting power at the United Nations between West and East. These members have since become states with the collapse of the Soviet Union. This UN practice reveals inconsistency and selectivity in dealing with groups of individuals. The question of whether it treats nongovernment organizations in a more satisfactory manner will be considered later.

Representation and Voting

Membership issues tend to merge with issues of representation. Even if the issue is considered solely from the perspective of state representation, defects abound in the UN system. The composition of the Security Council is the prime example: for most of the international organizations in the UN family, the executive body is controlled by a small number of states. This is in contrast to the plenary organ, where all members are represented, usually at an annual session, normally under the principle of one-state, one-vote. The voting mechanism in the Security Council ensures that each permanent member has a veto over any issue.[14] The other ten members of the council, the nonpermanent members, are elected for terms of two years with "due regard being specially paid, in the first instance to the contribution of Members of the United Nations to the maintenance of international peace and security and to the other purposes of the Organization, and also to equitable geographical representation."[15]

The membership of the Security Council was increased from eleven to fifteen in 1965, but this still fails to make the council representative of the whole UN membership. In 1945 the ratio of council members to total UN members was 11:51, nearly 22 percent; now it is 15:189, about 8 percent (forty-one members would have to be represented on the council to achieve the earlier ratio). Any UN member cannot be expected to be elected to the "club" for many years.[16] The membership of the Security Council needs to be increased if the organ is to be able to claim that it is acting on behalf of the whole membership as posited by article 24(1). A balance has to be maintained, however, between making the council more representative while recognizing its executive and responsive character. To increase the membership of the council to forty-one could endanger its efficiency. Reform proposals are becoming more concrete, with general agreement between twenty-five and thirty members but as yet with no clear consensus on the reform, abolition, or extension of the veto.[17]

Nonplenary organs have a similar bias toward the most powerful members, though this can sometimes be justified on the basis of the functions of the institution. The council of the ICAO, for instance, consists of thirty-three contracting states elected by the assembly, giving adequate representation to "the States of chief importance in air transport"; states "which make the largest contribution to the provision of facilities for international civil air navigation"; and other states "whose designation will ensure that all the major geographic areas of the world are represented on the Council."[18] The ICAO council thus contains the major aviation powers for obvious reasons but does not explicitly name any states. This is unlike the UN Security Council, where membership might well be given to states with the greatest military power, those who are major contributors to peacekeeping operations, as well as on the basis of equitable geographical representation. Such a composition could be justified along functional lines, in that the objectives of the council are to maintain international peace and security, not to secure lifelong permanent membership for a handful of states whose military and peacekeeping capacities are limited. Furthermore, as with the council of the ICAO, there would be no room for the veto within a functionally constructed Security Council.

Next I examine the democratic credentials of the General Assembly, in particular the governing principle of one-state, one-vote. Although this can be justified in the Security Council, where states represent regions or groups as well as themselves, in the assembly states vote primarily for themselves. The vast disparity in power and population among states signifies that the assembly is not truly democratic in representing the peoples of the planet. However, the current reform process seems to be firmly based on the notion that the assembly carries the democratic credentials of the United Nations. For instance, in his report of 16 July 1997 detailing a program for reform, the Secretary-General wrote that "the General Assembly is the organ of the United Nations which most fully embodies the universal and democratic character of the United Nations."[19] Giving each state equal voting power in the assembly appears to lead to equality of representation among states. However, although all states are formally equal in the assembly, in practice this has eroded.

The post-1945 institutional order has witnessed a move away from unanimity as the basis of decisionmaking in favor of majority voting. This has led to the factual decline of sovereign equality, in that decisions can be adopted over a minority of states. Decisions by a majority can affect the sovereign interests of a minority (or sometimes even a majority) of states, especially in the case of binding decisions as opposed to recommendations. Most organizations within the UN system have a recommendatory power, but a few have mandatory powers.

In the League of Nations, the normal rule was unanimity for both council and assembly, a requirement embodied in article 5 of the League's covenant. The contrast between this and UN organizations makes clear the move away from unanimity and sovereign equality. In regard to the UN Security Council, article 27 allows for a qualified majority for the whole council, as well as unanimity by the permanent members on substantive issues. The assembly adopts resolutions by qualified two-thirds majority.

Most organizations take decisions by a majority of some form or other. For example, the assembly of the ICAO can take decisions by a majority vote, whereas the general conference of UNESCO can adopt by a majority unless the constitution states otherwise, in which case it is two-thirds of those members present and voting.[20] Despite slight differences, organizations established under the principle of majority voting can adopt resolutions that affect the interests of a minority of states. The UN General Assembly, for instance, by the constant repetition of principles in resolutions, can add to and reinforce the corpus of international law and thereby bind states that originally voted against the resolution. Some immensely influential General Assembly resolutions have been adopted not by unanimity or by consensus but by majority decisions. For example, in 1962 the General Assembly adopted the Resolution on Permanent Sovereignty over Natural Resources that recognizes the right of states to expropriate foreign property.[21] Fourteen states were unwilling to vote for this resolution, including France. Subsequently, in one of the most pro-Western interpretations of the international legal principles governing expropriation, the French international lawyer and sole arbitrator in the 1977 award in the *Texaco v. Libya* case stated that the resolution reflected customary international law.[22]

In discerning the principles governing the indirect use of military force by one state against another, the ICJ in the *Nicaragua* case relied principally on General Assembly resolutions, namely, the 1965 Declaration on Non-Intervention, the 1970 Declaration on Friendly Relations, and the 1974 Definition of Aggression.[23] Although the latter two were adopted by consensus and only Britain abstained on the first, the importance of General Assembly resolutions as sources of custom can be seen. The court defined custom not only as general conformity of behavior by states but also reaction by the community when the customary rule has been broken. Such an approach considers the views of the law breaker and the victim, as well as the general critical reaction of the community.[24] The principle governing the nonuse of force in international relations embodied in article 2(4) of the UN Charter was upheld during the Cold War by the General Assembly, almost always by a majority vote. For instance, it repeatedly condemned the Soviet Union's armed intervention in Afghanistan until the Soviet withdrawal in 1989, resolutions voted for by the vast majority of states.[25] It adopted a similar resolution condemning the U.S. military intervention in Panama in 1989 by a smaller majority.[26]

Although the UN organization provides for majority voting in its organs, the basic principle is one-nation, one-vote. The smallest nations in the United Nations—the so-called microstates—have equal say in the General Assembly. The United States has been assessed for 25 percent of the regular budget, though this was reduced to 22 percent in December 2000, whereas the smaller nations pay 0.001 percent.[27] Japan and Germany are the second and fourth largest contributors to the regular budget, although neither is rewarded with a permanent seat on the Security Council and the right of veto. Under such a system resolutions can be adopted by a majority of states. This can result in greater expenditures for the organization, even though they are opposed by those states that contribute the most financially (but in practice decisions on budgetary matters will not be taken against the will of the major contributors).[28] It could be argued that while the United Nations has moved away from sovereign equality by allowing for majority decisionmaking, it has not fully or fairly done this to reflect the real interests and power of states. A further step away from formal sovereign equality, which would allow organizations greater formal and factual power to adopt decisions affecting the sovereign interests of states, would be the principle of weighted voting.

However, the flaw with weighted voting, whereby certain states are given more votes or voting power than others, is "the criterion on which extra weight should be given. Should it be population, national income, power, or some other criterion"[29] such as contributions to the budget of the organization? Weighted voting may be credible and acceptable in functional organizations whose purposes and powers are confined to achieving limited goals, but it seems inapplicable to political organizations such as the United Nations, which has such a vast array of goals that it would be impossible to agree on a set of criteria.

The main UN organizations that use weighted voting are the IMF and IBRD, for two reasons. First "their task is confined so precisely to one field that criteria for weighting can be found there."[30] Second, and perhaps more significant, the organizations would not have been as effective, indeed might not have been established, had the major donating states not obtained dominance in decisionmaking. The latter justification has led to domination of these organizations by Western states (the United States, Japan, Germany, France, and the United Kingdom).

A more equitable composition is found in the constitution of the ILO, founded in 1919 and brought into the UN sphere in 1945 as a specialized agency. Its purposes are outlined in the preamble to the ILO constitution, principally the improvement of working conditions. "The fact that the Organisation is designed to promote the interests of part of the Community *within the State,* as opposed to the interests of the State as such, has led to a form of representation of interests other than the

State interest which was unique at its inception."[31] This uniqueness of representation is reflected in the fact that all decisions within the organization's organs are taken on a tripartite basis. In the annual general conference each member is represented by a delegation consisting of two government delegates, one employer's delegate, and one worker's delegate, each delegate having one vote, requiring either a simple majority or qualified majority for a decision to be adopted. The governing body, according to article 7, shall consist of fifty-six persons, twenty-eight representing governments, fourteen representing the employers, and fourteen representing the workers. Of the twenty-eight persons representing governments, ten shall be of chief industrial importance, again reflecting the functional nature of the organization.

Although the ILO is seen as unique in its composition and representation, it is not impossible to imagine these principles being extended to other specialized agencies, though it is more difficult. There is no doubt that the specialized agencies rely heavily on experts, but they do not have voting rights, which belong solely to state representatives. Nevertheless, even "though officially organizations of governments, most specialized agencies have developed some degree of independence from governments. In fact, the technical people run the organization."[32] Thus an analogy to the ILO would suggest that the parts of the community within states who benefit or are affected by decisions of these specialized agencies, as well as the technical experts, should have some form of representation.

There is a greater need to involve nonstate actors in the specialized agencies and in the main UN organs. NGOs representing, at least in part, nonstate ideologies need to be incorporated in a more satisfactory manner.[33] NGOs are proving increasingly invaluable in the human rights field, and the accountability and democratic representation of the United Nations would be increased if it allowed a greater role for NGOs. At the moment NGOs have important roles in UN-sponsored conferences, and many have established consultative status with the specialized agencies and more formally with ECOSOC. Article 71 of the UN Charter states that ECOSOC "may make suitable arrangements for consultation" with NGOs "which are concerned with matters within its competence." ECOSOC has erected an elaborate structure detailing the basis of cooperation between it and NGOs. It has set several criteria NGOs must achieve before a relationship is established, such as having democratically adopted constitutions and the authority to speak for members. Three categories of NGOs have been established by ECOSOC. The first category has the closest relationship with ECOSOC, as they are directly concerned with its work and are closely involved with the economic and social life of the people they represent.[34]

Consultative status for these NGOs is achieved through ECOSOC's Committee on NGOs. Category I and II NGOs have the right to attend meetings; category III NGOs can attend meetings only in their field of competence. Category I and II NGOs can submit written statements to ECOSOC and in specific cases speak in ECOSOC.[35] The impact of NGOs within the main structure of the United Nations has been limited.[36] Despite the invocation of "the Peoples of the United Nations" in the preamble of the charter, NGOs do not have a role in the work of the Security Council or the General Assembly's work outside economic and social matters.[37]

Going even farther, UN Secretary-General Kofi Annan, in his *Millennium Report of the Secretary-General 2000* ("We the Peoples"), stated that the United Nations

> must be opened up further to the participation of the many actors whose contributions are essential to managing the path of globalization. Depending on the issues in hand, this may include civil society organizations, the private sector, parliamentarians, local authorities, scientific associations, educational institutions and many others.[38]

This would be a radical development and involve a corresponding reduction in the democracy deficit. However, it may be that the UN democracy deficit can be addressed not by looking solely at the lack of nonstate representation in the organization but also at the relationship between the state and its citizens.

The Democracy Deficit

Greater involvement of NGOs might well reduce the democracy deficit in the system, but this assumes that NGOs are representative of the wider community. Some liberal commentators contend that the UN's democracy deficit should be remedied by an elected second chamber in the General Assembly, as with the European Union.[39] Although an interesting proposal, it suffers from a simple elevation of the national democratic paradigm on to the international stage, ignoring problems of the connection of the elected body with the citizenry of the world, as well as the loyalty of the citizens to the institutions of government.[40]

Besides, the problem may not be lack of representation for individuals; it is the fact that state representatives do not reflect the will of the citizens but rather the government. Obviously if that government is not elected, then there will be no real democratic accountability to citizens on any matter.

However, the trend since the late 1980s has been toward democracy around the globe, and the vast majority of state representatives at the United Nations are representing democratically elected governments. The question is thus whether those representing the views of their governments also reflect the will of the citizens. The answer to the democracy deficit at the United Nations does not lie with the General Assembly and the plenary bodies of the specialized agencies but with national assemblies and parliaments. Do the national elected representatives in these bodies have sufficient independent input into their governments' foreign policy choices at the United Nations?

It is not possible to review the systems of democratic accountability within states. Here I look at a state that is naturally assumed to have a mature and effective system of democratic accountability—the United Kingdom—and focus on whether its UN policy is responsive to the will of the people reflected in the elected body—the House of Commons.[41] The issue has been highlighted by the United Kingdom's involvement in the March–June 1999 bombing campaign undertaken by the North Atlantic Treaty Organization (NATO) to prevent atrocities committed in Kosovo. Although not a UN-sanctioned operation, the problems and proposals for reform are of direct relevance to increasing democratic accountability at both the national and international levels. Below I consider the United Kingdom's system of democratic accountability as provided in constitutional law.

When considering the United Kingdom's decisions to commit troops to a conflict either of national or international concern, the reality is that in the United Kingdom the executive—the cabinet or a subgroup of that body—makes the decision. The House of Commons, representing the electorate, then has a chance to debate the matter. In recent times Parliament has acted as a significant control on the actions of the executive, in the sense that military action is subject to detailed questioning in the House of Commons and its committees. Although not playing a major role in Parliament's scrutiny of the executive's actions in times of conflict, the House of Lords can play a subsidiary role, principally in seeking information from the government.[42]

In reality, the controls exerted by Parliament on the actions of government in foreign affairs, including UN matters, are limited. Political control is limited as dissent about military action is seen as unpatriotic. Bipartisanship within Parliament is the norm. The main concern of the government is to keep public opinion onboard. It is only in this diluted sense that the electorate can influence decisionmaking. The government and large sections of the media attempt, often successfully, to maintain public support for the military operation. U.K. involvement in the NATO bombing campaign in Kosovo was the subject of parliamentary debate, though the government received the usual bipartisan support. In the foreign affairs select committee's report on Kosovo of 7 June 2000, the committee did not suggest that the overall objectives of the campaign were illegitimate, but it was highly critical of government decisions, especially on the international law basis for the operation.[43] In addition, it suggested reforms to national constitutional procedures for gaining parliamentary approval to deploy armed forces under international auspices. Its impact, coming a year after the end of the bombings, remains questionable. In the short term there has been very little publicity surrounding the report, although in the longer term its somewhat modest proposals for reform could be adopted.

However, the increased level of accountability in the case of Kosovo was due to the lack of a clear legal basis for the bombing campaign, which did not have the requisite mandate from the United Nations. When the deployment of U.K. troops occurs under UN authority, there is strong evidence of less scrutiny by the elected representatives, though the level does vary.[44] The basic constitutional position is that decisionmaking on issues of foreign affairs and the deployment of armed forces—whether or not as part of UN operations—are within the prerogative power of the Crown.[45] The Crown is the collective entity that in law stands for central government.[46] Central government is largely coterminous with the executive. Executive functions include "the execution of law and policy, the maintenance of public order . . . the direction of foreign policy, the conduct of military operations."[47] Thus the lack of democratic accountability spreads to most aspects of foreign affairs (including UN matters), not only the sovereign right to deploy troops. Thus when the U.K. government decides to become involved in *any* UN action, there is very little control by the elected representatives of the people.

The reality of the exercise of prerogative powers in the areas of foreign affairs and the disposition of armed forces is shown by the exchange in the House of Commons in 1982, when negotiations were taking place for the settlement of the Falklands conflict. The leader of the opposition claimed that "the House of Commons has the right to make judgment on this matter before any decision is taken by the Government that would enlarge the conflict." In response, Prime Minister Margaret Thatcher declared that "it is an inherent jurisdiction of the government to negotiate and reach decisions. Afterwards the House of Commons can pass judgment on the government."[48] Although the Falklands conflict did not involve UN-authorized military operations, the same political processes occur in the United Kingdom when UN authority is given.

Under U.K. constitutional theory the legislature controls the executive, as a government can be ousted by a vote of no-confidence in Parliament. However, the often decisive majorities commanded by the government in the House of Commons, produced by the first-past-the-post electoral system, signify that any control is limited. In effect a government with a large majority in the House of Commons is an "elective dictatorship" even in matters requiring legislation; this is more so in the case of prerogative powers.[49] There may often be lively debates in Parliament, primarily in the House of Commons, though limited discussion is found in the House of Lords. Furthermore, there is the questioning of ministers before the defense select committee or select committee on foreign affairs of the House of Commons. However, it is questionable whether these operate as robust controls on cabinet decisionmaking. Crucial decisions have already been made, making the controls appear, at best, retrospective. Higgins is correct when she states that

> Parliament's role in the formulation of British policy in the UN is at most marginal. Foreign affairs within the British system of Government are executive in character, and the function of Parliament in this respect is to criticize or approve the policies decided upon by the Cabinet.[50]

Ministers may, however, curtail their decisions when considering the possible adverse reaction of the House of Commons or the relevant select committee in the near future.

Parallels can be made between domestic and international decisionmaking. In the United Kingdom the executive, often a small part of it, makes decisions on foreign affairs; cabinet and parliamentary support will only be sought after that. At the UN level, the executive organ, the Security Council (or rather the P3 or P5) will make a decision, which will later be endorsed by the full Security Council and then possibly by the plenary body—the General Assembly. The latter will endorse an operation only after it has started. Lack of accountability seems to exist at the international level as well as the domestic level. At the international level there is the possibility of veto in the executive body, which is not present except in theory at the domestic level. Increased control of the executive, both at the national and international levels, seems desirable by increasing the role of the plenary bodies.

Although parliamentary scrutiny of the executive varies in different countries and depending upon the nature of the foreign affairs issue, there is an overall deficiency in domestic democratic structures when decisions are made on UN matters.[51] It is here that the democracy deficit needs to be tackled, at least primarily. Greater democratic accountability could be achieved at both levels. To increase the input of the citizens into the UN decisionmaking process, universal democratization of states, accompanied by an effective level of parliamentary control over government decisions at the national level, would go a long way. This, of course, assumes that there is a direct and continuing democratic link between the citizens and their elected representatives over and above the electoral process that occurs every few years. It is somewhat depressing to learn from the Secretary-General's *Millennium Report 2000* that although "in most countries a majority said that their elections were free and fair," "as many as two thirds of all respondents felt that their country, nevertheless, was not governed by the will of the people. Even in the world's oldest democracies many citizens expressed deep dissatisfaction."[52]

Nevertheless, properly scrutinized and accepted government decisions must be fed to the United Nations by the government through its UN representatives. In addition, to ensure that nonmembers of the Security Council have their citizens' views respected, there must be greater input into the decisionmaking process, even on military matters, by the General Assembly. A greater role for the national and international assemblies is also important to combat the lack of transparency in decisionmaking in national and international executives, both of which have a tendency toward excessive secrecy.

During the Kosovo campaign, it was argued that the ending of hostilities might bring pressure to change the constitutional procedures under which the United Kingdom goes to war. Despite greater parliamentary debate during the bombing campaign of March–June 1999, the criticism was, in regard to the British contribution to the campaign, that "in this particular conflict, this is a Prime Minister with a vast majority in Parliament, a pliant Labour Party and a habit of operating informally through those he trusts. This is a war run by the people who meet in the Prime Minister's study."[53] Senior members of Parliament argued that parliamentary approval should be sought before war is launched and that the select committees of Parliament, "which hardly function when fighting begins," should be much more involved in questioning and investigating executive decisions.[54] Despite the lengthy debates and questioning by the foreign affairs select committee, parliamentary debate went to decisions already made by the war cabinet. Yet bipartisanship on military action is still the norm, and so such debates are of reduced value. Although calls for reform were louder while the bombing campaign was going badly, they died down following the withdrawal of Serb forces from Kosovo. This is a pity; there should be proper accountability of the government during times of war. The exigencies of war should not be used as an excuse to deny initial parliamentary approval of the military action and proper scrutiny thereafter. The same argument applies to foreign affairs, where there is a need for greater democratic accountability in light of globalization.

The 7 June 2000 foreign affairs select committee report on Kosovo did not recommend a change in the prerogative powers of the executive to deploy troops. It did recommend that the government "should take a substantive motion in the House of Commons at the earliest opportunity after the commitment of troops to armed conflict allowing the House to express its view, and allowing Members to table amendments." The requirement that the government should win the argument over contrary proposals in the lower house and gain a positive vote would give "extra democratic legitimacy to military action."[55] The report thus recognizes the need for proper parliamentary approval of international action. It may also encourage a more critical attitude by Parliament toward government actions. It falls short of requiring that positive parliamentary approval be given prior to the government's decision and therefore will hardly help the democracy deficit in U.K. decisionmaking on foreign affairs, including UN matters.

Political Accountability

Thus there should be more involvement of plenary bodies, where all the member state representatives (the vast majority of which are representing democratically elected governments) sit. Yet the concentration of too much unaccountable power in the executive body is also a problem, with the Security Council increasingly acting as judge, jury, and executioner when acting under chapter VII of the charter. The relationships between the executive and plenary bodies in the agencies vary.

For instance, the structure of the ILO, with its smaller governing body, shares a feature with the United Nations and the ICAO, allowing membership to be affected by decisions adopted in a small organ by a majority vote. However, unlike the UN Security Council, the ILO governing body is limited to control over the secretariat and to preparing for meetings of the general conference.[56] In the case of the ILO, the nonplenary organ is subordinate to the plenary body, which will mean that sovereignty is not so easily impinged. Nevertheless, if the voting structure of the general conference is examined, majority decision-making still allows for decisions to be adopted against the interests of a minority.[57]

The difference between the ILO and the United Nations is that though both allow for the plenary body to adopt decisions by a majority or qualified majority, the United Nations, through the nonplenary Security Council, can adopt decisions that impinge on the sovereignty of the majority of members without their consent. However, it could be argued that by becoming members of the United Nations each state has consented, by article 25 of the UN Charter, to be bound by the decisions of the Security Council. Such an argument tends to forget that membership of the United Nations, although technically optional, is in fact essential for most states in the world, and there must be doubts about the nature of the consent given to the Security Council to take certain executive action.

In the case of the United Nations, despite the wording of article 24, which suggests that the Security Council is acting on behalf of the membership, there is no real constitutional method for the plenary body to control the activities of the Security Council. Similarly, the assembly of the ICAO, the plenary organ, delegates "to the Council the powers and authority necessary or desirable for the discharge of the duties of the Organization" in article 49 of the Chicago Convention. Nevertheless, the council of the ICAO has many independent powers, and as the permanent organ it runs the ICAO. The agencies vary in the formal relationship between the plenary and executive organs, but in practice the executive bodies are the most significant actors. Indeed, the role of executive bodies within the United Nations and UN agencies is not to execute the policies set by the plenary bodies. "In many cases boards combine executive and governing functions. The boards of organizations such as the IAEA, the IMO, the ICAO and the financial specialized agencies perform many independent functions while at the same time they are executive boards."[58]

There is thus a palpable need to formally strengthen the position of the plenary bodies to prevent manifest abuses of power by the executive bodies. The paradigm for this is the UN Security Council, though equally strong arguments can be made as to the IMF and World Bank.

The San Francisco Conference recognized the theory that the Security Council and General Assembly act as judges of their own competence.[59] This was compounded by the subsequent failure to build in any real checks and balances on the power of the Security Council in the charter. Yet there is still considerable Cold War practice when the General Assembly acted as the "conscience" of the Security Council despite the wording of article 12, which obliges the assembly to refrain from adopting recommendations while the Security Council is dealing with a dispute. For instance, the assembly condemned superpower military interventions and urged the adoption of mandatory sanctions against apartheid South Africa.[60] However, with the end of the Cold War the assembly has, to a degree, lost its critical attitude toward the Security Council.

Occasionally the General Assembly does criticize the action of the Security Council. For instance, in 1993 the assembly called for the lifting of the arms embargo against Bosnia. The embargo had been put in place for the whole of the former Yugoslavia by the Security Council in 1991. However, in the assembly's view, Bosnia was a sovereign independent state and as such was entitled to defend itself.[61] Other instances include the General Assembly's criticism of the Security Council over its failure to denounce Israel's shelling of the UN base at Qana in southern Lebanon in April 1996,[62] as well as the council's inaction over Israel's building of a new settlement in East Jerusalem in March 1997.[63]

In addition, the Secretary-General has occasionally evaluated Security Council action in terms of its constitutionality,[64] despite the fact that the Secretary-General's office itself has expanded far beyond the formal powers granted to it in the UN Charter.[65]

Although there is some political accountability of the Security Council to the General Assembly and to a lesser extent the Secretary-General, it merely includes criticism and pressure. In the absence of judicial review (see Chapter 5) or increased accountability to the political organs, there appear to be no practical limits on the Security Council's competence. In regard to the General Assembly, there do appear to be limits of a practical and constitutional nature. Its competence in peacekeeping and collective security is practically limited, as it is unable to act without the help of the P5. Thus even though it was responsible for the first real peacekeeping force in 1956, its role has been marginalized by the Security Council.[66] And although its competence regarding peace and security was greatly expanded during the Cold War, it stopped short of claiming external mandatory powers, recognizing that the charter constitutionally grants this power to the Security Council.

This was confirmed by the ICJ in the *Expenses* case and has acted as a legal limit on General Assembly expansionism.[67] Thus it has claimed the power to recommend enforcement measures, but it has not claimed a power to decide such measures. This constitutional limitation—in article 11(2) of the charter—has also been recognized in subsequent practice.

In other branches of the UN family there is a deficiency in real accountability, even though the UN Charter expressly provides for supervision of the specialized agencies by ECOSOC and, ultimately, the General Assembly. The constitutional links between ECOSOC and the specialized agencies are contained in articles 63 and 64. Article 64 provides that ECOSOC "may take appropriate steps to obtain regular reports from the specialized agencies." Article 63 creates the basis of a much stronger link by providing that ECOSOC can enter agreements with the agencies and can coordinate the activities of those agencies through consultation and recommendation.

One can even assess the agreements between the United Nations and its specialized agencies in optimistic terms:

> Clearly these agreements provide a useful basis for co-ordination. The submission of reports by the agencies, the examination of these reports by the Council and the power to make recommendations to the agencies are useful factors in securing co-ordination and avoiding duplication.[68]

This seems an unduly positive analysis of the agreements. First, these powers apply to the specialized agencies with the exception of the Bretton Woods bodies, which do not have to report to ECOSOC and have to "consider" the recommendations of the UN body.[69] Second, the other agencies, although under a more onerous obligation to report on whether an ECOSOC recommendation has been adopted, have in practice carved out a huge degree of autonomy. Historically, there has been very little control by ECOSOC due to its concern with voting victories over effective coordination of a huge and unwieldy system.[70] ECOSOC is criticized for too often using its recommendatory powers to condemn states along the lines of the General Assembly rather than concentrating on development and assistance matters.[71]

In theory and practice, then, the specialized UN agencies are not the "agents" of the world body in the full sense of that word. None subject themselves to the full authority of the United Nations, and some—the Bretton Woods bodies—are virtually independent. Thus in most economic and social matters there is a system of decentralization and, until recently, a system in disintegration.[72]

The ill-defined role of ECOSOC, especially in regard to the specialized agencies, has led to an ominous lack of central coordination between ECOSOC and the specialized agencies. According to P. Taylor,

> The system lacked any central brain, and remained very weak in its
> co-ordination mechanism . . . the immediate reason for this was that
> the United Nations system was pluralistic; its decentralized character
> allowed the member states to avoid the problems which would arise
> if the instruments of collectivity were to be strengthened.[73]

The problem of decentralization was compounded by the splintered effort in achieving the common goal of development. Developing states, dissatisfied with the domination of the world's financial and economic organizations by developed states, used their voting power in the UN General Assembly in 1962 to establish the United Nations Conference on Trade and Development as a subsidiary organ of the assembly under article 22 of the charter.[74] "UNCTAD's activities spanned the spectrum of concerns of [the] developing countries": international commodity trade, market access for exports of developing countries, international monetary and financial reform, and institutional change. By 1979 UNCTAD had effectively adopted the agenda of the NIEO, meant to redress the North-South imbalance, which had been put forward by the General Assembly in 1974.[75] Furthermore, various funds set up by ECOSOC to assist developing countries were brought together by the assembly in 1965.[76] The result was the formation of the UNDP,[77] the aim of which was "to coordinate the activities of the older institutions with regard to the development of the Third World."[78]

With the development of UNCTAD and UNDP, there was further loss of central control by ECOSOC. Although, ECOSOC has "failed . . . to coordinate the activities of the specialized agencies,"[79] those agencies are at least required to report to ECOSOC under the terms of article 64. In effect UNDP and UNCTAD have become "major rivals of ECOSOC as candidates for the role of policy maker and coordinator of the system."[80] A report by the UN's Joint Inspection Unit (JIU) in 1985 contained a scathing attack on the system, condemning the lack of an integrated or even coordinated approach; "inadequate analysis of the role assigned to the United Nations system in the general scheme of technical assistance requirements of the various countries"; "absence of a unified concept of development"; "lack of satisfactory machinery at the centre of local levels to ensure the preliminary work of coordination of contribution of the various agencies"; and "the vagueness of the terms of reference" of the various organizations and bodies concerned with the area, in particular the "similarity of jurisdiction between organs as important as the Economic and Social Council, UNCTAD, [and] the Second and Third Committees of the General Assembly," which "have created in the United Nations system a state of confusion."[81] The further lack of coordination with other international economic institutions such as the World Bank and the IMF has led to overlap, inefficiency, and fragmentation in the system. Reform has been limited, and further diffusion of control continues with conferences on the environment in 1992, world population in 1994,[82] and women in 1995, as well as the World Food Summit in 1996.

The General Assembly had already recognized this problem in the mid-1970s, and established the Ad Hoc Committee on the Restructuring of the Economic and Social Sectors of the United Nations,[83] whose report was endorsed by the assembly in 1977.[84] The report, although unimplemented, in many ways tried to reestablish the hierarchy, with the General Assembly concentrating on "over-all strategies, policies and priorities for the system as a whole in respect of international co-operation, including operational activities, in the economic, social and related fields." Under the general direction of the assembly, ECOSOC should concentrate on fulfilling its role "as the central forum for the discussion of the international economic and social issues," "to monitor and evaluate the implementation of over-all strategies, policies and priorities established by the General Assembly," and "to ensure the over-all co-ordination of the activities of the organization of the United Nations system." At the lowest level the resolution states that:

> All United Nations organs and programmes, the specialized agencies, the General Agreement on Tariffs and Trade, the International Atomic Energy Agency and *ad hoc* world conferences should co-operate in whatever measures are necessary for the effective discharge of the responsibilities of the General Assembly and the Economic and Social Council and should, in accordance with the Charter of the United

Nations and within the scope of their respective basic instruments, give full and prompt effect to their specific policy recommendations.

The attempt in 1977 to establish a clear chain of authority—from the assembly to ECOSOC and then to the agencies—although laudable, has proved extremely difficult in practice. It is no surprise that these aims remain valid and were repeated, for instance, twenty years later by the Secretary-General and the General Assembly.[85] However, the assembly and ECOSOC have reduced their desire to score political points, which may evolve into a more pragmatic attitude toward managing the system and controlling and coordinating the activities of agencies. It may be time to renegotiate the agreements of the immediate postwar period that regulate the relationship between the agencies and ECOSOC to provide more direction from, and greater accountability to, the center. ECOSOC needs to be more accountable to the General Assembly.

Furthermore, organizations such as the IAEA and the General Agreement on Tariffs and Trade (GATT; now the WTO) are not de jure specialized agencies of the United Nations as suggested by the 1977 resolution. They are independent organizations, which can coordinate with the United Nations in certain activities if they so choose. The director-generals of the IAEA and the WTO are both members of the ACC, yet the Institutional, Procedural, and Legal Sub-Committee of the Preparatory Committee of the WTO expressly stated in November 1994 that while it was necessary to have effective cooperation between the WTO and the United Nations, there were no grounds for establishing institutional links between the two organizations.[86] The WTO emerged from GATT as a new international organization on 1 January 1995, and it rejects the idea of coming within the UN family. Unlike the IMF and World Bank, the WTO appears unprepared to negotiate any agreement under article 63 allowing it autonomy. This suggests a move toward decentralization and lack of coordination.

It may be that the depoliticization of the assembly, ECOSOC, and the agencies' plenary bodies will make the UN system more attractive to outside organizations that fear political control and the inherent politicization of the system. Although the WTO may have developed some links with the UN system, especially the Bretton Woods organizations, since its inception in 1995, it is not formally a part of the UN system.[87] Whether this presents problems is beyond the scope of this book, but it can be argued that the WTO has respect for UN law anyway, eliminating the need to bring it into the system.[88] And the presence of the

WTO within the UN family would not by itself ensure consistency with UN law.

Thus the obvious way to create a framework for consistency is to bring all universal functional agencies within the UN system. The true measure of an organization's activities would not be its own constitution but that of the United Nations, with the charter at the apex. Then a full evaluation of the entity's compliance and furtherance of UN values could be undertaken. Although an organization outside the system may strive to bring its actions into line with UN law, that would appear to be a voluntary and nonreviewable decision on the part of the organization.[89]

The depoliticization of the UN system could make it attractive to current or future organizations operating outside it. If they were brought within the system, then they should conform with the overriding constitutional principles, including human rights, governing the UN system. It is desirable that the UN family be extended to cover such organizations, not for the sake of neatness or completeness but for the sake of consistency.

Mechanisms for Coordination

The picture, then, depicts an unwieldy system that lacks coordination. There are signs that the systemic problems are being addressed at a pragmatic level, especially under the guidance of UN Secretary-General Kofi Annan, who was elected on 1 January 1997. One of the main mechanisms for coordination is the much-derided Chief Executives Board for Coordination, formerly the Administrative Committee on Coordination (ACC). This body, established in 1946, initially consisted of the Secretary-General and the heads of the UN specialized agencies and has been depicted as a self-serving forum where the heads of the agencies ensured the autonomy and independence of their organizations from the UN center.[90] In recent years, however, there are suggestions that the ACC is much more dynamic and proactive. It has attempted to provide pragmatic direction to the system within the framework set by the constitution and the policy set by the General Assembly and ECOSOC. The ACC has added the heads of the UN funds and programs such as UNCTAD, UNEP, UNDP, UNICEF, and the WFP to its membership to ensure that programs and funds that have grown by necessity since 1945 do not overlap or duplicate the work of specialized agencies. Significantly, the head of the WTO has joined the head of the IAEA as a member of the ACC, representing IGOs outside the UN system.

The ACC's "main function now is that of facilitating increased co-ordination of the programmes approved by the governing bodies of the various organizations of the United Nations system and, more generally, promoting cooperation within the system in pursuit of the common goals of the international community."[91] Although this is the ACC's own assessment, there is greater evidence of coordination and coopera-tion through the ACC and its subsidiary bodies.[92] The ACC reports to ECOSOC, which provides overall policy guidance under the direction of the General Assembly. The ACC itself has claimed that since 1998 there has been "a substantial strengthening of the dialogue between" ECOSOC and the ACC. This period has also been "characterized by an intensive process of revitalization of [ECOSOC] and a more effective and participatory exercise by [ECOSOC] of its coordination functions; and a parallel strengthening of ACC's leaderships role within the system, *inter alia*, in bringing the system together in support of inter-governmental policy-making."[93]

There is also evidence of General Assembly direction being given to the UN system. In the triennial comprehensive policy review of op-erational activities within the UN system, the assembly's tone is much more pragmatic and directional. Its 1998 resolution urges cooperation and the reduction of overlap, then directs the ACC and the UN Secre-tary-General to improve the UN Developmental Assistance Framework. This aims to bring different UN activities within one country into a co-herent and mutually supportive whole, with the further development of a resident coordinator system utilizing the elements of the UN system as necessary. The tone is clear: the General Assembly is trying to manage the system instead of treating agencies as entirely separate. Direct men-tion is made of greater cooperation by the World Bank, which seems to be happening. The assembly also emphasizes the need for proper mon-itoring and evaluation.[94]

In the ACC there is a strong desire to develop a "United Nations voice" that would unify the system behind a shared vision. Moves to-ward this were evident in October 1999, when the meeting considered "that the broad concept of sustainable human security and development captured well the broad objectives of the United Nations system to pro-mote peace, development, democracy, social justice, the rule of law and human rights." "Sustainable human security and development can serve as the overarching objectives of a common agenda for the United Na-tions system."[95] Furthermore, in its April 2000 meeting the ACC recog-nized the importance of law in achieving these activities when it stated that the "key contribution of the United Nations system was to set norms and establish principles." This was especially important within the context of increasing globalization. The ACC stated that "international law and norms must become an integral part of the language of globalization."[96] Indeed, the phenomenon of globalization in the late 1990s and into the twenty-first century seems to be galvanizing the ACC. The ACC stated in April 2000 that

> globalization was more than an economic phenomenon. It had implications ranging from the application of labour standards and human rights to the management of population movements. It posed major challenges, from counteracting the spread of diseases to combating the expansion of criminal networks. Each organization had its own constituency and individual voice and was mandated to address specific aspects of the issue. It was only by working together that the United Nations system could tackle the overall challenge of globalization and help make it work for the world's people.[97]

The United Nations system is the only global mechanism that can address such problems. Its strengths are highlighted by the ACC:

> Universality: in terms of the scope of its membership, the range of its functions, its multicultural character and its capacity to give voice to the concerns of all; credibility and moral authority: value based orientation, underpinned by knowledge, giving expression and operating according to principles and acting for the common good; and convening power which enables the system to contribute to global agenda-setting, and to serve as a generator of normative standards and as a vehicle of international cooperation for their attainment.[98]

The weaknesses included:

> the system's inability to fully exploit the source of its own strength; insufficient coherence in setting goals and in implementing initiatives and in monitoring the realization of agreed plans and targets; and a certain propensity to be crisis-driven, that is to say, the reactive nature of the system.[99]

Greater contact with what the ACC calls "multistakeholders," in order to harness the resources of the private sector or to ascertain the concerns of "civil society," are part of the reforms that are being proposed and put into operation within the UN system.[100]

For example, the ACC has focused on initiatives already under way within the system, such as the "roll back malaria" initiative of the WHO and the "elimination of urban slums" initiative of the World Bank, to see how they can "best be reinforced and supported by the system as a whole."[101] The idea seems to be to work with existing UN structures to focus them on solving problems by facilitating and organizing combinations of organizations to address problems that "cut across the mandates of individual organizations."[102] This involves bringing in UN agencies that in the past have not always acted in co-ordination with other UN bodies, such as the World Bank, as well as organizations outside the UN system, for example, the WTO, NGOs, the private sector, and civil society organizations. The task is immense, but there is greater cooperation, though it is too early to evaluate its impact on the ground.

The Global Alliance for Vaccines and Immunization "is an excellent example of such a broad-based coalition alliance." Its aim is "achieving the long-standing goal of universal immunization for children." It brings together elements of the UN system as well as governments, foundations, and the private sector to ensure the manufacture of vaccines as well as procurement, training, education, and administration. Partners in the program include UNICEF, WHO, the World Bank, the Bill and Melinda Gates Children's Vaccine Program, the Rockefeller Foundation, the pharmaceutical industry, and representatives of governments.[103] A more UN-focused partnership is the ACC Network on Rural Development and Food Security, consisting of the FAO, IFAD, and WFP, the aim of which is to tackle problems at the country level to fight poverty. This was set up in 1997 following the World Food Summit of 1996, showing that UN-sponsored conferences can lead to positive and concerted action if the elements of the system are brought to bear by the ACC. By October 1999 a resident coordinator could be found in sixty-four countries, leading a team of experts to marshal the resources and skills of the various UN bodies to implement rural development programs.[104]

Another ACC-assisted initiative is UNAIDS, established in 1996. This program is cosponsored by UNICEF, UNDP, UNFPA, the United Nations Drug Control Programme, UNESCO, the WHO, and the World Bank. The goal of UNAIDS is to "catalyse, strengthen and orchestrate the unique expertise, resources and networks of influence that each of these organizations offers" to combat HIV/AIDS.[105] The United Nations is realistically the only organization capable of dealing with such a global epidemic. The ACC channels expertise and resources through resident coordinators, drawing on the various elements of the UN system that can assist.[106] Another example of interagency cooperation is the International Strategy for Disaster Reduction, drawing from the FAO, WMO, UNESCO, ITU, the World Bank, UNDP, UNEP, and the WFP. The aim is to strengthen the capacities of disaster-prone countries to cope more readily with disasters and to recover more quickly when they strike. The aim is to be preventative.[107]

The chain of authority—from the assembly to ECOSOC to the ACC and then to the agencies, funds, and programs—is showing signs of operating in a more pragmatic and results-oriented fashion. It remains to be seen whether this improvement will overcome the years of disintegration and apathy that have characterized the UN system in the past. It must be noted that there are other UN mechanisms that contribute to increasing the efficiency and coordination of the system.[108] The Office of Internal Oversight Services was established in 1994 by the General Assembly,[109] its mission "to promote effective programme management by identifying, reporting on and proposing remedies to address problems of waste, fraud, abuse and mismanagement within the Organization."[110]

Perhaps more significant in terms of development and improvement of the UN system as a whole is the JIU established in 1968 by the General Assembly[111] following the UN's financial crisis of the early 1960s. The JIU was made a permanent body, and a common subsidiary body within the UN system, following the promulgation of its statute in 1976.[112] The statute provides, inter alia, in article 5 that the inspectors (eleven independent experts on administrative and financial matters) "shall have the broadest powers of investigation in all matters having a bearing on the efficiency of the services and the proper use of funds." Article 5 also stipulates the mandate of the JIU, summarized as providing "an independent view through inspection and evaluation, aimed at improving management and methods and at achieving greater coordination between organizations"; and to "monitor that the activities undertaken by the organization are carried out in the most economical manner and that the optimum use is made of resources for carrying out these activities."[113] JIU reports are sent to the legislative organs of the organizations involved, which then choose whether to adopt the recommendations therein. The 300 or so reports of the JIU range from topics as diverse as UN publications to conflict prevention, in addition to the occasional systemwide report.[114] Their major weakness is "the lack of an appropriate 'follow-up' system for monitoring whether JIU recommendations approved by legislative bodies are implemented."[115]

Conclusion

The United Nations is in need of reform. The debates center on the membership of the Security Council, streamlining the Secretariat, and resolving the financial crisis at the United Nations.[116] These concerns are important. However, the issues of accountability and democracy go much farther. The increasingly supranational activities of the United Nations need to be supplemented by methods of political and legal control; otherwise the current dominance of the system by Western states is likely to appear more and more like an oligarchy, thereby undermining the system's legitimacy. The recognition that the Security Council is a functional organ dealing with peace and security should define its membership, and as a consequence the veto should not be formally recognized. The current UN practice of gaining consensus wherever possible with the fallback of qualified majority voting should be formally adopted.[117]

In the assembly, the more politicized organ, there is little alternative to the current one-state, one-vote system. Instead there should be a thorough reassessment of the financial contributions each state has to pay, leading to a more equitable system. Greater access to nonstate actors, including NGOs, and elements of civil society should be built in to the system. Without these reforms the United Nations will rightly be accused of double standards—of promoting democracy within countries but not within its own institutions, although democracy will be increased only with the advent of democratically elected governments sitting at the United Nations representing their respective peoples.

On the issue of accountability, the current approach, which leaves each organ as an autonomous entity subject to limited constitutional restraints (in the case of the Security Council such are virtually nonexistent), is unacceptable. There is a need to give the whole membership in the General Assembly some ultimate power over the Security Council. Such a power may require an exceptional qualified majority such as three-quarters or four-fifths, but it should include the power to annul acts of the Security Council that are unacceptable, whether for legal or political reasons, to the vast majority of the membership. The creation of an attorney general–type post would encourage the Security Council to consider the legality of acts more carefully than perhaps it does at present. It must be borne in mind, however, that in legal terms it is possible to depart from the formal language of the charter a considerable way before crossing the threshold of illegality. The threshold will be reinforced by the institutionalization of a more active ICJ regarding judicial review not only to cover Security Council activities but also those of the other organs and the specialized agencies (see Chapter 5).

The accountability of the specialized agencies needs to be improved by greater use of panels of independent experts mandated by the assembly or ECOSOC, along the lines of the JIU. Though normally used in human rights treaties to supervise state compliance, there is no reason why such depoliticized panels should not be created to help fulfill the UN's mandate to oversee the performance of the specialized agencies in their various functions. Greater coordination of the system needs to be provided by the ACC, although there are some signs that this is starting to happen. Pragmatism, though, should operate only within the UN legal order to further the values of the UN system.

Although these are mere suggestions, development and reform of the UN system has to address the more fundamental issues of democracy and accountability rather than the shorter-term issues of permanent membership, the size of UN bureaucracy, and funding.

Notes

1. Franck, *Fairness,* 26, 30, 41.
2. Art. 110(1) of the UN Charter provides that "the present Charter shall be ratified by signatory states in accordance with their respective constitutional processes."
3. *Admission of a State to the United Nations (Charter, Art. 4),* ICJ Rep. 1948, 65.
4. Schermers and Blokker, *Institutional Law,* 69.
5. See White, *International Organisations,* 66–69.
6. See Blum, "UN Membership." The FRY was admitted as a member of the United Nations by GA Res. 55/12, 1 Nov. 2000.
7. Schermers and Blokker, *Institutional Law,* 67.
8. 77 UNTS 143; Arts. 2 and 3.
9. 298 UNTS 48; Arts. 1 and 4.
10. GA Res. 3237, 22 Nov. 1974. See Blum, *Eroding,* ch. 4.
11. UN doc. S/20278 (1988).
12. Kirgis, *International Organizations,* 158–164.
13. GA Res. 32/9E, 4 Nov. 1977.
14. In practice the permanent members have ignored any formal restrictions on the exercise of the veto. See White, *Keeping the Peace,* 8–11.
15. Art. 23(1) of the UN Charter.
16. See report of Pakistan discussing the Equitable Representation Working Group's Report—GA 49th mtg., A/PV, 1 Nov. 1996.
17. Winkelman, "Bringing the Security Council."

18. Art. 50 of the Chicago Convention.

19. *Renewing the United Nations: A Programme for Reform,* UN doc. A/52/950, 16 July 1997, para. 97.

20. Art. 49 of the ICAO Convention; Art. 8(a) of the UNESCO Constitution.

21. GA Res. 1803, 1962.

22. (1977) 53 ILR 398, para. 97.

23. *Case Concerning Military and Paramilitary Activities in and Against Nicaragua,* ICJ Rep. 1986, 14 at 99–107. GA Res. 2131, 21 Dec. 1965; GA Res. 2625, 24 Oct. 1970; GA Res. 3314, 14 Dec. 1974.

24. ICJ Rep. 1986, 98. See Hart, *Concept,* 89.

25. Commencing with GA Res. ES-6/2, 14 Jan. 1980.

26. GA Res. 44/240, 29 Dec. 1989.

27. GA Res. 55/5, 23 Dec. 2000.

28. Zoller, "The Corporate Will," 633–634. GA Res. 41/123, 19 Dec. 1986.

29. Schermers and Blokker, *Institutional Law,* 520.

30. Ibid., 522.

31. Bowett, *International Institutions,* 109.

32. Schermers, "We the Peoples," 117.

33. On the variety of NGOs and their contribution to civil society, see Steiner and Alston, *International Human Rights,* 938–941.

34. Schermers and Blokker, *Institutional Law,* 129–130.

35. Ibid., 132.

36. Nicholas, *The United Nations,* 142–143; Schermers and Blokker, *Institutional Law,* 132. But see LeRoy Bennett, *International Organizations,* 272.

37. Beigbeder, *Le Role,* 32.

38. <http://www.un.org/millennium/sg/report/>, para. 46.

39. Franck, "The United Nations as Guarantor," 38. See also Franck, *Fairness,* 481–484.

40. Marks, *The Riddle,* 81–100.

41. For a thorough review of democratic accountability within a variety of states, see Jacobson and Ku, *Accountability.*

42. Loveland, *Constitutional Law,* 226.

43. Select Committee on Foreign Affairs, Fourth Report, 7 June 2000 <http:www.parliament.the-station...99900/cmselect/cmfaff/28/2806.htm>.

44. For details, see White, "The UK."

45. Lester and Oliver, *Constitutional Law,* 465–466, 476.

46. Bradley and Ewing, *Constitutional Law,* 253.

47. *Halbury's Laws of England,* 4th ed. (HMSO, 1973), col. 8(2), para. 9.

48. 23 H.C. Deb., 6th Ser., 11 May 1982, cols. 597–598.

49. Turpin, *British Government,* 361.

50. Higgins, *The Administration,* 55.

51. Damrosch, "The Interface."

52. <http://www.un.org/millennium/sg/report>, para. 62. This was based on a survey of 57,000 adults in sixty countries.

53. McSmith and Beaver, "Commander Blair Goes It Alone," *The Observer,* 18 April 1999, 14.

54. Ibid.

55. H.C. Foreign Affairs Select Committee Fourth Report, 7 June 2000, paras. 165–166.

56. Arts. 13(5) and 14, Constitution of the ILO.

57. For a thorough review of the balance of power in the organs of the UN specialized agencies, see Bowett, *Institutions,* 121–129.

58. Schermers and Blokker, *Institutional Law,* 290.

59. UNCIO, vol. 13, 709. Ciobanu, *Preliminary Objections,* 162–173.

60. See, for example, GA Res. 1663, 1961.

61. GA Res. 48/88, 20 Dec. 1993.

62. GA Res. 50/22C, 25 April 1996.

63. GA Res. 51/223, 13 Mar. 1997.

64. See, for example, the Secretary-General's statements on the legal basis of the naval operations in the Gulf in Lauterpacht, *The Kuwait Crisis,* 247.

65. Lavalle, "The Inherent Powers."

66. Luard, *The United Nations,* 46–47.

67. ICJ Rep. 1962, 151 at 163–164.

68. Bowett, *International Institutions,* 68.

69. See, for example, the 1947 agreement between the UN and the IMF, 16 UNTS 328.

70. Taylor, *International Organizations,* 127–129.

71. Williams, *Specialized Agencies,* 117.

72. See section below on mechanisms for coordination; see also Chapter 11.

73. Taylor, *International Organizations,* 115.

74. GA Res. 1785, 1962.

75. "UNCTAD and International Economic Reform," 249.

76. Sir Robert Jackson, *Study of the Capacity of the United Nations Development System* (1969).

77. GA Res. 2029, 22 Nov. 1965.

78. Taylor, *International Organizations,* 118.

79. Ibid., 127.

80. Ibid., 129.

81. JIU, *Some Reflections on Reform of the United Nations,* prepared by Maurice Bertrand, JIU/REP/85/9 (1985).

82. Taylor, *International Organizations,* 133–139.

83. GA Res. 2262 (S-7), 16 Sept. 1975.

84. GA Res. 32/197, 20 Dec. 1977.

85. SG, *Renewing the United Nations,* UN doc. A/51/950 (1997), para. 97; GA Res. 52/12, 19 Dec. 1997.

86. *Focus* (GATT Newsletter), vol. 112, Nov. 1994, 8.

87. Vines, "The WTO in Relation to the Fund and the Bank," 59. See also the International Trade Centre—part of the UN system that since 1968 has acted as a focal point between GATT/WTO and UNCTAD. It is a joint subsidiary organ of the WTO and UN—see <http://www.intracen.org>.

88. Petersmann, "How to Promote," 96–97. But see Enders, "The Role of the WTO," 65–66.

89. Although states that are members of the United Nations and the functional organization are obliged to give precedence to the UN Charter in the event of incompatibility. See Art. 103 of the UN Charter.

90. M. Hill, "The Administrative Committee on Co-ordination," in Luard, *Evolution*, 104.

91. <http://acc.unsystem.org/-about/>.

92. For a critical external view, see Idris and Bartolo, *A Better United Nations,* 91–138.

93. UN doc. E/2000/53, para. 12. See, for example, ECOSOC Res. 1999/66, 16 Dec. 1999.

94. GA Res. 53/192, 15 Dec. 1998. See SG Report A/53/226 and Add. 1–4; UN doc. ACC/1994, Annex II.

95. UN doc. ACC/1999/20, para. 8.

96. UN doc. ACC/2000/4, para. 21.

97. Ibid., para. 20.

98. UN doc. E/2000/53, para. 21.

99. Ibid.

100. Ibid., para. 30.

101. Ibid., para. 23

102. Ibid., para. 27.

103. Ibid., para. 28.

104. Ibid., para. 45.

105. <http://www/unaids.org/about/what.asp>.

106. UN doc. ACC/2000/4, para. 50.

107. Ibid., para. 67.

108. See also the General Assembly's Open-ended High-level Working Group on Strengthening the United Nations System, which looked at the system from 1995 to 1997. Its proposals were largely pragmatic, reflecting the current approach taken by the Secretary-General and the ACC. See GA Res. 49/252, 14 Sept. 1995; GA Res. 51/241, 31 July 1997; 53/239, 8 June 1999.

109. GA Res. 48/218B, 29 July 1994.

110. Office of Internal Oversight Services, "Its Genesis, Its Mission, Its Working Methods, Its Impact," DPI/1761, 1996.

111. See generally Munch, "The Joint Inspection Unit"; GA Res. 2360 (XXII), 19 Dec. 1967.

112. GA Res. 31/192, 22 Dec. 1976.

113. Munch, "The Joint Inspection Unit," 296.

114. Ibid., 298–299.

115. Ibid., 301.

116. See SG's statement to the GA introducing his report on "Renewing the United Nations," UN Press Release SG/SM/6284/Rev.2, GA/9282, 16 July 1997.

117. As is the case in the WTO, see Agreement on the WTO, (1993) 33 ILM 1, Art. 9.

5

The Legal Organs: Accountability and the Rule of Law

The ICJ is the principal judicial organ of the United Nations.[1] There are other judicial or quasijudicial organs in the UN system; some will be discussed in this chapter, others elsewhere. Examples include the ICTY, ICTR, and the ICC (see Chapter 8), the Law of the Sea Tribunal, the UN Compensation Commission on Iraq, the HRC (Chapter 9), and the Committee on Economic, Social, and Cultural Rights (CESCR; Chapter 9). Whereas the ICTR, ICTY, and Compensation Commission are subsidiary bodies of the UN Security Council, the others are established by UN-sponsored treaties and have greater autonomy than subsidiary organs. An important issue is the relationship, if any, between judicial bodies and the ICJ, the latter body being the primary focus of this chapter in assessing its contribution to the UN legal order.

Part 3 demonstrates that much of the UN's legal order is about producing laws, and so the ICJ's importance cannot be underestimated. The legitimacy of the system is enhanced many times if member states comply with the UN system's substantive regulatory laws and if the political organs observe the constitutional norms that shape the system. The rule of law within the UN system will be strengthened if the principal UN court plays a central role in upholding UN law.[2] This means settling disputes among member states as well as ensuring that the UN's organs, agencies, and bodies act intra vires (within the scope of their powers) and not ultra vires (outside the scope). However, the issue is whether the ICJ has the ability to apply that doctrine and, if so, whether the court is willing to do it.

The UN Charter states that the ICJ is a principal organ of the United Nations, alongside the General Assembly, the Security Council, ECOSOC, the Trusteeship Council, and the Secretariat.[3] There is no hierarchy in the structure of the United Nations, apart from article 24's reference to the "primary responsibility" of the Security Council for peace and security.[4] This raises the issue of the legal accountability of the political organs to the principal legal organ. Without a discernible UN hierarchy, the question is whether the ICJ can review the decisions of the political organs and other institutions.

A major aspect of this chapter is the critique of the other element of the rule of law, which requires that both governing institutions and those governed are subject to legal rules. The governed, that is, members of the UN community, are the primary litigants before the ICJ. The issue, then, is whether the ICJ protects and upholds the principles of the UN legal order. As stated by T. Franck:

> Yet it is only when the rule-writers make provision for an institutional process to apply the rules to specific disputes that a rule takes on the gravity which distinguishes it from the verbal shields and swords of diplomatic combat. Only an international law which is subject to case-by-case interpretation via a credible third-party decision making process is a *serious* norm.[5]

Furthermore, "like the law it applies, the Court's ability to pull states to compliance with its opinions depends on the general perception of the legitimacy and fairness of its opinion-forming process."[6] The issues of impartiality and fairness will be considered after an initial examination of the ICJ as the court of the United Nations.

The ICJ as the UN Court

Being the principal judicial organ of the United Nations, the ICJ bears a heavy responsibility, especially in upholding the rule of law within the UN system and by extension the international community.

The ICJ has special characteristics that distinguish it from other international judicial institutions. It is the only international judicial body that is open to all states, members as well as nonmembers. It is therefore qualified to become a general court for the international community. The incorporation of the ICJ within the UN Charter suggests that the United Nations considered itself to be representing the whole international community. Furthermore, on the basis of the definition of the so-called sources of law in its statute, the court is the only judicial

body that applies generally binding international law without limitation to
a defined treaty system or the restrictions of a specialized legal field. The
court is therefore in a better position than any other judicial institution to
contribute through its case law to the development of international law.[7]

According to G. Abi-Saab, this signifies that "its first and foremost
role is to uphold the global values of that community rather than to act
as a mere mediator between two disputing parties."[8] Unfortunately, one
of the legacies of its succession to the Permanent Court of International
Justice (PCIJ) under the League of Nations legal order was that for
many years the ICJ "acted as if it were an arbitral tribunal of the nineteenth century and not as an integral part of the UN."[9] Evidence of an
entrenched arbitral ideology operating within the court's structure and
decisionmaking processes will be illustrated below. This takes the shape
of national and ad hoc judges, reflecting the consensual nature of its
contentious jurisprudence, which indicate a continuation of "arbitraliza-
tion" or "transactional justice." In other words, the court is mainly concerned with resolving a dispute between parties and not necessarily acting in a wider context as the court of the "international legal order."[10]
Unfortunately, the drafters of the UN Charter did not create a sufficiently robust court to fulfill the prophetic words of the relevant committee at San Francisco.

> In establishing the International Court of Justice, the United Nations
> holds before a war-stricken world the beacons of Justice and Law and
> offers the possibility of substituting orderly judicial processes for the
> vicissitudes of war and the reign of brutal force.[11]

The court is restricted in its structures and powers from developing
into a powerful judicial organ of the United Nations and international
community. It is restricted in its contentious jurisdiction not only by the
fact that its binding decisions are not enforceable but also the continuation of the need to ground each case on the consent of the parties. Although an understandable restriction, the court has made little attempt
to question its severity even when faced with alleged breaches of norms
of *jus cogens* (fundamental laws) or obligations owed *erga omnes* (obligations owed to the international community as a whole) by states. In
the *Case Concerning East Timor,* brought by Portugal against Australia
in 1995, the court refused to grant jurisdiction on the basis that the case
would involve considering Indonesia's seizure and occupation of East
Timor in 1975. Given that Indonesia had not consented to the jurisdiction

of the court, the court, despite agreeing that the self-determination had the character of an *erga omnes* obligation, felt that it had no basis on which to ground its jurisdiction.[12] This was despite the fact that it had already defined obligations *erga omnes* in a previous case as the "obligations of a State towards the international community as a whole" as opposed to those arising between two states in a given dispute.[13] However, the court was unwilling to go against precedent on the requirement of consent, which is certainly applicable in pure interstate disputes but is less applicable in cases in which a state is breaching its obligations to the international community as a whole. The court, faced with a choice between the traditional paradigms of sovereignty and consent and the alternative paradigms of community and community values, chose, not untypically, the more conservative route.

Similarly, its jurisprudence in advisory opinions, although useful, has been of limited value given its stated unwillingness to act as a court of review testing the legality of the acts of the United Nations.[14] Yet the court is moving gingerly toward asserting legal guardianship over the UN Charter,[15] in terms of compliance with the charter by the United Nations itself and in terms of upholding fundamental UN values.[16]

Impartiality and Fairness of the ICJ

The statute of the ICJ attempts to establish a fair and neutral court. In regard to the caliber and independence of the fifteen judges, the statute provides that the "Court shall be composed of a body of independent judges elected regardless of their nationality from among persons of high moral character." Furthermore, no member of the court "may exercise any political or administrative function, or engage in any other occupation of a professional nature" or "act as agent, counsel, or advocate in any case." Finally, "every member of the Court shall . . . make a solemn declaration in open court that he will exercise his powers impartially and conscientiously."[17]

Although there is no substantial evidence to question the impartiality of the court, there are many examples of judges dissenting from a majority decision that rules against the dissenter's country of origin.[18] The dissents of Judge S. Schwebel in the *Nicaragua* case of 1986,[19] and also in the 1998 decision that found that the court had jurisdiction over the *Lockerbie* case[20] brought by Libya against the United States in 1992, are just two examples. Though the dissenting opinions were cogently argued, the fact that the U.S. judge disagreed with the overwhelming majority of the court, which had found against the United States, undermines confidence in the impartiality of individual judges when faced with a case in which their state is a party. It is ironic, however, that both the *Nicaragua* and *Lockerbie* cases enhanced the legitimacy of the court in the eyes of most states as "judicial independence in the face of a superpower's defiance."[21] The *Nicaragua* case certainly seems to have had a galvanizing effect on developing countries that were reticent to use the court prior to this decision but have been much more willing to use the court since.[22] Nevertheless, the vociferous U.S. dissent in the case was followed by the U.S. government's refusal to accept the judgment thereafter.

Instead of requiring judges to excuse themselves if their country of origin is a party, the statute leans the other way. Article 31 of the ICJ statute states that "judges of the nationality of each of the parties shall retain their right to sit in the case before the Court." Furthermore, it provides that "if the Court includes upon the Bench a judge of the nationality of one of the other parties any other party may choose a person to sit as judge." This idea of appointing ad hoc judges is questionable in light of the ideal that a court of law should not contain elements of bias or have the appearance of bias. Certainly the evidence is that ad hoc judges vote in favor of their appointing state, more so than established judges of the nationality of one of the parties.[23] Nevertheless, most commentators on the court support the institution on pragmatic grounds.

> These Provisions [of the statute] have given rise to controversy, principally on the ground that they distort the "international character" of the international magistrature and that they conflict with the principle that no man should be a judge in his own case (*Nemo judex in sua causa*). From the theoretical point of view this is undoubtedly true. However, . . . the notion of "national arbitrators" is deeply rooted in the practice of international arbitration, and indeed the facility to appoint them is probably a *sine qua non* for the success of the whole idea. The important thing for ensuring third-party judgment is not that national arbitrators or judges should disappear, but that the balance in the tribunal should be held by neutral judges. This is the conception which has been incorporated in the Statute, for in practice the outcome is rarely likely to be influenced by the views of the judges having the nationality of the parties who, in the nature of things, tend to cancel each other out.[24]

Although it is true that ad hoc judges and national judges do not generally affect the final decision of the court, this does not make their continuation satisfactory. Indeed, it appears somewhat perverse to claim that in the "light of the fragile foundations of international adjudication" the presence of ad hoc judges and the inclusion of their normally dissenting opinions "lends reality to the dictum that justice must not only be done but that it must be seen to be done."[25] The vigorous defense of ad hoc judges seems more to have to do with the defense of national judges, for if ad hoc judges are discounted then so must national judges. Yet the presence of both types of judges undermines the credibility of the court as an impartial and independent body. Their presence brings the ICJ closer to the institution of arbitration (especially when the technique of having small chambers is taken into account), which cannot be a good thing if the ICJ is to develop into an institution that is not subject to actual or perceived influence from a state party to the case before it.[26] Furthermore, it is not clear that the right to appoint an ad hoc judge is important in gaining the consent of a litigant state. It may even be argued that the removal of the opposing state's judge from the court would encourage it to consent.

On the issue of composition, the fact that the court shadows the composition of the Security Council is not encouraging given the council's distance from the general membership. Indeed, there is no justification for this in the statute, except for the fact that the size of the court corresponds to the current size of the council. Article 9 states that at every election of judges the Security Council and General Assembly shall bear in mind that the persons to be elected as judges should possess the necessary qualifications and that "in the body as a whole the representation of the main forms of civilization and of the principal legal systems of the world should be assured." There is no veto in the Security Council over the election of judges, with article 10 providing that an absolute majority is required in both the Security Council and the General Assembly.

The relative openness of article 9 has led to a series of "understandings which have either been negotiated diplomatically or have emerged *de facto* in the United Nations."[27] These understandings reflect the distribution of power in the Security Council with nationals from the P5 always being elected to the court, with the remainder reflecting the regional distribution of seats on the Security Council.[28] Though again an understandable development, especially within the strictures of the Cold War, the mimicking of the nonplenary political organ degrades the court's legitimacy. There is no justification, apart from the pragmatic, for filling five seats with nationals from the P5. The court should represent the international community, and it is only if the international community is defined as the Security Council, more specifically the P5, that its current composition can be justified.

State Disputes

The ICJ is the principal example of an international judicial body empowered to hear disputes between states. In many ways the ICJ is a traditional judicial institution being based firmly on the statute of the PCIJ of the League of Nations. Article 92 of the UN Charter states that the court shall function in accordance with its statute, which is "based upon the Statute" of the PCIJ. Article 92, which states that the ICJ is "the principal judicial organ" of the United Nations, thus contains a paradox as to whether to continue as a traditional, quasiarbitral judicial body settling disputes on a consensual basis among states, or whether it can become a world court upholding the rule of law based on the values of the international community. On balance it can be stated that the founders of the United Nations greatly enhanced the powers of the executive and legislative organs of the United Nations (the Security Council and the General Assembly), yet they failed to give the judicial body, the ICJ, any new teeth. Unlike the other organs, the ICJ can be seen as an unbroken continuation of the equivalent body in the League.

The state-based nature of the ICJ is emphasized in article 93, which states that all members of the United Nations are ipso facto parties to the statute of the ICJ, in addition to nonmember states, which "may become . . . part[ies] to the Statute . . . on conditions to be determined in each case by the General Assembly upon the recommendation of the Security Council." Switzerland, for instance, although not a member of the United Nations, is a party to the ICJ statute. The competence of the court as defined in the statute of the ICJ makes it clear that "only States may be parties in cases before the Court." The court's lack of mandatory jurisdiction to hear cases is emphasized by article 36 of the statute, which limits jurisdiction. Normally the ICJ depends upon the consent of the state parties to a dispute before it can hear it. This is made clear in article 36(1), which provides that "the jurisdiction of the Court comprises all cases which the parties refer to it and all matters specially provided for in the Charter of the United Nations or in treaties and conventions in force."

Consent to jurisdiction must be given by states in advance. The reference to "all matters specially provided for in" the UN Charter seems to have no effect, certainly none toward creating some sort of mandatory jurisdiction. The Security Council has the power to *recommend* to members that they refer legal disputes to the ICJ.[29] The fact that this recommendatory power cannot compel a state to submit to the jurisdiction of the ICJ was made clear by the ICJ itself in the *Corfu Channel* case, where the majority (in dictum) rejected the British argument to the contrary.[30] However, there are many "treaties or conventions in force" that provide for disputes to be referred to the ICJ. States that are party to these treaties may be brought before the ICJ by another state party on the basis of their treaty commitment, even though they would not wish the case in question to be decided by the ICJ. An example of this is article 14(1) of the 1971 Montreal Convention for the Suppression of Unlawful Acts Against the Safety of Civil Aviation, and article 36(1) of the statute of the ICJ, which formed the basis of Libya's 1992 applications to the court against the United States and United Kingdom in their attempts to extradite two Libyan terrorists accused in the Lockerbie bombing. Clearly the United States and Britain, when becoming parties to the Montreal Convention, did not foresee it as being used against them in this way.

Similarly, the FRY took ten NATO members to the court over the bombings of the FRY that started in March 1999 as a reaction to events in Kosovo. The FRY relied, in part, on article 9 of the Genocide Convention.[31] Although the court did not feel able to grant interim measures to the FRY, the case is proceeding to the merits, as are the *Lockerbie* cases. Both cases though show the weakness of relying on compromissory clauses to bring cases before the court. Libya brought the *Lockerbie* case under the Montreal Convention, but the real dispute is about the legality of Security Council resolutions. In the *Legality of the Use of Force (Yugoslavia)* cases, the FRY brought the cases, in part, under the Genocide Convention, when the real claim was for breach of article 2(4) of the UN Charter. In other words, the compromissory clauses in the two treaties were being used to force jurisdiction over related but separate legal issues. Compromissory clauses are, by themselves, an inadequate mechanism on which to ground an effective ICJ.

Article 36 also provides another source of jurisdiction for the ICJ, the so-called optional clause. Paragraph 2 provides that "the State parties to the present Statute may at any time declare that they recognize as compulsory *ipso facto* and without special agreement, in relation to any other state accepting the same obligation, the jurisdiction of the Court" in legal disputes. Although more than fifty declarations recognizing compulsory jurisdiction have been made, many are hedged with conditions and reservations to prevent disputes from being taken to the ICJ involving the vital interests of a state. In this respect states have reinterpreted article 36(3), which provides that the declarations under article 36(2) "shall be made unconditionally or on condition of reciprocity on the part of several or certain States, or for a certain time." Although allowing for certain conditions to be attached to the optional clause, article 36(3) does not expressly allow for such reservations. The ICJ has thus far managed to avoid determining the legality of reservations, which can, for instance, state that matters within the domestic jurisdiction of the state party as determined by that party are excluded from the jurisdiction of the court. The optional clause remains of doubtful value.[32]

The ICJ is the primary judicial forum for *states* to resolve international disputes. International organizations have no standing (i.e., the right to appear before the court), and although the ICJ can give advisory opinions on questions put to it by UN organs or other authorized agencies, opportunities to review the activities of UN organizations are rare.[33] In regard to its effectiveness in establishing the rule of law, the ICJ's consensual base means that it struggles to lift itself above the status of a standing arbitral body, often of minor cases. There are exceptions such as the *Nicaragua* and the *Lockerbie* cases. The former reasserted the fundamental principles of the United Nations and of the international community prohibiting the use of force. The latter gives the opportunity for the court to pronounce the limits of Security Council power as well as its own role within the UN system. In the *Nicaragua* case, the court asserted the rule of law over the most powerful state in the world, whereas in the *Lockerbie* cases the court has the opportunity to assert the rule of law over the most powerful element within the UN system. Furthermore, there is some evidence, starting in the 1990s,[34] that the court is being used more now than during the Cold War. However, even its most significant decisions concerning the indirect use of force have been undermined by noncompliance and even the refusal of the United States to appear before the court despite the fact that the court found it had jurisdiction.[35] Such actions by the most powerful states hardly indicate adherence to the principle of the rule of law. Furthermore, the outcome of the *Lockerbie* cases before the ICJ is still uncertain.

Judicial Review

The constitutional order of the United Nations would be strengthened by the presence of a constitutional court with competence to review the legality of actions by the various political components of the UN system. Even the most powerful entities within the UN system are bound by the provisions of the UN Charter, as well as fundamental principles of UN law and general international law. The presence of a constitutional court for determining abuse of power by political organs is a necessary prerequisite for a strong rule of law in the UN system. There are layers of political accountability within the UN system. The specialized agencies are accountable to ECOSOC as provided in chapter X of the UN Charter, with the further accountability of ECOSOC to the General Assembly.[36] However, such accountability does not necessarily respect the *legal* parameters within which the United Nations operates, and the evidence of the UN system being predicated upon legal accountability is much thinner.

One argument against legal accountability is that the presence of a constitutional court may well inhibit the development of an effective United Nations and that this should be the first concern. Such an argument places efficiency over legality and does not present a strong case against the emergence of a system of legal accountability over time. The arguments against a constitutional court are much weaker today than they were at the inception of the UN Charter, when the founders chose not to directly imbue the ICJ with such powers.[37] Although it can be debated as to whether a weak system should be predicated upon the rule of law or upon meeting the needs of its members in pragmatic ways, the United Nations today is much more activist, but it is still relatively inefficient.[38] The increased activism leads many to question whether the United Nations is stepping outside the powers granted to it. This necessitates the development of a method of legal accountability if the United Nations is to retain and increase its legitimacy.

Moreover, it is unusual to find the presence of a constitutional court within international organizations, which creates the impression that they are primarily vehicles for the achievement of common ends agreed upon by their creators, not legal orders based upon constitutional principles. Yet there is evidence that judicial bodies in the international system can play a constitutional role. The undoubted constitutional character of the European Court of Justice[39] has been reduced to a sui generis (unique, peculiar) character by some international institutional lawyers.[40] However, some economic integration organizations (e.g., the Economic Community of West African States [ECOWAS], the Andean Pact, and the Southern Cone [Mercosur]) have created a court with similar competence to the European Court of Justice. There is no real reason why this model could not be extended to a universal body such as the United Nations.

There is no established procedure in the UN Charter or in the statute of the ICJ for judicial review of decisions made by UN organizations and organs. The ICJ sometimes comments on the legality of UN actions pursuant to a requested advisory opinion, or if the matter arises in contentious proceedings between states under article 36 of the ICJ statute. Thus there is no judicial review granted per se to the ICJ, despite the fact that it has opportunities to either give guidance or to denounce UN action in advisory opinions and contentious proceedings. The issue is whether it does so given the fact that certainly in contentious proceedings, although the court is not given the express power to review lawfulness, "there exists no prohibition to perform such review if this is necessary."[41] Even though there is no *system* of judicial review, any ruling made by the court will at least give guidance on the political elements of the legal system and what they can and cannot do.

A review of the record helps one to see if there is a sufficient body of consistent constitutional law that can be applied to nonadjudicated decisions of the political bodies operating in the UN system. In relation to advisory opinions, the court has developed some jurisprudence. In discussing the creation of a peacekeeping force by the United Nations and the questions of which organs were entitled to mandate such a force, the court stated in the *Expenses* case of 1962 that the purposes of the United Nations as stated in article 1 of the charter "are wide indeed, but neither they nor the powers conferred to effectuate them are unlimited." However, "when the Organization takes action which warrants the assertion that it was appropriate for the fulfilment of one of the stated purposes of the United Nations, the presumption is that such action is not *ultra vires* the Organization."[42] Its tentative recognition of limits on UN power is qualified by the fact there was no established procedure for judicial review in the UN's structure unlike the legal systems of many states.[43] Nevertheless, the court was stating that any action that does not fulfill the purposes of the United Nations is ultra vires, thereby setting the parameters within which the United Nations should operate. This is not contradicted by the later *Namibia* advisory opinion of 1971 in which the court seemed to lean more toward the acceptance of resolutions at their face value; it stated that "a resolution of a properly constituted organ of the United Nations which is passed in accordance with the organ's rules of procedure, and is declared by the President to have been so passed, must be presumed to have been validly adopted." It further stated that the court "does not possess powers of judicial review or appeal in respect of the decisions taken by the United Nations organs concerned."[44] Yet in both the *Expenses* and *Namibia* cases it did review the actions of the Security Council and the General Assembly and found that both organs did indeed have the power to mandate consensual peacekeeping forces and to terminate the mandate of South Africa over Namibia respectively. The apparent contradiction (stating that the court was not a constitutional court while almost simultaneously reviewing the legality of UN resolutions) was necessitated by the many pressures within and without the court. Such pressures require it to tread carefully in relation to the other principal organs; it is a relationship of parity, not supremacy. Although the court was not prepared to state that it was some sort of UN supreme court, it did point out the limitations on the actions of other principal organs; overall it took a liberal and functionalist view of the powers of these organs.[45]

The court's generous approach to the powers of the United Nations is further exemplified by the *Effect of Awards* case of 1956. There it recognized the competence of the General Assembly to set up an administrative tribunal to ensure the protection of UN employees—a tribunal whose decisions were binding on the assembly itself.[46] Such advisory opinions seem almost to reflect the atmosphere of the Cold War in which the UN's effectiveness was at stake. The court seemed to be leaning far toward recognizing the legality of the rare decisions of the political organs to promote the effectiveness of the organization (in obvious ways such as the promotion of collective security, or in less obvious ways such as the "effective judicial protection of staff members of the UN").[47] The development of UN employment law can be seen, alongside the functional protection of employees recognized in the *Reparation* case, as necessary for the recruitment and retention of a high-quality UN workforce. Although recognizing the need for encouraging effectiveness in this lean period, the court still indicated that there are limits to which the principle of effectiveness can be used to develop implied powers.

With the increased effectiveness of the United Nations in the post–Cold War period, the court has moved toward a greater focus on the legal limitations upon political actions by UN bodies. The more activist UN bodies are straining against the legal frameworks within which they operate. Greater judicial activism is evidenced by the court's willingness in 1996 to find that the WHO had acted beyond its constitution in asking for an advisory opinion in *Legality of the Use by a State of Nuclear Weapons in Armed Conflicts*.[48] The court stated that "the mere fact that a majority of States, in voting on a resolution, have complied with all the relevant rules of form cannot in itself suffice to remedy any fundamental defects, such as acting *ultra vires*, with which the resolution might be afflicted."[49] This shows that the court is more willing to assert judicial authority, at least over the specialized agencies.[50] But the court did not confine its statement to the specialized agencies; it posited them as general principles.

Whereas the ICJ has moved toward asserting judicial review in its advisory opinions, there is less movement in its contentious jurisprudence. It appears that the court is about to recognize judicial review in cases that raise the issue of the competence of UN bodies. The dilemma facing the court is found in the continuing saga of the *Lockerbie* cases. The cases were first litigated in 1992 (request for provisional measures by Libya)[51] and then in 1998 (preliminary objections to the admissibility of the case and the jurisdiction of the court by the United States and United Kingdom).[52] One of the crucial issues was whether the Security Council acted lawfully in adopting binding decisions under chapter VII of the UN Charter. These decisions were designed to force Libya to hand over the two Libyan suspects. Although the cases have not reached the merits (and may never do so), they are worth considering in some detail.

Security Council Resolution No. 748, adopted on 31 March 1992 as a binding decision under article 25 and chapter VII, imposed economic sanctions against Libya while demanding compliance with U.K. and U.S. requests that Libya hand over the suspects. There can be no doubt that resolution 748 had a controversial legal pedigree. First, it was adopted without full and impartial fact-finding by the Security Council.[53] Second, it stretched the concept of what constitutes a "threat to the peace" under article 39 of the UN Charter, one of the three keys that unlocks the armory of chapter VII enforcement action, up to and arguably beyond the point of consistency with its previous determinations. Third, the resolution purported to circumvent an existing legal regime, contained in the 1971 Montreal Convention,[54] for the arrest, investigation, and punishment of persons suspected of acts of sabotage. On the basis of the compromissory clause in the Montreal Convention (article 14), which allowed a state party to take another party to the ICJ in the case of a dispute over the application of the convention, Libya was able to bring the cases against the United States and United Kingdom. All three states were parties to the convention. Such issues raise profound constitutional questions as to the limits of Security Council powers, as well as the question of the emergence of a hierarchy in international law whereby the Security Council can override the rights and duties of states under other treaty regimes.

The court has not yet commented on the lack of impartial investigation by the Security Council of the U.S. and U.K. allegations against Libya. J. Quigley notes that "without undertaking its own investigation, the Council imposed sanctions on Libya on the strength of information supplied by the United States and Britain."[55] Although article 34 of the UN Charter empowers the Security Council to undertake investigations of disputes, it does not oblige it to do so. However, the argument can be made that when the Security Council is purporting to act in a quasi-judicial way (i.e., imposing punishment on states for breaches of international law, in this case Libya's involvement in the bombing or at least harboring the suspected terrorists), it should observe "inherent" or "natural" rules of due process. In the separate context of considering the legality of the Security Council's establishment of the ICTY in 1993, Judge R. Sidwha stated that

> the discretion available to the Council in arriving at relevant conclusions under Article 39 . . . could not be measured in terms of any legal standards, other than that it had to be fair and not an arbitrary or a feigned exercise of power. The decision [to establish the ICTY] was based on *a proper appraisal of the evidence* and was reasonable and fair and not arbitrary or capricious.[56]

Although there is no doubt that proper fact-finding would increase the legitimacy of the Security Council, it is questionable, given the discretion accorded to the Security Council under article 34, whether this is a concrete legal limitation. Nevertheless, a recognition by the court, at the merits stage of the *Lockerbie* cases, of the lack of proper fact-finding as a weakness in the Security Council's dealings with Libya would indicate a development in constitutional law.

Certainly the Security Council, especially when acting under chapter VII, is a powerful body, and the court must tread carefully in considering whether the organ abused its power. The issue is complicated by the fact that there is a strong legal basis for claiming that the council can override the rights and duties of member states. Article 103 of the charter states that "in the event of a conflict between the obligations of the Members of the United Nations under the present Charter and their obligations under any other international agreement, their obligations under the present Charter shall prevail." Although not a direct obligation arising from the charter itself, mandatory decisions under chapter VII imposed by the Security Council give rise to obligations derived from the charter and therefore, according to article 103, prevail over obligations in other treaties. Libya has argued that the Montreal Convention (article 7) provides that Libya is under an obligation "to submit the case to its competent authorities for the purposes of prosecution" given that the two suspects at the time were in Libya. However, this obligation is subject to obligations imposed under the UN Charter.[57] The question the court must decide, then, is whether the obligations imposed by the Security Council on Libya had this effect. The court would then have to determine the legal effects of resolution 748. At that stage it might decide that it must consider the legal character of the resolution as well as its validity—that is, whether the resolution was adopted in accordance with the UN Charter.

In denying Libya's request for interim measures of protection in 1992, the court seemed to accept the supremacy of resolution 748. The court declared that the obligation imposed by the resolution on its face applied to all the parties and that this obligation prevailed over any other treaty obligation, including the Montreal Convention, in accordance with article 103.[58] The judgment leaves open the possibility of further review at the merits stage given that this was a decision on provisional measures. As Judge S. Oda noted, "The Court has *at present* no choice but to acknowledge that pre-eminence."[59] The dissenting and separate opinions of several judges hint at this, though most do not indicate the outcome.[60] In considering the U.K. and U.S. preliminary objections on admissibility and jurisdiction in 1998, the court sidestepped the main argument on the supremacy of Security Council resolutions, stating that the critical date for the determination of whether the court had jurisdiction over the case was the date on which the application to the court was filed by Libya on 3 March 1992. The mandatory resolutions of the council on Libya (748 and then resolution 883 of 11 November 1993) were adopted after this date. Thus the court found that it had jurisdiction on very narrow grounds.[61] Essentially this means the court can still decide at the merits stage that despite the fact that resolution 748 came after the court obtained jurisdiction the subsequent adoption of that resolution left the court with no choice but to reject the Libyan case. However, as counsel for the United States and United Kingdom pointed out in the 1998 cases, if the court was intending to do this it should have thrown the case out at the admissibility stage; to do otherwise would be a waste of the court's time.[62]

The fact that the court did not do this in 1998 suggests it is considering not accepting the Security Council's decisions at face value but that it will review them for their effects and legality. However, there is nothing in the 1998 judgments to suggest this is the court's intent. A review at the merits stage would center on whether the council was acting within its powers when adopting a binding decision directed at Libya in resolution 748, more specifically whether the council was legally justified in determining that a threat to the peace existed. Nevertheless, it is one thing to decide there are some limits to the concept of threat to the peace, quite another to decide that the ICJ has the power to declare a decision of the Security Council invalid because it has surpassed those limits.

The council's determination that Libya's support for terrorism constituted a threat to international peace within the meaning of article 39 was a departure for the council, but that does not necessarily make it unconstitutional. Indeed, the council has entrenched this position by subsequent practice in regard to Sudanese and Afghani support for terrorism. Terrorism, especially state-sponsored terrorism, is an activity that the Security Council should address under its collective security powers.[63] Indeed, this is preferable to unilateral actions taken by states to combat terrorism. However, it is for the court to decide whether such arguments are convincing. Combating the increasing threat of terrorism is within the council's competence, but if the court agrees, then it will be able to also limit the council's powers, providing greater clarity for judging the future actions of the council. Such an incremental, some would say conservative, approach to review is essentially the approach taken by the court in its advisory jurisprudence, exemplified by the *Expenses* case. The court found that the UN resolutions were lawful, yet it took the opportunity to circumscribe the council's powers.

It is argued that the *Lockerbie* cases provide a perfect opportunity to review if they proceed to the merits. However, given Libya's surrender of the two suspects for trial by a Scottish court sitting in the Netherlands in 1999, the trial, which concluded in 2001, may well lead to the end of the cases before the ICJ.[64] The arguments and issues raised by the cases, even though they might not be decided on the merits, illustrate the problems the ICJ faces if it wishes to be a court of review. The discussion below considers the arguments for and against review.

The charter itself does limit the council's powers in the purposes and principles, in particular article 1(1), which provides, inter alia, that the action must be taken "to maintain international peace and security." An isolated act of terrorism that has long since past would not be within the remit of the council's concern for current threats, but continuing support for terrorism would be.[65] Libya argues that a limitation can be found in article 1(1), which also states that such actions must be "in conformity with the principles of justice and international law." Libya suggests that Security Council resolutions that contradict international law (in this case the Montreal Convention) are ultra vires. However, this ignores the fact that the limitation applies only to "the adjustment or settlement of international disputes or situations which might lead to a breach of the peace." The necessity of Security Council action occasionally violating existing norms seems to have been recognized in the *travaux préparatoires* (preparatory work) and in the lack of such an express limitation in chapter VII of the charter. However, this cannot extend to violations of *jus cogens,* as stated in another contentious case currently before the court.[66] Resolutions 748 and 883 violated neither the object and purposes of the charter nor any norm of *jus cogens.*

Another limitation on the Security Council based on international law is that its decisions should not be adopted in bad faith.[67] This is a valid limitation on the exercise of power by the Security Council under chapter VII as well as chapter VI. But it is difficult to prove, especially given that it is not the bad faith of one or two members that must be established; there must also be an explanation of why the other members of the Security Council were not aware of the bad faith and, if they were, why they did not vote against the resolution.[68] Although the limitations of object and purpose, *jus cogens,* and bad faith appear to be firmly grounded in the charter and general international law, the limitation suggested by Judge Sidhwa in the *Tadic* case before the ICTY—that the council should investigate the facts before taking action—appears to be *de lege ferenda* (law as it should be).

Thus although there are developed and developing legal limitations on the concept of threat to the peace, Libya has to prove that they have been surpassed in the case of resolutions 748 and 883. This will prove a difficult if not insurmountable task, and certainly its arguments at the preliminary objections stage were not convincing.[69] However, even if Libya could present an overwhelming case of ultra vires, its success would still depend on the court recognizing that it had powers of review. The question of legal limits on the exercise of executive power and the issue of whether the court has the judicial power to review are distinct. Indeed, the United Kingdom recognized that the court could review decisions of the Security Council, but only in certain instances, which did not include determinations under article 39. The United Kingdom purported to limit the judicial function to "the issue of the formal validity of resolutions"[70] such as whether a resolution is a binding decision or whether it was validly adopted in accordance with the voting rules.[71] This position accepts that review is possible if the council exceeds at least one of the provisions of the charter, namely, article 27(3) on voting, but not others. This does not make sense. Because there are also legal limitations on the concept of threat to the peace, then such determinations are also potentially open to review. The legal limitations may be weak and are unlikely to be exceeded, but they are limitations nonetheless, and the court should be able to consider whether they have been surpassed in the case before it.

Nevertheless, to take this step when there is no real evidence of violation would be precipitous. All the court can do is hint at a possibility in the future in the eventuality the council steps outside the generous parameters of its constitution, in combination with the disputed resolution actually making its way before the court. There are legal limitations on the concept of threat to the peace; whether the court will recognize them and pronounce that it has the right to review resolutions allegedly adopted in violation of them is doubtful. In effect, two dissenting opinions in *Lockerbie* serve as a warning to the court not to take this leap.

Judges Schwebel and Jennings seemed to be in accord that "the Security Council is subject to the rule of law; it shall act in accordance with the Purposes and Principles of the United Nations and its decisions must be adopted in accordance with the Charter." However, both were of the opinion that the "discretionary competence" of the council to make determinations under article 39 was not limited in this way.[72] Although article 39 does give the council the power to determine what constitutes a threat to the peace, that discretion is not unlimited; it must at the very least be exercised in accordance with the purposes and principles of the charter.

Though equivocal on the constitutional limitations on the council, both judges are unequivocal on the issue of judicial review. Judge Schwebel stated that "it does not follow from the fact that the decisions of the Security Council must be in accordance with the Charter, and that the International Court of Justice is the principal judicial organ of the UN, that the Court is empowered to ensure that the Council's decisions do accord with the Charter."[73] Judge Schwebel puts forward a powerful thesis against judicial review. Recognizing that the charter is a "living instrument," he states that the development of judicial review would not be "evolutionary but revolutionary." He states it is not possible to imply such a power, as it is contrary to the constitutional structure of the United Nations, which gives the Security Council primary responsibility for collective security in article 24(1) of the charter. To place the ultimate power with the court would give it primary responsibility. On this basis Judge Schwebel suggests that by making a determination of ultra vires in relation to a council resolution, the court itself would be acting ultra vires.[74]

However, this argument is overstated. *Primary* responsibility is not the same as *exclusive* responsibility.[75] The court can have a role; indeed, the requirement in article 24(2) that the Security Council's decisions should be taken in accordance with the purposes and principles of the charter strongly suggests that it should. The court could develop this role if it so desired.[76] Furthermore, if it does so it will in all likelihood develop its review powers to reflect the court's position as the principal legal organ of the United Nations, having an equal status to the primary political body, the Security Council. In other words the court will probably adopt a doctrine of "concurrent review"—"that no one organ of the United Nations has a final say on the interpretation of the Charter and that a decision of the Court must be respected in the case that it resolves but not necessarily in future cases"—rather than a doctrine of "judicial supremacy," "under which the 'constitutional' holdings of the Court are binding on all other organs of the United Nations in all future cases."[77]

In addition, even if the court develops powers of review, the chances of it preventing the council from carrying out its primary responsibility are remote, for several reasons. First, there will be no systematic review of council decisions, as there is no suggestion of a state having the right per se to challenge the legality of council decisions before the court. Second, the vast majority of Security Council resolutions will be intra vires, and spurious challenges will not hamper the Security Council, especially if it commands the support of the membership. Third, Security Council resolutions will presumably be valid until the unlikely event they are declared otherwise.[78]

If the court decided to move in the direction of review at the merits stage it would not be acting ultra vires. It is, however, a question of choosing the right moment. As M. Shaw eloquently states, at the moment the court is caught between "the Scylla of supreme court constitutionalism and the Charybdis of judicial abstinence."[79] The hostility of the United States and United Kingdom to judicial review is a major roadblock. However, they have made strong arguments to the effect that resolutions 748 and 883 were perfectly lawful exercises of the council's collective security powers. So why are they afraid of review?

The ability to obtain judicial guidance and direction on what constitutes a lawful exercise of power will enable the Security Council to enhance its legitimacy by acting within its constitution. Given the flexible and organic nature of the charter, and the fact that there are only a limited number of restrictions on the exercise of the council's discretionary power under article 39, judicial review is not something that should be resisted; rather it should be welcomed as another stage in the development of the organization. Furthermore, given that the Security Council's own subsidiary judicial organ, the ICTY, has itself reviewed the Security Council decisions that established it in the *Tadic* case, and given the rarity of an opportunity for review arising again before the court, it may feel that the time is ripe to cautiously embrace judicial review. The court should do this by making clear the limitations on the council's discretionary powers under article 39 and by indicating that it would declare invalid a decision that was in violation of them.

"The unique character of the UN system may ensure that judicial review of Security Council resolutions occurs incidentally, indirectly, and infrequently, but it does occur."[80] Given that the Security Council presents the court with the greatest difficulty not only in the discernment of legal limits but also in its relationship to the council, the potential for review in this inhospitable terrain should indicate to the other organs, agencies, and bodies that the court might be able to develop a significant body of constitutional law. The fact that it has not yet done so is a weakness in the development and protection of the rule of law in the UN system. Until the right to seek judicial review is granted to member states of the UN organizations, the ICJ will be able to give only occasional determinations and guidance on crucial constitutional matters.[81] The rule of law is thus upheld in a tenuous, inconsistent, and unsatisfactory way.

Subsidiary Judicial Bodies

Part 3 of this book considers the application of the UN's principles in practice.[82] Other bodies set up by the Security Council fulfill its functions in maintaining international peace and security: principally, the International Criminal Tribunals (former Yugoslavia and Rwanda),[83] the Boundary Commission (Iraq/Kuwait), and the Compensation Commission (Iraq).[84] However, their creation raises questions on constitutionality: Did the Security Council have the power to create them? Again, this may be an academic debate, and it can be argued that they are ultra vires, but the absence of an effective review mechanism in the shape of the ICJ undermines the usefulness of such a finding.

The details of the compensation system and demarcation imposed on Iraq in 1991, as well as the intrusive disarmament regime, all of which were imposed on Iraq after its defeat by the Coalition pursuant to a mandatory chapter VII resolution, will be discussed in Chapter 6.[85] However, the implications of some of the powers to the Security Council, and therefore their delegation to subsidiary organs, are problematic. The special commission created for the partial disarmament of Iraq can be seen as a power implied from the Security Council's general powers for the formulation of disarmament.[86] However, the Boundary Commission and Compensation Commission are more difficult to reconcile with the UN Charter given that settlement usually occurs within the confines of chapter VI of the UN Charter and is therefore consensual. Although Iraq agreed to the terms of the cease-fire, placing the conditions within a binding chapter VII resolution reflects the fact that the council was not predicating the cease-fire on agreement but on obligation.[87]

Although the development of mandatory settlement powers is not entirely out of the question, it certainly raises the possibility of the Security Council acting ultra vires. Iraq does not have any competence to challenge the decision of the Security Council before the ICJ. This raises the question of why rogue states like Iraq should be given this option. The answer lies in the credibility of the rule of law. Although Iraq breached international law in invading Kuwait, this does not necessarily mean that the UN responses to the invasion and its aftermath are lawful.

Similar issues arise with the creation of the ICTY/ICTR. In the *Tadic* case, the appeals chamber of the ICTY addressed the issue of the constitutionality of the ICTY. One of the appellant's arguments was that "the Security Council is constitutionally or inherently incapable of creating a judicial organ, as it is conceived in the Charter as an executive organ, hence not possessed of judicial powers which can be exercised through a judicial organ."[88] The chamber's response is not entirely convincing, stating that the "Security Council has resorted to the establishment of a judicial organ in the form of an international criminal tribunal for the exercise of its own principal function of maintenance of peace and security, *i.e.*, as a measure contributing to the restoration and maintenance of peace in the former Yugoslavia." In other words, the Security Council is capable of creating organs, including judicial organs, that fulfill its functions even though it does not have judicial power itself.[89] In effect the ICTY was reviewing the legality of its own creation and thus, somewhat fortuitously, there is judicial review in this instance. However, it would have been better had review come from the principal judicial organ of the UN system rather than a subsidiary organ facing the charge that it was not properly constituted. Allowing a state such as the FRY to seek review on the issue before the ICJ would strengthen the rule of law in the system. At the moment though there is no provision for Iraq or the FRY to do that.

Other judicial or quasijudicial bodies operating in the UN system are the products of treaties sponsored by the United Nations. The jurisprudence of the HRC operating under the ICCPR; the CESCR operating under the International Covenant on Economic, Social, and Cultural Rights (ICESCR); and the various supervisory committees established under UN-sponsored treaties protecting specific human rights such as the Committee Against Torture created by the Convention Against Torture and Other Cruel, Inhuman, or Degrading Treatment or Punishment will be reviewed in Chapter 9. One issue is the compatibility of jurisprudence among these and other bodies created under UN-sponsored treaties, such as the Law of the Sea Tribunal established by the 1982 Law of the Sea Convention,[90] with that of the ICJ, which has well-established jurisprudence in the areas of law of the sea[91] and human rights.[92] The absence of a formal hierarchy, given that these bodies are created by separate treaties and are not in a formal relationship with the United Nations, may create problems, although recognizing that they are part of the UN system can help ensure consistency. However, the problems worsen when there are quasijudicial bodies operating outside the UN system, such as the WTO's Dispute Resolution Panel, and dealing with issues within the UN's field of competence. The issues then become the respect paid not only to the jurisprudence of the ICJ[93] but also UN law in general. Although an organization outside the system can strive to bring its actions into line with UN law, that would appear to be a voluntary and nonreviewable decision, both politically and legally.[94]

Conclusion

Given limits on the ICJ's powers, it is difficult to agree with Franck's positive assessment of the court. Franck states that "although it is an institution of low visibility and depends for credibility primarily on its powers of reasoning, the International Court of Justice stands at the apex of international legal development."[95] Although the court is the main judicial organ in the UN system, it is still hampered by its arbitral character. Even then the court's impact is limited, for "only a handful of disputes have actually been decided by the Court."[96]

Its contribution to the development of a rule of law though *could* be immense. Some decisions indicate the court will act as the upholder of UN law in relation to members and the political organs. Thus the court has the opportunity to become the "judicial sheet anchor of an ordered international society."[97] Furthermore, with the proliferation of other judicial and quasijudicial bodies of a specialist nature operating within the UN system, there is a need not only for review procedures to be strengthened but also to recognize and entrench a hierarchy of courts, with the ICJ at the apex, capable of dealing with many more cases. It is also desirable to bring judicial bodies operating in areas of UN concern but outside the UN system within a developing UN legal system. There is no doubt that a good deal could be done to increase the effectiveness of the ICJ, but an increased caseload should not come at the expense of consistency and should not subvert the court's primary function: upholding the fundamental values of the UN's constitutional order.[98]

Notes

1. Art. 92 of the UN Charter.
2. See generally Brownlie, "The Powers of Political Organs," 91.
3. Art. 7 of the UN Charter.
4. Rosenne, *The World Court,* 36.
5. Franck, *Fairness,* 317.
6. Ibid., 316–317.
7. Simma, *The Charter,* 979.
8. Abi-Saab, "The International Court as a World Court," 7.
9. Ibid., 6.
10. Ibid., 11–12.
11. UNCIO XIII, 413.
12. *Case Concerning East Timor (Portugal v. Australia),* ICJ Rep. 1995, 90 at 102. See Burchill, "The ICJ Decision in the Case Concerning East Timor."
13. *Barcelona Traction Case,* ICJ Rep. 1970, 32.
14. See, for example, its weak opinion in *Legality of the Threat or Use of Nuclear Weapons* (1996) 35 ILM 809.
15. *Lockerbie* cases (provisional measures), ICJ Rep. 1992 (*Libya v. United States*), 138 (separate opinion of Judge Lachs).
16. See, for example, Akande, "The Role of the International Court."
17. Arts. 2, 16, 17, and 20 of the ICJ Statute.
18. Rosenne, *The World Court,* 60–61.
19. *Nicaragua v. United States,* ICJ Rep. 1986, 14 at 249.
20. *Lockerbie* cases (preliminary objections), ICJ Rep. 1998.
21. Franck, *Fairness,* 319.

22. Ibid.

23. Ibid., 324–325.

24. Rosenne, *The World Court*, 73. See also Merrills, *International Dispute Settlement*, 137; Franck, *Fairness*, 324; Weiss, "Judicial Independence," 123. But see Nsereko, "The International Court, Impartiality," 207.

25. Rosenne, *The World Court*, 74.

26. Arts. 26 and 31(4) of the ICJ Statute.

27. Rosenne, *The World Court*, 55.

28. Ibid., 55–56.

29. Art. 36(3) of the UN Charter.

30. *Corfu Channel Case,* ICJ Rep. 1947–1948, 31–32.

31. *Legality of the Use of Force (Yugoslavia)* cases, (1999) 38 ILM 950.

32. Merrills, *International Dispute Settlement,* 123.

33. Art. 96 of the UN Charter.

34. Highet, "The Peace Palace Heats Up."

35. *Case Concerning Military and Paramilitary Activities in and Against Nicaragua* (jurisdiction and admissibility), ICJ Rep. 1984, 392.

36. See Art. 60 of the UN Charter.

37. UNCIO, XIII, 709–710.

38. See Rawls, *A Theory of Justice,* 542.

39. Due, "A Constitutional Court," 8.

40. Amerasinghe, *Principles,* 12.

41. Tomuschat, "International Law," 302.

42. *Certain Expenses of the United Nations,* ICJ Rep. 1962, 168.

43. Ibid.

44. *Legal Consequences for States of the Continued Presence of South Africa in Namibia (South West Africa) Notwithstanding Security Council Resolution 276 (1970),* ICJ Rep. 1971, 21–22, 45.

45. Bowett, *International Institutions,* 337–338.

46. *Effect of Awards of Compensation Made by the UN Administrative Tribunal,* ICJ Rep. 1956, 77.

47. Tomuschat, "International Law," 301.

48. ICJ Rep. 1996, 66.

49. Ibid., 82.

50. Some agencies provide rights of appeal to the ICJ from their own dispute resolution organs. See, for example, *Appeal Relating to the Jurisdiction of the ICAO Council (India v. Pakistan),* ICJ Rep. 1972, 46.

51. *Questions of Interpretation and Application of the 1971 Montreal Convention Arising from the Aerial Incident at Lockerbie (Libya v. United States, Libya v. United Kingdom)* (provisional measures), ICJ Rep. 1992, 3, 114 [hereinafter *Lockerbie* cases].

52. *Lockerbie* cases (preliminary objections), ICJ Rep. 1998.

53. Quigley, "Security Council Fact Finding," 192.

54. (1971) 10 ILM 1151.

55. Quigley, "Security Council Fact Finding," 192.

56. *Prosecutor v. Tadic*, IT-94-1-AR72, 2 Oct. 1995, para. 61 (separate opinion, emphasis added). See also Lauterpacht, *Aspects,* 42.

57. Libya also argued that the United States and the United Kingdom breached Article 11 of the Montreal Convention by not assisting Libya in its investigations—*Lockerbie* case, ICJ Rep. 1998 (*Libya v. United Kingdom*), paras. 30–32.

58. *Lockerbie* case, ICJ Rep. 1992 (*Libya v. United States*), 126.

59. Ibid., 129 (emphasis added).

60. *Lockerbie* case, ICJ Rep. 1992 (*Libya v. United States*), 138 (Judge Lachs); 142 (Judge Shahabuddeen); 143–159 (Judge Bedjaoui); 165–166, 176 (Judge Weeramantry). See also Franck, "The 'Powers of Appreciation.'"

61. *Lockerbie* case, 1998 (*Libya v. United Kingdom*), paras. 38 and 44.

62. Ibid., para. 46.

63. But see Lamb, "Legal Limits," 379.

64. (2001) 40 ILM 582.

65. *Lockerbie* case, ICJ Rep. 1998 (*Libya v. United Kingdom,* dissenting opinion of Judge Schwebel), at 4.

66. *Application of the Convention on the Prevention and Punishment of the Crime of Genocide (Bosnia and Hezegovina v. Yugoslavia [Serbia and Montenegro])* (provisional measures), ICJ Rep. 1993, 325 at 439–482.

67. Franck, "The *Bona Fides* of Power," 191. See also Gowlland-Debbas, "Security Council Enforcement Action," 93–94.

68. Cryer, "The Security Council and Article 39," 169.

69. See White, "To Review or Not to Review."

70. Verbatim Record of the Proceedings, 14 Oct. 1997, CR/97/17, para. 12.

71. Ibid., 20 Oct. 1997, CR/97/22, para. 3.5.

72. *Lockerbie* case, 1998 (*Libya v. United Kingdom,* dissenting opinion of Judge Schwebel), at 9–12 (dissenting opinion of Judge Jennings), at 9.

73. Ibid., at 10 (Judge Schwebel) and at 10 (Judge Jennings).

74. Ibid., at 9 and 13.

75. *Expenses* case, ICJ Rep. 1962, 162.

76. Watson, "Constitutionalism," 14.

77. Ibid., 39.

78. Bailey and Daws, *The Procedure,* 319.

79. Shaw, "The Security Council," 219.

80. Lamb, "Legal Limits," 365.

81. See generally Bowett, "The Court's Role," 187–192.

82. See also the World Bank Inspection Panel reviewed in Chapter 11. See also Schlemmer-Schulte, "The World Bank."

83. Reviewed in Chapter 8.

84. Reviewed in Chapter 6.

85. SC Res. 687, 3 April 1991.

86. Art. 26 of the UN Charter.

87. See Roberts, "United Nations Security Council Resolution 687," 613–614.

88. *Tadic* case, IT-94-AR72, 2 Oct. 1995, 16.

89. Ibid., 19. See Greenwood, "The Development of International Humanitarian Law," 103–104.

90. Merrills, *International Dispute Settlement,* 185–196.

91. Quintana, "The International Court," 367.

92. Gowlland-Debbas, "Judicial Insights," 340–342.

93. Schermers, "The International Court of Justice," 261.

94. Apart perhaps from the effects of Article 103 of the UN Charter.

95. Franck, *Fairness,* 318.

96. Merrills, *International Dispute Settlement,* 164.

97. Shahabuddeen, "The World Court," 9.

98. See generally Peck and Lee, *Increasing the Effectiveness of the International Court.*

PART 3

Implementation and Protection

6

Peace and Security

Traditionally, the UN's primary purpose has been the maintenance of international peace and security.[1] Throughout the complex negotiations among the great powers (the United States, the United Kingdom, the USSR, and, to a much lesser degree, China and France) that led to the 1945 founding conference in San Francisco, the emphasis was on creating a strong executive body—the Security Council. It would have "primary responsibility" for the maintenance of peace and would be imbued with exceptionally strong powers to enable it to fulfill that function.[2] The great powers saw themselves as the world's police force, acting within the framework of the Security Council. However, with the start of the Cold War the Security Council quickly slipped into being the embodiment of a balance of power based on opposing camps. This led to a shift in the division of competence in the United Nations toward recognizing a subsidiary role for the veto-free General Assembly.

The great powers did not foresee the assembly playing any role in collective security, intending it to be a meeting place for states to exchange views but not to formulate or implement policy. However, the smaller powers at San Francisco managed to secure some basic provisions in the UN Charter that would enable the assembly to carve out in practice a role in maintaining peace and security.[3] Although it remains the "town meeting place of the world" and "the open conscience of humanity,"[4] the assembly's competence regarding peace and security is founded on the inherent qualities of such a universal body. Indeed, despite the increased activism of the Security Council in the post–Cold War world, the role of the General Assembly in the area of collective security is of continuing importance.

The UN's predecessor, the League of Nations, failed to keep the peace because the idea of collective security was far too weak, with states preferring to protect their own national interests; the mechanisms of collective security reflected as much. The driving force behind the League, U.S. President Woodrow Wilson, saw the organization as replacing the previous precarious balance of power by institutionalizing the idea that the most powerful states would act in concert, as trustees, so to speak, for world peace.[5] The U.S. Congress refused to join the League, meaning it was flawed from the start. For a universal system of collective security to work, the world's most powerful states must be persuaded to join and contribute to the maintenance of peace.

The covenant of the League did contain innovative provisions for collective security, attempting to prohibit aggression through embargoes and military measures against transgressing states.[6] However, the requirement of unanimity in the League's council and assembly for most substantive decisions, combined with the lack of collective will to keep the peace, resulted in a dilution of power. Sanctions under article 16, for example, became a decision by each individual member of the League. Loopholes in the covenant were exploited and obligations ignored as the world descended again into war.[7]

The United Nations has its origins in the collection of Allies that were eventually victorious in World War II. In January 1942 these powers declared themselves to be "the United Nations," at least in the sense of their unity against the Axis powers.[8] The idea was that this alliance would continue after the end of the war to maintain peace and security. By October 1943, in the Moscow declaration, the United States, United Kingdom, Soviet Union, and China aimed to create a general international organization to fulfill this purpose.[9] Comprehensive proposals from the four powers were discussed at Dumbarton Oaks between August and October 1944.[10] They agreed on the basic shape of the Security Council and introduced the concept of the veto, with the big four plus France having permanent representation with special voting rights, thereby ensuring that no action would be taken by the council without their agreement. The right of veto—the greatest weakness in the structure of the new organization—was further refined at the Yalta Conference in February 1945 and was presented to the smaller powers at San Francisco on a take-it-or-leave-it-basis.[11]

The veto would come to blight the Security Council during the Cold War; though used less frequently today, its potential use shapes what the council can and cannot do in the post–Cold War era.[12] Nevertheless, the UN Charter contained a far greater centralization of collective measures and machinery than did the League covenant. In addition to a complex set of provisions in chapter VI for the peaceful settlement of disputes, the executive body under chapter VII had sharper teeth. It enjoyed unprecedented power to take mandatory economic and military action, not only to combat an aggressor but also any situation that threatened international peace and security. The concept of a threat to the peace has been widely interpreted by the Security Council to include internal situations of extreme violence that have actual or potential international repercussions (see Chapter 3). If the Security Council acts under these mechanisms, states would be obliged to take economic measures or supply military forces under UN control. The potential power of the Security Council is enormous. Furthermore, chapter VII of the UN Charter has been used to create novel enforcement mechanisms (e.g., against Iraq for its 1990 invasion of Kuwait, as well as the creation of international criminal tribunals for the former Yugoslavia and for Rwanda; see Chapter 8).

The potential of the Security Council went unfulfilled for more than four decades due to the intense ideological rivalry and arms race between the two superpowers. The collective security system was eclipsed by the reemergence of the balance-of-power system, in this case of two opposing "defensive" alliances: NATO and the Warsaw Pact. Although the world was restricted to a cold peace and not a hot and catastrophic nuclear war, the balance of power inevitably collapsed with the disintegration of the Soviet Union beginning in 1989 and the rapid dissolution of the Warsaw Pact. One of the telling issues is whether the UN collective security system has stepped in to fill the vacuum.

Although the Security Council has been much more active in taking military measures, the system is again in crisis, with controversial military operations being undertaken by Western states against Iraq after the 1991 cease-fire and by NATO against the FRY in 1999. Thus I begin by examining the doctrine of collective security as developed by the Security Council in this context. The veto threat will also be discussed in light of powerful states stepping outside the UN system for collective security. I then move on to a discussion of UN collective security action of both a military and nonmilitary nature.[13]

The Charter Scheme for Military Measures

In 1945 the UN's collective security role was premised on the ability of the council to use military measures to enforce the peace. The military option was contained in article 42, which permits the Security Council "to take such action by air, sea, or land forces as may be necessary to restore international peace and security." Further, the article provides that "such actions may include demonstrations, blockade, and other operations by air, sea, or land forces of Members of the United Nations." Article 43 then details the mechanism whereby armed forces are to be made available, namely, by "special agreements" made by members, detailing the numbers, location, and state of readiness of such forces. These agreements were to be reached as soon as possible. Although the Military Staff Committee (MSC) established under article 47 of the charter reported to the Security Council by April 1947 on the basic principles that should govern the UN's armed forces, Cold War tensions prevented any consensus.[14]

Without consensus among the permanent members, the idea of a UN army was shelved. The collective security vision of command and control by the United Nations was therefore unachievable. What developed instead, starting with Korea in 1950, was a decentralized system of collective security whereby the United Nations delegated authority to a state or group of states under chapter VII to take military enforcement action on behalf of the members. This in essence brings military enforcement action under article 42 of chapter VII very close to the system envisaged for regional organizations under chapter VIII. Article 53 provides that "the Security Council shall, where appropriate, utilize such regional arrangements or agencies for enforcement action under its authority." The UN's supremacy in collective security matters of a coercive nature is underlined by article 53: "No enforcement action shall be taken under regional arrangements or by regional arrangements without the authorization of the Security Council." Although there are debates as to whether regional organizations have autonomy as to economic sanctions, the charter prohibits military enforcement action without UN authority.[15] Collective defensive military action by regional organizations or ad hoc alliances is permitted under article 51 of the charter when a member state comes under armed attack and "until the Security Council has taken measures necessary to maintain international peace and security."

Furthermore, centralized UN command and control has arisen to a greater extent for consensual peacekeeping operations (but through the Secretary-General, not the MSC) due to the less intrusive nature of such operations. States are more willing to submit to UN command and control in this context, whereas there is reluctance, especially by the United States, to submit to UN command and control under chapter VII military enforcement actions.[16] Hence, in these operations command is delegated to a state or group of states. When more muscular peacekeeping operations are created with explicit enforcement duties, it creates difficulties. This led to problems when the United Nations Operation in Somalia (UNOSOM II) took over from the U.S.-led Unified Task Force (UNITAF) in 1993, when the core peacekeeping force was under UN command but was supplemented by three different U.S.-led elements that in differing ways were not subject to UN command and control.[17]

The Decentralized System of Collective Security

"Collective security" can be defined as the combined usage of the coercive capacity of the international community to combat illegal uses of armed force and situations that threaten international peace.[18] Collective security experts recognize degrees of collective security; a system might not match an ideal, but that does not mean it is not a collective security system. Indeed, there are considerable disagreements on what constitutes the ideal system.[19] Nevertheless, the greater the international consensus behind the operation, the greater its legitimacy. Certainly, questions surface as to the composition of the UN Security Council and its ability to represent the international community.[20] This in turn calls into question whether a council mandate lends legitimacy to the operation. Until there is a major reform of the council, the legitimacy of military operations will be increased if they also have the support of the General Assembly.[21] Indeed, it is not correct to state that only the Security Council, acting on behalf of the United Nations, can authorize enforcement action; rather, it is only the United Nations, normally acting through the Security Council, that can authorize such action.[22]

Collective security or police actions taken outside the ambit of the United Nations are more problematic, for they normally lack legitimacy and legality. Although the Security Council is in need of reform, it does represent the United Nations when taking action for peace and security.[23] The international community has granted the Security Council this function. Even if states had a collective police power before 1945, at that point they embodied it, for better or worse, in the UN Security Council.[24] It seems more precise to state that the existence of a collective power before the advent of the UN Charter was, legally speaking, doubtful. By establishing the UN Charter the vast majority of states decided to establish a body with novel competence.

The adoption of the UN Charter in 1945 was a defining moment in the sense of creating a new world order, with the charter becoming in effect the constitution of the international community. Thereafter the United Nations possessed powers that states did not; it can be argued that only the United Nations could delegate its collective security powers of enforcement to a state or states. Two objections can be raised. First, empowerment of the Security Council in article 24(1) of the charter is "in order to take prompt and effective action." Second, the Security Council, by the same provision, has only primary, not exclusive, responsibility. Thus it can be argued that if the Security Council does not take action to remedy a threat to or breach of the peace, then responsibility would revert to states or other international organizations to take collective action.[25]

However, the reference to "primary responsibility" for peace and security in article 24(1) relates to the division of competence within the United Nations. It is the General Assembly and, to a lesser extent, the ICJ that have subsidiary competence regarding international peace and security, not states acting unilaterally or multilaterally.[26] It will be argued, then, that Security Council inaction means the General Assembly has competence to recommend military enforcement action. Furthermore, the idea of rights reverting back to states in the event of Security Council inaction assumes that they possessed such rights before 1945 and that they could reclaim them. Both these claims have little legal pedigree.[27] Specifically, they violate the fundamental norm of the international community prohibiting the threat or use of force.[28] Collective security action is, in effect, locked into the United Nations.[29]

In the absence of agreements under article 43 of the charter, the Security Council has produced a loose, decentralized system of collective security. The norm is for the Security Council to authorize a state or group of states under chapter VII of the UN Charter to take military action to maintain or restore international peace and security. Command of these operations is vested in those states forming the multinational force (or "coalition of the willing"). The Security Council's main mechanism for controlling the operations are the enabling resolution and reporting system. Here the contributing states provide information to the Security Council, usually via the Secretary-General, on the military action. This is a far cry from the formal provisions of chapter VII of the UN Charter, whereby command and control was meant to be centralized under the MSC and, ultimately, the Security Council.[30]

Strategic control by the MSC and overall political control by the council may appear necessary for collective security under the charter, in that they embody centralization for the collective use of force. This argument can be used to criticize the council when it has delegated authority and control to a state or group of states. However, dismissing a viable alternative because it does not match the text of the charter is too formalistic.[31] The council can authorize one state to use force, but it is still a collective authorization in that it represents the collective will of the council on behalf of the United Nations. This is all the more so when the council authorizes a group of states to carry out such a function.[32] The question remains whether control by the council and the MSC is essential to fulfilling the collective security function. It could be argued that the provisions of chapter VII are formalities that, if in operation, would facilitate the use of the power contained in article 42. They can be seen as just one method of allowing the council to fulfill its collective security role. Thus it would appear to be unnecessary to make such formalities a prerequisite to the use of military enforcement action by the council.[33]

This decentralized system is erratic, kicking in when dominant states' interests are at stake; it can easily be blocked by the veto of a permanent member. However, with the end of the Cold War the system has started to operate in a fashion closer to that envisaged in 1945. The council has not yet "decided" to use military force; it has recommended or authorized states to do so for particular purposes. Inevitably, the voluntary nature of the military option undermines the collective security ideal that every aggression is met with counterforce, for there may be few willing volunteers, and even they can withdraw without legal hindrance.[34] However, it is difficult to argue against the volunteer system of UN-authorized military action under chapter VII when chapter VIII explicitly accepts it under article 53 in regard to regional arrangements.

The thin line between military actions under chapter VII versus those under chapter VIII is more illusory in light of the NATO actions in Bosnia and Kosovo under UN authority (after the NATO bombings). Security Council resolutions mandated military enforcement actions, culminating in the endorsement of the Implementation Force (IFOR) following the Dayton Accords of November 1995[35] and the Kosovo Force (KFOR) following the FRY's withdrawal in June 1999.[36] These can be seen either as deriving from chapter VIII, thereby treating NATO as a "regional arrangement," or as authorizations to each individual member state of NATO, including other contributors to IFOR/KFOR, to form multilateral forces under chapter VII. Both are equally plausible, thereby illustrating the decentralized model based on UN authorization.

Although not matching the original charter scheme, the decentralized military option that has been developed by the Security Council is a lawful evolution of its powers to maintain and restore international peace and security. But the system does have legal parameters. At the very least there must be an authorizing resolution from the Security Council,[37] which must be construed narrowly.[38] In the United Nations there is consensus that the phrase "all necessary measures" or "all necessary means" in combination with an "authorization" "under Chapter VII" signifies that military enforcement action is being sanctioned. Other language will not do.

For example, U.S. and U.K. attempts to interpret Security Council resolutions condemning Iraq for noncompliance with weapons inspections during 1998 to authorize military measures were not convincing. The resolutions only used the phrase "serious consequences" and indicated that the Security Council would decide what those would be if Iraq failed to comply. Furthermore, there was insufficient support for the U.S.-U.K. position, especially from Russia and China and many other members of the Security Council.[39] Failure to secure the necessary authorizing language in a resolution signifies a lack of consensus on military action. It is disingenuous for certain states to then claim that they can unilaterally interpret resolutions as sanctioning military action. That is an unjustified claim to take military action. The same must be true for any military action taken "in support of" Security Council resolutions. None of the relevant resolutions on Iraq after the cease-fire in 1991 and the FRY in 1999 provided authority for military actions against those states.[40]

Although binding chapter VII resolutions were breached by Iraq (relating to arms reduction) and the FRY (relating to repression of the Kosovar Albanians), this is not a sufficient justification for the "unilateral enforcement of the collective will."[41] The lack of consensus in the Security Council that a chapter VII resolution condemning and demanding certain action can give rise to military action by willing states if the resolutions are ignored is telling. Indeed, if Western states continue to utilize resolutions in this way, there will be no agreement on any type of chapter VII resolution in the future.[42] The collective security system has been stretched by Western states and is generous to them, but they must seek and gain the Security Council's mandate. The desire of Western states to base their military actions on Security Council resolutions is significant, for it seems to undermine the argument that the NATO bombardment of the FRY and the intervention in northern Iraq reflect the reemergence of a unilateral right to humanitarian intervention.[43]

Examining the claims of NATO states before international and national forums and in pleadings before the ICJ in May 1999, N. Krisch concludes that despite the odd and inconsistent statements by the United States and United Kingdom that seemed to favor unilateral humanitarian intervention, they and the other NATO members tried to justify their action on the basis of the collective authority of the United Nations rather than on the right of humanitarian intervention.[44] "Thus, a purely unilateral humanitarian intervention seems even more difficult after the case of Kosovo than before."[45] In trying to force the military actions under the UN umbrella, NATO states probably did more damage to the precarious and dangerous doctrine of humanitarian intervention. In addition, they have breached, and therefore undermined, the constitutional parameters of the UN collective security system they helped create.

The failure of the Security Council to condemn the NATO bombing of the FRY (rejecting a Russian draft on 26 March 1999 by a 12–3 vote) cannot be seen as an authorization or endorsement of the bombing.[46] A major concern for many states voting against the resolution was its lack of balance: it failed to condemn the brutality of the repressive measures taken by the FRY.[47] Above all, a failure to condemn cannot be seen as an authorization to use force.

Acting on Behalf of the "International Community"

Although the intervenors in Iraq and Kosovo weakened the doctrine of humanitarian intervention, probably beyond repair, there is the question of whether military intervention taken "in support of" or "in the spirit of" Security Council resolutions is a new and accepted concept in international law. In the absence of a clear mandate from the Security Council, the intervening states have invoked the argument that they are acting on behalf of the "international community." The Security Council resolutions represent the will of the international community, and the states are merely enforcing that will. This "international community" seems to be the concept underpinning the recent actions in Iraq and Kosovo. Much derided in the past by powerful states, this idea is necessitated when military intervention is taken to uphold fundamental norms of the international community prohibiting crimes against humanity, which were undoubtedly being committed in northern Iraq and Kosovo.[48]

It is easy for a state to invoke the international community to legitimize military intervention, but who or what is it?[49] The dangers of

basing it on international law alone are clear, for there is a huge leap
from recognizing laws prohibiting crimes against humanity to recognizing that states have the right (unilaterally or with allies) to enforce those
norms. Such a system will rapidly descend into self-help, whereby the
international community becomes a cloak for military interventions and
hegemony. However, in the case of Kosovo and Iraq, some of the discretion was removed by the Security Council resolutions recognizing
the gravity of the human rights abuses in those countries. Does this not
lend a certain objectivity? Yes, but discretion remains, for this new form
of intervention is claimed as a legal right, not a duty, often cloaked in
the rhetoric of moral obligations.[50] Furthermore, it is somewhat disingenuous to claim that the international community's will is *embodied* in
a Security Council resolution when that organ has the capacity to formally *express* its will. The determination of a threat to the peace is not
the same as a mandate to take military action. The argument fails to recognize the gap between statements of law and their enforcement.

However, in the case of Kosovo, but not Iraq, there was an authorization from an international organization—NATO. Do nineteen democracies acting in concert represent the international community? Can
such an organization breach international law? The fact that NATO is
composed of liberal democracies does not suggest that it is the fulcrum
of the international community. In fact, in wartime decisionmaking
many of the constitutional checks and balances that exist in liberal
democracies are not applicable. The power rests within the executive;
the legislature generally does not approve of such actions in advance. In
the case of the United Kingdom, the decision to go to war is taken by
the cabinet; the war itself is run by a small part of the cabinet with military advisers. Parliament debates, but the decision is set, and it would
cause a constitutional crisis if Parliament were to vote against actions
already taken by the executive. The only real democratic control on
such military actions is public opinion. Put simply, NATO cannot claim
to represent the international community.

The legality and legitimacy of the NATO action in Kosovo in 1999
is undermined by the NATO treaty. Although NATO claimed the right to
take non–article 5 operations (i.e., military action not taken in self-
defense), that cannot be determined by NATO alone.[51] NATO can operate only within the framework of international law and the UN Charter,
which has supremacy over any other international treaty given conflicting obligations.[52] Although NATO members by consensus can arguably
reinterpret their own treaty, they cannot opt out of the UN system to

become a collective security competitor to the United Nations.[53] Thus the U.S. undersecretary of state, Strobe Talbott, was incorrect to state that "we must be careful not to subordinate NATO to any other international body."[54] The whole international security system is based on a hierarchy with the United Nations at the apex. To allow smaller alliances or organizations the right of "self-authorization" to take enforcement action would lead to competing claims to intervention.[55]

Still, the United States and United Kingdom assert the paramountcy of the UN Charter over other conflicting treaty regimes when it suits them. The essence of their arguments in the *Lockerbie* cases is that the obligations imposed on Libya by the Security Council prevail by virtue of the UN Charter over Libya's rights and duties contained in the 1971 Montreal Convention.[56] It is inconsistent to argue the supremacy of the UN Charter in the case of Libya and yet dismiss it in the case of the NATO intervention in Kosovo.

The United Nations represents the vast majority of states (189 in September 2001); only it has a legitimate claim to be acting on behalf of the international community. In 1945 it was imbued with exceptional powers that no state or organization could possess unless they received authority from the United Nations. It was because the United Nations represented "the vast majority of the Members of the international community" at the time, and now more so, that it has the powers of the international community.[57] Within the United Nations, it is the General Assembly that is reflective of the political will of the organization. "The special value of the General Assembly is its universality, its capacity to be a forum in which the voice of every member state can be heard."[58]

Security Council or UN Authority?

Although it is argued here that the United Nations is the only source of authority for collective military action beyond self-defense, the weakness of the system is the veto in the Security Council. There are strong arguments that the General Assembly has residual enforcement powers in exceptional cases, and it should have been the fall-back forum for seeking authority to undertake the bombing of the FRY in 1999. NATO's argument that it had no choice but to undertake the bombing without authority, in the form of a recommendation, from an organ that truly represents the international community is thus incorrect. Indeed, if any forum can legitimately claim to represent or embody the international community, then it has to be the General Assembly of the United Nations. The General Assembly not only has subsidiary competence regarding collective security; it has primary competence on issues of human rights.[59] Claims to intervene in Kosovo to protect human rights would thus have all the attributes necessary for the assembly to grant authority, but only if the action was supported by a two-thirds majority.[60]

Debates over this sort of competence in the General Assembly tend to be clouded by questions over the legality of the Uniting for Peace resolution adopted by the General Assembly in 1950.[61] The reason for the resolution was the return in August 1950 of the Soviet Union to the Security Council. In fact, the assembly had already adopted an "enforcement" resolution on Korea after the Soviets had returned to the Security Council but before the Uniting for Peace resolution was adopted.[62] The reasons for Uniting for Peace went beyond Korea. The Western-influenced majority in the General Assembly saw the frequent use of the Soviet veto during the period 1946–1950 as an abuse of that right and that the ideal of great power unity was no longer attainable. The Western states wanted an alternative form of collective security based not on P5 agreement but on the will of the majority in the assembly.

Such a concept of collective security, though opening the potential for economic and military actions against transgressors, might also allow the General Assembly to recommend military action against one of the P5. A more likely scenario would be for the assembly to recommend military action that would affect the interests of a permanent member. Because this system of collective security was potentially dangerous, the resolution restricted the assembly's power to recommend military measures for flagrant violations of international peace— namely, breaches of the peace or acts of aggression—and did not expressly permit the assembly to take measures as a response to threats to the peace.

The Soviet Union objected to the resolution; it argued that the resolution violated the charter requirement that coercive power was granted solely to the Security Council.[63] In 1962, the ICJ in the *Expenses* case stated that "action," which is the preserve of the Security Council, refers to coercive action, but it failed to state whether this excluded the assembly from recommending coercive measures.[64] At some point, the ICJ suggested that "action" is restricted to mandatory coercive action ordered by the Security Council. In other words, the assembly did not appear to be barred from recommending enforcement action as part of its responsibility for maintaining peace as recognized by the court.[65] Furthermore, despite the wording of the Uniting for Peace resolution, there appears to be no cogent argument against allowing the assembly to recommend military measures to combat a threat to the peace.[66]

However, in the context of the ban on the use of armed force—a rule of *jus cogens* from which no derogation is allowed—doubts can be cast on the legality of the Uniting for Peace resolution and therefore the power of the assembly to recommend military measures. The exceptions to article 2(4) include action only in self-defense under article 51 and military action authorized by the Security Council under articles 42 or 53. To state that the General Assembly can recommend military action creates a third exception, which would appear to be contrary to the *jus cogens* in article 2(4). However, the Security Council is authorizing military action on behalf of the United Nations, and so the exceptions are those undertaken in legitimate self-defense and those mandated by the United Nations. The question of which UN organ issues the mandate is an internal issue and does not affect the legitimacy of UN action vis-à-vis a transgressing state.[67] The internal issue can be resolved with both organs having the ability to mandate military action, given that the assembly has all those recommendatory powers possessed by the council, albeit at a supplementary level.[68]

The Uniting for Peace resolution—whereby the assembly can be activated in the face of a deadlocked Security Council by a procedural vote in the council that is not subject to the veto—has been used in the past to gain UN authority for innovative military actions. Facing military intervention by two permanent members in the Suez crisis of 1956 and a threat to the peace in the Congo in 1960, the Security Council, unable to take substantive action itself due to the veto, transferred the matter to the assembly.[69] The assembly duly became the organ of authority in the case of UNEF, a traditional peacekeeping force, and temporarily in the case of ONUC, which acted in a more muscular fashion. Although it may be argued that these two operations were more peacekeeping than enforcement—and thus are not precedents for seeking an enforcement mandate for intervention in Kosovo—the Congo operation came very close to enforcement.[70]

In addition, the General Assembly had, even before the adoption of the Uniting for Peace resolution, become involved in the Korean enforcement operation. In fact, the assembly made a substantial contribution to UN action in Korea by passing a resolution that allowed the UN force to continue its operations to establish "a unified, independent and democratic government of Korea" after the Security Council had been deadlocked by the return of the Soviet representative.[71] This resolution was seen as sanctioning General Douglas MacArthur's crossing of the 38th Parallel and thus constituted enforcement action. British Foreign Secretary Ernest Bevin, who was instrumental in the resolution, thought it was essential to have UN authority for the intervention in North Korea.[72]

The charter procedure for convoking a special session is not significantly different from the Uniting for Peace resolution.[73] Both allow for the transfer of matters from the Security Council by a procedural vote or by a majority of members in the General Assembly.[74] In addition, the Uniting for Peace resolution specifically grants to the assembly power to recommend collective measures and establishes machinery to enable it to carry them out. Article 10 recognizes the power of the assembly to recommend measures, so in a normal, special, or emergency special session it has the same powers as those granted by the Uniting for Peace resolution. Indeed, its actual powers are wider than Uniting for Peace, for it can act to combat threats to the peace as well as breaches of the peace and acts of aggression.[75] The sponsors of the Uniting for Peace resolution may have been confused as to whether the assembly could recommend enforcement measures. They failed to take account of the valid argument in favor of the assembly having this power, which it had already utilized in the Korean situation.

The procedure advocated by Western states in 1950 was conveniently forgotten in Kosovo. The cumbersome nature of convening a special or emergency special session of the assembly is no excuse given that NATO first threatened to use force without express authority in October 1998. The matter could have been put forward by NATO members, the coalition of the willing, before the assembly during its annual session. Indeed, the assembly did consider the situation of human rights in Kosovo and adopted a resolution on 9 December 1999 that was critical of the FRY and supportive of the Security Council.[76] This represented an opportunity for NATO to seek authority for its air strikes.

UN-Authorized Military Operations: A Mixed Record

I now review some of the chapter VII enforcement actions undertaken on behalf of the United Nations to assess the strength of the system.

The UN collective security system overlaps with the collective self-defense regime when the international community is responding to armed aggression—one state invades another. It has been argued by some jurists that the United Nations, in the two cases where it has authorized a response to aggression, is merely legitimating the right of collective self-defense under article 51.[77] However, the real legal basis of the operation is chapter VII, article 42, as a UN military operation fulfilling UN aims and objectives.[78] It is not defined by the customary law of self-defense. The United Nations has the legal power to authorize responses to aggression under articles 39 and 42, and in the cases of Korea in 1950 and Iraq in 1990 the organization did that.

In Korea in 1950, the Security Council recommended "that the Members of the United Nations furnish such assistance to the Republic of Korea as may be necessary to repel the armed attack and to restore international peace and security in the area."[79] The mandate goes beyond the purely defensive—repelling the attack by North Korea. It seems to permit the UN-authorized army to take offensive action if necessary to restore international peace and security. The mandate is ambiguous, and doubts as to whether the mandate was adequate to make a crossing of the 38th Parallel into North Korea were dispelled by the General Assembly's resolution quoted just above. The assembly had to take over as the organ of authority given that the Soviet Union's return to the Security Council ensured deadlock.

The UN-authorized response to the North Korean intervention eventually led to a return to the status quo in the Korean Peninsula, although only after the U.S.-led operation had been pushed out of North Korea by the Chinese army. The dangers of attempting to enforce peace on an aggressor seemed to influence the extent of the military operation undertaken against Iraq in 1991. Security Council Resolution No. 678 of 29 November 1990 authorized member states "to use all necessary means to uphold and implement Security Council resolution 660 and all subsequent resolutions and to restore international peace and security in the area" unless Iraq withdrew before 15 January 1991. Despite the permissive language, the Coalition restricted operations to the removal of Iraq from Kuwait. Although the air campaign did penetrate deep into Iraq and was aimed at industrial as well as military targets, and the ground offensive did involve a temporary occupation of large parts of southern Iraq, those actions merely ensured the successful liberation of Kuwait.

The Coalition was successful, but the wider aim of restoring peace and security to the area was through an intrusive cease-fire at the end of hostilities in Security Council Resolution No. 687 of 3 April 1991. It attempted to address the source of aggression using a disarmament regime supervised by the United Nations Special Commission and the IAEA. In addition, the resolution provided a system whereby Iraq would have to contribute 30 percent of its oil revenues to compensate its victims, as well as a demarcation of the disputed boundary between Iraq and Kuwait. The regime was to be enforced by the harsh sanctions regime against Iraq, though this was alleviated by humanitarian exceptions and an oil-for-food agreement, which was finally achieved between the United Nations and Iraq in 1996.[80]

This regime is predicated on the fact that the council will enforce Iraqi compliance through economic sanctions; military sanctions were to be decided anew by the Security Council. In effect, the air strikes against Iraq in 1993 and from December 1998 onward, primarily by the United States and United Kingdom in order to enforce the disarmament regime, have no authority in UN law. Attempts to resurrect the initial resolution of November 1990 to legitimate these actions ignore the fact that in resolution 687 of April 1991 the council revoked its mandate to the Coalition, the latter having achieved the objective of liberating Kuwait.[81] A similar lack of UN authority can be seen as to the so-called no-fly zones imposed after the cease-fire by Western states over northern and southern Iraq to protect Kurds and Shi-ite Muslims, the military intervention in northern Iraq in April and May 1991, as well as all subsequent air strikes to protest Iraqi attempts to reassert authority over northern Iraq (e.g., September 1996). Resolution 688, adopted on 5 April 1991 in the face of Iraqi repression of the Kurds and Shi-ite Muslims, did not authorize military action.[82]

Both the Korean and Kuwaiti operations were successful in that they repelled the aggressor. The wider aims of collective security—in particular, trying to tackle the source of the aggression—have presented problems. In the case of Korea, this nearly resulted in a worldwide conflagration as the UN-authorized army's crossing into North Korea provoked a massive Chinese military intervention. In the case of Iraq it was decided by the Security Council to address the issue in a nonmilitary way after the Coalition had freed Kuwait. Frustration at the perceived lack of success of this regime has led Western states to step outside UN authority when taking military actions, despite attempts to stretch the cloak of UN authority over their actions.

The confusion that exists between UN-authorized military operations and those that take place outside UN authority is compounded when command and control is in the hands of states. In the Korean operation, the UN Secretary-General wished for UN command and control, but the United States rejected that idea and led and dominated the force.[83] Similarly in the Gulf, the United States commanded the army. However, both the Korean and the initial Gulf operations had UN authority; the United Nations merely delegated its power to a group of states and similarly delegated command and control. The United States may have commanded the air strikes since 1991, but it lacks the legal power to do so, not having received authority from the United Nations.

Of course the UN record on aggression must be judged in light of the many attacks and breaches of the peace since 1945.[84] The United Nations has taken military action in response to only two. Of course states can take action without council authority to combat aggression in individual or collective self-defense under article 51 of the UN Charter (e.g., the U.K. response to Argentina's invasion of the Falkland Islands). Similarly, the U.S. response to the terrorist attacks of 11 September 2001 was based on self-defense. Although the Security Council condemned the terrorist acts as threats to international peace and then imposed chapter VII measures on all states to block the financing of terrorism, it did so in recognition of the right of self-defense.[85] In the cases of council-authorized responses to aggression, the two taken against North Korea and Iraq were perhaps the most flagrant "wars" of aggression. In this respect the UN responses may deter future aggressors.

The UN's response to threats to the peace is equally patchy. During the Cold War the response was virtually nonexistent, at least at the military level (the U.K. Beira patrol to stop the importation of oil by southern Rhodesia being an exception).[86] Post–Cold War the United Nations has been much more active, with varying levels of success. On one hand there are the debacles of Somalia, Rwanda, and Bosnia (pre-Dayton), balanced by successes in Haiti and Albania.[87] In the balance hang the UN-authorized operations in Bosnia, Kosovo, and East Timor. A few general comments can be made in regard to some of the UN-authorized operations to date.

The danger of "mission creep" was especially prevalent in Somalia, where the initial humanitarian aims of the UNITAF operation stated in 1992 were supplanted by the desire to build a state.[88] Although statebuilding is a legitimate and desirable aim, especially when faced with a failed state, the lesson of Somalia is that it cannot be achieved easily by force of arms. The failure to quell the factions in Somalia and the resultant ignominious withdrawal of UNOSOM II in 1995 are testament to this. Some degree of consent is needed. Even then, more time and resources are needed to restore both the negative and positive peace compared to the initial military operation. The initial success based on the mere threat of a U.S.-led intervention in Haiti in 1994 must be soberly balanced against the struggles of the UN peacekeeping and peacebuilding operations thereafter.[89]

Further evidence is seen in the UN-authorized operations in Bosnia after the Dayton Accords of 1995 and in Kosovo beginning in June 1999 following the unauthorized NATO bombings of the FRY. The cycle of violence that has stretched back for centuries in that region is not going to be broken easily and requires a long-term commitment: a military presence as well as a civilian administration. There are no short-term solutions to the underlying problems. States must be prepared to support, resource, and fund continuing multifaceted operations if peace is to be permanently brought to these zones of violence.[90]

Economic Sanctions: A Blunt Weapon?

Chapter VII, article 41 states that the Security Council can utilize measures short of the use of armed force. These "may include the complete or partial interruption of economic relations and of rail, sea, air, postal, telegraphic, radio, and other means of communication, and the severance of diplomatic relations." The power contained in article 41 was intended to allow the imposition of mandatory enforcement measures after the council had made a determination of a threat to the peace, breach of the peace, or act of aggression under article 39. However, on many occasions the council has been unwilling to take mandatory action, settling for voluntary measures or sanctions. Although the charter base for such powers is inconclusive, there is no doubt that the council has developed such a power, the evolution of which lies in political compromise. Voluntary sanctions, as the term implies, are breached with impunity and are relatively ineffective except in a symbolic role.[91]

The council has used the weapon of mandatory sanctions only once against an aggressor, a state breaching interstate peace. In the case of Iraq, sanctions were first imposed by resolution 661 of 6 August 1990, following Iraq's refusal to comply with the council's mandatory ceasefire and withdrawal call in resolution 660 of 2 August 1990, the day Kuwait was invaded. Sanctions in this case were imposed quickly, and as the terms of resolution 661 show, they were comprehensive. The council also decided to establish a committee to examine the implementation of sanctions by member states. In analyzing these reports, support for resolution 661 reached well over 80 percent of the UN membership. Many nonmembers responded positively, although at least one, Switzerland, stated that it was not under a legal obligation to impose sanctions against Iraq.[92] In 1990 economic sanctions looked likely to be effective as a means of enforcing international law given that oil-rich Iraq was a one-product economy.[93]

Thus the Security Council adopted a series of resolutions to fine-tune the embargo, including an authorization to navies to intercept suspected sanctions-breaking ships in the Gulf.[94] Sanctions were imposed in August 1990; by January 1991, when the UN-authorized military campaign started, sanctions did not appear to have weakened Iraq's resolve, although they may have affected its military capacity.

Nevertheless, questions must be raised as to the effectiveness of sanctions. Sanctions were continued against Iraq by resolution 687 of 3 April 1991 after military action successfully ousted Iraq from Kuwait. The purpose of the continuing sanctions regime was to secure Iraq's compliance with the resolutions' provisions on disarmament and compensation, although the hidden agenda must have been to undermine the regime of Saddam Hussein. Resolution 687 provides for a review of the sanctions regime against Iraq "every sixty days in the light of the policies and practices of the Government of Iraq." The sanctions have remained in place ever since.

The aim of sanctions was not to starve the people of Iraq into submission but to weaken Iraq's hold on Kuwait and then force it to comply with its obligations to disarm and to compensate states and individuals for its aggression. This was made clear from the outset by resolution 661 adopted on 6 August 1990 and elaborated upon by resolution 666 of 13 September 1990. The latter outlined a mechanism whereby the UN Sanctions Committee would monitor the food situation in Iraq and determine which needs ought to be met. The committee struggled with avoiding "starvation as a weapon."[95] Nevertheless, the direct effect of the sanctions was on the Iraqi people themselves.

The civilian population has and continues to suffer from malnutrition and an increase in diseases. The Security Council has tried to alleviate this by permitting exports of oil under UN supervision for the purchase of foodstuffs. This offer was originally made in August 1991 but was not accepted by the Iraqi regime until December 1996.[96] Nevertheless, the sanctions regime is not a sufficient weapon to harm those responsible for the invasion, namely, the Iraqi regime of Saddam Hussein. Ordinary Iraqi citizens appear to be the ones who are suffering.

Care must be taken that UN economic sanctions do not result in the violation of fundamental UN values, especially basic human rights. This was made clear in 1997 by the CESCR in a general comment.[97] The committee, concerned about the increasing frequency of sanctions regimes, emphasized that "such sanctions should always take full account of the provisions of the International Covenant on Economic, Social and Cultural Rights." By taking the narrow view that the covenant is directly applicable only to the state parties to it, the committee struggled with the applicability of the covenant to sanctions regimes imposed by the Security Council under chapter VII. It failed to view norms embodied in the covenant, and before that in the UDHR, as part of the UN's own constitutional law and therefore as a limitation on the activities of the organization as well as states.

Nevertheless, the committee felt that despite this the United Nations should have regard for the rights contained in the covenant. Sanctions regimes "often cause significant disruption in the distribution of food, pharmaceuticals and sanitation supplies, jeopardize the quality of food and the availability of clean drinking water, severely interfere with the functioning of basic health and education systems and undermine the right to work." The humanitarian exceptions often built into the sanctions regimes by the United Nations do not necessarily alleviate these problems, and so the committee strongly recommended that basic human rights "must be fully taken into account when designing an appropriate sanctions regime." The premise behind the committee's refreshing approach is that "lawlessness of one kind must not be met by lawlessness of another kind which pays no heed to the fundamental rights that underlie and give legitimacy to any such collective action."

It is possible to argue that sanctions—a blunt instrument incapable of removing aggression—are more suitable for threats to the peace; they are directed at those who must change the internal situation—the rulers and the ruled. The sanctions regime against Iraq aimed to resolve a threat to the peace rather than the initial aggression, but its effects are on the ordinary citizens of Iraq, as well as the peoples and governments that traditionally traded with the target state. The Iraqi sanctions regime illustrates that the Security Council was powerless to address the immediate economic plight of other states such as Jordan despite the fact that article 50 provides that such states have "the right to consult the Security Council with regard to a solution of those problems."

Whether or not sanctions provoke a change in the Iraqi regime, either by fostering discontent in the population or by forcing the regime to change the system, the failed experiment suggests that economic coercion alone is not an alternative to military coercion. Sanctions are not an adequate weapon for enforcing collective security. Furthermore, unless used with precision and care, sanctions regimes can actually violate UN law.

In addition to the case of Iraq, the Security Council has used mandatory sanctions for many threats to the peace, including comprehensive regimes against southern Rhodesia between 1968 and 1979 and against Yugoslavia (Serbia and Montenegro) from 1992. More selective regimes have been imposed: against Libya, 1992–1998; Haiti, 1993–1994; Sudan from 1996; Angola from 1993; and Sierra Leone from 1997. Arms embargoes have also been imposed: against South Africa, 1977–1994; Somalia and Liberia from 1992; and Rwanda, 1994–1995. During the Cold War the council was reluctant to use its full powers under article 41, but since the decline of the superpower veto the council has frequently used its article 41 powers, further evidence that it believes in its collective security role.

The case of Rhodesia is a mixed bag. The council's committee established to monitor the sanctions regime suggests that from 1968 the Rhodesian economy improved.[98] There is evidence that after 1974 with the combined effects of Mozambique's independence (Portugal, the colonial power, was a major sanction-breaker), the guerrilla war, and the sanctions regime, the domestic situation began to decline. Although sanctions did not immediately achieve the goals of the Security Council (ending the unilateral declaration of independence by forcing the regime to negotiate or forcing internal change by ruining the Rhodesian economy), they led to the fulfillment of other goals that must be viewed as a success: limiting the conflict mainly to Rhodesian soil, preventing foreign military intervention, and encouraging the white regime to negotiate.

The sanctions against Rhodesia and Iraq suggest that the only way to affect a strong state economy is to impose an immediate comprehensive embargo. Limited embargoes are insufficient; even if they target weak areas of the economy, the unsanctioned areas will compensate. However, there are humanitarian considerations, and the effectiveness of full embargoes must not be overestimated.

There was an arms embargo against South Africa, but the strong economy and natural resources enabled it to produce its own weapons. But if used against a country totally dependent on outside states for arms, especially if there is no real prospect for domestic arms production, an arms embargo can be useful, as in Somalia (resolution 733 of

23 January 1992). However, the Somalia resolution contained no machinery for monitoring arms shipments, and the council is relying on
UN members' obligation to honor a mandatory decision of the council.

The council's mandatory arms embargo against Liberia (resolution
788 of 19 November 1992) seems to have had a greater impact, although the performance of the ECOWAS peacekeeping force, which
was exempted from the embargo, accounts for most of the progress
there. The effect of a mandatory oil and arms embargo against another
extremely poor country, Haiti (resolution 841 of 17 June 1993), seems
to have been more dramatic, with the military regime agreeing to the
restoration of democracy under the deposed president on 2 July 1993.
However, there was no follow-up implementation of the agreement; the
Security Council reimposed the oil and arms embargo in October 1993,
accompanied by the authorization to member states to stop suspected
sanctions-breaking ships.[99] Although sanctions were further expanded in
May 1994,[100] it took the threat in July 1994 of a UN-authorized, U.S.-
led military operation for the military dictatorship in Haiti to step down
in October 1994, consenting to a U.S. and then a UN force to oversee
the return to democracy. Again it seems that sanctions alone, without
the threat or use of military force, were inadequate for the tasks.

Nevertheless, this provides limited evidence that sanctions can be
effective if the target state is very weak; it does not necessarily require
a comprehensive embargo to be effective. Indeed, a comprehensive embargo against a state whose population is below the poverty line would
seem inhumane in the extreme and may well result in a violation of the
UN's human rights values.

A slightly different approach was taken on the civil war in Angola
following the breakdown in the peace process, with the Security Council imposing a mandatory arms and oil embargo only against areas held
by the National Union for the Total Independence of Angola (UNITA).[101]
This approach was again adopted in September 1994 when the Security
Council imposed a more comprehensive regime against the Bosnian
Serbs.[102] In these cases, sanctions were directed at the faction responsible for the continuation of the internal conflict, but this more "just" approach is perhaps possible only in a state that is divided politically, eth-
nically, and geographically.

A more comprehensive embargo was imposed against war-torn former Yugoslavia by resolution 757 of 30 May 1992. The council condemned the continued intervention by Yugoslavia (Serbia and Montenegro) and Croatia in the former republic and emerging state of Bosnia.

The resolution built on the mandatory arms embargo imposed against the whole of Yugoslavia by resolution 713 of 25 September 1991. Clearly, the aims of the arms embargo resolutions against Somalia, Haiti, Liberia, and the former Yugoslavia were to prevent the escalation of civil wars that would occur if outside states supplied arms to one faction or another.

The aim of the more comprehensive sanctions regime against Serbia was to prevent its forces from assisting Bosnian Serbs in their struggle to gain more territory in Bosnia. Unlike the arms embargo, which is to prevent escalation, the aim of the regime against Serbia was to punish it for its intervention and for its support of ethnic cleansing. The continuation of the sanctions was intended to coerce Serbia into withdrawing military support for Bosnian Serbs and to force that faction to agree to peaceful settlement. Although the evidence is that the sanctions were inadequate to the task, the economy was hit hard; and the Serbs only consented to the Dayton Accords after suffering military setbacks against a joint Croatian-Muslim offensive in combination with UN-authorized NATO air strikes in August 1995.

Another development in sanctions occurred after the terrorist attacks on the United States on 11 September 2001, when the Security Council imposed chapter VII measures on all states, aimed at preventing and suppressing the financing of terrorism.[103] The Security Council may be developing its sanctions policy to more accurately target individuals responsible for terrorism. In so doing it has bolstered its lawmaking powers, which in the past have been directed at specific states accused of supporting terrorism (e.g., Libya, Sudan, Afghanistan) by exercising a general legislative competence over all states. The resolution, inter alia, requires states to "criminalize the wilful provision or collection . . . of funds by their nationals or in their territories . . . in the knowledge that they are to be used, in order to carry out terrorist acts."

Peacekeeping: From Keeping Negative Peace to Promoting Positive Peace

Military enforcement action has the purpose of coercing a resisting state or party to accept UN policy. In contrast, peacekeeping, a military option often deployed by the Security Council and exceptionally the General Assembly, is less intrusive, essentially nonaggressive, and consensual. Although the UN Charter does not expressly provide for the deployment of peacekeepers, their creation by the Security Council and the General Assembly lies within the penumbra of the UN Charter, as the ICJ recognized in the *Expenses* case.[104] Articles 36 and 40 can be the basis for peacekeeping, in that peacekeepers traditionally oversee provisional measures such as a cease-fire and withdrawal and, as seen more recently, oversee the implementation of a peace agreement. Peacekeeping, then, is something more than peaceful settlement—it involves the deployment of military forces under a UN mandate—but less than an enforcement action. For this reason, it is sometimes stated to be an implied power located somewhere between chapters VI and VII of the UN Charter. But the forces deployed can vary; sometimes it resembles an enforcement action, especially when a force is deployed in internal conflicts.

Peacekeeping developed out of the UN's need to observe the cease-fires it brokered in the first decade after World War II. The struggle for decolonization led to the need for observers in Indonesia in 1947 as that country struggled for independence from the Netherlands.[105] Decolonization also led to conflicts between newly independent states over disputed areas like Kashmir, claimed by India and Pakistan. The initial conflict ended in stalemate in July 1949 with a bilateral accord granting observation functions to the United Nations Military Observer Group in India and Pakistan (UNMOGIP), established by the Security Council.[106] This team of unarmed observers has reported on the cease-fire ever since, though it has been powerless to prevent occasional breaches of the cease-fire.

The emergence of the state of Israel in 1948 also fostered the idea of peacekeeping. The first Arab-Israeli war ended with acceptance of Security Council resolutions calling for a cease-fire. The detailed functions of the UN Truce Supervision Organization (UNTSO) emerged out of the armistice agreements of 1949 between Israel and Jordan, Syria, Egypt, and Lebanon. The functions of UNTSO were recognized by the Security Council in 1949, although the force had been in situ since 1948 to supervise the truce negotiated by the Truce Commission with the authority of the Security Council.[107] This haphazard emergence of UNTSO's mandate illustrates how peacekeeping developed in the formative years, with the council responding to the requirements of the parties to the dispute rather than taking the initiative. Indeed, UNTSO has remained in the Middle East; its force of 200–600 unarmed observers has performed various functions in the region, observing cease-fires after the 1956, 1967, and 1973 wars, as well as the Palestinian and Israeli withdrawal from Beirut in 1982–1983. UNTSO is another force that the Security Council has found essential in a volatile region.

Peacekeeping took a major stride in 1956, when the Suez crisis led to the establishment of the first full peacekeeping force, UNEF I. This differed from the earlier observation teams in three ways. First, the force was larger (more than 6,000 troops at its height). Second, the troops had arms, although they were light arms. Finally, the functions were also to secure and supervise the cessation of hostilities, including the withdrawal of the armies of the United Kingdom, France, and Israel.[108] Once this was achieved, the force became a buffer between Israel and Egypt. However, the force was emplaced only after the belligerents had accepted the cease-fire and agreed to withdraw.

Although active in separating the warring parties, UNEF I was not empowered to step in if major hostilities broke out again, as it was armed for defense, not enforcement. Peacekeeping comes if the parties accept a cease-fire and withdrawal, then consent to the peacekeepers on their soil. The principle of consent was illustrated in 1967, when UN Secretary-General U Thant ordered the withdrawal of UNEF I after the president of Egypt made it clear that Egypt's consent had been withdrawn. Although it can be argued that the General Assembly, as the author of UNEF's mandate, was responsible for its status and that the assembly—not the Secretary-General—had the power to withdraw the force, U Thant's decision vis-à-vis Egypt was essentially correct.[109] Indeed, it is highly likely that at least some contributing states would have withdrawn their troops if U Thant had not withdrawn UNEF I.[110] Nevertheless, the withdrawal of UNEF I and the ensuing Six Day War illustrated the limits of peacekeeping. Ironically, the fourth major Arab-Israeli conflict, the Yom Kippur War of 1973, made states realize once again the usefulness of peacekeeping. The Security Council created UNEF II, which successfully supervised the renewed cease-fire between Israel and Egypt between 1973 and 1979, when the Camp David Accords finally established peace between the two states.[111]

Interstate forces such as UNEF, UNMOGIP, the United Nations Iran-Iraq Military Observer Group (1988–1991), and the United Nations Disengagement Observer Force (in the Golan Heights between Israel and Syria since 1974) have the traditional task of supervising a cease-fire and the withdrawal to positions occupied before the conflict started, both of which have already been consented to by the parties. An examination of interstate forces reveals that they are almost always successful within the limited objectives of their mandates. In the case of *intrastate* peacekeeping forces, the mandates must sometimes change to cope with the situation. The difficulties of a civil war–type situation mean that the principles of peacekeeping—namely, consent, impartiality, and limited self-defense—are harder to achieve, as the UN's experience in the Congo between 1960 and 1964 illustrates.

The UN operation in the Congo was sent under the authority of the Security Council at the request of the government of the Congo in July 1960. It was to provide assistance until the Congolese security forces could take over following the breakdown of order upon Belgian decolonization.[112] As soon as ONUC arrived it was in a precarious position, with fighting continuing in the Congo, rival governments being established, and the attempted secession of the Katanga region with the active assistance of Belgian troops and mercenaries. A simple UNEF-type mandate and operation was insufficient to prevent the collapse of the Congo altogether, which led the General Assembly, and then the Security Council, to adopt resolutions that seemed to authorize the offensive use of force by the almost 20,000-strong UN force.[113] ONUC tried to keep within the principles of peacekeeping, especially before the adoption of resolution 161, by negotiating cease-fires and staying impartial. However, it had to use force to subdue the Katangese rebellion in April 1961, December 1961, and between December 1962 and January 1963.[114] It is difficult to see ONUC as a true peacekeeping operation, in that it was authorized to use force beyond self-defense, was not impartial, received little cooperation, and there was no real government in the Congo for a period until August 1961 thereby raising doubts over the issue of consent. Yet ONUC was not an enforcement action like that undertaken by the UN-authorized force in Korea, for instance.[115]

The United Nations has utilized the dangerous combination of peacekeeping and enforcement in subsequent conflicts, principally in Bosnia between 1992 and 1995, and Somalia, where UNOSOM (pure peacekeeping), UNITAF (enforcement action led by the United States), and UNOSOM II (muscular peacekeeping) were successively emplaced between 1992 and 1995. Although the UN's actions in the Congo were successful, it failed in Bosnia and Somalia, leading to questions about using peacekeeping forces in an aggressive way, indeed, whether it is even compatible with the impartial nature of peacekeeping.

In a recent report on peace operations, however, a distinguished panel headed by Lakhdar Brahimi recommended that traditional peacekeeping virtues could be developed to allow a force not only to defend itself but also to defend individuals under its charge.[116] Although a limited suggestion, if adopted it could very well push UN peacekeepers into conflicts. Of course, the massacres in Rwanda in 1994 and Srebrenica in 1995 indicate that UN forces should follow Brahimi's proposal, but in order to do so they must be provided with adequate troops and equipment as well as mandate. If the distinction between peacekeeping and enforcement is to be maintained, however, it should be recognized that enforcement action should be undertaken by a coalition of the willing as opposed to UN blue helmets.

Whereas the quasienforcement approach to peacekeeping appears to undermine the credibility of the UN's role as a peace broker, the integrated and pacific approach, which has also developed since the end of the Cold War, can be seen as a natural development of the principles of peacekeeping. This method pressures the parties to accept a peacekeeping force and to a recommendation for settlement, whether from the Security Council, General Assembly, Secretary-General, outside states, organizations, or individuals. Thus the force performs traditional functions, such as supervising a cease-fire, and supervises the implementation of the peace agreement. More precisely, two or three separate forces—or one force with two or three distinct elements, including a traditional peacekeeping component, a civilian police element, and a civilian component (normally for election supervision)—oversee the implementation of the agreed settlement process.

The origins of this approach can be traced to the Cold War, when the Netherlands and Indonesia sought and were granted General Assembly approval for the creation of a UN Temporary Executive Authority and the UN Security Force on West Irian in 1962. The approach was reapplied in Namibia in 1989–1990 (see Chapter 7). The Security Council has used this approach with varying degrees of success, ranging from effective operations in Nicaragua, El Salvador, Cambodia, and Mozambique to abject failures in Western Sahara, Angola, and Rwanda, where the peace process collapsed under the genocide committed by the Hutu government against the Tutsi minority in April 1994. Nevertheless, despite serious setbacks, the Security Council appears ready to continue with this approach, supplementing it with greater support for a country after its first UN-supervised election or referendum.[117] Indeed, the current UN operations in East Timor and Kosovo, both started in 1999, show that on certain occasions the United Nations is prepared to take over the running of a territory pending a UN-supervised, democratically based, peaceful settlement (see Chapter 7).

Conclusion

The UN's record is patchy, although there has been a significant improvement in the post–Cold War era. Lessons have to be learned. Peacekeeping forces should be deployed in situations where there is peace to keep, economic sanctions should be used precisely and carefully to avoid suffering, and military action should be mandated more precisely and be subject to greater UN control. Selectivity should be reduced in all areas of UN activity. Running through all the conflicts is the necessity for the international community, through the United Nations, to commit to long-term postconflict assistance.

Other regional or security organizations and states can deploy peacekeeping operations and in certain circumstances utilize economic sanctions to preserve or restore the peace. Such rights exist under international law and do not breach articles 2(4) and 53 of the UN Charter. However, the function of collective military action beyond self-defense rests solely in the hands of the United Nations. It was imbued with this unique power in 1945. One of the greatest dangers the United Nations faces today is that powerful states, frustrated with the intransigence of the Security Council in certain conflicts, will take the law into their own hands.

It can be argued that in the Kosovo crisis of 1999, as with Iraq after the cease-fire of 1991, the Security Council failed to take the necessary military action to combat breaches of Security Council resolutions despite threats to the peace. In this sense it failed to fulfill its duties as envisioned in 1945. Even assuming that the Security Council was being paralyzed by an illegitimate veto threat, states cannot take it upon themselves to enforce UN resolutions. Such a contention presumes that states had these powers before they "collectivized" them in the Security Council, which is very doubtful. It also ignores the fact that such powers must be expressly returned or granted to them by the United Nations.

Furthermore, when the UN Charter speaks of the Security Council having "primary responsibility" to maintain or restore international peace and security, it is recognizing that the General Assembly has secondary responsibility for peace and security that can be invoked when the Security Council is unable to act. Indeed, when combined with its undoubted competence in matters of human rights and its legitimate claim to represent the international community, the General Assembly is the natural alternative. The need to honor the authority of the United Nations is clear:

> Often a real or imagined evil will exert a tremendous centrifugal pull on most of us to support forceful action. Nonetheless, the perils associated with warfare—that great powers can use humanitarian concerns to mask geopolitical interest; that major air strikes such as those

threatened against Iraq and Serbia in 1998 have serious consequences in lives lost, destruction caused and the resulting destabilization; that warfare is of limited utility as a means of solving complex, long-standing, underlying problems; that a world order that allows individual or coalitions of nations to deploy offensive military might for what they deem are worthy causes amounts to anarchy—these perils require that force be only used as last resort as determined by a world body.[118]

The United Nations, which acts through the Security Council and sometimes the General Assembly, is that world body. If the Security Council were unable to act because of legitimate concerns that the situation does not require it to exercise its primary responsibility to authorize military action, then it would be unconstitutional for the assembly to have exercised its competence. However, if there is a genuine threat to the peace, breach of the peace, or act of aggression so dangerous and overwhelming that it requires a military response, then the assembly is entitled, indeed obliged, to act. In the Kosovo crisis, the Security Council had determined there to be a threat to the peace, and there was strong evidence of massive repression and crimes against humanity. However, instead of pushing the matter before the Security Council to see if the Russians and Chinese would actually veto the resolution authorizing the bombing, it was merely assumed such would be the case. Furthermore, forcing a veto would have freed the NATO states to put forward a procedural resolution before the council transferring the matter to the General Assembly, where a vote on the proposed NATO action should have been held. Assuming it gained support, then NATO would have obtained a sound legal basis upon which to launch its air strikes.

Why NATO did not follow this course remains a matter of conjecture. At least on the surface, it does not appear to have been on the agenda. Three reasons may have been pertinent. First, there was the fear that the method of military action being put forward—bombing—would not be acceptable to two-thirds of the membership. Bombing in the name of humanity may be cause for concern for the international community. [119] The main reason why this was the only option on the table for NATO was "a desire, understandable in itself, to minimize NATO casualties."[120] Second, securing UN authority would have created an expectation, though not a legal obligation, that NATO would launch military action, thereby restricting NATO's freedom of choice.[121] Third, a fear that the use of the General Assembly to authorize military action would set a dangerous precedent and could be used against NATO states in the future. This ignores the fact that the precedents for securing

assembly authority are already there; they have been conveniently forgotten, and bombing without any UN authority sets an even more dangerous precedent.

Notes

1. Art. 1(1) of the UN Charter.
2. Art. 24(1) of the UN Charter.
3. Arts. 10, 11(1), and 14 of the UN Charter.
4. (1946–1947) *Yearbook of the United Nations,* 51.
5. Saksena, *The United Nations,* 8–10.
6. Arts. 10, 11, and 16 of the League of Nations Covenant.
7. See, for example, Arts. 12(1), 13(4), 15(6), and 15(7) of the covenant.
8. Declaration by the United Nations; text in Russell and Muther, *A History of the United Nations,* App. C.
9. For text, see World Peace Foundation, *The United Nations in the Making: Basic Documents,* 9–10.
10. UNCIO 3, 2–17.
11. Ibid., 713. The veto is contained in Art. 27(3) of the UN Charter.
12. Tabulation in Bailey and Daws, *The Procedure,* 231.
13. It is not proposed here to review in any detail the UN's use of its peaceful settlement powers. The Security Council under chapter VI, the General Assembly under chapter IV, and the Secretary-General under chapter XV all have significant competence in this area and have produced thousands of resolutions and initiatives over the years. These may bear fruit themselves as the state parties or the factions within a country accept the initiatives. However, for intractable conflicts, it is often necessary for the Security Council, and exceptionally the General Assembly (but only in a recommendatory fashion), to deploy one or another of the mechanisms discussed here, illustrating the necessity of the United Nations having teeth and of using those teeth effectively. For more detail, see White, *Keeping the Peace,* 80–98, 193–198, 229–231.
14. UN SCOR, 2nd Sess., Special Supp. No. 1, 1947.
15. See generally Walter, "Security Council Control of Regional Action."
16. See U.S. Presidential Decision on U.S. Participation in UN Operations (1994) 33 ILM 795.
17. UN Blue Book Series, *The United Nations and Somalia, 1992–1996,* 33.
18. Saksena, *The United Nations,* 4–5.
19. Claude, *Power,* 110–168. Kupchan, "The Case for Collective Security," 42–44.
20. See White, *Keeping the Peace,* 141.
21. The Korean action received support from the General Assembly in GA Res. 376, 7 Oct. 1950. Less obvious support was forthcoming in the military response to the invasion of Kuwait—see, for example, GA Res. 46/135, 17 Dec. 1991. See also GA Res. 49/27, 5 Dec. 1994, on Haiti; GA Res. 49/206, 23 Dec.

1994, on Rwanda; GA Res. 48/146, 20 Dec. 1993, on Somalia; and GA Res. 50/193, 22 Dec. 1995, on Bosnia. Clearly, most of these endorsements were retrospective. See also Franck, "The United Nations as Guarantor," 25.

22. But see Sarooshi, *The United Nations,* 27–29.

23. Art. 24(1) of the UN Charter.

24. Sarooshi, *The United Nations,* 26–32.

25. See the resolution adopted by the North Atlantic Assembly of November 1998 (NATO Doc. AR 295 SA), cited in Simma, "NATO, the UN, and the Use of Force," 16.

26. *Expenses* case, ICJ Rep. 1962, 164–165.

27. Simma, "NATO, the UN, and the Use of Force," 17.

28. Art. 2(4) of the UN Charter; Charney, "Anticipatory Humanitarian Action," 835.

29. Franck, "Lessons of Kosovo," 860.

30. Arts. 45–47 of the UN Charter.

31. But see Quigley, "The United States and the United Nations."

32. This seems to be envisaged by Article 48 of the UN Charter, which provides in paragraph 1 that "the action required to carry out the decisions of the Security Council for the maintenance of international peace and security shall be taken by all the Members of the United Nations or by some of them, as the Security Council may determine." See also paragraph 2, which envisages such action by member states acting in "appropriate international agencies."

33. Gill, "Legal and Some Political Limitations on the Power of the UN Security Council," 61.

34. But see Sarooshi, *The United Nations,* 150.

35. SC Res. 1031, 15 Dec. 1995.

36. SC Res. 1244, 10 June 1999.

37. Lobel and Ratner, "Bypassing the Security Council," 125–127.

38. Sarooshi, *The United Nations,* 44.

39. See, for example, SC Res. 1154, 2 March 1998; White and Cryer, "Unilateral Enforcement of Resolution 687," 274.

40. SC Res. 688 of 5 April 1991 re OPERATION PROVIDE COMFORT (1996) in northern Iraq; SC Res. 687 of 3 April 1991 re, for example, OPERATION DESERT FOX (1998) against Iraq; SC Res. 1199 of 23 Sept. 1998 and 1203 of 24 Oct. 1998, re OPERATION ALLIED FORCE (1999) against the FRY.

41. Krisch, "Unilateral Enforcement of the Collective Will," 59.

42. Ibid., 94.

43. But see Cassese, "Ex Inuria Ius Oritur," 23.

44. See, for example, *Case Concerning Legality of the Use of Force (Yugoslavia v. United Kingdom),* Request [by the FRY] for Provisional Measures, 2 June 1999. The court refused to grant the request, although it did express its concern both at the loss of life in Kosovo and "with the use of force in Yugoslavia," which "under the present circumstances raises very serious issues of international law"—paras. 15–16.

45. Krisch, "Unilateral Enforcement of the Collective Will," 93. See his analysis of NATO claims at 81–86. The same can be said of the use of force by

Western states to protect the Kurds in northern Iraq in 1991, followed by airstrikes thereafter—see White, "The Legality of Bombing in the Name of Humanity," 34.

46. UN doc. S/1999/328.

47. See SC 3989th mtg, 26 March 1999.

48. Grieco, "Anarchy and the Limits of Cooperation," 485.

49. See generally Tsakaloyannis, "International Society at a Crossroads," 19; Hurrell, "International Society and the Study of Regimes," 49; Bull, "The Importance of Grotius," 71.

50. See debate in House of Commons, H.C. Deb., 25 March 1999, cols. 542–543 (re Kosovo).

51. Resolution on "Recasting Euro-Atlantic Security," adopted by North Atlantic Assembly, NATO doc. AR 295 SA (1998).

52. Art. 103 of the UN Charter.

53. In particular, Arts. 42 and 53 of the UN Charter. See McCoubrey, "Kosovo, NATO," 32–34.

54. Cited in Simma, "NATO, the UN, and the Use of Force," 15. See also the position of the United Kingdom reflected in the House of Commons Defence Select Committee in its Third Report, 31 March 1999, in which it declared that "insistence on a UN Security Council mandate for such [non–Article 5] operations would be unnecessary as well as covertly giving Russia a veto over Alliance action. All 19 Allies act in accordance with the principles of international law and we are secure in our assertion that the necessity of unanimous agreement for any action will ensure its legality"—para. 176.

55. Simma, "NATO, the UN, and the Use of Force," 20.

56. *Cases Concerning Questions of Interpretation and Application of the Montreal Convention Arising from the Aerial Incident at Lockerbie (Libya v. United Kingdom, Libya v. United States)*, ICJ Rep.1992, 3 and 114 (provisional measures); (1998) 37 ILM 587 (preliminary objections).

57. *Reparation* case, ICJ Rep. 1949, 185.

58. *Report of the Commission on Global Governance*, 242.

59. White, *Keeping the Peace*, 169–172.

60. Abstentions do not count as votes, so the required number of votes in favor of military action may not be as high as thought—see Kirgis, *International Organizations*, 213.

61. GA Res. 377, 3 Nov. 1950.

62. GA Res. 376, 7 Oct. 1950.

63. GA 301st plen. mtg., 1950.

64. Art. 11(2) of the UN Charter.

65. *Expenses* case, ICJ Rep. 1962, 162–165.

66. Bailey and Daws, *The Procedure*, 296.

67. *Expenses* case, ICJ Rep. 1962, 168.

68. Arts. 10 and 14 of the UN Charter.

69. SC Res. 119, 31 Oct. 1956 (United Kingdom and France voted against); SC Res. 157, 17 Sept. 1960 (USSR voted against).

70. White, *Keeping the Peace*, 254–261. But see the *Expenses* case, 177.

71. GA Res 376, 7 Oct. 1950.

72. See Farrar-Hockley, *The British Part in the Korean War,* 209.

73. Art. 20 of the UN Charter.

74. Simma, *The Charter,* 346.

75. Ibid., 235.

76. GA Res. 53/164, 9 Dec. 1998. Adopted by 122-3-34. Russia voted against the resolution and China abstained. The Russian vote against was explained in the GA Third Committee debate on the draft on the basis that the resolution did not sufficiently respect the territorial integrity of the FRY—UN Press Release GA/SHC/3511, 18 Nov. 1998.

77. Stone, *Legal Controls,* 234–237; Malanczuk, *Akehurst's Modern Introduction,* 392, 397; Rosow, "Until What?" 506–510; Schachter, "United Nations Law," 459–460; Lavalle, "The Law of the United Nations," 3, 62.

78. White and Ulgen, "The Decentralized Military Option"; Bowett, *United Nations Forces,* 45–47.

79. SC Res. 83, 27 June 1950.

80. (1996) 35 ILM 1095.

81. Gray, "After the Cease-Fire," 155, 173.

82. White, "Commentary on the Protection."

83. Lie, *In the Cause of Peace,* 334.

84. White, *Keeping the Peace,* 49.

85. SC Res. 1368, 12 Sept. 2001; SC Res. 1373, 28 Sept. 2001.

86. SC Res. 221, 9 April 1966.

87. On Operation ALBA, see Kritsiotis, "Security Council Resolution 1101."

88. SC Res. 794, 3 Dec. 1992.

89. SC Res. 940, 31 July 1994.

90. See Report of the Panel on United Nations Peace Operations (The Brahimi Report), UN docs. A/55/305, S/2000/809, 21 Aug. 2000.

91. See generally Drezner, "Bargaining, Enforcement, and Multilateral Sanctions."

92. Bethlehem, *The Kuwait Crisis,* xxxiv–xxxvi; UN doc. S/21585 (1990).

93. Bethlehem, *The Kuwait Crisis,* xliii.

94. SC Res. 665, 25 Aug. 1990.

95. Provisional records of the Sanctions Committee, 5th mtg., 31 Aug. 1991, in Bethlehem, *Kuwait Crisis,* 797.

96. SC Res. 706, 15 Aug. 1991.

97. General Comment No. 8, UN doc. E/C.12/1997/8. See also Reisman and Stevick, "The Applicability of International Law."

98. UN doc. S/12265 (1975).

99. SC Res. 873, 13 Oct. 1993, and SC Res. 875, 16 Oct. 1993.

100. SC Res. 917, 6 May 1994.

101. SC Res. 864, 15 Sept. 1993.

102. SC Res. 942, 23 Sept. 1994.

103. SC Res. 1373, 28 Sept. 2001.

104. ICJ Rep. 1962, 151.

105. For more detail on all forces, see UN, *The Blue Helmets: A Review of United Nations Peacekeeping,* 3rd ed. (1996).

106. SC Res. 47, 21 April 1948.

107. SC Res. 73, 11 Aug. 1949.

108. GA Res. 998, 3 Nov. 1956.

109. UN doc. A/6370 (1956). But see Garvey, "United Nations Peacekeeping."

110. Higgins, *Peacekeeping,* vol. 1, 339.

111. SC Res. 340, 25 Oct. 1973.

112. SC Res. 143, 17 July 1960.

113. GA Res. 1474, 20 Sept. 1960; SC Res, 161, 21 Feb. 1961, and SC Res. 169, 24 Nov. 1961.

114. UN doc. S/5240 (1963).

115. *Expenses* case, ICJ Rep. 1962, 177.

116. Report of the Panel on United Nations Peace Operations, UN docs. A/55/305, S/2000/809, 21 Aug. 2001, paras. 49–50.

117. For current peacekeeping forces, see <www.un.org/Depts/dpko>.

118. Lobel and Ratner, "Bypassing the Security Council," 153.

119. See McCoubrey, "Kosovo, NATO," 35–36, 38–39. Also contains a discussion on whether the bombing breached the requirements of the *jus in bello.*

120. Ibid., 38.

121. But see the case of Zaire, where the multilateral force under Canadian command decided not to intervene during 1996–1997 upon its own assessment of the refugee crisis, despite receiving authorization from the Security Council—SC Res. 1080, 15 Nov. 1996.

7

Support for Democracy

In this chapter I contend that support for democracy is not a post–Cold War phenomenon at the United Nations. Rather, democracy and support for democracy are grounded in the UN Charter, in the purposes and principles of the organization. The rights and duties this creates for the United Nations and its member states will be discussed throughout this chapter. In general terms, the firmer the foundation in the UN Charter, as developed by subsequent practice, the greater the potential support for democracy has for sustained development and increased legitimacy, namely, the ability to pull the UN community to compliance.[1] An examination of the development of the basic constitutional principles of self-determination and peace by the United Nations, accompanied by the development of democracy from the right to self-determination, will reveal not only the legal basis of support for democracy in the United Nations but also the legal principles that should govern it. I argue that the norms governing support for democracy have come from the HRC operating under the ICCPR.

My focus will then turn to the main mechanisms of support for democracy provided by the United Nations for emerging or established states. For reasons of space, I concentrate in particular on the procedural aspects of democracy (principally electoral assistance) rather than the substantive development of democracy within the wider concerns of good governance. The latter would demand that I cover the activities of the UNDP, as well as several specialized agencies like UNESCO, the IMF, and the World Bank.[2] Such activities can typically occur in an effort to deepen and strengthen democracy following a UN-supervised election. Thus I primarily look at the first (procedural) stage and only touch on the second (substantive) stage (see Chapter 11 for more on this).[3]

Whereas consensus can be achieved on the legal principles governing the first stage, the second stage tends to be dominated by political and economic concerns. The analysis of the first stage will have two main components: an examination of electoral assistance as an aspect of multifunctional UN peacekeeping forces, and an examination of the assistance provided by the UN's Electoral Assistance Division (EAD).[4] The principles under which support for democracy is provided on the ground by the United Nations need to be discerned in order to ensure compatibility with constitutional principles.

The Promotion of Democracy

The question of whether the United Nations is founded upon constitutional principles or is a product of a mere "interstate compact" has been considered in Chapter 1.[5] It was seen that there is an increasing recognition that the UN Charter "has become the constitution of the international community."[6] As depicted in Chapter 3, the purposes and principles of the constitutional order are elaborated in the preamble as well as articles 1 and 2: peace, self-determination, human rights, sovereign equality, qualified nonintervention, and, more recently, protecting the environment. The purposes and principles are the standards set for the United Nations and its members; many have developed into recognized legal rights belonging to peoples and individuals. Others remain at the level of rights and duties of members and the United Nations itself. By firmly establishing democracy as an aspect of internal self-determination, it can be shown that states are under a duty to respect and uphold it and that the United Nations is under an obligation to promote it within states in accordance with article 55 of the UN Charter.[7] The point is that democracy is not discretionary or optional for member states or for the United Nations in promoting it within member states.

However, democracy, or greater democratization, is probably optional for the United Nations itself. As the United Nations moves toward constitutionalism, its defects become manifest—the lack of true separation of powers and a democratic deficit within the United Nations despite the words of the preamble—"We the Peoples of the United Nations." Although this chapter is not concerned with exploring the lack of democracy within the United Nations itself (see Chapter 4), it does impact the UN's increasing concern with democratization within member states. The legitimacy of the UN's concern with democracy within states will be enhanced if UN reforms move toward direct representation at the United Nations itself. The involvement of NGOs in the workings of ECOSOC is not sufficient by itself.

It was argued in Chapter 4 that the issue is one of democracy in member states more so than increasing direct representation in the United Nations. Democratically elected governments should be able to represent peoples more effectively at the United Nations than non-democratically elected ones. However, the fact that this is not always the case indicates that a deepening of democracy is needed within member states to enable elected governments to represent the will of the people on the international stage, not just at home. This is not to eschew reform of the United Nations itself, where too much concentration of power in the Security Council, combined with the weaknesses of the other principal organs, means that many of the UN's more meaningful decisions are unrepresentative. Reform of the United Nations is required, including the involvement of nonstate actors. However, given that the core character of the United Nations as an intergovernmental organization is unlikely to change, the most effective way to develop democracy at the United Nations is to promote a type of democracy within states that makes elected governments accountable to the electorate for their foreign policy decisions. In this way the member states' representatives at the United Nations will be truly representative.

Self-Determination and Democracy

It was argued in Chapter 3 that democracy is a development of self-determination, which through UN practice has become the most established third-generation right. Given the rapid evolution of UN democracy promotion, it is important to elaborate upon this development. Article 1(2) posits that a purpose of the United Nations is the development of friendly relations among nations "based on respect for the principle of equal rights and self-determination of peoples." The principle of self-determination is also found in article 55, said to create a general obligation on the United Nations, in particular the General Assembly, which under article 13 is given general competence regarding human rights. The UN Charter does not elaborate on the principle of self-determination, though it can be argued that the declaration on non–self-governing territories contained in articles 73 and 74, creating certain obligations for administering powers, is the only concrete application of the principle in the charter.

The importance of UN practice in relation to non–self-governing territories must not be underestimated in the development of democracy assistance. The Trusteeship Council developed a practice from 1956 in regard to British Togoland in sending observers to monitor and, in later cases, oversee preindependence plebiscites, elections, and referenda.[8] Furthermore, "although the UN had an express legal right to intervene in and validate the democratic process within trust territories, it also found grounds for exercising a supervisory role in colonial elections and referendums immediately prior to independence."[9]

The growth in UN practice through the Trusteeship Council and the General Assembly from non–self-governing territories and colonial possessions culminated in the UN Transition Assistance Group (UNTAG) in Namibia in 1989. UNTAG bridges the Cold War era and the post–Cold War era and shows that democracy assistance is not a recent phenomenon. A continuity in this type of democracy assistance can also be discerned in the recent popular consultation conducted under UN auspices with the people of East Timor on 30 August 1999.

In addition to practice on the ground, the United Nations developed the principle of self-determination in its declaratory, or lawmaking (in a soft law sense), role. Through this process self-determination has been elevated to a general legal right recognized by the ICJ.[10] The development of the right has occurred primarily through two General Assembly resolutions: the Declaration on the Granting of Independence to Colonial Countries and Peoples of 1960,[11] and the Declaration on Principles of International Law Concerning Friendly Relations and Co-operation Among States in Accordance with the Charter of the United Nations (the Declaration on Friendly Relations) of 1970.[12] In addition, there are the two UN-sponsored International Covenants on Human Rights of 1966, which both guarantee in article 1 the right of peoples to self-determination. The protection of self-determination by the committees empowered to uphold the two covenants has provided content to the right.

The current status of UN law on self-determination is summarized: "a rule of international law by which the political future of a colonial or similar non-independent territory should be determined in accordance with the wishes of its inhabitants, within the limits of the principle of *uti possidetis*." Identifying this as the "external aspect" of self-determination, the author contends its "internal aspect" "may require that governments generally have a democratic base, and that minorities be allowed political autonomy."[13] It is from the internal aspect of self-determination that the value of democracy has grown apace with the end of the Cold War. However, unlike self-determination, democracy is not a people's right but can be seen as an individual right. "While democracy invokes the right of each *person* to participate in governance, self-determination is about the social right of a *people* to constitute a nation state."[14]

The democratic entitlement also reinforces other core principles of the UN system—justice, human rights, and peace. The concept of "positive peace" covers all these aspects (see Chapter 3) and has culminated in the General Assembly including within it respect for democracy.[15] Such a peace is reinforced by the fact that democracies rarely wage war, especially against one another.[16] Further, fully democratic governments are less likely to use force against their own people.[17] The link between democracy and peace can be seen in many of the UN-brokered peace agreements, of which electoral assistance is but a part (discussed below).

Democracy and Human Rights

The institutionalization of democratic entitlement from abstract value to concrete individual right has occurred through the practice of UN organs, agencies, and bodies set up under UN-sponsored treaties. This has occurred through the principle of self-determination, which has developed into a right belonging to a people, and also through the principle of individual human rights protection.

In setting the general standards to which the United Nations and member states should aspire, the work of the HRC operating under the ICCPR is of primary importance. The ICCPR provides further support for the right of democracy in article 25, which builds on article 21 of the assembly's 1948 UDHR.[18] The UDHR remedied the lack of substantive human rights provisions in the charter, but its form as a General Assembly resolution and consequent lack of immediate legal obligation led to the drafting of the two international covenants in the UN Human Rights Commission. With this method the United Nations developed an international bill of rights, which forms an important pillar of UN law and, through its development by the HRC, provides some fundamental principles upon which the promotion of democracy should be based.

There is no requirement in the UN Charter that states be democratic; article 4 of the UN Charter requires only that member states be "peace-loving."[19] And though the conditions on membership have not changed, states have been able to agree on the need for democracy, or at least the procedural aspects in the form of elections.

The 1948 UDHR, in article 21, provides "that everyone has the right to take part in the government of his country, directly or through freely chosen representatives." Article 25 of the ICCPR builds on article 21 of the UDHR by stipulating that

> every citizen shall have the right and the opportunity . . . without unreasonable restrictions: (a) to take part in the conduct of public affairs, directly or through freely chosen representatives; (b) to vote and to be elected at genuine periodic elections which shall be by universal and equal suffrage and shall be held by secret ballot, guaranteeing the free expression of the will of the electors.

This provision is probably the most important source in the search for a legal standard for the promotion of democracy by the United Nations and is cited as such by the UN bodies operating in the field. Under the ICCPR, alleged breaches of article 25 can be the subject matter of individual claims under the optional protocol. This has permitted the HRC to develop jurisprudence on the obligations created under article 25 for state parties, thus ensuring that the norm does not exist at the abstract level like so many others in international law. Although not legally binding upon the state parties to the covenant, the decisions and views of the HRC are the most authoritative interpretation of its provisions. Even more important is the HRC's recently produced general comment on article 25 setting out a more general interpretation.[20]

Although the term "democracy" appears only twice in the general comment, the HRC emphasizes at the outset that "whatever form of constitution or government is in force," "Article 25 lies at the core of democratic government based on the consent of the people."[21] The covenant does not call for a specific democratic model to be adopted by state parties. Article 25 does seem to provide the minimum foundations upon which a democracy can be built. In fact, the general comment includes all the essential conditions attributed to a democratic system. Starting from a broad conception of "the conduct of public affairs" in article 25(a), including the exercise of legislative, executive, and administrative powers, the HRC continues that

> it is implicit in Article 25 that, where citizens participate through freely chosen representatives, those representatives do in fact exercise governmental power and that they are accountable through the electoral process for their exercise of that power. It is also implicit that the representatives exercise only those powers which are allocated to them in accordance with constitutional provisions. Participation through freely chosen representatives is exercised through voting processes which must be established by laws which are in accordance with paragraph (b).[22]

This link between paragraphs (a) and (b) of article 25 affirms the fundamental concept of popular sovereignty. However, an important restriction
on participation in public affairs is found in the 1992 HRC decision in
Mikmaq People v. Canada. The Canadian prime minister had refused to
allow the Mikmaq people specific participation at special constitutional
conferences convened for the purpose of clarifying aboriginal rights. In
response to the claim by the Mikmaq, the HRC stated that

> it cannot be the meaning of Article 25(a) that every citizen may deter-
> mine either to take part directly in the conduct of public affairs or to
> leave it to freely chosen representatives. It is for the legal and consti-
> tutional system of the State party to provide for the modalities of such
> participation. Article 25(a) cannot be understood as an unconditional
> right to choose the *modalities* of participation in the conduct of pub-
> lic affairs.[23]

The UN Centre for Human Rights, in considering the modalities for UN
electoral assistance, has correctly stated that this case is "a useful general principle with regard to political participation, indicating the importance of respect for the legal principles of a particular state."[24]

In relation to article 25(b), the HRC's general comment clarifies
common electoral principles: universal and equal suffrage, secret bal-
loting, and free elections. Although no electoral system is posited by the
HRC, it does state that the principle of one-person, one-vote must apply.
The choice is between majority and proportional representation systems.[25] Furthermore, as to the meaning of "genuine" elections, the HRC
emphasizes that "genuine periodic elections are essential to ensure the
accountability of representatives. . . . Such elections must be held at in-
tervals . . . which ensure that the authority of government continues to
be based on the free expression of the will of electors." Read together
with the HRC statement that "political parties play a significant role in
. . . the election process,"[26] this corroborates the conclusion that an election process in which voters have no meaningful choice between parties
or candidates and cannot express that choice without compulsion or fear
is not "genuine" but constitutes a violation of article 25.[27] In effect the
HRC's jurisprudence is at odds with the one-party political system.[28]

However, the rights contained in article 25 are, according to the language of that provision, subject to reasonable restrictions. From various
individual complaints upheld by the HRC, the deprivation of all political rights for fifteen years by a military regime is unreasonable.[29] But
for difficult questions relating to such issues as financial support for
candidates during the election campaign, there is no jurisprudence. Such

matters will hopefully come before the HRC as its jurisprudence develops and may well, in the meantime, be resolved in a practical way by the Secretary-General and the EAD when providing electoral assistance on the ground. For guidance, the UN machinery should have regard for the developed jurisprudence of the European Court of Human Rights in the promotion of democracy.[30]

The General Assembly, Elections, and Democratization

Other sources of UN support for democracy are the General Assembly's declaratory resolutions on the matter. The assembly's concern with election supervision and democratization derives from its authority over the Trusteeship Council under article 85 of the UN Charter, as well as its general competence over self-determination and human rights matters under article 55 of the charter. The end of the Cold War has enabled it to adapt its previously restricted competence over trusteeship and colonial territories to neocolonial situations (Namibia, East Timor), the emergence of new states (Eritrea), and, increasingly, independent states.

This new concern corresponds with the end of the Cold War. However, rather than being an aspect of the agenda of the Western victors,[31] the assembly's concern with elections and democratization is reflective of a much more profound support among nation-states for democracy,[32] which arose with the ending of ideologies based on dictatorship and the one-party state.

The General Assembly made a tentative start in the late 1980s.[33] In resolutions 43/157 and 44/146 (the so-called elections resolutions), its support for the principle of periodic and genuine elections embodied in the UDHR and ICCPR focused on apartheid in South Africa. The 1989 resolution did state that "determining the will of the people requires an electoral process that provides an equal opportunity for all citizens to become candidates and put forward their political views, individually and in co-operation with others within constitutional and national legislation," thereby establishing very basic principles—what could be called UN law on elections.

However, the resolution also reiterated that states are free to choose their own electoral systems after emphasizing the principle of sovereign equality.[34] The sovereignty principle was strengthened through a balancing resolution on respect for the principles of national sovereignty and noninterference in the internal affairs of states in the electoral process. Resolution 44/147 (the so-called sovereignty resolution) emphasized article 2(7) of the UN Charter and affirmed that it "is the sole concern of peoples to determine methods and to establish institutions regarding the electoral process"; it also expressed support for the majority in South Africa and the Palestinian people.[35] The Cold War feel of this resolution was reflected in the fact that eleven Western states voted against it. However, the greater UN concern with free and fair elections was reflected in the fact that the more positive resolution—44/146—was adopted without a vote.[36]

These two resolutions reflect the increasing intrusiveness of the General Assembly and the diminishing majority opposing it. In addition, the resolutions evince an increasing specification of UN law on the democratic entitlement. The 1991 elections resolution recognized that "electoral verification by the UN should remain an exceptional activity . . . to be undertaken in well-defined circumstances, *inter alia,* primarily in situations with a clear international dimension," which appears to be a step backward. Yet this was balanced by the fact that the resolution recognizes the value of electoral assistance provided by the United Nations via the technical and advisory services of the UN Human Rights Centre. The recognition of practical assistance, albeit in exceptional circumstances, moves the United Nations from reinforcing an abstract value to concrete action.[37] The 1991 sovereignty resolution—46/130—remained essentially unchanged and yet attracted less support.[38]

The development of practical help can be seen in the elections resolutions of the 1990s. Resolution 47/138 welcomed the Secretary-General's decision to establish the Electoral Assistance Unit within the Secretariat. The resolution did not refer to exceptional circumstances but to the principle of electoral assistance provided to member states at their request, on a case-by-case basis according to guidelines prepared by the Secretariat.[39] Later resolutions noted the need for: adequate time to carry out a mission; the existence of conditions which would allow for free and fair elections; and significant postelection assistance to strengthen a pluralistic civil society.[40] The consolidation of democracies is recognized in 1997's resolution 52/129, which states the need to support the process in subsequent elections in countries that have already had first-time democratic elections. The United Nations should help in national electoral institutions, in civic education, and in the overall consolidation of the democratization process. The resolution also recommends that UN electoral assistance be geared towards comprehensive observation of the electoral process, beginning with registration and other pre-election activities and continuing through the campaign, election day and the announcement of the election results, in instances where more than technical assistance is required by the requesting state.[41]

This is a far cry from the exceptional provision of electoral assistance promulgated in the 1991 resolution.

The terminology of the UN resolutions in this area has changed as well. The terms "democratization," and "elections" have been referred to increasingly in the elections resolutions, signifying a deeper concern than the facilitation of elections. In 1995 this led to a new line of assembly resolutions (the so-called democracy resolutions) promoting and consolidating new or restored democracies.[42] These resolutions are abstract, referring to values such as "peace, democracy, justice, equality, the rule of law, pluralism, development, better standards of living and solidarity" and continue to attract consensus; they seem to support the elections resolutions.[43] The 1998 democracy resolution—53/31—again adopted without a vote, expresses the assembly's appreciation of the Secretary-General's report that recommends

building a political culture through human rights observance, mobilization of civil society, electoral assistance, free and independent media, enhancing the rule of law, and improving accountability, transparency and quality of public sector management and democratic structures of government.[44]

Although providing principles on which UN support for democracy should be based, the General Assembly also affirms the two fundamental tenets upon which the United Nations operates in this area. First, there is recognition of "the legitimacy of different national, political, economic and cultural systems."[45] Although not as clear as the HRC on the incompatibility of one-party systems, the General Assembly's elections and democracy resolutions are based on multiparty democratic entitlement. Second, there is the UN's impartiality in this area among competing elements and in its treatment of different countries. In UN peacekeeping missions, although the United Nations generally maintains impartiality within each country, it is guilty of not treating like cases alike. Selectivity, unfortunately, is present in the UN system.

Multifunctional Peacekeeping Operations

In recognizing the link between democracy and peace, peacekeeping operations have moved from traditional UN Emergency Force operations, which tried to keep the parties from fighting, to sophisticated multifaceted operations as in Namibia, Nicaragua, Cambodia, and elsewhere.[46] Here I consider electoral supervision within peacekeeping operations under a consensual mandate. Such operations, although elaborate, can still be seen as supporting democracy. Their complexity stems from the fact that the United Nations is helping the state, and the people, gain freedom from war through the development of positive peace. Although normally assisting the peace process with agreement of the parties, the United Nations has occasionally, in the cases of West Irian (1962–1963) and Cambodia (1991–1993), assumed temporary sovereignty over a country, administering it during the transitional period.

This type of operation was resurrected toward the end of the Cold War with the UN operation in Namibia in 1989. UNTAG entailed a peacekeeping operation to supervise not only a cease-fire between the South West African People's Organization and South African forces but also free and fair elections leading to an independent state. The combination of elections and peacekeeping, though successful in Namibia after initial breaches of the cease-fire, is a high-risk strategy. The UNTAG operation shows that the process will often need to be conducted within a regional context if the democratizing country is to remain stable during the transition. Furthermore, crucial to success is the need for continuing consent and cooperation, especially after the polls are closed and the results announced. The lack of adequate impartial UN security personnel can lead to a breakdown in order as defeated factions try to fill the constitutional and political void before the new government takes office. In East Timor in 1999 a free and fair ballot was followed by violence that went unchecked by the Indonesian armed forces and police. The 5 May 1999 agreement between the United Nations, Portugal, and Indonesia that led to the referendum on the status of East Timor was not only vague as to Indonesia's commitments on security but also focused almost exclusively on Indonesia's responsibilities in the period leading up to the ballot.[47]

The United Nations has to be scrupulously fair and treat all factions equally. This is difficult in multifunctional operations compared to traditional peacekeeping (when it is difficult enough). The postponement of the referendum in Western Sahara is evidence of this. The small number of monitors (about 350) under the United Nations Mission for the Referendum in Western Sahara (MINURSO) compounded the problem of drawing up the list of those entitled to vote, with the inevitable result that the United Nations was accused of bias toward Morocco.[48] With two of the basic principles of peacekeeping in jeopardy, namely, cooperation and impartiality, prospects for success in this long-running dispute are doubtful.

The win-or-lose electoral contest presents difficult issues for the United Nations. The organization has slowly realized that elections cannot be the sole method of transition from war to peace, from a one-party state to democracy. This partly explains the greater involvement of UNDP in later operations in Mozambique, for example. Although the UN-supervised elections of September 1992 in Angola were deemed free and fair by the Secretary-General's representative, they did not bring peace and democracy.[49] The losers in the election, UNITA, took up arms again despite attempts by the Security Council to restore the peace process. The Security Council's last mandated operation was withdrawn in February 1999.[50]

In contrast, one can point to the success of democratization in Mozambique. In October 1997 free and fair elections were held under UN auspices. The elections were

> a culmination of a major success story in United Nations peacemaking, peace-keeping, and humanitarian and election assistance. Through a complex, multifaceted and highly innovative strategy which broke new ground in how the United Nations dealt with parties in a conflict situation, a formerly socialist Government, committed to a one-party State, negotiated with an armed, rebellious group to create peace for their country.[51]

The mandate of the UN Operation in Mozambique (ONUMOZ) was to verify and monitor the implementation of the peace agreement signed by the government of Mozambique and the Mozambique National Resistance in Rome on 4 October 1992. The peace accords required the United Nations to supervise the cease-fire between the two parties, provide security for key transport corridors, monitor a comprehensive disarmament and demobilization program, coordinate and monitor humanitarian assistance operations throughout the country, and provide assistance and verification for national elections.[52]

UN supervision of the election was the last stage in the settlement but the first stage in democratization. Preparation for the elections was substantial, with the United Nations concentrating on converting the warring factions into peaceful political parties through finance as well as advice and assistance from the EAD and UNDP.[53] After a considerable number of obstacles were overcome, and with UN encouragement, the parties finally approved the National Elections Commission and a system of elections by proportional representation.[54] The National Elections Commission laid down a timetable and was responsible for the "conduct, preparation and organization of the elections."[55] The electoral division of ONUMOZ

> established its own network of monitoring activities, with 148 officers stationed throughout the provinces to cover voter registration, civic education, political campaigns and party political access to, as well as impartiality of, the media, polling, vote counting and vote tabulation at the provincial counting centres. Complaints of alleged irregularities in the electoral process were to be transmitted to the [National Elections Commission], while ONUMOZ was mandated to carry out separate investigations.[56]

In the end there were 2,300 observers from the United Nations, European Union, and NGOs as well as up to 35,000 monitors from the different parties—again illustrating the greater emphasis on the parties to undertake settlement.[57] This contrasts, for example, with the earlier UN Transition Assistance Authority in Cambodia (UNTAC), where a considerably larger force (more than 20,000) was deployed and the emphasis was to push through a UN settlement of the conflict.[58] The electoral process in Mozambique was peaceful, and the United Nations declared the elections free and fair despite a last-minute boycott of the first day of the three-day voting period.[59]

The success of ONUMOZ is explained by the Secretary-General as being due to "the deep desire of the Mozambican people—and of the principal parties involved in the process—for peace."[60] The involvement of the parties in the institutions and mechanisms from cease-fire to election is essential if the United Nations is to succeed with a smaller force. Parties' lack of commitment to the peace process can lead to its unraveling under a small force, as in the case of Angola, so a much larger force is needed, as evidenced by the United Nations Angola Verification Missions (UNAVEM II to UNAVEM III) and by the significant presence of UNTAC in Cambodia. ONUMOZ illustrates the importance of UN impartiality in the process and shows how the process is strengthened if the parties agree on all aspects of the transition to democracy, from the constitution to the method and procedures of election. ONUMOZ shows the value of democracy *assistance* by the United Nations, as opposed to some form of democracy *imposition*.

However, in the case of ONUMOZ some 6,500 UN troops were needed to ensure security during the elections. ONUMOZ compares favorably to the United Nations Assistance Mission in East Timor (UNAMET), which initially only had 280 civilian police in addition to referendum monitors.[61] The Security Council, when mandating UNAMET on 11 June 1999, also authorized sending fifty military liaison officers.[62] The United Nations realized before the ballot result was announced on 3 September 1999 that its low level of involvement was a high-risk strategy. Indeed, the Secretary-General stated in May that many East Timorese had "unrealistic expectations" of the United Nations—"which cannot be met."[63]

The problem was evident during the signing of the agreement with Indonesia on 5 May 1999, when at a press conference no satisfactory answer was given to a pointed question directed to the Secretary-General: "How can you say that Indonesia will be in charge of security when it has been the perpetrator of violence in East Timor for 23 years and killed about 200,000 Timorese?"[64] The Secretary-General's response was that "realistically" the United Nations had to address the Indonesian government and accept its position that it was to be in charge of security. Did the United Nations have to accept this position? It is easy to say with hindsight that it did not, but the extremely low level of UN involvement in such a volatile and long-standing conflict was inadequate.

Despite difficulties for peacekeepers in Angola, Western Sahara, and East Timor, the successes in Nicaragua, El Salvador, Namibia, Cambodia, and Mozambique have ensured the development of this precarious but potentially rewarding method of settlement. Nevertheless, the strain on the UN's budget, the uncertainties about the success of election supervision, and the extent to which the world community sees election supervision as part of the right to democracy call into question whether the UN's combined approach to peacekeeping and election supervision will continue. Current signs are that it will, as illustrated by the UN's commitments in Guatemala, Liberia, the Central African Republic, and, more recently, in Sierra Leone and East Timor.

Mechanisms for the Promotion of Democracy

Although multifunctional forces are still on the agenda, the trend seems to be toward less intrusive assistance. Although recognizing the need to deploy multifaceted peacekeeping operations in violent and volatile situations, the United Nations has developed other forms of support for democracy.[65] Indeed, it is noticeable how quickly, at least in UN terms, the organization developed a sophisticated set of responses, allowing flexibility in requests for assistance.[66] However, even though the numbers are impressively high, the low level of assistance in some situations smacks of tokenism.[67]

The United Nations provides seven basic types of electoral assistance:[68]

1. The organization and conduct of the electoral process. This is the deluxe service whereby the United Nations does virtually everything in regard to the preparation for and conduct of the elections, including, if necessary, the provision of a peacekeeping force, as witnessed in Cambodia.

2. Supervision of the electoral process. Here the United Nations certifies all stages of the electoral process in order to guarantee the legitimacy of the result. This is most useful in the context of decolonization and often forms part of a peacekeeping operation, as in Namibia.

3. Verification of the electoral process. This is still a high level of UN involvement, as the purpose is to verify the free and fair nature of elections conducted by national authorities. The United Nations has to commit enough personnel to cover the country and make a declaration as to the fairness of the elections. This is often used as part of a peacekeeping operation in a sovereign independent state, for example, in Angola, El Salvador, Haiti, Nicaragua, Mozambique, and South Africa.

The operation in East Timor in 1999 seems to fit in this third category, but as with South Africa, it was not a robust UN presence. However, UNAMET, not the Indonesian authorities, was responsible for the organization and conduct of the ballot on 30 August 1999.[69] This suggests that it was not a verification presence but a supervision mission (i.e., level two). This was made clearer by the Security Council after the ballot result was announced, in which the East Timorese rejected autonomy and therefore opted for independence by an overwhelming majority. The Security Council, in condemning the violence, not only endorsed the verdict as "an accurate reflection of the views of the East

Timorese people" but also thanked the Secretary-General and UNAMET for *organizing* and *conducting* the consultation.[70] This makes the incongruity between the reality of UNAMET, with its limited resources, and its mandate even greater. The Secretary-General made it clear that UNAMET was not a level-four operation, as it was not responsible for coordinating international observers.[71] UNAMET therefore seems to sit uncomfortably between levels two and three, reflecting the compromises that gained the consent of the Indonesian government. If the Namibia model had been truly followed, and this is the most suitable, then a military component of at least 5,000 armed troops should have been mandated, along with a larger police element (UNTAG had 1,500 police) in addition to the election monitors. Whether this would have been sufficient to prevent the violence is not clear.

The next four levels of assistance are:

4. Coordination of international observers. This level of assistance appears to be the third most frequently provided (after levels six and seven) due to "its effectiveness and relative economy."[72] Here the United Nations coordinates all the international observers requested by the government. The United Nations effectively molds a disparate collection of individuals into a joint international observer group by briefing the observers on basic standards of election observation. Since this lower level does not involve direct UN observation, the United Nations does not make a final statement on the conduct of the elections.

5. Support for national observers. Here the EAD trains national observers to create an internal method for validating the elections. This was used in 1994 in Mexico, a relatively stable state in which the legitimacy of the election process was nonetheless under scrutiny. "This approach is best applied in countries that are relatively well developed and pluralistic, and possess a viable community of [NGOs] willing to participate in national election supervision."[73]

6. Observation. Here a small team or a single observer is sent to observe an electoral process and report to the Secretary-General. However, the United Nations recognizes that this could be used to give legitimacy to an electoral process and could be seen as largely symbolic. The United Nations therefore recognizes that it will be provided only in special circumstances, though the nature of those circumstances is unclear and is perhaps contradicted by the many examples of this level.

7. Technical assistance. Although designated the lowest level of assistance, in reality it must rank higher than level six. It is also the most frequently requested. Examples include advice to electoral authorities; design of electoral systems; computerization of electoral rolls; voter education; advice on drafting electoral laws; advice on constitutional reform; training of poll officers; preparation of an identity-card system; advice on security at elections; purchase of electoral materials such as ballot papers; and advice on counting. The increasing provision of post-election assistance perhaps ought to be included at this level and may include reform of the electoral system and the civil service.[74]

Regarding the conditions for providing electoral assistance, there is a divide between the first three levels as compared to the rest. In the first three the United Nations is prepared to declare that the elections are free and fair. This confers considerable international legitimacy on national elections. The high level of UN involvement at level one almost guarantees that there will be such a declaration, whereas there can be no such guarantees at the next two levels. In all three, there are certain risks to the UN's credibility, and so it is not surprising that a formal mandate is required from either the Security Council (in the case of high security risks—levels one and two) or the General Assembly (mainly level three).

Levels four through seven can be undertaken by the EAD controlled by the Secretary-General. The Secretary-General will report annually on all levels to the assembly, as well as on specific operations under council mandate to the Security Council as well, which acts as the ultimate control mechanism. Although there are mechanisms of political accountability by which the UN organs can review the actions of the Secretary-General and the EAD, there is the need for legal guidance from the ICJ, especially after the debacle in East Timor, where the UN's own guidelines were not followed.

The mandate (levels one through three) or the actions of the EAD (level four through seven) depend on a prior request by the country to the Secretary-General, at least three months before the proposed election. This request will be followed by a needs assessment mission, which must assess the degree of support for elections and elections assistance within the country and determine whether the basic conditions are present for a democratic process.[75] Although not stated as a prerequisite, it is normal for the United Nations to secure the consent of all factions rather than just the government. This reflects the need to have in place more than mere formal legal requirements. Although with peacekeeping and electoral supervision operations the consent of the government is a legal prerequisite, in reality true consent is obtained only by gaining the agreement of all factions and, ideally, of the civilian population.

Although earlier UN documents also referred to there being "a clear international dimension to the situation" before any level of assistance is authorized, this reflects an early approach that saw assistance as exceptional.[76] This requirement has been dropped in later guidelines, although in reality it may well still apply, certainly as to the higher-risk assistance operations.

One final condition that reflects the strong support for state sovereignty in the General Assembly is that UN electoral assistance "does not seek to impose any given political model"; rather it is based on the premise that there are a variety of models of democracy reflecting the "particular needs, aspirations and historical realities of the people involved, *taken within the framework of international standards.*"[77] Of course, sovereignty is ultimately protected by the requirement of consent, though in exceptional cases, that is, where the denial or removal of democracy is deemed to be a threat to the peace by the Security Council, it can use economic and military measures to impose or reimpose democracy.[78] Even after a consensual UN operation that leads to an election, the Security Council may need to ensure stability by authorizing a chapter VII military enforcement operation. Such was the case on 15 September 1999, when the Security Council authorized an Australian-led multinational force to restore peace and security in East Timor.[79]

The Australian-led coalition of the willing managed to restore order on the island and was able to hand over to the UN Transitional Administration in East Timor (UNTAET) in February 2000. This chapter VII–mandated operation,[80] along with the UN Interim Administration in Kosovo (UNMIK), also created under chapter VII,[81] represent a new development for UN peacekeeping or peace support operations, though Cambodia and Bosnia are partial precedents from the 1990s. UNTAET has a mandate that includes the maintenance of law and order, the establishment of an effective administration, the development of social services, capacity-building for self-government and sustainable development, as well as humanitarian assistance. Election monitoring is a part of the UN's support for democracy, itself a significant part of the UN's state-building enterprise. UNMIK's mandate covers law and order and other similar elements to UNTAET. The crucial difference is that whereas East Timor is being prepared for statehood, the future status of Kosovo within the FRY is uncertain. UNMIK's mandate is to establish substantial autonomy and self-government and to facilitate processes to determine the province's future. Nevertheless, both UNTAET and UNMIK share many features, making them the effective sovereign authority in the two territories. In many ways this represents a new form of peace-keeping, although its origins can be traced to earlier concepts of trustee-ship and protectorate.

State-building is exceptional; support for democracy in the form of election monitoring is the norm. These operations are typically not mandated under chapter VII and thus consent is the basis. In this context, the constraining international standards derive from the embodiment of self-determination (and democracy) as fundamental purposes of the UN Charter and, furthermore, as specific rights in article 21 of the UDHR and article 25 of the ICCPR.[82] Other standards affirmed by the United Nations include nondiscrimination, freedom of opinion, freedom of expression and information, freedom of assembly, freedom of association, and an independent judiciary. These abstract concepts, drawn from the same legal instruments, translate into concrete conditions that provide the UN framework for assistance operations. Some of these derive from the legal instruments mentioned above; others are legitimate practical extrapolations.[83] They are: the need for a secret ballot; universal suffrage; one-person, one-vote; periodicity (one-time elections will not suffice);[84] a multiparty system; a free and independent media; transparency of the election process; the recognition of the rule of law and the establishment of a judicial system with the power of review; and politicians and public officials who serve the public, not themselves.[85] These are the elements necessary to ensure the commencement of the process of democratization by means of a free and fair election, whereby the political will of the people is fully expressed.[86] "In essence, these standards represent the views of the international community as a whole."[87] Of course, the achievement of these standards by a state with the help of the United Nations is only the first real step along the path to democracy. However, there is no doubt that such an achievement is an essential precondition for the further development and entrenchment of democracy within a state, a process that may well need assistance from other elements of the UN system.

Conclusion

There has been an evolution in the UN's involvement in support for democracy. From abstract concepts of human rights and self-determination in the UN Charter, now there is a recognized democracy entitlement, embodied in the UDHR and the ICCPR and based on "the ideal of political power based on the will of the people," respect for the rule of law, and human rights.[88] The General Assembly, based on its trustee and colonial experiences, has since the 1990s developed a set of general principles on electoral assistance. These have been converted into practical modalities for providing assistance by the Secretary-General, the UN Centre for Human Rights, the Electoral Assistance Division, and, increasingly, the UNDP.

Although maintaining respect for the sovereignty of member states by insisting on the need for consent and by respecting the individuality of peoples and cultures, the United Nations has shaped a convincing legal framework within which it will operate. It has thus produced an increasingly concrete set of requirements for free and fair elections. Although there is room for choice by member states, they cannot step outside the parameters if they require the imprimatur of the United Nations. The United Nations must be careful not to relax these parameters, except on rare occasions, but on the whole elections are capable of being declared free and fair. Furthermore, the United Nations must be careful not to be drawn into tokenism, enabling a state to illegitimately claim the UN seal of approval. Finally, the United Nations must ensure that the level of assistance rendered is commensurate with the task. East Timor provides a stark reminder to the United Nations of this requirement.

Although some of the elements of the UN framework principles can be viewed as promoting a liberal view of democracy—multiparty democracy based on the rule of law—this is acceptable to the vast majority of states. The direction a fledgling democracy develops after a UN-supervised election is a politically charged issue. The legal framework regulates the political choices, but the aim of promoting democracy is to remove the one-party state and dictatorships and reduce corruption in civil society. There is no direct coercion of the international community of states in this direction, although individual states may be coerced by the Security Council. There is an irrepressible movement toward democracy within the UN membership.

Notes

1. Franck, *Fairness,* 89.
2. In particular the work of the UNDP Management Development and Governance Division starting in 1989 and giving support in the following areas: governing institutions, decentralized governance, public sector management

and accountability, urban development, governance in crisis countries, and capacity development. <http://magnet.undp.org/about-us/Mdgdbro.htm>. See also "UNDP and Governance: Experience and Lessons Learned," <http://magnet.undp.org/Docs/gov/lessons1.htm>.

3. See Joyner, "The United Nations and Democracy," 340–341.

4. The UNDP has become increasingly involved with the first stage as well as the second—see note 2 above.

5. Arangio-Ruiz, "The Federal Analogy," 9.

6. Simma, *The Charter,* 1117. See also Tomuschat, *The United Nations at Age Fifty,* ix.

7. Cassese, "Political Self-Determination," 160.

8. Franck, *Fairness,* 95–96.

9. Ibid., 97. See also Beigbeder, *International Monitoring,* 98.

10. *Namibia* case, ICJ Rep. 1971, 31. *Western Sahara* case, ICJ Rep. 1975, 31–33.

11. GA Res. 1514, 14 Dec. 1960.

12. GA Res. 2625, 24 Oct. 1970.

13. Harris, *Cases and Materials,* 113. See also GA Res. 47/135, 18 Dec. 1992; Art. 27 of the International Covenant on Civil and Political Rights.

14. Franck, *Fairness,* 92.

15. GA Res. 51/101, 12 Dec. 1996.

16. Crawford, "The Charter of the UN," 113.

17. Joyner, "The United Nations and Democracy," 350.

18. GA Res. 217A (III), 10 Dec. 1948.

19. There were some discussions at the 1945 San Francisco Conference as to whether conditions for membership should include references to the form of government. See Rosas, "Democracy and Human Rights," 22.

20. See General Comment No. 25, 12 July 1996; UN doc. CCPR/C/21/Rev.1/Add.7.

21. Para. 1 of the General Comment.

22. Para. 7 of the General Comment.

23. See Communication No. 205/1986 in (1993) 14 *Human Rights Law Journal,* 16.

24. UN Centre for Human Rights, *Human Rights and Elections: A Handbook on the Legal, Technical, and Human Rights Aspects of Elections* (1994), para. 87.

25. Para. 21 of the General Comment.

26. Paras. 9 and 21 of the General Comment.

27. Partsch, "Freedom of Conscience," 240.

28. See also *Bwalya v. Zambia,* Communication No. 314/1988 in (1993) 14 *Human Rights Law Journal,* 408–410.

29. See the *Massera* case, no. 5/1977, Human Rights Committee, selected decisions under the optional protocol, UN doc. CCPR/C/OP/1, 40–43; the *Altesor* case, no. 10/1977, 105–109; the *Weinberger* case, no. 28/1978, 57–60; the *Tourón* case, no. 32/1978, 61–63; the *Landinelli Silva* case, no. 34/1978, 65–66; and the *Pietraroia* case, no. 44/1978, 76–80.

30. See Mowbray, "The Role of the European Court of Human Rights," 703.

31. But see Mutua, "The Ideology of Human Rights," 589; Farer, "Collectively Defending Democracy," 716.

32. Franck, *Fairness,* 85, 88. Franck notes that by 1994 at least 130 governments were committed to democracy in the form of "open, multiparty, secret ballot elections with a universal franchise." See also Ndiaye, "International Cooperation to Promote Democracy," 23; Marks, "International Law," 533.

33. GA Res. 43/157, 8 Dec. 1988, requested that the Human Rights Commission look into the matter. See generally Beigbeder, *International Monitoring,* 100–105.

34. GA Res. 44/146, 15 Dec. 1989.

35. GA Res. 44/147, 15 Dec. 1989.

36. See, however, the following year's pair of similar resolutions. The resolution respecting national sovereignty (45/151, 18 Dec. 1990) was adopted by a similar majority, but the resolution supporting the principle of periodic and genuine elections was adopted by 129-8-9 (45/150, 18 Dec. 1990). Its move toward the provision of practical help by the United Nations probably explains this reaction by a minority of states.

37. GA Res. 46/137, 17 Dec. 1991, 134-4-13.

38. GA Res. 46/130, 17 Dec. 1991, 102-40-13. The sovereignty resolutions over the years have remained essentially the same and yet have attracted less support. GA Res. 47/130, 18 Dec. 1992, 99-45-16. GA Res. 48/124, 20 Dec. 1993, 101-51-17. GA Res. 49/180, 23 Dec. 1994, 97-54-14. GA Res. 50/172, 22 Dec. 1995, 91-57-21. GA Res. 52/119, 12 Dec. 1997, 96-58-12.

39. GA Res. 47/138, 18 Dec. 1992, 140-0-20.

40. GA Res. 48/131, 20 Dec. 1993, 153-0-13; GA Res. 49/190, 23 Dec. 1994, 155-1(Iran)-12; GA Res. 50/185, 22 Dec. 1995, 156-0-15.

41. GA Res. 52/129, 12 Dec. 1997, 157-0-15.

42. GA Res. 50/133, 20 Dec. 1995.

43. GA Res. 51/31, 6 Dec. 1996; GA Res. 52/18, 21 Nov. 1997.

44. GA Res. 53/31, 23 Nov. 1998.

45. Ndiaye, "International Cooperation to Promote Democracy," 28.

46. The main examples of such forces are: UNAVEM I, II, and III (Angola, 1989–1997); UNTAG (Namibia, 1989–1990); the United Nations Observer Group in Central America (Nicaragua, 1989–1992); MINURSO (Western Sahara, 1991–); the United Nations Observer Mission in El Salvador (1991–1995); UNTAC (Cambodia, 1991–1993); ONUMOZ (Mozambique, 1992–1994); the United Nations Observer Mission in Liberia (1993–1997); the United Nations Mission in Haiti/United Nations Support Mission in Haiti (1993–1997); the United Nations Mission in Guatemala (1997); the United Nations Mission in the Central African Republic (1998–2000); and the United Nations Assistance Mission in Sierra Leone (1999–).

47. UN doc. A/53/951, Annex III.

48. First established by SC Res. 690, 29 April 1991.

49. (1992) 29(4) *UN Chronicle* 9.

50. SC Res. 1299, 26 Feb. 1999. See SG report, UN doc. S/1999/202.

51. UN Blue Book Series, *The United Nations and Mozambique, 1992–1995* (New York: UN, 1995), 3.

52. Ibid., 4. On the Rome Agreement, see UN doc. S/24635 (1992). On the mandate, see SC Res. 797, 16 Dec. 1992.

53. SG report, UN doc. A/49/675, 11 Nov. 1994, 20.

54. UN doc. S/1994/89.

55. UN Blue Book Series, *Mozambique,* 56.

56. Ibid., 57.

57. UN doc. S/1994/1196.

58. See Vu, "The Holding of Free and Fair Elections in Cambodia," 1177.

59. UN doc. S/1994/1282.

60. UN Blue Book Series, *Mozambique,* 67.

61. UN doc. S/1999/595.

62. SC Res. 1246, 11 June 1999.

63. UN doc. S/1999/595.

64. UN Press Release, SG/SM/6980, 6 May 1999.

65. Although the United Nations is unlikely to intervene in many postcoup situations unless they constitute threats to the peace. See Suy, "Democracy in International Relations," 128. See generally Pierce, "The Haitian Crisis," 477.

66. Ebersole, "The United Nations' Response," 91; Stoelting, "The Challenge of UN Monitored Elections," 371.

67. Between 1989 and 1996 the United Nations authorized the following types of assistance: organization and conduct (3); supervision (1); verification (8); coordination and support (25); support for national observers (1); observation (27); and technical assistance (48). See UN doc. A/51/512 (1996).

68. See SG report, UN doc. A/49/675, 17 Nov. 1994, Annex III ("Guidelines for Member States considering the formulation of Requests for Electoral Supervision").

69. SG report, UN doc. S/1999/595.

70. Presidential statement, S/PRST/1999/27, 3 Sept. 1999.

71. UN doc. S/1999/595.

72. SG report, UN doc. A/49/675, Annex III, para. 11.

73. Ibid., para. 15.

74. See generally Gassama, "Safeguarding the Democratic Entitlement," 287.

75. UN doc. A/49/675, para. 4.

76. Centre for Human Rights, *Human Rights and Elections,* para. 13.

77. Ibid., para. 17 (emphasis added).

78. See, for example, SC Res. 940, 31 July 1994 (Haiti).

79. SC Res. 1264, 15 Sept. 1999.

80. SC Res. 1272, 25 Oct. 1999.

81. SC Res. 1244, 10 June 1999.

82. Centre for Human Rights, *Human Rights and Elections,* para. 17.

83. Many of these are now contained in GA Res. 55/96, 4 Dec. 2000, 157-0-16.

84. Ibid., paras. 61–72.

85. SG report, UN doc. A/50/332 (1995), paras. 14, 23, 32, 94, 104, and 115. See also SG report, UN doc. A/51/512 (1996), paras. 11, 44, and 63. See generally SG report, UN doc. A/52/513 (1997).

86. Centre for Human Rights, *Human Rights and Elections*, paras. 62–63.

87. Fox, "The Right to Political Participation," 252.

88. Joyner, "The United Nations and Democracy," 335.

8

International Criminal Justice

Although the concept of justice is broad and underlies all UN values, the concept has taken on a specific legal form. The United Nations has developed norms of international criminal law whereby individuals and states bear criminal responsibility for certain actions that can loosely be categorized as crimes against humanity. Furthermore, there is an evolving system of international criminal justice whereby certain mechanisms assert jurisdiction over international crimes. Together these norms and mechanisms constitute a distinct and significant development regarding the abstract concept of justice.

In theory, international crimes give rise to universal jurisdiction over individual suspects. "Universal jurisdiction" means "the power of a state to punish certain crimes committed, without any required connection to territory, nationality or special state interest."[1] However, given the common lack of state interest in asserting jurisdiction over fugitive international criminals, the concept of universal jurisdiction has existed less in actual practice. Prosecutions for crimes against humanity typically occur in the state where the acts were committed (e.g., in Rwanda for the genocidal acts there).[2] In addition, there are occasional prosecutions by the suspect's own state (as when the United States prosecuted the lieutenant alleged to be responsible for the My Lai massacre in Vietnam).[3] The first type is often dependent on a change in government; the second is dependent on the state's willingness to make an example of its own. Even in cases where universal jurisdiction is asserted, as in the trial of Adolf Eichmann by Israel in 1961, the state usually has a special interest in undertaking the prosecution.[4]

States possess discretion in considering whether to assert jurisdiction over international criminals, meaning they can too often decline to prosecute even the most horrible crimes. This explains the increasing involvement of the United Nations in international criminal law and justice.[5]

Although its early record is scattered, the latest developments, including the sponsorship of the statute on the International Criminal Court adopted in Rome in 1998, reveal a much more systematic approach.[6] These developments counter the idea that international criminal law cannot exist in a world of equal states.[7]

The UN's Concern with International Criminal Justice

Prior to the UN Charter of 1945, there were prohibitions against international crimes such as piracy, war crimes, and slavery. However, the legal structures were primitive. For example, the 1926 Convention to Suppress the Slave Trade and Slavery,[8] sponsored by the League of Nations, did not label slavery as an international crime; it did not provide universal jurisdiction over slavers or any mechanisms for supervision or enforcement of the obligations under the convention.[9]

Although there is nothing concrete in the UN Charter to build a system of international criminal justice, the United Nations went about laying some of the building-blocks. The ILC's projects on state responsibility and crimes against peace, although they have yet to come to fruition, encapsulate a two-pronged assault on international criminal activity.[10] Article 19 of the draft articles on state responsibility (1996) was concerned with international crimes of states, namely, breaches of international obligations "so essential for the protection of the international community," such as aggression, denial of the right of self-determination, slavery, genocide, apartheid, and massive pollution of the atmosphere and the seas.[11] The draft code of crimes against peace (1996) recognizes that many of these acts can also give rise to individual criminal responsibility, although its list is slightly different: aggression, genocide, crimes against humanity, crimes against UN personnel, and war crimes, reflecting a focus on the individual rather than the state.[12]

Despite progress on the criminalization of individual actions (e.g., by sponsoring the statute on the ICC), the ILC's progress on criminalizing state actions has stalled. Indeed, the 2001 draft articles on state responsibility are a step backward.[13] Instead of labeling certain serious breaches as international crimes, the final draft of article 40 refers only to the concept of a "serious breach by a State of an obligation arising under a peremptory norm of general international law." There is no longer any categorization of such breaches as international crimes of states; neither is there any list of such breaches. Such dilution was needed to mollify some states that opposed the identification of certain breaches of international law as crimes of state.

The concept of imposing *individual* criminal responsibility is a huge departure from the traditional approach that breaches of international law only give rise to state responsibility. Indeed, the ILC's approach endorses greater entrenchment of individual responsibility for breaches of international criminal law. Historically, the telling break was the Nuremberg Tribunal prosecuting Nazi war leaders for crimes against peace, crimes against humanity, and war crimes. The tribunal stated:

> It was submitted [by the defendants] that international law is concerned with the actions of Sovereign States, and provides no punishment for individuals; and further, that where the act in question is an Act of State, those who carry it out are not personally responsible, but are protected by the doctrine of sovereignty of the State. . . . Crimes against international law are committed by men, not by abstract entities, and only by punishing individuals who commit such crimes can the provisions of international law be enforced.[14]

The UN General Assembly affirmed these principles, and the United Nations commenced building a body of law and a set of mechanisms on international crimes.[15] The United Nations brought international criminal justice within the system in three ways. First, it incorporated certain norms and mechanisms under the traditional value of peace and security. Second, under the rubric of human rights, the United Nations developed core human rights norms that gave rise to individual criminal responsibility. Finally, the abstract notion of justice found in article 1 of the UN Charter was developed by formulating, through the ILC, norms on state responsibility for international crimes (now "serious breaches") and individual responsibility. However, the latter shows that the line between the three is blurred. The ILC has developed a draft code of crimes against *peace*. The draft code is not meant to be the elaboration of an international penal code for the whole range of international crimes, and so it does not include slavery, piracy, and other acts that could not be said to be crimes against peace.[16]

Crimes Against Peace

Here I focus on whether concrete actions have been taken to bring individuals to justice by invoking peace, a primary value of the UN system.

Arguably, armed aggression is the core crime of the UN system, combining the value of peace with the desire to do justice. The crime of aggression is recognized by the ILC against the state (at least until 2000) and the individual. However, it has not played a role in the ad hoc international criminal tribunals created by the Security Council; neither is it properly embedded in the statute of the ICC adopted in 1998.

Although the planning, preparation, initiation, or waging of a war of aggression was recognized as a crime giving rise to individual responsibility at Nuremberg, very little has been achieved since. The criminalization of aggression was not without controversy at Nuremberg given that the Pact of Paris of 1928, which outlawed war, only seemed to envisage state responsibility (and then only civil rather than criminal responsibility).[17] However, it has been accepted, at least in theory, as manifested in article 16 of the ILC draft code of crimes against peace, which states that "an individual, who, as leader or organizer, actively participates in or orders the planning, preparation, initiation or waging of aggression committed by a State, shall be responsible for the crime of aggression."[18]

In 1974, after decades of negotiations, the General Assembly finally adopted, by consensus, a definition of "aggression."[19] The definition states that "a war of aggression is a crime against international peace" and that "aggression gives rise to international responsibility." However, it is generally contended that the resolution "was intended to assist the General Assembly and the Security Council by clarifying a key concept (see its use in Article 1 and 39, Charter) in the United Nations scheme for the maintenance of international peace and security."[20] Although the number of determinations of "aggression" has increased since the definition, primarily against Israel and South Africa during apartheid, there has been no attempt by the Security Council to link them to the issue of state or individual responsibility.[21] Furthermore, the idea that the 1974 resolution could define aggression for the purposes of individual responsibility was finally rejected when the 1998 Rome Conference on the ICC failed to agree on any definition of aggression, although aggression (left undefined) is recognized as a core crime in article 5 of the statute.

This failure to criminalize aggression in the wake of Nuremberg is disappointing given that the entire system is based on the maintenance of peace and security. This lack of progress can be attributed to member states' self-interest, especially on the part of the United States.[22] An accurate definition of aggression would inhibit, in legal terms, states that readily use military force against other states. For example, if the U.S.-U.K. bombings of Iraq in December 1998 were not authorized by the Security Council or under the rubric of self-defense, then those actions would be "crimes of aggression" under any sensible definition and would impose criminal responsibility on the states and their political and military leaders.[23]

The crime of aggression implies individual responsibility yet in many ways blurs the distinction between state and individual. The lack of accountability for aggressive war reflects a lack of desire to criminalize the activities of political and military leaders. Few calls have been made to try individual leaders for aggression on an ad hoc basis, notably Saddam Hussein for Iraq's invasion of Kuwait in 1990.[24] And the ad hoc ICTY was not granted jurisdiction over the crime of aggression, despite the fact that there is a strong case against the political leaders of Serbia and Croatia for their aggressive involvement in the war in Bosnia as well as for their responsibility for war crimes and crimes against humanity, which are within the jurisdiction of the tribunal.[25]

Terrorism

Although the United Nations has not been able to agree on the definition of "crime of aggression," the Security Council has used its mandatory, coercive collective security powers under chapter VII in other areas of international criminal law. The creation of the criminal tribunals for the former Yugoslavia in 1993 and Rwanda in 1994 will be analyzed in the next section.

Another dramatic intervention by the Security Council arose from the Lockerbie incident. The majority of those killed on PanAm Flight 103 were U.S. or U.K. nationals, and in November 1991 a warrant was issued for the arrest of two Libyan nationals suspected of planting the bomb. This was quickly followed by a declaration by the United States and United Kingdom (and France for a separate aerial incident) calling upon Libya to hand over the two suspects for trial in Scotland or the United States.[26]

Libya did not comply and cited the Montreal Convention, which in article 1 states that an individual commits an offense if he

unlawfully and intentionally . . . places or causes to be placed on an aircraft in service, by any means whatsoever, a device or substance

which is likely to destroy that aircraft, or to cause damage to it which
renders it incapable of flight, or to cause damage to it which is likely
to endanger its safety in flight.[27]

Libya stated that it was also complying with article 7 of the convention,
which states that:

> The Contracting State in the territory of which the alleged offender is
> found shall, if it does not extradite him, be obliged, without exception
> whatsoever and whether or not the offence was committed in its terri-
> tory, to submit the case to its competent authorities for the purpose of
> prosecution. Those authorities shall take their decision in the same
> manner as in the case of any ordinary offence of a serious nature
> under the law of that State.

This "extradite or prosecute" formula is a common provision in
many so-called suppression conventions and embodies a treaty form of
universal jurisdiction.[28] However, the weaknesses became manifest in
the Lockerbie affair, where the suspects were Libyan nationals (indeed,
they were officers in the Libyan intelligence services) taking refuge in
Libya. This, combined with the prosecutorial discretion recognized to
exist in the suppression conventions, rendered any trial of the two suspects in Libya, or the handing over of the two suspects to the United
Kingdom or United States, highly unlikely.[29] Both of those states had
jurisdiction over the offense under article 5 of the convention as, respectively, the territorial state and the state in which the aircraft was
registered.

The failure of the existing UN-sponsored convention to provide effective mechanisms for bringing individual suspects to trial,[30] combined
with allegations against Libya of state-sponsored terrorism, led to the
United States and United Kingdom taking the case to the Security
Council in January 1991.[31] In response, Libya went before the ICJ under
article 14 of the Montreal Convention, alleging that the other states
were breaching the provisions of the convention.[32]

The Security Council adopted resolutions on the matter (see Chapter 5). Of importance here is the use of chapter VII in resolution 748
adopted on 31 March 1992. Determining a threat to international peace
and security, the council decided that Libya must make a "full and effective response" to the U.K. and U.S. requests for the extradition and
renounce its support for terrorism. The resolution imposed an arms and
air embargo on Libya in an attempt to enforce the mandatory decision.

The ICJ's preliminary decisions on Libya's application under the Montreal Convention have been discussed in Chapter 5. The issue of the legality of the Security Council's involvement, in particular the application of the concept of "threat to the peace" to terrorist activities, remains to be decided by the court. In defense of the Security Council, it is difficult to see how state-sponsored terrorism is not an issue of collective security over which the organ has competence. Of much greater significance are the legal effects of resolution 748; the obligations it imposes prevail over any other international agreement by virtue of article 103 of the UN Charter.[33] This signifies that the Security Council can override legal regimes like the Montreal Convention.

Although controversial, the use of supranational powers to prevail over any other conflicting treaty provides a more vertical legal structure, arguably necessary for a functioning and effective system of international criminal justice. Indeed, the Security Council has built on this practice in the case of Sudan, which refused to hand over the three suspects wanted in connection with the attempted assassination of President Hosni Mubarek of Egypt in June 1995.[34] Similar action was taken in 1999 against the unrecognized Taliban regime in Afghanistan for allowing suspected terrorist Osama bin Laden to operate from its territory.[35]

Indeed, following the attacks against the United States on 11 September 2001, the Security Council took further action to combat terrorism. While a U.S.-led coalition commenced military action against terrorist bases and Taliban forces on 7 October 2001 on the basis of self-defense, the Security Council condemned the attacks against the United States as a threat to international peace (12 September 2001) and took action under chapter VII on the basis of its growing competence in criminal justice matters.[36] The determination that such acts of terrorism constitute threats to international peace and security enabled the council to take these further steps. On 28 September 2001, the Security Council adopted a chapter VII resolution that binds all states to prevent and suppress the financing of terrorism by criminalizing the "wilful provision or collection of funds . . . by their nationals or in their territories with the intention that the funds should be used, or in the knowledge that they are to be used, in order to carry out terrorist acts."[37] The resolution also binds all states, inter alia, to freeze the assets of terrorist organizations; prevent the supply of weapons to terrorists; prohibit terrorists from being based on their territories; prosecute terrorists within their territories; prevent the movement of terrorists; and provide mutual assistance with states attempting to prosecute terrorists. These actions are taken according to the determination in the resolution that terrorism is contrary to the purposes and principles of the charter. A committee of the Security Council is established to monitor state compliance, and states are under an initial obligation to respond within ninety days. By this resolution the Security Council is legislating for the international community (including nonmember states).[38] The resolution develops previous actions to combat terrorism, which, although binding on all states, were directed against certain states for their involvement in terrorism. Its effectiveness remains to be seen, though it appears to be an innovative and legitimate attempt to harness the powers of the Security Council in a worldwide effort to combat terrorism.

Despite the fact that the United Nations is purportedly based on sovereign equality, it does have a built-in hierarchy in the form of the Security Council. However, the effectiveness of the council in this field must not be overestimated, given that its efforts to secure the extradition of the two suspects from Libya did not succeed. Indeed, it seems that the combined effects of the litigation among the parties led to the compromise (a trial of the two suspects in the Netherlands before a Scottish court sitting without a jury). The suspects arrived in the Netherlands in April 1999. The trial focused on the criminal responsibility of the two individual suspects, one of whom was convicted of murder on 31 January 2001.[39] It did not address the responsibility of their political superiors.

Suppression Conventions

Unfortunately, even though the Security Council has clear competence in matters of peace and security, its activities are selective. It would be too naive to expect the council to extend its competence on a regular basis to international crimes. One way the United Nations has attempted to overcome the weakness of the extradite-or-prosecute approach of the antiterrorist conventions identified above is through methods of supervision, though rarely enforcement.

There is a distinct contrast between the UN-sponsored convention that addressed the most repugnant international crime—genocide—and the later conventions that attempted to suppress international crimes such as torture. The Convention on the Prevention and Punishment of the Crime of Genocide does designate that genocide is a "crime under international law" in article 1.[40] Furthermore, it does contain a definition in article 2 that has stood the test of time despite deficiencies in the definition (e.g., not including political groups within groups that can be the victims of genocide). However, the convention fails to universalize the crime in any effective way.[41] Article 6 recognizes territorial jurisdiction or jurisdiction by an "international penal tribunal" over the crime. This reference lay dormant until the ICTY and ICTR were granted jurisdiction over genocide in relation to the conflicts and atrocities in the former Yugoslavia and Rwanda. The latter has started convicting individuals for the crime of genocide.[42] The ICC will also have jurisdiction over this crime when its statute comes into force (late 2002).

In addition, establishing state responsibility is possible under article 9 of the Genocide Convention. This provides that disputes between the contracting parties over the application or fulfillment of the Genocide Convention "including those relating to the responsibility of a State for genocide . . . shall be submitted to the International Court of Justice at the request of any of the parties to the dispute." Certain state parties have weakened this provision by making reservations.[43] The first case under article 9 was brought by Bosnia against Yugoslavia (Serbia and Montenegro) in 1993. The fact that the case is still proceeding to the merits illustrates the weakness of relying on the ICJ, though it did order Serbia to desist from its alleged involvement in genocidal acts in 1993 as an interim measure.[44]

The later UN-sponsored Convention Against Torture and Other Cruel, Inhuman, or Degrading Treatment or Punishment of 1984[45] can be taken as a model human rights instrument that is stronger in terms of supervision. The Committee Against Torture (CAT) was created under article 17, consisting of ten independent experts. CAT has competence to review regular reports on compliance submitted by the state parties (articles 19 and 20), as well as to receive state and individual petitions under an optional system whereby state parties can accept these mechanisms (articles 21 and 22). Furthermore, although not designated as an international crime, torture as defined in article 1 is universalized as a crime through the extradite-or-prosecute formula (article 5). Although this improves on the Genocide Convention model, there are weaknesses that counter any assertion that the Convention Against Torture contains methods of enforcement. First, the CAT is supervisory; its decisions are not binding and cannot be enforced against states or individuals who have committed torture. This has led many to doubt whether it renders individuals criminally responsible for torture.[46] Second, states can become parties to the convention without accepting the state or individual complaint procedures. Finally, though torture is recognized as giving rise to universal jurisdiction, the extradite-or-prosecute formula is not extended to other undefined "acts of cruel, inhuman or degrading treatment" (article 16).

Other human rights instruments will be discussed in Chapter 9. International criminal justice is not merely the identification and enforcement of international crimes; it includes protections through fair trial and due process for the individual accused. Human rights instruments have remedied many of the defects of the Tokyo and Nuremberg trials in this regard.[47]

Here I am concerned with other treaties and instruments that attempt to suppress crimes of an international nature.[48] These conventions adopt some or all of the mechanisms outlined above in the various suppression conventions. For instance, the Convention Against the Taking of Hostages of 1979 adopts the extradite-or-prosecute formula,[49] whereas the 1988 Convention Against Illicit Traffic in Narcotic Drugs and Psychotropic Substances also uses supervisory mechanisms based on the UN Commission on Narcotic Drugs.[50] The 1973 Convention on the Suppression and Punishment of the Crime of Apartheid establishes supervisory mechanisms while improving on the Genocide Convention's approach to jurisdiction by replacing territorial jurisdiction with universal jurisdiction.[51]

Most of these conventions were drafted following the adoption of declarations by the UN General Assembly. In other instances, the law-making process has only reached the stage of a declaration. A recent important example is the Declaration on the Protection of All Persons from Enforced Disappearances of 1992.[52] The declaration states in article 1 that "any act of enforced disappearance is an offence to human dignity"; like the conventions it purports to oblige states to criminalize such an offense in their national laws. However, even though the declaration was adopted by consensus, its legislative status is doubtful.[53] And unlike the suppression conventions, it does not provide a precise definition of the offense or provide universal jurisdiction.[54] Finally, there is no mechanism for supervision. Nevertheless, "its passage signifies at least the beginning of a trend towards international criminality, analogous to the passage of the Declaration on Torture in 1975."[55] These deficiencies can be remedied if the declaration leads to a suppression treaty, though the lack of enforcement mechanisms within the suppression conventions themselves cast doubt about their efficacy in upholding the UN's value of justice.

The Ad Hoc International Criminal Tribunals

The Security Council's expanding notion of threat to the peace has led that body into areas of international criminal justice. The changing concept of peace has led the Security Council to establish two international criminal tribunals to bring lasting peace to the former Yugoslavia and Rwanda. The creation of a special court for Sierra Leone adds to this development.[56] In so doing, the Security Council adds an element of enforcement via punishment to the UN's evolving system of international criminal justice. The idea of punishment has taken hold within the United Nations with the adoption of the ICC statute in Rome in 1998, promising a greater universalization of punishment.

Though the idea was not envisaged by the UN Charter, the Security Council utilized its powers in 1993 under chapter VII to establish the ICTY[57] with jurisdiction over genocide, war crimes, and crimes against humanity committed in the territory of the former Yugoslavia since 1991.[58] This was followed in 1994 by the creation of the ICTR[59] for prosecuting individuals responsible for genocide and other serious violations of international humanitarian law committed in Rwanda in 1994.[60] Both tribunals were established in the firm belief that they would contribute to restoring peace and after determining that the violations of international criminal law constituted, by themselves, threats to international peace and security.

The link between the council's primary function—the maintenance and restoration of international peace and security—and the creation of the tribunals was legally necessary.[61] In the *Tadic*[62] and *Kanyabashi*[63] cases, the ICTY (appeals chamber) and ICTR (trial chamber) rejected jurisdictional objections submitted on the basis that the Security Council did not have the power to create tribunals possessing criminal jurisdiction. Both tribunals emphasized the fact that the tribunals were created as part of the Security Council's primary function and that such a power could be implied from the nonexhaustive list of nonmilitary measures in article 41 of the charter.[64]

Nevertheless, it is not enough to blindly accept this link. Thus it is worth investigating the actual contribution of the ICTY and ICTR to peace and to the development of international criminal justice. There is no doubt about the contribution of the tribunals to international criminal justice by the development and application of international criminal law, but their contribution to the establishment of peace in Bosnia and

Rwanda can be questioned. First of all, the tribunals do appear to suffer from the "legacy of having been established to cover the failure of the international community to actually stop the war and the atrocities committed in Former Yugoslavia" and Rwanda.[65] It can be argued that peace and justice—inseparable for establishing a lasting peace—are separable while negative peace is restored by coercive nonmilitary and military measures or by negotiation. It is not immediately clear that war-crimes trials are effective in bringing about the ending of a conflict. It can be contended that they should take place after the establishment of a negative peace, at least according to the Nuremberg model.

Furthermore, the indictment of political and military leaders can hamper negotiations for peace, as those leaders' consent may be necessary. The Bosnian Serb leaders, Radovan Karadzic and Ratko Mladic, have been indicted for war crimes, crimes against humanity, and genocide, including the killing of 6,000 Muslim men following the fall of Srebrenica in 1995.[66] Rule 61 proceedings, which resemble a trial in absentia[67] in which a prima facie case has been made by the prosecutor, followed against Karadzic and Mladic.[68] International arrest warrants have been issued, inter alia, to the state members of the NATO-led peace implementation force. The arrest and trial of these leaders, however, is likely to take place only once they have been isolated politically, and the decision to arrest mainly depends on the states contributing to the NATO force exercising its "discretionary" powers in Bosnia.[69]

In addition, "the threat of prosecution may actually contribute to an escalation of the conflict. . . . The only incentive is to win and keep killing."[70] It may be because of this that the role of the ICTY was played down in Dayton during November 1995.[71] The jurisdiction of the ICTY extends to the whole of the former Yugoslavia. With this in mind, the threat of prosecutions failed to deter criminal actions as evidenced by the atrocities commited in Kosovo in 1998–1999. Deterrence is just one of the many claims made by advocates of the tribunals. Here is a concise list of those claims:

> Those who pushed for the creation of these tribunals argued that, as with earlier trials of major Nazi and Japanese wartime leaders, properly conducted international criminal trials, brought by and on behalf of the international community, would: threaten those in positions of power to deter further violence; make possible atonement for the perpetrators and honor the dead; provide a mechanism to enable victims and their families to receive needed psychological relief, identify remains, restore lost property, and otherwise help heal wounds; channel

victims' thirst for revenge towards peaceful dispute settlement; affirm the Nuremberg Principles at international level while restoring faith in the rule of law generally; tell the truth of what occurred, thereby preserving an accurate historical account of barbarism that would help prevent its recurrence; and, perhaps most important, restore the lost civility of torn societies to achieve national reconciliation.[72]

The purpose of such tribunals is closure, enabling a line to be drawn between past and future, to enable both the devastated society and the international community to start again. This is done by trying and convicting individuals rather than attributing collective responsibility.[73] However, such an approach will work only if the vast majority of individuals who actually committed violations of international humanitarian law are indicted and convicted by the tribunals.[74] Otherwise the cycle of revenge and violence is likely to continue. There must also be doubt as to the ability of tribunals to provide an accurate historical accounting of atrocities, considering the rather simplistic account given in the *Tadic* case of the descent into violence in Bosnia in 1991–1992 from a state of ethnic harmony to one of evil barbarity.[75] However, tribunals help in a more modest way, enabling ruptured societies to start again: "Societies in which such divisive issues are not raised *at least in a courtroom* face a greater danger of having these questions vetted in renewed mass atrocities instead of in more controlled settings."[76]

The UN's experiments with international criminal justice within the context of collective security have been inconclusive. The tribunals have made important contributions to the normative framework, in particular by the international criminalization of internal atrocities, thus recognizing that individual criminal responsibility is attached to violations of common article 3 of the Geneva Conventions.[77] However, the establishment and maintenance of international criminal tribunals are not sufficient per se to protect UN values. State cooperation is required, especially in arresting indicted war criminals. Although the ICTY is not in the advantageous position of administering "victor's justice" as in Nuremberg, it is backed up by the supranational mandatory powers of the Security Council. This signifies that states are under a *duty* to cooperate with the ICTY and ICTR,[78] and the Security Council has extended this to nonstate entities such as the Bosnian Serb republic.[79]

Yet the ICTY and ICTR remain dependent upon the Security Council to enforce the tribunals' decisions.[80] This is a considerable weakness, compounded by the decision of states contributing to the NATO-led force, made clear when the Security Council authorized it.[81] Contributing states declared that they had no obligation to arrest indicted war criminals but would do so at their discretion. Nevertheless, the year 1997 "may well have been a turning point" for the ICTY, especially in light of the number of NATO arrests.[82] It has a long way to go "in bringing to justice those responsible for the appalling violations of humanitarian law in the former Yugoslavia, let alone contribute to the maintenance of international peace—the ostensible reason for its creation."[83] Nevertheless, a breakthrough occurred on 29 June 2001, when Slobodan Milosevic, the former president of the FRY and one of the principal actors in the violence, was transferred to the ICTY to stand trial, initially on charges of crimes against humanity committed in Kosovo in 1998–1999.

The ICTR has faced even more intractable problems, including an insufficient budget, the fact that Rwandan courts are administering rough justice to thousands of suspects, and the lack of a police force to arrest indicted criminals.[84] The latter difficulty is not as great as it appears, with several high-ranking Hutu leaders, including the prime minister of Rwanda at the time of the genocide, being tried and convicted by the tribunal.[85] The defeat of the Hutu regime resulted in something like victor's justice and has made it easier for surrounding countries to comply with their obligations to the ICTR and the Security Council by arresting indicted suspects. Although by no means rehabilitated after its disastrous start, the ICTR is starting to apply international criminal law to the appalling atrocities in Rwanda, belatedly upholding the UN's values of justice and peace.

The International Criminal Court

The biggest criticism of the ad hoc international criminal tribunals is their selectivity, which raises questions about legitimacy. Why only the former Yugoslavia, Rwanda, and Sierra Leone? Why not Burundi, Liberia, Angola, Chechnya, and East Timor? If justice, especially international criminal justice, is truly part of the UN system's values, then international criminal courts need to have jurisdiction over suspects irrespective of nationality and the location of the crimes. Put simply, there is a pressing need for a court of humanity with universal jurisdiction over crimes against humanity.

The idea of an international criminal court is not new (article 6 of the Genocide Convention of 1948 referred to an international penal tribunal). The idea was not given any priority during the Cold War, but was not beyond revival. During the late 1980s the Soviet Union and Trinidad suggested an international court be established with jurisdiction over terrorism and drug-trafficking.[86] Ironically, terrorism and drug-trafficking, along with other so-called treaty crimes, were excluded from the Rome statute of 1998 in favor of "customary crimes," which created fewer jurisdictional problems.[87] In 1989, the General Assembly requested that the ILC restart its work on drafting a statute for an international criminal court, on its agenda since 1948.[88] The ILC adopted a draft statute in 1994,[89] and the General Assembly established the United Nations Preparatory Committee on the Establishment of the Court (Prepcom),[90] whose sessions led to a diplomatic conference in Rome in July 1998. After much horse-trading and pessimism, and against all odds, a statute of the ICC was adopted by the conference on 17 July 1998,[91] by 120 votes in favor with seven against (China, Israel, United States, Libya, Iraq, Qatar, and Yemen) with twenty-one abstentions. The statute is now open for signature by all states and will come into force upon receiving sixty ratifications (articles 125 and 126). Although sponsored by the United Nations, the ICC will be independent to ensure judicial impartiality, though cases can be referred by the Security Council under article 13(b). Article 2 also provides that "the Court shall be brought into a relationship with the United Nations through an agreement to be approved by the Assembly of State Parties to this Statute," a relationship analogous to the UN's agreements with the IAEA, for example.[92]

Though the statute has several weaknesses, highlighted below, it is a remarkable achievement. The experiences of the ad hoc tribunals, specifically the horrendous atrocities that led to their creation, combined with the greater sense of international community that emerged with the end of the Cold War, to produce a breakthrough. The contrast between the rapid establishment of the ad hoc tribunals and the slow process toward the ICC can be explained: the ICC represents a move toward the universal application of international criminal law rather than the selective application of that law. This explains the strong opposition from powerful states, principally the United States.[93] The United States prefers a realist vision of international relations wherein the state is not subject to regulation or control by international bodies or courts—a horizontal international system in which the United States claims extraterritorial enforcement powers, allowing it to seize and try international criminals in its own courts.[94]

But the real reason for the delay was that too many states are guilty of committing, sanctioning, or condoning international crimes. There

were many self-serving objections: Russia and China objected to jurisdiction over crimes against humanity committed outside of an armed
conflict; the United States objected to jurisdiction over isolated war
crimes, arguing it should try only those committed as part of a policy or
widespread occurrence; France and other Western states objected to the
inclusion of the use of nuclear weapons as a war crime; France objected
to the inclusion of collateral damage as a war crime; Israel objected to
the transfer of civilian populations into occupied territories as a war
crime; the Holy See objected to the inclusion of enforced pregnancy as
a war crime; the United States objected to the use of children in an
armed conflict as a war crime; China, India, Indonesia, Pakistan, and
Turkey objected to the inclusion of common article 3 of the Geneva
Conventions of 1949 regarding acts committed in internal conflicts;
Russia objected to the inclusion of crimes over and above common article 3 in relation to noninternational armed conflicts; and finally the
United States and other permanent members of the Security Council objected to jurisdiction over aggression as a crime.[95]

One of the disappointing features is that the ICC will have jurisdiction over only a small part of international criminal law, loosely violations of international humanitarian law—genocide, crimes against
humanity, and war crimes (article 5). Although these are distinct categories, there is a considerable overlap. For instance, a single act of rape
by a soldier against a civilian in time of armed conflict is a war crime
under article 8(2)(b)(xxii) and article 8(2)(e)(vi); if it is "committed as
part of a widespread or systematic attack directed against any civilian
population, with knowledge of the attack" under article 7(1)(g), then it
is also a crime against humanity; and finally if it is "committed with intent to destroy, in whole or in part, a national, ethnical, racial or religious group" under article 6, it will possibly amount to genocide. Each
offense is more serious than the last, and the criminal intent is increasingly difficult to prove, but the act of rape is the same. With this in
mind, jurisdiction reflects a narrow consensus as to the core of international crimes.

Although the definition of "genocide" remains that of the 1948 convention (including the glaring absence of political groups as protected
groups), the definitions of crimes against humanity and war crimes are
broader. For instance, article 7 (crimes against humanity) adds to the
Nuremberg charter—namely, murder, extermination, enslavement, de-
portation, and persecution—to include, inter alia, imprisonment, torture,
rape, sexual slavery, enforced prostitution, forced pregnancy, enforced

sterilization, enforced disappearances, and apartheid. The list of war crimes in international armed conflicts goes way beyond grave breaches under the 1949 Geneva Conventions, which are principally acts of physical harm to persons or property protected by the conventions. The Rome statute includes, inter alia, attacks on UN personnel, certain collateral damage, the transfer of civilian populations to occupied territories, sex crimes, and the conscription of children under the age of fifteen into the armed forces or using them in hostilities.

Furthermore, the list of war crimes in noninternational armed conflicts goes beyond common article 3 of the Geneva Conventions, which protects the physical integrity of persons taking no part in the hostilities. The Rome statute includes, inter alia, some of the acts identified as war crimes in international armed conflicts such as attacks on UN personnel, sex crimes, and the use of children under fifteen in the armed forces (article 8).

Although the list of war crimes in international and internal conflicts is impressive, there are serious limits to the ICC's jurisdiction. Under article 8(1), isolated war crimes in an armed conflict will not normally give rise to jurisdiction: "The Court shall have jurisdiction in respect of war crimes in particular when committed as part of a plan or policy or as part of a large scale-commission of such crimes." This makes the overlap between war crimes and crimes against humanity even greater, again restricting the court's competence. There are other restrictions to jurisdiction. For common article 3 violations the statute does not apply to mere "internal disturbances or tensions, such as riots, isolated and sporadic acts of violence." For crimes beyond the core of common article 3, an even stricter set of conditions applies by repeating the preceding formula and adding that the provisions only cover "armed conflicts that take place in the territory of a State when there is protracted armed conflict between governmental authorities and organized groups or between such groups."

Although the court's jurisdiction will not be retroactive, there is a final protection provided to states concerned about the propensity of their armed forces to commit war crimes. Article 124 provides that

> a State, on becoming a party to this Statute, may declare that for a period of seven years after the entry into force of this Statute for the State concerned, it does not accept the jurisdiction of the Court with respect to the category of crimes referred to in article 8 [war crimes] when a crime is alleged to have been committed by its national[s] or on its territory.

The provision is so cynical it requires no further comment.

Although the ICC statute helps to expand and clarify core crimes, any chance for prosecution of individuals is slim. In theory the easiest to prove is a war crime, but only the most horrific circumstances will yield up individuals to justice. The value of justice is fully protected only by providing that the ICC has jurisdiction over any war criminal in cases where national courts are "unable or unwilling" to try them.[96] Furthermore, although aggression is listed as a core crime, the court will exercise jurisdiction only if a definition of aggression has been adopted, according to article 5(2). The ineffective inclusion of the core crime against peace is hugely disappointing. Furthermore, although article 123 provides for the extension of the list of crimes by means of a review conference, the ICC as currently empowered will not have jurisdiction over future aggressors, terrorists, and torturers. However, arguments may be made that certain terrorist atrocities can amount to crimes against humanity. If the intention was to create a court to try future Saddams for aggression, Pinochets for torture, and Lockerbie-type bombers for terrorist acts, then the plan has failed unless the Security Council bypasses the jurisdiction limitations on an ad hoc basis.[97]

An international court possessing universal jurisdiction over all international crimes would entrench the value of justice in the UN system. Whether there will be a truly "international" court depends on the number of ratifications to the statute. The final issue is thus universal jurisdiction. The small number of "customary" core crimes actually strengthens the case for universal jurisdiction, as they are recognized as giving states universal jurisdiction. This argument means that the court would have

> jurisdiction over all . . . the core crimes, committed worldwide and regardless of whether the State on the territory of which the crime was committed, the custodial State, the State of the victim of the crime, or the country of origin of the offender . . . have consented to the exercise of the jurisdiction of the Court.[98]

In fact this was objected to by too many states and in the end the ICC, under article 12, has jurisdiction if the state in which the crime was committed, or the suspect's state of origin, is a party to the statute. With no inherent jurisdiction over core crimes, the court's ability to apply basic principles of justice without fear or favor is reduced. Furthermore, under article 17 the court's jurisdiction is complementary to the jurisdiction of national courts and will be activated only when the national authorities are "unable or unwilling" to prosecute. This is a step backward from the ad hoc tribunals, which are supranational in character, having "primacy" over national courts.[99] Although this is an explicable retreat, it nevertheless adds to the air of conservatism hanging over the establishment of the ICC.

Parts of the ICC statute counter these state-centered provisions. There were unsuccessful attempts to restrict the ICC's competence if the Security Council was addressing the matter under chapter VII of the charter;[100] article 16 requires a positive resolution of the Security Council adopted under chapter VII to block a prosecution. The attainment of such a blocking resolution will be much harder to achieve, and even if adopted the block is effective only for twelve months, after which a further Security Council resolution is required. In addition, the triggers for initiating proceedings are generous. Although individuals cannot bring a case against another individual, article 13 permits the independent prosecutor to initiate proceedings. In many ways the success of the court will depend on the strength of personality and dynamism of the prosecutor, who under article 15(1) is empowered to "initiate investigations *proprio motu* on the basis of information on crimes within the jurisdiction of the Court." Horse-trading can be expected, although article 42(4) of the statute requires the prosecutor to be elected only by an absolute ballot of the members of the assembly of state parties.

Conclusion

The enhancement and protection of the core UN value of justice in the specific form of international criminal justice illustrates the inherent dynamism of the UN system. From abstract value, to formulation of specific international crimes, to concrete embodiment in the form of the ICC, the United Nations has advanced toward a system of international criminal justice that will provide adequate mechanisms for protecting basic human rights. The recognition that criminal acts entail individual responsibility, and that violators can be tried and sentenced by courts of humanity established by the United Nations, are momentous achievements in a world of generally self-interested states. However, the effectiveness of these courts—the ICTY, the ICTR, the special court for Sierra Leone, and the ICC—has yet to be gauged. The former two are convicting and sentencing many individuals guilty of heinous crimes, but they are yet a drop in the ocean when considering the number of international crimes still being committed around the globe. The impact of the ICC has yet to be evaluated, but the preliminary assessment is not optimistic in light of its jurisdictional limitations.

The United Nations has contributed to a substantial body of international criminal law prohibiting aggression, slavery, torture, forms of terrorism, drug-trafficking, hostage-taking, and other crimes, yet it has failed to provide adequate mechanisms for enforcement. Its overreliance on states to prosecute individuals, the cumbersome actions of the Security Council in punishing terrorists, and the supervisory mechanisms of core human rights treaties are insufficient to address even minor breaches of international criminal law. The advent of the ICTY and ICTR is an improvement, as is the ICC. The need for international judicial mechanisms to protect the UN's value of justice is self-evident. The half-century delay in creating such bodies, in particular the ICC, is inexcusable; the list of unprosecuted international criminals is testament to that. Now that the ICC exists, the United Nations must develop and expand its jurisdiction and powers, moving it toward becoming a strong international criminal court upholding basic justice in the face of barbarism.

Notes

1. Malanczuk, *Akehurst's Modern Introduction,* 113.
2. Alvarez, "Rush to Closure," 2074.
3. *United States v. Lt. William Calley* (1971) 46 CMR 1131.
4. *Attorney General of the Government of Israel v. Eichmann* (1961) 36 ILR 5.
5. See, for example, GA Res. 3074, 3 Dec. 1973.
6. (1998) 37 ILM 999.
7. Schwarzenberger, "The Problem of an International Criminal Court."
8. 6 LNTS 253.
9. Murphy, "International Crimes," 995.
10. See Rosenne, "State Responsibility," 146.
11. UN doc. A/51/10 (1996).
12. UN doc. A/51/332/Corr.1 (1996).
13. UN doc. A/CN.4/L.602/Rev.1, 26 July 2001.
14. Judgment of the Nuremberg Military Tribunal, (1947) *American Journal of International Law* 41, 172.
15. GA Res. 95(I), 11 Dec. 1946.
16. Ortega, "The ILC Adopts the Draft Code," 285.
17. 94 LNTS 57.

18. UN doc. A/51/332/Corr.1 (1996).

19. GA Res. 3314 (XXIX), 14 Dec. 1974.

20. Harris, *Cases and Materials,* 949.

21. White, *Keeping the Peace,* 50.

22. Zimmermann, "The Creation of an International Criminal Court," 199.

23. White and Cryer, "A Threat Too Far."

24. Ferencz, "An International Criminal Code and Court," 386.

25. Schuett, "The International War Crimes Tribunal," 102–107. Milosevic was indicted on 27 May 1999 (IT-99-37) but in relation to the suppressive acts taken by the FRY in Kosovo during 1998–1999.

26. UN doc. S/23308 (1991).

27. 974 UNTS 177.

28. See Art. 5(2) of the Montreal Convention, which obliges each state to establish jurisdiction over the offenses "in the case where the alleged offender is present in its territory and it does not extradite him."

29. Harris, *Cases and Materials,* 715.

30. Other UN-sponsored treaties dealing with aspects of "aerial" terrorism: Convention on Offences and Certain Other Acts Committed on Board Aircraft (1963), 704 UNTS 219; Convention for the Unlawful Seizure of Aircraft (1970), 860 UNTS 105; Convention for the Suppression of Unlawful Acts of Violence at Airports Serving International Civil Aviation (1988), 27 ILM 267.

31. SC 3033 mtg., 21 Jan. 1992.

32. Libyan application, 3 March 1992, ICJ General List No. 88.

33. See *Lockerbie* cases (provisional measures), ICJ Rep. 1992, para. 39.

34. SC Res. 1044, 31 Jan. 1996; SC Res. 1054, 26 April 1996.

35. SC Res. 1267, 15 Oct. 1999.

36. SC Res. 1368, 12 Sept. 2001.

37. SC Res. 1373, 28 Sept. 2001.

38. See Art. 2(6) of the UN Charter.

39. (2001) 40 ILM 582.

40. 78 UNTS 277.

41. Though universal jurisdiction is recognized in customary international law—Ratner and Abrams, *Accountability for Human Rights Atrocities,* 40.

42. *Akayesu* case, ICTR-96-4-T, 2 Sept. 1998. But see the *Jelisic* case before the ICTY, IT-95-10, 19 Oct. 1999.

43. UN doc. ST/LEG/SER.E/15, 86–88. See also *Reservations to the Convention on Genocide* case, ICJ Rep. 1951, 15.

44. *Application of the Convention on the Prevention and Punishment of the Crime of Genocide, Provisional Measures,* ICJ Rep. 1993, 325 (preliminary objections judgment, 11 July 1996). Croatia made an application to the ICJ against the FRY on 2 July 1999. The FRY made an application against ten NATO states for their involvement in the bombing of Serbia in 1999–see provisional measures judgment in *Legality of the Use of Force (Yugoslavia)* cases, (1999) 38 ILM 950.

45. (1985) 24 ILM 535.

46. D'Zurilla, "Individual Responsibility for Torture," 210–214.
47. Warbrick, "International Criminal Courts."
48. Murphy, "International Crimes," 999.
49. (1979) 18 ILM 1456, Art. 8.
50. (1989) 28 ILM 493, Arts. 21–22.
51. (1974) 13 ILM 50, Arts. V and IX.
52. GA Res. 47/133, 18 Dec. 1992.
53. It must be noted that "enforced disappearances of persons" is listed in the Rome Statute of 1998 establishing the ICC as one of the acts that can constitute a crime against humanity if "committed as part of a widespread or systematic attack directed against any civilian population, with knowledge of the attack"—Art. 7(1)(i).
54. But see the third preambular paragraph.
55. Ratner and Abrams, *Accountability,* 116.
56. UN doc. S/2000/915, 4 Oct. 2000; Frulli, "The Special Court."
57. O'Brian, "The International Tribunal."
58. SC Res. 827, 25 May 1993.
59. Lee, "The Rwandan Tribunal."
60. SC Res. 955, 8 Nov. 1994.
61. Warbrick, "The United Nations System," 260.
62. IT-94-1-AR72, 2 Oct. 1995.
63. ICTR-96-15-I, 18 June 1997.
64. Greenwood, "The Development of International Humanitarian Law," 102–106.
65. Malanczuk, *Akehurst's Modern Introduction,* 359.
66. Indicted on 16 November 1995, IT-95-18.
67. Greenwood, "The Development of International Humanitarian Law," 112.
68. Cases IT-95-5-R61, IT-95-18-R61, 11 July 1996.
69. But see Figa-Talamanca, "The Role of NATO in the Peace Agreement."
70. Mak, "The Case Against," 555–556. See also D'Amato, "Peace vs. Accountability."
71. (1996) 35 ILM 75.
72. Alvarez, "Rush to Closure," 2032.
73. Ibid., 3033–3034.
74. Ibid., 2041.
75. Ibid., 2045. But see Harris, "Progress and Problems," 1.
76. Alvarez, "Rush to Closure," 2088–2089.
77. *Tadic* case. See Art. 4 of the ICTR Statute 1994. Examples of important cases that develop international humanitarian law—*Celebici* case, IT-96-21-T, 16 Dec. 1998 (ICTY—re command responsibility); *Furundzija* case, IT-95-17, 10 Dec. 1998 (ICTY—rape as a war crime); *Kupreskic* case, IT-95-16 (ICTY—crimes against humanity); *Blaskic* case, IT-95-14, 3 March 2000 (crimes against humanity).
78. SC Res. 827, 25 May 1993, para. 4.
79. SC Res. 942, 23 Sept. 1994.

80. *Blaskic* case, IT-95-14-T, 18 July 1997.

81. SC 3607 mtg., 15 Dec. 1995.

82. Greenwood, "The Development of International Humanitarian Law," 98.

83. Ibid., 97.

84. See reports of the Secretary-General on the ICTR starting with the second report—UN doc. S/1995/533 (1995).

85. *Kambanda* case, ICTR 97-23-S, 4 Sept. 1998.

86. Harris, "Progress and Problems," 3.

87. See Boister, "The Exclusion of Treaty Crimes."

88. GA Res. 44/39, 4 Dec. 1989.

89. Crawford, "The ILC's Draft Statute"; Crawford, "The ILC Adopts a Statute."

90. GA Res. 51/207, 17 Dec. 1996.

91. (1998) 37 ILM 999.

92. Cryer, "Commentary on the Rome Statute," 274.

93. Ferencz, "An International Criminal Code and Court," 385–388.

94. See, for example, *Yunis v. Yunis* (1993) 30 ILM 403.

95. Zimmermann, "The Creation of a Permanent International Criminal Court," 177, 187, 189, 191–192, 195–197, and 199.

96. See Art. 17 of the ICC Statute.

97. But see Art. 13(b) of the ICC Statute.

98. Zimmermann, "The Creation of a Permanent International Criminal Court," 205.

99. See, for example, Art. 9(2) of the Statute of the ICTY (1993) 32 ILM 1203.

100. Gowlland-Debbas, "The Relationship," 99.

9

Human Rights

The international law of human rights, as well as the mechanisms for its supervision and enforcement, is not solely the product of the UN system. But the UN's activities have "contributed in a very large measure to the task of creating, shaping and implementing" the international human rights regime that has grown since the immediate post-1945 order.[1] Indeed, placing human rights on the international agenda at that time represented a significant development in international relations; by the very nature of human rights, the focus is on the individual rather than the state.

The proliferation of norms, processes, and organs concerned with human rights has been seen as chaotic, lacking any "systemic" or "rational" coherence.[2] Although there is confusion and overlap in the system, it does have a basic integrity; there has been evolution and development, a process not entirely accidental. There has been a deliberate effort to, first, establish the standards in a series of documents such as the UDHR of 1948. This has been followed by attempts to entrench standards in international law and establish mechanisms for the implementation of norms. The system has created political as well as legal mechanisms for the promotion and protection of human rights.

I am concerned with identifying the norms and mechanisms operating within the UN system, and I comment on their effectiveness. However, effectiveness is a subjective concept; some may be "satisfied with a focused discussion in an international forum," but "others might insist upon a formal condemnation or at least the establishment of a fact-finding and reporting mechanism," and still others "might be unsatisfied with anything less than the imposition of sanctions or even the mounting of a military exercise designed to restore respect for human rights."[3] Evaluations of the effectiveness of the UN system for the protection of human rights vary given different assumptions about what is "effective" protection of human rights.[4] This is compounded by the difficult issue of causality, meaning the problem of identifying whether it was the United Nations, other factors, or a combination that helped to alleviate an abusive situation.[5]

Given the relative nature of the concept of effectiveness, as well as the problematic nature of causation, I evaluate UN action against the standards outlined in Chapter 3 at two levels. First, I consider the implementation of standards by the various mechanisms and techniques. Second, I consider the effect of those actions on the ground in general terms; the reader can then make an informed decision about the effectiveness of the United Nations.

Political Mechanisms

The UN chain of authority for human rights runs from the General Assembly, to ECOSOC, to the UN Commission on Human Rights,[6] to the Subcommission on the Promotion and Protection of Human Rights (before 1999, known as the Subcommission on Prevention of Discrimination and Protection of Minorities).[7] Although the latter is a subsidiary body consisting of twenty-six independent experts, the others are political bodies comprising representatives of states. Furthermore, the subcommission's independence is not absolute, with members often having a close affiliation with their national governments.[8] It is inevitable that this aspect of the system will tend toward domination by state concerns and that human rights will be used as a weapon in the hands of the majority against certain states. Concern for protecting the human rights of *individuals* has not been a major facet of this system. It is rare for this part of the system to alleviate abuses of individuals within an oppressive state, though condemnation and isolation can eventually have an effect on abuses in general. Of course, this assumes there is a causal link between condemnation and alleviation, and it can be argued that isolation of especially oppressive states leads to greater abuse.

The political aspects of the system can penetrate the hard shell of the state by the use of special rapporteurs, ad hoc committees, and the High Commissioner for Human Rights. The latter is a post created in

1993 following the Vienna World Conference on Human Rights with the mandate of promoting and protecting human rights throughout the world and undertaking tasks assigned by the competent bodies within the UN system.[9] Such mechanisms enable the United Nations to obtain information on abuses within states, though actual visits on the ground are based on consent. This system may reveal the level and type of human rights abuses occurring within a country.

However, the end-product of this process, namely, criticism and condemnation, is directed against the state and does not always alleviate the suffering. Of course, if the human rights situation (usually in combination with an armed conflict) is a threat to the peace, then the collective security powers of the Security Council can be invoked, leading to the possibility of economic sanctions, criminal tribunals, and military measures. However, economic sanctions are a blunt weapon and often do more harm than good (see Chapter 6). International criminal tribunals are rare and tend to remedy human rights abuses retroactively. Military measures can be successful in protecting human rights, but collective humanitarian intervention under UN authority is sporadic and limited by member states' fear of losing military personnel. However, human rights protection in postconflict situations in the context of multifaceted peacekeeping operations can prove to be more effective. This occurred in El Salvador from 1991 to 1995, and in Kosovo and East Timor since 1999.

The international covenant system sponsored by the United Nations allows individuals greater freedom under international law to bring legal cases against governments. However, it is doubtful whether individuals possess full rights on the international plane. The problems— lack of universal ratification, reservations, and the optional schemes for individual complaints—could be alleviated by the political arm of the system, creating effective mechanisms for protecting human rights. UN member states would then be subject to the constitutional law of the system built up by the political organs, for instance, in the shape of the UDHR. Enforcement would not depend on a member state being a party to the relevant covenant and accepting all the obligations therein but would be a product of its UN membership.

The hub of the political system—the UN Commission on Human Rights, consisting of fifty-three state representatives—has concentrated on identifying and setting standards and then the application of standards to states. In 1967 ECOSOC authorized the commission to consider allegations of gross violations of human rights, especially those

revealing a consistent pattern of human rights violations.[10] The aim is to
reveal and condemn the most serious violators and has resulted in a
"well established public procedure for the investigation of human rights
violations by particular states."[11] This consists of the appointment of a
special rapporteur whose report is discussed in open sessions of the
commission. In the past this process has been so politicized as to raise
questions over its legitimacy.

There is no doubt that the special procedures that are focused on
country situations, inasmuch as they are contentious and denunciatory,
carry political overtones. With the exception of persistent situations
(southern Africa, Israel, Chile), there appears to be a growing reluctance
among the UN membership to make country situations the object of
public scrutiny. The country approach has been on the retreat, and instead the so-called thematic approach has come into favor.[12]

The commission's approach toward abusive states is limited, and its
handling of individual petitions has been less than convincing. The
domination of the nation-state within the UN system in 1946 led the commission to adopt the shameful position of refusing to consider petitions
from individuals alleging human rights abuse by their government.[13] This
victory for absolute sovereignty was relaxed somewhat in 1959, when
ECOSOC made available to the commission communications received
from individuals and gave copies to the member states named in the complaints (with the individual remaining anonymous).[14] However, it was
clear that the commission could not take any action on the matter.

The gradual erosion of sovereignty has continued, although it is by
no means satisfactory. In 1970 ECOSOC authorized the subcommission
to establish a procedure for reviewing petitions from individuals from
any UN member state. Again the aim was to refer to the commission
only those situations that from the evidence before the subcommission
"appear to reveal a consistent pattern of gross and reliably attested violations of human rights."[15] This may lead to the appointment of an ad
hoc committee whose investigation is dependent on the consent of the
state in question. The end result is that the commission can report to
ECOSOC and make recommendations. Again the procedure is not really
centered on upholding the rights of individuals but on revealing the
presence of abusive states. In a sense this is as far as the UN system has
progressed. Here is a sober evaluation:

> Whereas the Commission's monitoring and enforcement work . . . is un-
> doubtedly worthwhile in the sense that it results in reports evidencing
> state conduct and requires states to defend themselves at Commission

sessions, there are limits to its value. Although attention may be focused beneficially on situations of real concern for human rights, politics clearly influence the choice and treatment of particular cases. There are no mandatory powers to hear witnesses or to enter territory to conduct investigations. Where infringements of human rights are found, the Commission's powers are restricted to persuasion, public criticism and, in the most serious cases, attempts at isolation of the offending state; there are no legally binding sanctions available.[16]

By creating a process for the correct and accurate identification of the facts (but only in certain cases), the UN Commission on Human Rights has taken the first step in creating a process for the enforcement of human rights norms—in which the facts are established and the law is enforced. At the moment the commission has contributed to the recognition by states that there is a body of international human rights law applicable to domestic situations, but the problem is one of enforcement of those norms.[17] Of course the development of this type of legal system is an expression of idealism in international relations, where states only reluctantly qualify their sovereignty. However, there is progress within the more narrowly defined legal regimes set up under the international covenants.

The absence of mandatory and coercive powers affects the other main UN bodies concerned with human rights. The UN Centre for Human Rights, for instance, which the Vienna declaration of 1993 identified as playing an "important role in co-ordinating system wide attention for human rights," merely administers the UN's involvement in human rights and has no proactive role.[18] Even the UN High Commissioner for Refugees, created in 1950 under article 22 of the UN Charter as a subsidiary organ of the General Assembly, has essentially a supervisory role.[19] This is recognized in article 35 of the 1951 Convention Relating to the Status of Refugees.[20] In addition, the UNHCR is dependent upon state consent, as there are no mandatory or coercive powers to ensure the protection of refugees.[21] Refugees therefore have rights in a relative, not absolute, sense. The status of the refugee on the international plane is shaped more by state sovereignty, and the consequent lack of international institutional protection, than it is by abstract notions of rights.[22]

Legal Mechanisms

The Vienna declaration of 1993 concentrates more on the reinforcement of established standards and the setting down of new ones than on improving the coordination and efficiency of the increasingly elaborate structure of institutions that addresses human rights. One development has been the proliferation of organs under the binding treaties developed at the United Nations to protect specific human rights. However, early human rights treaties sponsored by the UN General Assembly concentrated on setting standards rather than creating the machinery for implementation. The leading example is the Convention on the Prevention and Punishment of the Crime of Genocide of 1948 (see Chapter 8).

Later UN-sponsored human rights treaties lay down standards and create the machinery for overseeing the implementation of these standards. Coordination of these separate human rights regimes is evidenced by the fact that the UN Secretary-General since 1993 has held annual meetings of the chairs of the treaty bodies, the aim of which is to adopt specific measures for coordination. An early move toward greater institutional protection of human rights can be found in the International Convention on the Elimination of All Forms of Racial Discrimination of 1966,[23] which inter alia establishes the Committee on the Elimination of All Forms of Racial Discrimination (CERD), consisting of eighteen independent experts. CERD receives periodic reports from the parties on the issue of the implementation of the convention. In addition, there are little-used systems providing for interstate claims, whereby one state can complain of another state's nonimplementation of the convention; as well as an optional system, which has only recently been activated, for petitions to CERD by individuals.[24] CERD has no power to make binding decisions in any of these matters, its competence being limited to recommendations and suggestions.[25]

Despite CERD's limited powers, its record has improved, with evidence that its reports and procedures have caused many states to amend their internal legislation and even enforce it.[26] As with all treaty regimes, the impact on human rights is insufficient when compared to racial discrimination around the world. Nevertheless, some progress has been made on tackling deep-rooted historical enmities within states. In general, though, CERD suffers from the same systemic weaknesses as the committees operating under the general international covenants reviewed below.

A similar structure is to be found in later UN-sponsored human rights treaties such as the Convention Against Torture and Other Cruel, Inhuman, or Degrading Treatment or Punishment (1984).[27] This treaty provides that torture is a crime of universal jurisdiction in article 5(2) and establishes the Committee Against Torture of ten independent experts. CAT has competence to hear state party reports on implementation and state party complaints on nonimplementation by other parties; under article 22, an optional procedure is established whereby individual petitions can be heard. Again there are no powers given to CAT to make binding decisions, let alone enforce its findings. For example, in *Qani Halimi-Nedzibi v. Austria,* article 12 of the Convention Against Torture had been found to be breached.[28] CAT asked the state party to ensure that similar violations would not occur in the future and report to CAT any relevant measures taken by the state in conformity with its views. However, in another case, *Balabou Mutombo v. Switzerland,* CAT stated that Switzerland had "an obligation to refrain from expelling" the complainant, who faced torture upon return to his native Zaire.[29] CAT was not attempting to make a binding decision; it was using stronger language to remind the state party of its obligations under the Convention Against Torture, in this case article 3.

The later conventions prohibiting racial discrimination and torture are an improvement over the simple standard-setting of the early Genocide Convention. However, the lack of mandatory and enforcement powers means the committees act as mere watchdogs, relying on publicity and pressure, as well as treaty obligations, to ensure compliance. Furthermore, not all recent treaties go as far in the empowerment of the supervisory body. The Convention on the Rights of the Child of 1989[30] contains very thorough standards regarding the treatment of children but only empowers the Committee on the Rights of the Child to hear state reports and to make suggestions and recommendations thereon,[31] there being no provision for state complaints or the right of individual petition. The Committee on the Elimination of Discrimination Against Women, established under the 1979 Convention on the Elimination of All Forms of Discrimination Against Women,[32] has only recently been empowered by an optional protocol allowing individual complaints.[33] This is combined with an investigatory power when there is evidence of grave or systematic abuses, though on-site investigation can occur only with state consent.

The failure to extend the rights of the child, and until recently those of women, to include complaints to an impartial body undermines the completeness of these rights. Indeed, even under the treaties—which do contain the right of individual petition—the optional procedure still places ultimate control with the state. The fundamental contradiction at the heart of human rights law is that it does not grant full rights to individuals on the international plane. The granting of those rights is still under the sovereign command of the state, which has the option of not ratifying the treaty at all, or of ratifying the treaty but not agreeing to the optional system, if available, that allows individuals to complain of abuse.

In some ways creating a treaty framework to protect the human rights listed in the UDHR can be seen as an attempt to bypass the UN political system, with its bedrock of state sovereignty and its political machinations. However, more recent evidence, shown by the thematic approach, suggests that the elements are working together to tackle human rights problems at different levels and in different ways but with the same aims and objectives: the protection and promotion of human rights. Fundamental in this regard are the general human rights regimes created by the ICCPR[34] and the ICESCR[35] adopted by the UN General Assembly in 1966. These treaties were the final product of a drafting process started in the Human Rights Commission in 1947. The treaties themselves did not enter into force until 1976.

The treaties split the list of human rights contained in the UDHR. The strongest justification was that civil and political rights (so-called first-generation human rights) had an absolute character requiring immediate state compliance, whereas economic and social rights (second-generation human rights) were relative, depending upon the development of the state in question. Such arguments are reflected in the obligations on state parties, contained in article 2(1) of each; civil and political rights being subject to an absolute and immediate obligation, whereas economic and social rights are subject to a qualified and progressive obligation.[36] In reality the driving force behind the division was the ideological divide between the West, which advocated civil and political rights, and the socialist bloc, which advocated economic and social rights. The division weakened the covenants, which have not yet been ratified by the full membership of the United Nations.

The systems of supervision differ, the institutional framework being much more advanced in the case of civil and political rights. Article 28 of the ICCPR establishes the HRC, consisting of eighteen independent experts. The HRC's primary function, according to article 40, is to review state reports every five years on the "measures they have adopted which give effect to the rights" contained in the treaty. Part of the review process involves public questioning of state representatives on aspects of their reports. Governments may well attempt to hide abuses in the reports, and so by informal procedure HRC members receive reports from NGOs. The HRC will often conclude its cross-examination of representatives with a critical series of observations and transmit to the

state parties general comments on overall compliance.[37] However, the
HRC has interpreted article 40(4) as prohibiting country-specific reports. The system thus relies on states to incorporate any comments into
their domestic legislation and procedures for protecting human rights
before the next report has to be submitted in five years. This method of
supervision is "implementation" only in a broad sense, as it depends on
a haphazard system of fact-finding beyond the facts presented by governments.[38] There is no method of ensuring compliance beyond relying
on the next round of reports.

The ICCPR also provides, in article 41, an optional system of state
application to allege treaty violations by another state. No such applications have been made. More successful has been the First Optional
Protocol to the ICCPR which has about 100 state parties.[39] Under article 1 of this protocol state parties recognize "the competence of the
Committee to receive and consider communications from individuals
subject to its jurisdiction who claim to be victims of a violation by that
State Party of any of the rights set forth in the Covenant."[40] This system
has proved a greater success, with the HRC finding in ninety-three of
120 cases it heard by 1996 that breaches had been committed.[41] Nevertheless, the HRC itself recognized the limitations in protecting human
rights under the optional protocol:

> The Committee is neither a court nor a body with a quasi-judicial man-
> date, like the organs created under . . . the European Convention on
> Human Rights. . . . Still, the Committee applies the provisions of the
> Covenant and the Optional Protocol in a judicial sprit and performs
> functions similar to those of the European Commission on Human
> Rights, in as much as the consideration of applications from individu-
> als is concerned. Its decisions on the merits . . . are, in principle, com-
> parable to the reports of the European Commission, non-binding rec-
> ommendations. The two systems differ, however, in that the Optional
> Protocol does not provide explicitly for friendly settlement between the
> parties, and, more importantly, in that the Committee has no power to
> hand down binding decisions as does the European Court of Human
> Rights. State parties to the Optional Protocol endeavour to observe the
> Committee's views, but in cases of non-compliance the Optional Proto-
> col does not provide for any enforcement measures or for sanctions.[42]

Furthermore, "compliance with the HRC's views has been disappointing although some states have shown a willingness to co-operate
with the HRC and give effect to its views."[43] Overall, the HRC presents
a limited avenue of redress for individuals who have suffered human

rights abuses and compares unfavorably to the more established regional systems.

Nevertheless, the impact of HRC decisions goes beyond criticism of individual states. Its decisions have a wider significance in that the standards it sets create expectations as to how governments should behave toward citizens. Its position as a fulcrum for human rights consciousness-raising is bolstered by its universality, its impartiality, and the weight that its decisions carry. The HRC's early jurisprudence focused heavily on violations of the rights to be free from torture, inhumane and degrading treatment, and arbitrary arrest, as well as the right to a fair trial. Its decisions tended to be perfunctory determinations that certain behavior constituted a breach of particular provisions of the ICCPR. This is epitomized in the glut of cases against Uruguay in the late 1970s and early 1980s, where there were obvious breaches by the military regime. For instance, the HRC determined that an eighteen-month period of detention between arrest and trial constituted a breach of article 9, on the right to trial within a reasonable period of time.[44] The HRC also determined that article 7 was breached when an individual suffered serious physical injuries during detention; the HRC did not specify whether this constituted torture or something less.[45]

Later decisions developed the law, thereby increasing the protection of individuals. For example, in *Mukong v. Cameroon,* the HRC stated that "arbitrariness" in the sense of "arbitrary arrest" in article 9 was not to be equated with "against the law" but must be interpreted more broadly to include elements of inappropriateness, injustice, lack of predictability, and due process of law.[46] This approach reduces states' ability to enact laws and establish national standards that fall short of international standards.

In another significant development, the HRC made a determination in *Mojica v. Dominican Republic* that an individual's right to life under article 6 was violated by the state when that person "disappeared" and the government presented no convincing evidence that it was not involved.[47] Placing the burden of proof on the government is a recognition of the vast discrepancy in resources and power between the individual and the state, and the decision constitutes an attempt to reduce the arbitrary exercise of power.

A final example is the HRC's decision to uphold a law that made it a criminal offense to challenge the correctness of the conviction of war criminals at Nuremberg. In *Faurisson v. France,* the HRC found that the application of this law to an individual who denied the existence of the

Nazi gas chambers did not violate that person's right to freedom of expression under article 19 of the covenant, because the rights of others prevailed.[48] The HRC felt that the government had correctly exercised its power to restrict freedom of expression given that it had the valid aim of halting the spread of anti-Semitism in France.

The assignment of relative weight to rights in different situations is the sign of a maturing jurisprudence that recognizes that granting rights to individuals also creates duties.

These are just some examples; their actual impact on the ground is questionable. Arbitrary arrests, the "disappeared," and Holocaust denials continue to plague many states. The theoretical development of the law by the HRC increases the gap between law and reality, at least in some states. Nevertheless, the development of human rights standards, and at least some supervision of those standards by the HRC, pressures recalcitrant state parties to implement and uphold human rights. The machinery of the UN system can utilize this framework to pressure UN member states, but that pressure consists of condemnation and prodding rather than coercion and punishment.

The ICESCR has even more limited institutional machinery to ensure compliance with its provisions.[49] The treaty (articles 16–22) places responsibility for overseeing the implementation of rights contained therein on ECOSOC. The failure of ECOSOC or its Working Group, consisting of state representatives, led to the creation of the CESCR, modeled on the HRC.[50] The CESCR's competence is much more straightforward, in that it reviews five-year state reports according to articles 16 and 17. It does not have an individual complaint mechanism, though there have been proposals.[51]

Like the HRC, the CESCR has had problems with state parties not submitting reports.[52] The CESCR examines reports in public hearings along the lines of the HRC and makes critical comments in its concluding observations. The CESCR can also make "suggestions and recommendations of a general nature on the basis of its consideration of" national reports. This reporting process has the same defects as for the ICCPR, although strangely the CESCR has developed more formal procedures than the HRC for receiving factual information from NGOs and the UN specialized agencies.[53] A member of the CESCR assessed the reporting procedure as follows:

> In general terms, the potential effectiveness of the reporting procedure clearly lies less in the formal exchanges between the Committee and

the state party and more in the mobilization of domestic political and
other forces to participate in monitoring government policies and providing a detailed critique (assuming that one is warranted) of the government's own assessment of the situation.[54]

The fact that the system relies on domestic public opinion is flawed.
Public opinion plays a formal or informal role in lobbying a government
to change its policy—a role that is often lacking in an abusive state.[55]
The development of a civil society that can pressure government to
change policy is more prevalent in democratic states, which guarantee
human rights within a democratic framework. The fact that a government is subject to periodic elections makes it much more susceptible to
public pressure. The end result is that there can be marginal human
rights improvements in the majority of states, but they are offset by a
deterioration of rights among the minority. The process of "naming and
shaming" these states, embodied in the CESCR, tends to have limited
effect on the human rights situation.

The Thematic Approach

In analyzing thematic approaches to human rights and state compliance,
extensive use has been made of *For the Record 1999: The UN Human
Rights System,* produced by Human Rights Internet, a Canadian-based
NGO. This annual review of the UN record on human rights protection
commenced publication in 1997. Its usefulness is pointed out by Lloyd
Axworthy, the Canadian minister of foreign affairs, in the preface to the
1999 report: the "United Nations has, over the years, developed a comprehensive structure to monitor the performance of states as measured
against their commitments to international standards."[56] This encapsulates the issue: the problem is not the lack of human rights standards
and mechanisms but the willingness of states to comply with obligations. The law is binding on states; the lack of enforcement is a combination of institutional deficiency and state unwillingness. In a consensual international legal system, institutional deficiency is endemic; the
real problem is lack of goodwill on the part of states.

Bearing in mind that the thematic approach now dominates the UN
human rights system, the list of thematic mechanisms and approaches
found in the 1999 record defies rational classification. They are all, of
course, human rights issues, dealing with groups (e.g., children, migrants,

minorities, women), activities covered by legal regimes (disappearances, torture), basic essentials of life (food, poverty, development), and current crises in health (HIV/AIDS, toxic waste). Although the list is longer, it reflects concerns and is not representative of a coordinated, coherent attempt to protect interrelated human rights across the board. This may reflect a desire to move away from the classification of human rights into first-, second-, and third-generation rights, but the lack of an alternative framework can produce a simple checklist approach.

Within each theme, relevant UN actions are coordinated, but only to a certain extent. In this section I look at two themes: disappearances and torture. The first is a problem that concerns many human rights, especially the right to life. The second theme concerns the right to be free from torture. These two themes, narrow as they are compared to, say, poverty, nonetheless illustrate that there is a proliferation of mechanisms and procedures.

The UN's work on disappearances is gaining strength and builds on the jurisprudence of the HRC. The Working Group on Enforced or Voluntary Disappearances was established in 1980 by the Human Rights Commission. It has developed a competence, unique among working groups, of receiving individual complaints.[57] The Working Group reported in 1999 that it had information on disappearances in seventy countries, illustrating the extent of the problem.[58] The report identified features of the disappearances plus characteristics of the victims but was unable to go any farther than advocate the full implementation of the nonbinding Declaration on the Protection of All Persons from Enforced Disappearances, adopted by the General Assembly in 1992.[59] The Working Group criticized the immunity of perpetrators and advocated criminal prosecution in accordance with the declaration. The problem is that the perpetrators often operate under the umbrella of the state. Designating such actions as international crimes may be more productive, but mechanisms for enforcement are few (the ICC statute includes disappearances only as one component of crimes against humanity).

The UN system is attempting to adopt a binding convention, a draft treaty being prepared by the Subcommission on the Promotion and Protection of Human Rights in 1998.[60] The treaty would create the Committee Against Forced Disappearances, with the same three-tiered competence as the CERD, CAT, and HRC—state complaints, state reports, and an individual complaint procedure. Significantly, it would possess the power to undertake procedures to seek and find persons who have disappeared. The advent of a quasienforcement power within a committee acting under a human rights treaty, if it comes to pass, will be a big step toward an effective UN human rights system. Of course, having the power is one thing; using it to good effect another. There is still a long way to go considering the depth of the problem.

The UN concern as to torture reached a higher level compared to disappearances when it adopted the 1984 treaty accompanied by the establishment of the CAT. The legal regime governing torture is at a more advanced stage of development. However, it is interesting to see whether the UN record on torture has produced any breakthrough since 1984. The special rapporteur's 1999 reports to the Human Rights Commission and the General Assembly indicated that torture is still a serious (and possibly increasing) problem.[61] The special rapporteur transmitted 113 urgent actions to forty-one countries in the first eight months of 1999 compared to 712 appeals to eighty-three countries in the previous five years. Such figures indicate that the UN system is not reducing the number of cases of torture, at least significantly.

This perception is enhanced by the fundamental problems identified by the special rapporteur, namely, prolonged detention without communication; conditions that give the opportunity for torture; the presumption against torture endemic in many prosecutors and judges within countries; and widespread immunity given to the perpetrators. The special rapporteur's recommendations to the UN's political bodies also indicate that the United Nations has not made progress in eradicating torture. The main recommendations were that detention not be permitted beyond forty-eight hours; that the ICC statute be ratified (though again it must be noted that torture per se is not a crime under that statute); and the enactment and implementation of national legislation requiring prosecution. These basic issues (apart from the maximum period of detention) do not go much beyond the legal principles already recognized under UN law. It is noticeable that neither the Human Rights Commission nor the UN General Assembly adopted the rapporteur's recommendation regarding maximum period of detention.[62]

A significant development since 1992 has been the Human Rights Commission's Working Group, mandated to establish a draft optional protocol to the Convention Against Torture to establish a preventive system of regular visits to places of detention.[63] This would develop the existing procedure under article 20 of the convention for on-site visits (with state consent) when there is strong evidence of systematic torture.[64] The possible development of an inspection regime by the United Nations, albeit under an optional protocol, is an encouraging sign and shows the United Nations can move beyond the establishment and re-finement of standards and fact-finding mechanisms toward enforcement and prevention.

The Specialized Agencies

In considering the UN's record on human rights, the role of two spe-cialized agencies—the ILO and UNESCO—must not be forgotten.

Under the ILO constitution, the ILO is concerned with economic and social rights such as the right to work, the right to the enjoyment of just and favorable conditions of work, the right to form trade unions and join the trade union of one's choice, the right to social security, and the right to an adequate standard of living. Civil and political rights covered include freedom of expression, freedom of association, and the right of peaceful assembly.[65]

The ILO has a good record on workers' rights. This is due to its unique, equitable composition. All decisions within ILO organs are taken on a tripartite basis. In the annual General Conference each member is represented by a delegation consisting of two government delegates, one employers' delegate, and one workers' delegate, each delegate having one vote, requiring either a simple majority or a qualified majority for a decision to be adopted. The fact that all the relevant interest groups are represented ensures that the output of the ILO, in the form of over 180 conventions and 190 recommendations, achieves greater acceptance.

The output of the ILO is legislative. The organization uses its pow-ers of treaty-making and resolution adoption in a sophisticated and combined manner. Initial recommendations can lead to a binding treaty. This is not uncommon in the UN's other bodies, but the ILO can also supplement a framework convention with more detailed recommenda-tions.[66] Formally, recommendations have less legal force than binding treaty commitments, but in practice the two methods of lawmaking are interwoven; it would be difficult for a member state to accept a con-vention but not its clarifying or explanatory recommendations. For in-stance, the 1951 ILO Convention Concerning Equal Remuneration for Men and Women Workers for Work of Equal Value[67] lays down a gen-eral principle of equal pay, and the Recommendation Concerning Equal Remuneration for Men and Women Workers for Equal Value adopted by the General Conference of the ILO that same year[68] indicates methods in which the members could implement the general principle.

This legislative nature is heightened by the fact that the secretariat of the ILO, the International Labour Office, has not permitted reservations to the ILO conventions. This practice has been accepted by member states, although it is out of line with the normal law of treaties, which permits reservations unless stated otherwise in the treaty and unless contrary to the object and purposes of the treaty.[69] In 1951 the International Labour Office justified this approach on the grounds of the unique tripartite nature of the conference and by the fact that the ILO constitution contemplates, in article 19(5)(b) and (d), the adoption or rejection of a convention as a whole by the legislative bodies of member states. To allow reservations would be to allow one of the tripartite elements—the government—to block rights acceptable to both employers and employees. The ILO conventions are to be agreed within the ILO, and it is in that forum that changes and modifications should be proposed, not unilaterally within legislatures.[70]

Thus there is a higher degree of congruence between the laws adopted and compliance by member states. The organization breaks down the normal relationship between state and organization by its tripartite nature; the output is viewed as legislative. Conventions adopted by the ILO are supervised in a way rarely found within the United Nations (e.g., the two international covenants sponsored by the Human Rights Commission). Although some states objected to the ILO's first conventions because states lacked complete control, the ILO's practice was quickly accepted. Furthermore, article 19(5)(e) of the ILO constitution provides that members must bring the convention before the municipal authorities for the enactment of legislation and to report on the result; if the member does not ratify the convention

> it shall report to the Director General of the International Labour Office, at appropriate intervals as requested by the Governing Body, the position of its law and practice in regard to the matters dealt with in the Convention, showing the extent to which effect has been given . . . to any of the provisions of the Convention . . . and stating the difficulties which prevent or delay the ratification of such Convention.

In other words, a member state that has not ratified a convention must justify its position and also report on the discrepancies between its practice and the convention—despite the fact it is not a party. A recalcitrant member can thus be pushed into ratification.[71]

Upon this impressive constitutional foundation there sit the normal supervisory mechanisms for compliance.[72] These include periodic reporting by states on the measures they have taken to implement the treaties to which they are a party. These are considered by a committee of experts, which transmits its observations to the General Conference.[73] There is also an interstate procedure, whereby a member can allege that another has not been complying with a relevant convention to which both states are a party. There is then provision for the establishment of a quasijudicial commission of inquiry by the governing body, and ultimate recourse can be made to the ICJ.[74]

In addition, a representation can be made to the International Labour Office by an association of employers or workers that a member government has not complied with an ILO convention to which it is a party. The governing body of the ILO can communicate this to the government, which can respond. A committee appointed by the governing body then hears the case and reports back with recommendations. The governing body decides whether to accept the recommendations and, if a breach of the convention is found, can publish the original allegation.[75] Finally there is a special mechanism to consider issues of freedom of association, with the establishment in 1951 of the Committee on Freedom of Association, drawn from each of the tripartite elements of the ILO. After examining complaints, the committee submits reports to the governing body with recommendations that can be adopted by that organ. Considerable activity has occurred under this mechanism, with more than 1,600 cases having been considered by the end of 1991.[76] The Fact-Finding and Conciliation Commission can be used to deal with sensitive cases, although it operates with the consent of the state and has heard very few cases.[77]

The ILO is a different type of organization, both in structure and lawmaking. Indications are that it is more successful as a result. Although there is progress yet to be made, the ILO's raft of conventions and resolutions, combined with its reasonably effective supervisory mechanisms and above all its makeup, have ensured that the legal regulation in this area is detailed and states are subjected to scrutiny. It has also been creative, not only in developing the law but also in taking practical steps to ensure implementation. Since 1953, for instance, it has also focused on indigenous peoples and tribal populations, culminating in a revised treaty, the Indigenous and Tribal Peoples Convention of 1989.[78] In addition to developing the only legal instruments the UN system has on this issue, the ILO has since the early 1950s carried out technical assistance programs, ranging from infrastructure to training.[79] Efforts in this regard have been intensified since the adoption of the revised convention.[80]

Although the ILO has worked well within the UN system as to indigenous peoples, jurisdictional disputes have arisen.[81] For instance, the 1990 Convention on the Rights of Migrant Workers and Their Families has not yet entered into force.[82] This treaty was not sponsored by the ILO but by the United Nations. One of the reasons for nonratification is that the ILO has competence over migrants as workers whereas the United Nations has competence over them as aliens, so that the issue of migrant workers should be addressed under ILO law.[83] This point seems to forget that the ILO is part of the UN system, and ILO law is part of the wider UN legal order, of which the 1990 convention is a part. Territorial disputes over competence seem, in this case, to be a self-serving argument by reluctant states rather than disputes between two different organizations operating within the UN system.

Allegations of overreaching have been leveled at the ILO and UN-ESCO. In 1977 the United States withdrew from the ILO, stating that the ILO had "become increasingly and excessively involved in political issues which are quite beyond the competence and mandate of the organization."[84] The politicization of the ILO is evidenced by a 1974 resolution directed at the continued Israeli occupation of Arab territories, declaring that any occupation of territory was a violation of human and trade union rights. It condemned Israeli violation of trade union freedom in the occupied territories and called on the ILO director-general to use all means to end the violation.[85] Although focused on trade union issues, the resolution reflected the condemnatory approach of the majority of states in the UN General Assembly, which has consistently called for the end of Israeli occupation. The ILO's resolution adds nothing to the substance of the assembly's resolutions and distracts it from its principal activities.[86]

Similar politicization led to the withdrawal of the United States and the United Kingdom from UNESCO in 1984 and 1985.[87] UNESCO was created in 1945 as the principal agency promoting international collaboration through education, science, and culture. Admittedly, UNESCO has carried the political agenda of the majority of states by selectively and rather ineptly condemning South Africa, Israel, and other pariah states (e.g., adopting resolutions on archaeology in Jerusalem, which amounted to an attack on the occupying power).[88] Although undermining the credibility and effectiveness of UNESCO, the constitutions of the ILO and UNESCO invite the discussion of bigger issues than the development of standard working conditions and the level of primary education.[89] The preamble of the ILO constitution states that "universal

and lasting peace can be established only if it is based upon social justice" and that "conditions of labour exist involving such injustice, hard-
ship and privation to large numbers of people as to produce unrest so
great that the peace and harmony of the world is imperilled."

The UNESCO constitution also makes an explicit link between its
primary area of work and wider political issues, especially peace and
security, by declaring in its preamble that "since wars begin in the
minds of men, it is in the minds of men that the defences of peace must
be constructed"; and further that

> a peace based exclusively upon the political and economic arrange-
> ments of governments would not be a peace which could secure the
> unanimous, lasting and sincere support of the peoples of the world,
> and that peace must therefore be founded, if it is not to fail, upon the
> intellectual and moral solidarity of mankind.

The explicit link between peace and security and education, science,
and culture is made in article 1, which defines UNESCO's purposes. In
many ways, it is not possible to accuse the majority in UNESCO or the
ILO of acting ultra vires when they adopt resolutions that concentrate
on security issues as well as labor and education issues.

Furthermore, the political condemnations by UNESCO and the ILO
only take up a small part of their time and resources. More than one-
third of UNESCO's budget is expended on programs designed to improve the quality of education in developing countries. Other areas include scientific cooperation on research and projects. Social sciences,
culture, and communications are also centers of activities, programs, and
research, all coordinated and financed by UNESCO. UNESCO's competence in human rights matters is perhaps not as extensive as the ILO's,
but it has developed considerable practice regarding educational rights,
cultural rights, and information rights. UNESCO's 1960 Convention
Against Discrimination in Education is a case in point.[90] By a 1962 protocol the Conciliation and Good Offices Commission was created to facilitate settlements between state parties under the convention. In addition,
since 1978 the executive board of UNESCO has established a procedure to
address individual allegations of human rights abuse within the primary
areas of UNESCO's competence. The Committee on Conventions and
Recommendations considers the complaints and, under a confidential procedure, attempts to facilitate a "friendly solution designed to advance the
promotion of the human rights falling within UNESCO's fields of competence."[91] Although the figures look encouraging, with the committee

settling 241 cases out of the 414 cases considered between 1978 and 1993, it "is unclear how successful the procedure has been, in view of the strict confidentiality which binds it, the length of time to produce results and the high proportion of cases declared inadmissible."[92]

Conclusion

An impressive body of human rights law has been produced by the UN system. There are mechanisms and procedures to ensure implementation, ranging from state reporting procedures (usually to an independent committee of experts) to an optional procedure for hearing individual complaints. However, most of these mechanisms are not subject to overarching UN control through ECOSOC and the General Assembly. This is where greater coordination should come from, just as it does in the area of labor law from the ILO, where an organization monitors treaties, not a series of stand-alone committees. However, coordination of action is not the real problem with the UN system of human rights; rather, it is states failing to accept their legal obligations under treaty regimes.

The lack of commitment is seen in the ratification of treaties and the level of state reporting under each treaty. The state reporting procedure is the very minimum for a human rights system. And ratification alone is insufficient, as that can indicate paper compliance as opposed to real compliance. If states are not prepared to fulfill their reporting commitments, then there is little that monitoring mechanisms will do. The legal principles have been established, the procedures put in place; the real task is for states to comply with the procedures. Only then will the United Nations be able to gauge whether human rights are being honored.[93]

Unless UN member states accept human rights obligations, it is difficult to say that there is an effective UN human rights system. The appalling human rights records in some countries will not be alleviated by reporting alone, but failure to comply with the minimum requirements of the system is an indication of profound cynicism that needs to be removed if the system is to be improved.

It is clear that there is a twofold need within the UN system. First, there must be a move toward the unification of the various treaty regimes to form a clear body of UN constitutional law binding on all UN members, accompanied by a rationalization of the treaty bodies. The ILO model should be followed in this regard, although ultimately the ILO should also be integrated into the UN human rights system. Second, there needs to be more intrusive implementation, such as that being proposed for torture and disappearances. Ultimately, though, the system can be improved dramatically only if all member states start to take their human rights commitments seriously.

Notes

1. Alston, "Appraising the United Nations," 1.

2. Ibid., 2.

3. Ibid., 13.

4. Donnelly, "International Human Rights"; Forsythe, *The Internationalization,* 77; Henkin, *The Age of Rights,* 24; Allott, *Eunomia,* 288. Summarized in Alston, "Appraising the United Nations," 17–18.

5. Alston, "Appraising the United Nations," 18.

6. Created by ECOSOC Res. 5(I), 16 Feb. 1946; Res. 9(II), 21 June 1946.

7. Created by the Commission in 1947 under the authority of ECOSOC granted by ECOSOC Res. 9(II).

8. Tolley, *The UN Commission,* 166–167.

9. GA Res. 48/141, 20 Dec. 1993. See Alston, "Neither Fish nor Fowl."

10. ECOSOC Res. 1235, 1967.

11. Harris, *Cases and Materials,* 629.

12. Van Boven, "Political and Legal Control Mechanisms," 44.

13. ECOSOC Res. 75 (V), 1947.

14. ECOSOC Res. 728F (28), 1959.

15. ECOSOC Res. 1503 (XLVIII), 27 May 1970.

16. Harris, *Cases and Materials,* 630.

17. Ibid.

18. Gibson, *International Organizations,* 199–201.

19. GA Res. 428(V), 14 Dec. 1950.

20. 189 UNTS 150.

21. Para. 8 of the UNHCR Statute, in GA Res. 428.

22. See also Goodwin-Gill, *The Refugee,* 131.

23. 640 UNTS 133.

24. Arts. 8, 9, 11, and 14 of the Convention Against Racial Discrimination. The first petition by an individual under Article 14 was *Yilmaz-Dogan v. Netherlands,* CERD Report, 43 UN GAOR, Supp. No. 18, 1988, 59.

25. For a succinct analysis of the CERD, see Harris, *Cases and Materials,* 705–707.

26. Shaw, *International Law,* 233.

27. (1985) 24 ILM 535.

28. (1995) 2(1) IHRR 190.

29. (1994) 1(3) IHRR 122. See also *Alan v. Switzerland* (1997) 4 IHRR 66.

30. (1989) 28 ILM 1488.

31. Arts. 43–45. For examples, see (1994) 1(3) IHRR 162–192.

32. (1980) 19 ILM 33, Art. 22.

33. UN doc. E/CN.6/1999/10, Annex 11.

34. 999 UNTS 150.

35. 993 UNTS 3.

36. Sieghart, *Human Rights,* 25–26. But see the Committee on Economic, Social, and Cultural Rights, General Comment No. 9 (1998), UN doc. E/1999/22, Annex IV, para. 2.

37. See generally Boerefijn, *The Reporting Procedure.*

38. McGoldrick, *The Human Rights Committee,* 500.

39. 999 UNTS 302.

40. On the meaning of "victim," see *Aumeeruddy-Cziffra v. Mauritius* (1981) 1 Selected Decisions HRC 67.

41. Harris, *Cases and Materials,* 652.

42. HRC Report (1989) 44 UN GAOR Supp. No. 40, 14.

43. McGoldrick, *Human Rights Committee,* 500.

44. *Burgos v. Uruguay* (1981) HRC 176.

45. *Weinberger v. Uruguay* (1981) HRC 114. See also *Ambrosini v. Uruguay* (1979) HRC 124.

46. (1995) 2 IHRR 131.

47. (1995) 2 IHRR 86.

48. (1996) 4 IHRR 444.

49. See generally Craven, *The International Covenant.*

50. ECOSOC Res. 1985/17.

51. Steiner and Alston, *International Human Rights,* 777.

52. Harris, *Cases and Materials,* 697.

53. ECOSOC Res. 187/5; Rule 69, Committee on Economic, Social, and Cultural Rights, Provisional Rules of Procedure, UN doc. E/C.12/1990/4.

54. Alston, "U.S. Ratification of the Covenant," 371.

55. Kirgis, *International Organizations,* 911.

56. <http://www.hri.ca/fortherecord1999>.

57. Steiner and Alston, *International Human Rights,* 642.

58. UN doc. E/CN.4/1999/62.

59. GA Res. 47/133, 18 Dec. 1992.

60. UN doc. E/CN.4/Sub.2/1998/19.

61. UN docs. E/CN.4/1999/61 and A/54/426.

62. E/CN.4/RES/1999/32, 30 April 1999; GA Res. 54/156, 17 Dec. 1999.

63. For progress, see UN docs. E/CN.4/1999/59 + Add.1, 29 April 1999; E/CN.4/2000/58, 2 Dec. 1999; A/C.3/55/L.30, 25 Oct. 2000.

64. Steiner and Alston, *International Human Rights,* 775.

65. Centre for Human Rights, *United Nations Action in the Field of Human Rights* (1994), 29.

66. Valticos, "The International Labour Organization," 134–135.

67. 165 UNTS 303.

68. ILO Recommendation 90 (1951).

69. Art. 19 of the Vienna Convention on the Law of Treaties, 1969, 1155 UNTS 331.

70. (1951) 34 *ILO Official Bulletin,* 274 at 287–288.

71. A similar though less onerous clause can be found in the WHO Constitution, Art. 20.

72. See Davidson, *Human Rights,* 73–74; Shaw, *International Law,* 249–252.

73. Art. 22 of the ILO Constitution.

74. Arts. 26–29 and 31–33 of the ILO Constitution.

75. Art. 24 of the ILO Constitution.

76. Centre for Human Rights, *United Nations Action in the Field of Human Rights* (1994), 124.

77. Ibid. They concerned the rights of public sector workers in Japan (1965), Greece (1966), Chile (1975), Lesotho (1975), the United States (Puerto Rico, 1981), and South Africa (1991).

78. (1989) 28 ILM 1382.

79. Although a Working Group of the General Assembly has prepared the Draft Declaration on the Rights of Indigenous Peoples—UN doc. E/CN.4/1999/82.

80. Centre for Human Rights, *United Nations Action in the Field of Human Rights,* 196.

81. See *For the Record 1999: The United Nations Human Rights System* <http://www.hri.ca/fortherecord1999/vol11/indigenous.htm>.

82. (1991) 30 ILM 1521.

83. *For the Record 1999* <http://www.hri.ca/fortherecord1999/vol11/migrant.htm>.

84. UN doc. A/C.5/1704 (1975).

85. *Record of Proceedings,* ILC, 59th session, 808 (1974).

86. See also Emmeriji, "The International Labour Organization," 111.

87. For U.S. reasons, see *Department of State Bulletin* 84 (1984), 41.

88. Williams, *Specialized Agencies,* 57.

89. Mourik, "UNESCO: Structural Origins," 123.

90. 429 UNTS 93.

91. UNESCO decision 104.EX/3.3 (1978).

92. Shaw, *International Law,* 253–254.

93. A sample taken from *For the Record 1999* shows the extent of the problem. On one extreme we have countries like Angola, where there are appalling atrocities being committed every day. Peversely, Angola is a party to the main human rights treaties—the two international covenants, as well as the treaties protecting the human rights of women and children. It has, however, submitted no reports under those treaties as it is required to do. At the other end of the scale there are states, such as the United Kingdom, who have widely ratified human rights treaties (though often with reservations), and have complied

with their reporting requirements thereunder. The bulk of states, though (e.g., Pakistan, Saudi Arabia, Sri Lanka, El Salvador, Haiti, Mexico, Croatia, Russia, Israel, and the United States), fall between these two poles by ratifying some treaties, and under those treaty regimes failing to comply fully with the reporting requirements. <http://www.hri.ca/fortherecord1999>.

10

The Environment

The development of legally binding environmental standards is a recent phenomenon in the United Nations.[1] The formalist approach to international law largely denies the existence of a body of international environmental law. It sees environmental law as a weak attempt to limit the freedom of states or grudgingly accepts it as so-called soft law, which has a limited impact.[2] Although UN practice in setting and implementing environmental standards has increased, the UN institutions in this area have limited aims.

States are prepared to countenance human rights standards and supervision, but they are less inclined to accept hard environmental targets. Human rights standards and organizational supervision do not necessarily impinge on "national security and maintaining economic growth."[3] However, national interests restrict the development of UN institutions whose aim is to protect the environment, as well as the development of the right to a clean environment. The evidence is that international environmental organizations are dominated by states. The individual has little power to enforce environmental standards on the international stage.[4]

Of course, environmental protection does not necessarily require the recognition of an individual right. Adequate protection could occur as a result of state-based initiatives. The evidence, however, is that the United Nations has a long way to go before this is achieved, understandable given the recent emergence of the environment as a UN value. Still, the fact that the United Nations has managed to place this issue firmly on the international agenda in the last three decades is, in itself, an achievement.

Given the dominance of sovereign concerns in this area it is contended that "organized international responses to shared environmental problems will occur through cooperation among States, not through the imposition of government over them." This signifies that UN institutions set up to protect the environment will be relatively weak and will only be able to "promote change in national behaviour that is substantial enough to have a positive impact, eventually, on the quality of the natural environment."5 This pragmatic assessment belies the fact that cooperation among UN states can itself be a mirage.

UN actions in this area are beset by conflicting aims. On one hand, it promotes economic and industrial development through UNDP and UNIDO; on the other it protects the environment through UNEP. Developing states tend to congregate around the desire for development, whereas most developed states support global environmental protection. It can be argued that the UN's institutional activity in the area is weak. The Stockholm declaration of 1972 marked the beginning of the UN's legal and institutional developments in this area; the Rio declaration of 1992 was made when the world faced mounting evidence of long-term environmental degradation. Between the two declarations environmental concerns actually became subordinated to development concerns.6 This can be seen as an inherent aspect of globalization as the majority of developing states' desire for industrial development is married to consumer economies in the developed world.

The United Nations and the Environment

Beginning in 1972, the United Nations has moved toward setting environmental standards, sometimes in the form of binding treaty commitments, but usually in the form "of framework or 'umbrella' treaties or of non-binding declarations, codes, guidelines, or recommended principles." Such soft laws are "not law in the sense used by [Article 38 of the ICJ statute] but none the less they do not lack all authority."7 Unfortunately, this illustrates the weakness of environmental law as well as of the principal organization that has helped to develop it. It also shows the potential weakness of UN organs, committees, and agencies set up by environmental treaties to implement standards.

Aside from standards, environmental law is an undeveloped area. Human rights debates have been held for centuries and led to universal standards. Furthermore, UN bodies have defined these standards through their practice and decisions. Debate on international standards for protecting the environment is more recent and different from the debate on first- and second-generation human rights.[8] "We can see that what 'pollution' means is, like the term 'environment,' significantly dependent on context and objective. While it is possible to talk of an obligation to prevent pollution, or to protect the environment, such an obligation has a very variable content, and there is little point attempting a global definition."[9] The relativity of the right to a clean environment is much greater than for individual human rights.

Such uncertainty extends to many of the concepts underpinning environmental law, partly the result of political and ideological compromises within UN bodies. However, once created, these concepts shape the actions of UN bodies to achieve implementation of them and their derivatives. An example is the notion of the common heritage of mankind. States and jurists have different views on this. In the case of states, it varies on whether they think resources should be shared, benefits redistributed, and technology transferred from the North to the South. In addition, there are unresolved arguments over whether the concept of the common heritage is applicable to resources or areas beyond national jurisdiction, such as the deep sea-bed and the moon, or whether it extends to areas within national boundaries, such as the Amazon rain forest. The application of the concept entails some sort of trusteeship or stewardship, with responsibility to present and future generations. Nevertheless, it is unclear how far the concept extends, and its content can vary according to the interests of states.[10]

Other areas of environmental law developed by the United Nations have become accepted as international legal principles. Principle 21 of the UN Stockholm Conference, although not presented at the time as a binding commitment, has been accepted as an international legal principle.[11] The principle posits that states have "the responsibility to ensure that activities within their jurisdiction or control do not cause damage to the environment of other States or of areas beyond the limits of national jurisdiction."[12] The so-called no-harm principle, which limits the sovereignty of states, is in many ways the bedrock of international environmental law. However, its use to prevent or remedy harm is limited, illustrating the limitations of the law and the institutions designed to implement it. Nevertheless, the principle is a point of reference for diffuse national and international responses at both governmental and nongovernmental levels to prevent catastrophes like Chernobyl.

In general the United Nations has not moved toward the supervision and enforcement of environmental laws such as principle 21 or of standards laid down in so-called soft law instruments. As in other areas such as international criminal law,[13] there is a limited exception when environmental concerns overlap with the collective security system in the shape of a functioning UN Security Council.[14] The latter body held Iraq "liable under international law for any direct loss, damage, *including environmental damage and the depletion of natural resources,* or injury to foreign Governments, nationals and corporations, as a result of Iraq's unlawful invasion and occupation of Kuwait" in August 1990, in a binding chapter VII resolution adopted after the end of the military conflict in April 1991.[15] The further extension of the collective security umbrella to cover environmental matters was flagged by the special Security Council summit of world leaders held in January 1992. That summit declared that "non-military sources of instability in the economic, social, humanitarian and ecological fields have become threats to the peace and security."[16] As in other areas, the collective security machinery of the United Nations can provide an avenue for enforcing environmental laws, but only in extreme situations amounting to threats to international peace. This will lead to a very selective enforcement system.

Institutional Structure

Unlike the protection of human rights, which receive brief but express mention, protection of the environment does not appear in the UN Charter. Nevertheless, the United Nations has developed an extensive competence in the area (see Chapter 3). Apart from the role of the UN's specialized agencies (reviewed below), UN competence is divided between the General Assembly, ECOSOC, and the United Nations Environment Programme, with the latter performing the most active role.

UNEP was established pursuant to the 1972 Stockholm Conference, called by the General Assembly. The Stockholm Conference adopted a declaration of general principles, some of which have become part of customary international law; it also laid down an action plan on environmental policy and established the United Nations Environment Fund, based upon voluntary contributions from states.[17] Instead of being established as an autonomous specialized agency, UNEP was created by a General Assembly resolution in 1972 under article 22 of the UN Charter, which allows the assembly to establish subsidiary organs.[18] The assembly's resolution established a subsidiary organ with an autonomous

status equipped with a separate budget, secretariat, and organs, something halfway between a subsidiary organ and a specialized agency.[19]
The resolution was not adopted by consensus but by an overwhelming
majority of states, who were "convinced of the need for prompt and effective implementation by Governments and the international community of measures designed to safeguard and enhance the environment for
the benefit of present and future generations of man," requiring the establishment of "a permanent institutional arrangement within the United
Nations system for the protection and improvement of the environment."

As well as a secretariat serving "as a focal point for environmental
action and co-ordination within the [United Nations] headed by an executive director, the assembly established the UNEP governing council
of fifty-eight members elected by the assembly and representing different regions. This body is responsible for promoting international cooperation, laying down policy guidance, reviewing reports on the implementation of UNEP environmental programs received from the executive
director, reviewing the world environmental situation, and promoting
knowledge about environmental problems. The governing council is
under a duty to annually report to the assembly via ECOSOC.

Advances have been made by UNEP developing principles of international environmental law, both soft and hard. UNEP's approach is
"based on first formulating the scientific positions, then developing legal
strategies, and in the process building political support with an important
role accorded to the negotiation of 'soft law' guidelines, principles etc."[20]
A good example is UNEP's regional seas program to address polluted wa-
ters such as the Mediterranean and Caspian Seas by a combination of
conventions, soft laws, and diplomatic conferences.[21] Also worthy of
mention is UNEP's attempted regulation of chemicals, in particular its
sponsorship of the new Convention on Persistent Organic Pollutants,
which hopefully will enter into force by 2004.[22] In general terms,

> in the support-building process many compromises have to be arrived
> at especially in the interests of maintaining the "sustainable develop-
> ment policy" propounded by the World Commission on Environment
> and Development. Thus the conventions are replete with constructive
> ambiguities in relation both to definition and the more controversial
> issues are generally left to the "soft law" processes, the procedures
> and status of which are often made deliberately obscure.[23]

In the soft law area, only the World Charter for Nature, adopted by
the UN General Assembly in 1982 following a UNEP special session,
seems to be of a peremptory character.[24] Other declarations and principles

adopted by UNEP and the assembly, on mining, pollution, waste management, and chemicals, place no real obligations on states.[25] Ambiguous treaties negotiated and drafted by UNEP include the 1985 Vienna Convention for the Protection of the Ozone Layer.[26] Although UNEP has set many standards, the compromises needed to overcome the North-South polarization have undermined its effectiveness. Furthermore, UNEP possesses none of the review and supervisory functions found in human rights bodies; it can review environmental implementation in a general sense, but there is no duty on states to report on implementing standards. Furthermore, a resolution provided for the Environmental Coordination Board to attempt to "provide for the most efficient coordination of United Nations Environment programmes," but this was soon made redundant, and the job given to the more unwieldy ACC.

The United Nations held another international conference on the environment at Rio in 1992 to improve international protection of the environment, but it resulted in further obfuscation of the core issues and a lack of concrete obligations. Both UNEP and ECOSOC called on the General Assembly to convene the UN Conference on Environment and Development in 1989.[27] The content of the assembly's resolution, which was adopted by consensus, reveals the major difficulty, if not impossibility, of agreeing on significant environmental controls. The assembly begins by recognizing that despite Stockholm and UNEP there has been a "continuing deterioration of the state of the environment and the serious degradation of the global life support systems," which if allowed to continue "could disrupt the ecological balance, jeopardize the life-sustaining qualities of the earth and lead to an ecological catastrophe." The assembly also recognized the "global character of environmental problems, including climate change, depletion of the ozone layer, transboundary air and water pollution, the contamination of the oceans and the seas and degradation of land resources."

In attempting to direct the conference toward adopting measures for protecting the environment, the assembly disabled its potential impact. It did this by *condemning* economic development and its accompanying pollution in industrialized countries while *encouraging* development, alongside environmental protection, in developing countries. The overall aims of the conference, according to the assembly, should have been to "elaborate strategies and measures to halt and reverse the effects of environmental degradation in the context of strengthened national and international efforts to promote sustainable and environmentally sound development in all countries." One way to reconcile these disparate aims would be for advanced nations to fund clean development in developing countries while cleaning up their own industries and cutting back on consumer demand. Although this is suggested in the assembly's resolution, its naïveté is revealed in the negotiations and outcome of the 1992 conference.[28]

The UN's Rio Conference, also known as the Earth Summit, held in June 1992, produced two treaties for formal ratification by states. First, it produced the Framework Convention on Climate Change, which contains guiding principles and vague commitments on greenhouse gases.[29] Second, it produced the Convention on Biological Diversity, another framework treaty to create general obligations for the conservation of ecosystems, species, and diversity of species.[30] Although both treaties are beset by compromise and ambiguity, they create institutions to promote compliance and contain financial mechanisms to ease the burden on developing states. These institutions and mechanisms will be reviewed later.

In addition to the two formal treaties, the Rio Conference produced two nonbinding declarations and a program of action known as Agenda 21. One of the declarations was a statement of principles on the management, conservation, and sustainable development of all types of forest. The Statement of Principles on Forests restates principle 21 of the Stockholm declaration; countries that deplete forests within their own jurisdiction are responsible for the consequent deterioration in the climates of other countries. However, the statement then makes it clear that "states have the sovereign and inalienable right to utilize, manage and develop their forests in accordance with the development needs and level of socio-economic development and on the basis of national policies consistent with sustainable development."[31]

The more significant Rio Declaration on Environment and Development represents a greater emphasis on sovereignty and development than found twenty years earlier at Stockholm.[32] The subjugation of environment to development is present in the majority of the principles contained in the document; principle 4 states that "in order to achieve sustainable development, environmental protection shall constitute an integral part of the development process and cannot be considered in isolation from it." Principles that seem to support environmental protection are ambivalent; principle 11 states that

states shall enact effective environmental legislation. Environmental standards, management objectives and priorities should reflect the environmental and developmental contexts to which they apply. Standards applied by some countries may be inappropriate and of unwarranted economic and social concern to other countries, in particular developing countries.

The same emphasis on economic issues is found in Agenda 21. Instead of emphasizing environmental standards for all states irrespective of development, Agenda 21 dilutes environmental standards by making them relative to socioeconomic factors.[33] Agenda 21 addresses the issue of international institutional arrangements.[34] Urging UNEP and UNDP to develop and expand activities in the environmental and developmental fields, Agenda 21 also urges the creation of another institution within the UN framework. The aim of this institution would be to "rationalize the intergovernmental decision-making capacity for the integration of environment and development and to examine the progress in the implementation of Agenda 21 at the national, regional and international levels." Such a commission would be created under article 68 of the charter and would report to ECOSOC and the assembly, identified as the "supreme policy-making forum that would provide overall guidance to Governments, the United Nations system and relevant treaty bodies."

The General Assembly recommended the creation of the Commission on Sustainable Development "as a functional commission of" ECOSOC.[35] The commission consists of fifty-three state representatives elected by ECOSOC; its mandate is to: monitor progress in the implementation of Agenda 21 by examining reports from organizations and bodies concerned with environment and development; "consider information provided by Governments . . . in the form of . . . national reports regarding the activities they undertake to implement Agenda 21"; review Agenda 21 commitments such as the transfer of technology; review the progress toward the UN target of 0.7 percent of GNP of developed countries for development assistance; and receive and analyze reports from NGOs.

The mandate contains a breakthrough in the monitoring and supervision of standards by providing for a state reporting system. However, this advance is checked by the wider range of activities to be monitored in the integrated areas of environment and development. In its second session report of 1994, the commission received many communications by many governments and organizations submitted on a voluntary basis.[36] However, development assistance was down by 10 percent, and there was scant evidence of any transfer of environmentally sound technology from

North to South as advocated by Agenda 21. Overall, the report and the subsequent assembly resolution emphasize the lack of financial commitment by the richer nations to achieve the goals of Agenda 21.[37] Nevertheless, the commission's review of the range of environmental issues specified in Agenda 21 appears to be gaining momentum. In its annual sessions the commission has gained greater legitimacy by its methodical, fact-based, and nonpolitical review,[38] achieved with the backing of the General Assembly.[39]

The Specialized Agencies

The UN's approach to environmental issues is to create political institutions such as UNEP to set and monitor environmental standards. The political compromises in these bodies means development and the environment are linked, with development issues taking precedence. The fact that the majority (i.e., the developing states) has to make concessions to the minority (i.e., the developed states) to reach consensus has resulted in soft law.

A functional critique would state that this is an inevitable result of empowering a political body, such as the United Nations, with the solution of these problems. Organizations that address common problems may be better able to focus on setting and implementing environmental standards. This would mean that instead of attempting to achieve global consensus on environmental principles and ending up with ambiguous concepts such as "sustainable development" (the heart of Agenda 21), there would emerge a series of concrete and practical principles and standards.[40] The UN's specialized agencies have had success, as have some of the treaty bodies established by UN-sponsored conventions. Inevitably there are going to be areas such as greenhouse gases and biodiversity that escape the net of the agencies, but there are several UN-sponsored treaties dealing with these areas, most of which contain monitoring machinery.

In regard to the successful specialized agencies, the IMO produced widely ratified conventions such as the International Convention for the Prevention of Pollution of the Sea by Oil of 1954.[41] UNESCO is responsible for the Convention for the Protection of the World Cultural and Natural Heritage of 1972, including environmentally significant areas.[42] The WHO's international health regulations cover such things as water quality and have had a major impact in setting environmental standards on matters directly relating to health. The WMO provides essential information on climate and weather, indicative of man-made changes in the environment.

On the negative side, the FAO's Committee on Fisheries has been less successful in developing global mechanisms for fish stock conservation. However, the UN Convention on Straddling and Highly Migratory Fish Stocks of August 1995 may make some difference in this regard.

The World Bank is worthy of some attention (see Chapter 11). There, the world community has attempted to achieve a compromise between development and environmental protection. The World Bank has been accused of "bankrolling ecological and economic disaster in the developing world, by promoting developmental projects that have denuded forests, depleted soils, and increased dependence on unsustainable energy sources." Furthermore, "gestures by the Bank to introduce greener policies in response to these criticisms have been met with deep scepticism and accusations of superficial 'greenwashing.'"[43] World Bank projects "are often massive infrastructure or industrialization programs"[44] and have a "failure rate staggering even by internal assessments,"[45] leading inevitably to ecological and social damage.

The World Bank's drive to fund development was tempered in the late 1980s by green guidelines "designed to incorporate environmental considerations into loan decisions." These standards are meant to mitigate "negative effects of loans for traditional development projects in all areas including, among others, the power sector and agriculture." However, they are not encouraging given that "environmental considerations rarely, if ever, prevent the World Bank from making a loan, limiting the ultimate benefit of the new guidelines."[46] However, a much more positive greening occurred in March 1991 with the establishment of the Global Environmental Facility by the World Bank, UNDP, and UNEP to fund environmental projects in the developing world.[47] The greater cooperation between UNEP and the World Bank is not yet matched by UNEP and the WTO, which is formally outside the UN system. Tentative moves were made in 1998 in the form of communications from the UNEP secretariat to the WTO Committee on Trade and Environment.[48]

The GEF marks a tentative move toward cooperation between the United Nations and the World Bank, separated for all practical purposes since the Bretton Woods institutions were established in 1947. Before the GEF was created, the UN's environmental competence was divorced from the Bank's concern with economic issues. Furthermore, the Bank's one-dollar, one-vote structure conflicts with the UN's one-state, one-vote principle, leading to divergent agendas, with developed states dominating the Bank and developing states dominating the United Nations, at least in the assembly, UNDP, and UNEP.

Inevitably the World Bank was criticized at Rio in 1992. The Rio declaration was indirect but relatively clear in principle 7, which states that "the developed countries acknowledge the responsibility that they bear in the international pursuit of sustainable development in view of the pressure their societies place on the global environment and of the technologies and *financial resources* they command."[49] Furthermore, in chapter 38 of Agenda 21, the recommendations state the Commission on Sustainable Development should monitor reports on the implementation of Agenda 21 from organizations, "including those relating to finance."

The developed states, which dominate the World Bank, agreed to the Rio declaration and Agenda 21; they had already agreed to the establishment of the GEF, allowing for greater UN say (including developing states) in the World Bank. Initial reports of the GEF are discouraging, with control firmly in the hands of developed countries,[50] though the GEF has attempted to implement improvements.[51] Furthermore, GEF's incorporation into the UN Convention on Biological Diversity and the UN Framework Convention on Climate Change adopted at Rio in 1992 is a more positive sign. The Climate Change Convention places developing states (through the Conference of Parties) in control of the GEF. The convention in article 11 states that a "financial mechanism" to fund projects to address climate change "shall function under the guidance of and be accountable to the Conference of the Parties, which shall decide on its policies, programme priorities and eligibility criteria." The GEF is appointed as the financial mechanism on an "interim basis" by article 21(3), reviewable after four years according to article 11(4).

Institutional balance between developed and developing states in the GEF and other UN bodies is essential for a concomitant (and workable) balance between environmental and developmental concerns.

Limits on World Bank autonomy are to be welcomed. Nevertheless, ambiguity persists as to the commitments under the Climate Change Convention, Agenda 21, and the Rio declaration. Simply adding these to Bank criteria for funding projects does not necessarily produce environmental benefits. But recent evidence suggests that the GEF is starting to accommodate the interests of developing states, dependent, of course, on financial commitment by developed states.[52]

The principle of "sustainable development," beyond the amalgamation of development and environment, is troublesome. Although UNEP has been mandated to develop international environmental law on sustainable

development, progress has been slow.[53] Indeed, sustainable development is an ambiguous compromise between North and South, incorpo-
rating the North's environmental concerns and the South's developmental concerns. Sustainable development encourages the belief "that
continued economic growth and development, as well as population
growth, can take place in a manner that will bring the global population
to an acceptable overall standard of living, without damaging the life
support system so much that it prevents this goal from ever being attained."[54] Not firmly grounded on scientific fact, this is contrary to the
spirit of the so-called precautionary principle. This principle provides
that "where there are threats of serious or irreversible damage, lack of
full scientific certainty should not be used as a reason for postponing
measures to prevent environmental degradation."[55] It could be argued
that by promoting sustainable development states and the United Nations are violating the reasoning behind the precautionary principle.

Behind sustainable development is the belief "that science and en-
gineering can overcome our environmental problems and allow us to
continue expanding resource extraction and use, producing products and
raising the material standard of living of the earth's people indefinitely,
even as the population increases."[56] Principle 12 of the Rio declaration
embodies this contradiction, attempting to reconcile environmental protection and economic growth: "States should co-operate to promote a
supportive and open international economic system that would lead to
economic growth and sustainable development." The United Nations is
not going to protect the environment if basic goals and principles are
unattainable. Although a sort of compromise between developed and developing states has been achieved on sustainable development, it lacks
content. There is no real agreement on how to integrate development
and environment in a way that protects the environment.

The 1997 adoption of the Benchmark Draft of the Earth Charter by
the United Nations Conference on Environment and Development
(Rio+5) Forum is important. Its drafters (mostly NGOs) state that it will
"serve as a universal declaration of the environmental standards required for sustainability."[57] However, the draft does not develop the
concept of sustainable development; it contains instead exhortations:
"we the peoples of the world commit ourselves to action . . . [to] live
sustainably, promoting and adopting modes of consumption, production
and reproduction that respect and safeguard human rights and the
regenerative capacities of Earth." Further there is a commitment to
"promote social development and financial systems that create and

maintain sustainable livelihoods, eradicate poverty and strengthen local communities."[58]

The draft contains few concrete legal obligations, merely repeating the rhetoric of the Rio declarations. Thus as to sustainable development, the first step in the legal process—the adoption of laws—has not been achieved. Without this there is little possibility of implementing standards. The United Nations is a long way from defining "sustainable development" and, beyond that, defining it in a way that works to produce global environmental protection.

Institutions Created by
UN-Sponsored Environmental Treaties

The impact of UN bodies on environmental protection is less than in the areas of collective security and human rights. Yet there is some progress, principally in the creation and activities of organs created by UN-sponsored environmental treaties. There is also better coordination of secretariats under the auspices of UNEP.[59]

Older environmental conventions did not contain machinery to review implementation of treaty obligations; beginning in the late 1950s, treaties began to include institutions, usually in the form of a review conference.[60] This is an inefficient way to supervise treaties, especially when measures must be taken by consensus. There is recent evidence that treaty machinery is becoming more sophisticated, with majority voting, as well as commissions representing state parties. Nevertheless, the supervisory bodies created by treaty, "whether a meeting of the parties or a Commission, is in substance no more than a diplomatic conference of States, and the existence in some of these cases of a separate legal personality does not alter the reality that the membership of these institutions is in no sense independent of the States they represent."[61]

Despite their relative crudity, review conferences and commissions are effective in promoting international environmental law, more so than judicial or quasijudicial methods of dispute settlement.[62] Individual civil and political rights, as well as economic and social rights, are suited to the judicial process; a collective right (e.g., to a clean environment) is perhaps less so. Besides, environmental law has not developed along the same path as human rights; individuals have virtually no environmental rights as such on the international plane. Furthermore, the aims of environmental law have developed beyond damage done by one state to another toward preventing environmental harm as embodied in the precautionary principle.

In many ways a system of judicial remedies for damage done by pollution is a secondary method, especially given the underdeveloped, consent-based judicial system that operates at the state level. Here the ICJ has a limited role to play in promoting environmental law, as there have been very few significant environmental decisions. The *Corfu Channel* case of 1949 did not directly raise environmental issues, although it did establish the basis of state responsibility developed by principle 21 of the Stockholm declaration of 1972.[63] The aging body of ICJ and arbitral decisions on the environment does not create a legal framework to prevent deterioration in the environment and address new problems.

Although the ICJ may begin to tackle environmental matters, the supervisory bodies created by UN-sponsored treaties play the larger role.[64] Yet key environmental treaties fall outside the system and are resistant to UN control, even though that would help achieve consistent, enforceable standards. The prime example is the Antarctic Treaty System (ATS), established in 1959.[65] Although a reasonably effective system, ATS suffers from a lack of representation; decisions, although unanimous by the state parties, are made by a minority of states making up the international community. The argument for the very reason for its success—the small and therefore workable nature of its consultative meetings—is countered by evidence from more representative systems.

The Convention on International Trade in Endangered Species of 1973 has more than 100 state parties, all entitled to be represented and to vote at the conference of the parties. The most important function of the conference is to review and amend the species listed in the appendices to the convention. So-called Appendix I species are those threatened with extinction and in which trade is prohibited, whereas trade is controlled in regard to species listed in Appendix II. It is surprising that such a fundamental treaty system operates independently of the United Nations.

A move toward greater international enforcement of environmental norms was the 1987 Montreal Protocol on Substances That Deplete the Ozone Layer. Empowering a treaty review body with the ability to bind states by majority decision, this is a much more intrusive instrument than its parent treaty—the UNEP-sponsored 1985 Vienna Convention for the Protection of the Ozone Layer.[66] The latter was weak in substance and machinery in that it obliged the parties under article 2(1) "to take appropriate measures in accordance with the provisions of this Convention . . . to protect human health and the environment against adverse effects resulting or likely to result from human activities which modify or are likely to modify the ozone layer." This was an uneasy compromise between developed countries wishing to restrict chlorofluorocarbons (CFCs) and developing countries who did not. Structurally the Vienna Convention provides, in article 7, for a secretariat and, in article 6, for a conference of the parties to review implementation based in part on information received from state parties. The conference can, according to article 8, adopt new protocols to further the obligations in article 2. Although a limited departure from consensus is permitted by article 9(3) for amendments to the convention or to protocols, the assumption is unanimity, in contrast to the 1987 Montreal Protocol.

The 1987 protocol is more intrusive, substantively and institutionally. It includes firm targets for the reduction and eventual elimination of ozone-depleting substances, a reporting obligation, and innovative technology-transfer provisions. Although the basic organ is the meeting of the parties to the protocol, majority voting exists, and decisions have mandatory force. Article 2(9) (as amended in 1990) allows parties to adjust the targets and the substances prohibited. Subparagraph (c) provides that consensus ought to be achieved, but as a last resort a two-thirds majority is sufficient subject to certain conditions, ensuring decisions are supported by separate majorities of developing as well as developed countries. Article 2(9)(d) provides that "the decisions . . . shall be binding on all Parties."

Subsequent developments have shown the meeting of parties moving toward enforcement. Article 8 permits parties to create mechanisms to determine noncompliance and punishment. The state parties agreed in 1990 that an implementation committee should hear complaints on the basis of a unilateral application by a state party. That committee seeks an amicable solution and if one is not forthcoming the meeting of the parties can then decide on steps for full compliance. Furthermore, in November 1992 the noncompliance procedure was expanded to include measures that might be taken by the meeting of parties, including cautions, suspension of rights and privileges, and availability of resources under the financial mechanisms.

Unfortunately, this dynamic development faltered under the Rio conventions on biological diversity and climate change. The Biological Diversity Convention has few innovative institutional mechanisms. Its provisions create a supervisory conference of the parties to which state parties report and a secretariat (articles 23, 24, and 26)—standard fare—with no mandatory powers and limited majority decisionmaking powers, although article 25 does provide for a subsidiary body on scientific, technical, and technological advice.

The Climate Change Convention has greater institutional development. Article 10 creates a subsidiary body for implementation of the treaty, in addition to the standard supervisory conference of the parties and the secretariat (articles 7 and 8), and a subsidiary body for scientific and technological advice (article 9). Furthermore, article 7(3) does permit the conference of the parties to adopt its own "decision-making procedures for matters not already covered by decision-making procedures stipulated in the Convention. Such procedures may include specified majorities required for the adoption of particular decisions," thus explicitly allowing the conference to move toward majority decisionmaking on more issues. Nevertheless, progress has been weak on targets for the reduction of greenhouse gases. Limited reductions of on average 5.2 percent were agreed in the Kyoto Protocol of 1997, although that agreement was subject to questionable concessions allowing for emissions-trading.[67] In essence emissions-trading

> involves establishing individual quotas for each participating country as to the amount of greenhouse gases that country can emit. If a country does not utilise all of its quota, it can sell the remainder to another participating country who can make use of it so as to allow further emissions without being contrary to its obligations under the Protocol.[68]

No agreement on the implementation of Kyoto was achieved at a climate change conference held at The Hague in November 2000. Indeed, the whole process seemed to unravel as the United States refused to ratify the protocol after failing to gain concessions. This indicates that despite relatively sophisticated institutional design, the Climate Change Convention is still dependent on achieving consensus, which cannot happen if major players such as the United States are unwilling to cut emissions.

Conclusion

The failure of the UN conference at The Hague to agree on further implementation of the treaty regime to reduce greenhouse gases reflects the current state of UN efforts in protecting the environment. There has been limited progress in promulgating and implementing specific obligations on states, restricting their traditional freedom to pollute. The need to develop laws and institutions that act as a brake on the increasing depletion of the world's environment is an imperative. Although the United Nations has made significant institutional advances in the shape of UNEP and the Commission on Sustainable Development, they are intergovernmental and by no means supranational. Even where majority decisionmaking is allowed, consensus is the norm. Arguably, in the absence of supranationality, consensus decisionmaking is necessary given that global environmental measures must be taken by states together.

In terms of standard-setting, there has been progress regarding environmental degradation, but mechanisms for their implementation are lacking. The limited impact of the ICJ, the principal judicial means of compliance, is testimony to this. However, beyond the UN-sponsored framework conventions on environmental matters, standard-setting has itself been limited. The overriding search for a comprehensible definition of "sustainable development" has undermined less grandiose and achievable norm-setting. The gradual development of the GEF, under joint UNEP–World Bank stewardship, has proven that a pragmatic approach to environmental protection can pay dividends. The Bank and the WTO have had difficulty adopting effective environmental policies, reflecting an inherent conflict between the agendas (e.g., economic development versus the environment). Sustainable development is an attempt to reconcile development and the environment at an abstract level; more success can be achieved in the practical world.

Deficiencies abound at all three levels of the UN's legal order on the environment. In terms of standard-setting, interpretation, and enforcement, the UN system is lacking. States are more reluctant to make concessions in this area than in many others—perhaps all except peace and security. Protecting the environment is in many ways the most difficult UN value to achieve, for if it is not done by all states, or at least the vast majority, including the most powerful, then it cannot be achieved. The United Nations has made great strides in raising environmental awareness, but this is really the prelegal stage. It has to move on to more comprehensive environmental legislation accompanied by effective implementing mechanisms if it is to meet its greatest challenge.

Notes

1. Birnie, "Environmental"; Boer, "The Globalisation."
2. Birnie and Boyle, *Environment,* 1, 10.

3. Haas, Keohane, and Levy, *Institutions*, 1.

4. Birnie and Boyle, *Environment*, 86.

5. Haas, Keohane, and Levy, *Institutions*, 4–5.

6. Pallemaerts, "International Environmental Law," 17.

7. Birnie and Boyle, *Environment*, 10, 27.

8. Boyle, "The Role of International Human Rights Law," 43. But see Dommen, "Claiming," and Lee, "The Underlying."

9. Birnie and Boyle, *Environment*, 102.

10. Kiss and Shelton, "La Notion," 129.

11. Detter de Lupis, "The Human Environment," 222.

12. Kiss and Shelton, *Environmental Law*, 129.

13. See Chapter 8.

14. Fitzpatrick, "The United Nations General Assembly and the Security Council," 11–20.

15. SC Res. 687, 3 April 1991 (emphasis added).

16. UN doc. S/23500 (1992).

17. UN doc. A/CONF.48/14 (1972), reproduced in (1972) 11 ILM 1416. Sohn, "The Stockholm Declaration," 423.

18. GA Res. 2997, 15 Dec. 1972.

19. Bowett, *Institutions*, 57–58.

20. Birnie and Boyle, *Environment*, 50.

21. Marotta, "Regional Seas."

22. Heyvaert, "Regulation."

23. Birnie and Boyle, *Environment*, 50. On the World Commission on Environment and Development, see Pallemaerts, in Sands, *Greening*, 3–4.

24. GA Res. 37/7, 28 Oct. 1982.

25. Birnie and Boyle, *Environment*, 50–51.

26. (1987) 26 ILM 1529.

27. UNEP Res. 15/3 (1989); ECOSOC Res. 1989/87 (1989).

28. GA Res. 44/228, 22 Dec. 1989.

29. (1992) 31 ILM 848.

30. (1992) 31 ILM 818.

31. UN doc. A/CONF.151/6/Rev.1 (1992), reproduced in (1992) 31 ILM 882.

32. UN doc. A/CONF.151/5/Rev.1 (1992), reproduced in (1992) 31 ILM 876.

33. UN doc. A/CONF.151/26 (1992), ch. 2.

34. Ibid., ch. 38.

35. GA Res. 47/191, 22 Dec. 1992.

36. UN doc. E/1994/33/rev.1 (1994).

37. GA Res. 49/111, 19 Dec. 1994.

38. Williams, "UN Commission" (1996).

39. Williams, "UN Commission" (1997).

40. UN Doc. A/CONF.151.26 (1992), ch. 1.

41. 327 UNTS 3.

42. UKTS 2 (185), Cmnd. 9424.

43. Werksman, "Greening Bretton Woods," 65.

44. Guyett, "Environment and Lending," 889.

45. Werksman, "Greening," 68.

46. Guyett, "Environment and Lending," 897. See also Di Leva, "International Environmental."

47. See also Shihata, "Implementation."

48. "Statement by the United Nations Environment Programme to the WTO Committee on Trade and Environment," *International Environmental Affairs* 10(4) (1998), 290. See also Winter, "Reconciling the GATT"; Wofford, "A Greener."

49. Emphasis added.

50. Werksman, "Greening," 82.

51. Bloch, "Global," 552.

52. Ibid., 556.

53. But see A-Khavari and Rothwell, "The ICJ," 518–525.

54. Cameron, "The GATT and the Environment," 115.

55. Ibid.

56. McCluney, "Sustainable Values," 16–18. See also Lipshutz, "Wasn't the Future," 35.

57. Anderson, "The Benchmark," 109.

58. Ibid., 113–115.

59. "United Nations Environment Programme," (1996) *Yearbook of Environment Law* 450 at 451.

60. White, *International Organisations,* 270–271.

61. Birnie and Boyle, *Environment,* 165.

62. Ibid., 136–139.

63. ICJ Rep. 1949, 72.

64. *Case Concerning the Gabcikovo-Nagymaros Project* (1998) 37 ILM 162. But see A-Khavari and Rothwell, "The ICJ."

65. 402 UNTS 71.

66. (1987) 26 ILM 1529, 1550.

67. Ott, "Global Climate," 179. Breidenich et al., "Kyoto," 323–325.

68. French, "Kyoto Protocol," 235.

11

Economic and Development Matters

In this chapter I focus on the World Bank and the International Monetary Fund, the twin pillars of the UN system of finance known as the Bretton Woods institutions. The chapter will also look at the other elements of the UN system concerned with economic and development matters, as well as the World Trade Organization. The WTO, although formally outside the UN system, is increasingly a part of it.

To a large extent the gradual incorporation of the WTO into the UN system is a fulfillment of the three-pillar vision many held at Bretton Woods in the mid-1940s. It was envisaged that the UN's economic and financial legal order would consist of a regime for international trade based on an international trade organization; a regime for monetary affairs administered by the IMF; and a regime for reconstruction and development under World Bank supervision.[1] The failure of the founding fathers to create an international trade organization, and the subsequent separate path taken by the General Agreement on Tariffs and Trade, meant that when the WTO was created in 1995 (building on the foundation of GATT) it proved much harder to reconcile the WTO with the UN system. However, it was less so in relation to the Bretton Woods organizations, as their philosophy and functions are much closer to the WTO than the other elements of the system. This has led to stronger ties between the WTO and the Bretton Woods institutions.

But structural debates should not blind us to the fact that development and economic welfare are essential components of the UN system. They must be achieved if the UN's basic values of peace and security are to be protected. Indeed, all the values are worth less if a minimum standard of individual economic and social well-being is not achieved. The problem lies in the profound disagreement over the methods to achieve that. Should it be based on redistribution of wealth from North to South, or should it be based on encouraging poorer countries to become wealthier through debt? Should rich nations be obliged to provide aid and assistance to poorer countries without strings, or should assistance be in the form of repayable loans and credits?

Inevitably, the system is a mixture. In the area of human rights the ideological divisions that separated civil and political rights from economic and social rights have largely disappeared. However, there is as yet no fundamental agreement on the exact nature of the legal order upon which development is built, although a liberal ideology is the most dominant. Yet it is possible to adopt a liberal approach to economic development while protecting universal human rights, and not necessarily only those that are equated with liberalism (civil and political rights).

The Bretton Woods Institutions and the UN System

The two UN financial institutions—the World Bank and the IMF—are concerned with financial and economic welfare. The ideology from the outset is liberal: "The IMF and the World Bank were founded on the basic notion that liberal rules of free trade, free payments, monetary stability and capital mobility would best promote international economic welfare."[2] In many ways these are difficult to reconcile with other UN values such as human rights, self-determination, democracy, justice, and the environment.

Such dichotomies were less obvious in the period before the 1970s, when the financial institutions and other elements of the UN system respected sovereignty to a great extent and did not overtly intervene in the domestic economic policies of member states. In addition, a competing vision of the world economic order emerged, one based on sharing and redistribution and promoted by the group of developing countries in UNCTAD and the General Assembly. However, with the demise or nonadoption of the tenets of the New International Economic Order, coupled with the end of the Cold War, the liberal vision of economic welfare—and hence the profile of the Bretton Woods organizations—predominated.

The World Bank adopted a wider and wider definition of "development." The IMF requires more and more information and influence to control the roller-coaster exchange-rate system in the wake of the demise of the par value (gold standard) system in 1971. These developments mean more intrusive regulation, extending far beyond what was intended in the immediate postwar period. This led to a conflict between the activities of the World Bank and the IMF and the other elements of the UN system. However, there are signs this is being addressed and reconciled, although the system is by no means satisfactory. Put simply, world economic and financial stability should not be achieved at the cost of basic human rights.

The IMF and World Bank entered their UN relationship by agreement under article 63 of the UN Charter as specialized agencies in November 1947. The agreements recognized the necessity that they (i.e., the Bank and IMF) operate as "independent international" organizations.[3] Although all specialized agencies are autonomous IGOs having separate personalities, the IMF and World Bank have greater autonomy than all others. There are few obligations; the IMF and IBRD must give "due consideration" to agenda items proposed by the United Nations; formal recommendations can be presented only after "reasonable prior consultation."[4] The IMF and IBRD will have due regard to decisions of the Security Council under articles 41 and 42 of the UN Charter,[5] and both boards of governors agreed in 1951 to have due regard to the recommendations of the General Assembly under the Uniting for Peace resolution.[6] Nevertheless, there is no substantive obligation to report on the implementation of UN resolutions or to supply regular reports on IMF/IBRD activities to ECOSOC or the General Assembly, as with the other specialized agencies. Article 64 of the UN Charter provides that ECOSOC "may take . . . steps to obtain appropriate reports from the specialized agencies" and "may make arrangements . . . on steps taken to give effect to its own recommendations." Thus reports from the specialized agencies are expected but not necessarily required. Certainly in the case of the Bretton Woods institutions, there is no real accountability to ECOSOC.

The WTO was created in 1995 and was not brought in as a UN specialized agency, yet the IMF has a detailed agreement with the WTO. This agreement provides, in general, for consultation "with a view to achieving greater coherence in global economic policy making."[7] There is a similar agreement between the World Bank and the WTO. There is a functional overlap between the major trade and financial organizations, one of which requires the organizations to cooperate. However, the compatibility of their policies and actions with the UN legal order is not assured by a system in which the IMF and the World Bank are not

bound by the charter or even the agreements to follow relevant UN resolutions. Furthermore, the WTO is arguably outside the UN legal order.
But practical links with the Bretton Woods institutions and the United
Nations itself (e.g., WTO membership of the ACC) indicate that the
WTO will be subject to UN law (e.g., on the environment and human
rights). The Bretton Woods institutions, recognizing that legitimacy depends on acting within the UN legal order, have increased their cooperation and consultation with the United Nations.[8]

The IMF, Monetary Affairs, and Human Rights

The purposes of the IMF, stated in article 1 of the IMF Articles of
Agreement, are: to promote international monetary cooperation; to facilitate the expansion and balanced growth of international trade; to
promote exchange stability; to assist in the establishment of a multilateral system of payments; to give confidence to members by making
resources of the IMF available to them; and to shorten and lessen the
disequilibrium in the international balance of payments by members.
    Here is a rather benign description of the IMF:

> It is neither a development bank, nor a world central bank, nor an
> agency that can or wishes to coerce its members to do very much of
> anything. It is rather a cooperative institution that 182 countries have
> voluntarily joined because they see the advantage of consulting with
> one another in the forum to maintain a stable system of buying and
> selling their currencies so that payments in foreign money can take
> place between countries smoothly and without delay.[9]

However, the IMF, although not a directly coercive organization, has a
much greater influence over states, especially poorer ones, than this
suggests.
    The IMF's activities are threefold. First, it undertakes surveillance
and consultation to appraise members states' exchange-rate policies.
Second, it provides financial assistance via credits and loans to members with balance-of-payment difficulties. This includes initiatives such
as the Heavily Indebted Poor Countries Initiative (HIPC), which since
1996 has provided assistance to reduce external debt burdens to sustainable levels, enabling countries to service debt without going further
into it. Finally, the IMF provides technical assistance.
    Technical assistance helps the development of productive resources
of member countries by enhancing the effectiveness of economic policy

and financial management. It is sometimes linked to surveillance of exchange-rate policies under article 4(3) of the IMF agreement, although it is still based on consent.[10] Technical assistance programs were started in 1964, when many newly independent Afro-Asian nations sought help in setting up their own central banks and ministries of finance. Today the IMF provides technical assistance in four broad categories: the design and implementation of fiscal and monetary polices; institution-building, such as the development of central banks, treasuries, tax, and customs departments; drafting and review of economic and financial legislation; and training of officials.[11]

The IMF also has rule-making functions and has created "international monetary law" in three areas.[12] The first is exchange-rate stabilization, though this is soft law, with a dilution of obligations following the amendments to article 4 of the IMF agreement in 1976 to abandon the system of fixed exchange rates.[13] Second, there is balance-of-payment stabilization based on article 5 of the agreement and consisting of the use of Special Drawing Rights (SDRs) as a first step forward in "international monetary collaboration." Finally, an international payments regime is founded on articles 6 and 8 of the agreement, aimed at promoting a system of international payments "that would be secure, non-discriminatory and free from undue governmental restrictions." This means that governments can restrict capital movements, but only with IMF approval, for making payments and transfers for current international transactions.[14]

In the period up to 1971, when the par value system based on the gold standard collapsed, the IMF was concerned with relatively narrow issues. "It monitored its Member States' international monetary policies to ensure that they were consistent with the maintenance of their currencies' par value. The IMF was also expected to provide its members with short-term financing when they experienced balance of payment difficulties."[15] Although for different reasons, both institutions changed in roughly the same period—the World Bank because of the need to change from reconstruction to development, the IMF because of the change from the par value system to a market-oriented exchange system that allows currencies to fluctuate in value. Both changes complicated their work.

In the case of the IMF, a floating exchange-rate system "becomes only one of many economic variables that can influence the country's balance of payments." "Floating exchange rates allow a country to correct a balance of payments problem by making adjustments either in the value of its currency or in its domestic economy."[16] This meant that the IMF

had to address an increasing number of domestic economic matters in consultations derived from article 4 of the agreement. Issues such as "labor,
health, and agricultural polices can directly affect the value of a country's
currency and its ability to adjust changes in its balance of payments."[17]

With its increasing concern for domestic matters, the IMF has a direct impact on human rights issues, in consultations as well as its loan
conditions. The IMF's concern with health care, social security, and
labor laws and policies impacts economic and social rights. A wider
concern with good governance allows the IMF to influence civil and political rights. As with the World Bank (see below), there are problems
with selectivity, in that the

> extent of the IMF's influence will vary depending upon the identity of
> a Member State. If the State has a healthy economy or is rich enough
> that it is unlikely to need the resources of the IMF, it is free to accept
> or reject the IMF's views. On the other hand poor States or those
> States that are using or expect to use the IMF's financing facilities can
> not treat the IMF's advice so dispassionately.[18]

The IMF has more than 180 members; although described as a "co-
operative institution" that has "no effective authority over the domestic
economic policies of its members," it does have *influence* over member states' economic policies.[19] First, the quota system favors the
stronger economies. By contributing 18 percent of the quota subscrip-
tion to the IMF, the United States can borrow more from the IMF, has
more special assets (i.e., SDRs), and more voting power than any other
member. The next highest contributors are Germany and Japan at 5.67
percent each, followed by France and the United Kingdom at 5.1 percent each; weighted voting allocations follow accordingly.

This gives the IMF's executive board tremendous power, though its
twenty-four executive directors rarely adopt decisions other than by
consensus. However, five of the directors hold about 40 percent of the
voting power, which in combination with other directors from Western
countries gives like-minded states dominance.

The structures are similar in the World Bank, where it is calculated
that in 1995 the Group of Seven industrialized states (G7; G8 including
Russia) held 43.3 percent of votes on the board, the Western-dominated
Organization for Economic and Cooperative Development 57.5 percent.[20] This dominance is disguised by the desire to achieve consensus
as in IMF and World Bank decisionmaking. Consensus decisionmaking
against the background of rules that allow for a qualified majority or

majority voting will often force a disgruntled member not to dissent for fear of retribution (e.g., the dissenting member knows that a vote against will not change a thing).[21] The majority, in contrast, must decide whether to force the recalcitrant member's hand to produce a negative vote, destroying the appearance of consensus and undermining the legitimacy of the decision.

Thus consensus decisionmaking without real veto power is not the ideal painted in IMF literature. The same applies to the World Bank and WTO (though there is no weighted voting in the WTO), which also operate a system of consensus decisionmaking against a backdrop of qualified majority voting.[22] Furthermore, consensus decisionmaking places power in the chairman or director (in the IMF it is a European; in the World Bank it is an American), who must try to achieve a convergence of interests.[23] This process normally takes place "beyond the public eye,"[24] and so the pressures brought to bear against the minority and the deals made to achieve consensus are mysteries to outside observers.[25]

Each member state is obliged to inform the others about its exchange-rate policies and mechanisms, which since the abandonment of the gold standard can vary from free flotation to the pegging of a currency. Member states also refrain from restricting the exchange of its own money into foreign currency and also increase wealth compared to the whole membership in an orderly way.[26]

These treaty obligations are not without supervision from the IMF, which undertakes surveillance[27] of underlying economic policies, arguably necessary in a system that relies on the open market to set currency levels.[28] Developing from the express power of surveillance, annual consultations take place wherein the IMF collects economic data and has discussions with high-ranking officials. In addition, "special consultations" with economically powerful countries "review the world economic situation."[29] Surveillance and consultations influence member states' economic policies, producing—along with the prevailing global economic ideology—conformity among policies and mechanisms. The greater need to manage the world financial system in light of globalization and instability means that the IMF has strengthened its consultations, surveillance, and data-collection functions to take preventive (as opposed to reactive) measures.[30]

Although the degree of IMF leverage over recalcitrant members is an open question, the IMF carries great influence over borrowers to stem and reverse balance-of-payment problems. For instance, in the financial crises of the mid-1990s, the IMF extended very large credits to

Mexico ($18 billion) and Russia ($6.2 billion), and in the late 1990s it extended $20.4 billion to Russia and more than $35 billion to Indonesia, Korea, and Thailand.[31] Such loans are only extended if the money is going to be used effectively. This means that loan conditions are attached requiring reforms by the borrower. Typically this involves reduction in government expenditures, tightening of monetary policy, and addressing certain structural weaknesses, such as the need to privatize inefficient public undertakings.

Since the mid-1990s the conditions have come to include adequate welfare provision to prevent poor populations from suffering unduly from adjustments deriving from the IMF's loan. Further conditions include "good quality government spending" (e.g., on health and education), as well as "good governance" aimed at reducing corruption and increasing transparency in decisionmaking on financial matters.[32] The more the IMF endeavors to ensure that its loans achieve stability, the more intrusive it has to be and the more it seems to veer toward a uniform, one-size-fits-all brand of liberal capitalism. The paradoxes are apparent: conditions that require reductions in government spending contrast with the IMF's desire to protect the poor and increase "good" government spending.

The UN's financial institutions have been criticized by the CESCR operating under the UN-sponsored ICESCR. The implication of several CESCR country reports is that World Bank and IMF loans and assistance should be in accordance with the ICESCR's obligations to "protect vulnerable groups and members of society."[33] Of course, the CESCR cannot directly call for such observance, as such obligations extend only to the parties of the ICESCR. Nevertheless, the CESCR comes as close as possible to imputing the fundamental obligations to the UN's financial organizations.

In its 1999 report on Cameroon, the CESCR noted that the government's economic reform measures, which implemented the structural adjustment program approved by the IMF and the World Bank, "while increasing the real GDP growth rate [have] impacted negatively on the enjoyment of economic, social and cultural rights by increasing poverty and unemployment, worsening income distribution and causing the collapse of social services."[34] In a May 2000 meeting to review Egypt's report, Paul Hunt, a member of the CESCR, noted that "wide-ranging macroeconomic reforms, supported by the World Bank" and the IMF, had been implemented by Egypt. Although these generally had positive results, "as in many other States, those economic reforms had had a significant impact on economic, social and cultural rights." Further-more, he suggested that the government should, "in its negotiations with the international financial institutions," "use the Covenant as a tool to help it resist reforms that would harm the most vulnerable groups in Egyptian society."[35] This was taken up by the whole CESCR in its 2000 report on Egypt.[36]

Furthermore, the CESCR, in its 2000 report on Italy, encouraged that country "as a member of international organizations," especially the World Bank and the IMF, "to do all that it can to ensure that the policies and decisions of those organizations are in conformity with the obliga-tions of States parties to the Covenant."[37] Thus the CESCR has used its supervisory power over ICESCR parties to encourage powerful states to ensure that financial organizations do not violate human rights, also suggesting to weaker parties that they should use the ICESCR as a shield to ward off attempts by financial institutions to impose overly re-strictive monetary regimes that might violate human rights.

In addition, the CESCR has used to good effect its power to issue general comments, in combination with its specific power under ICE-SCR article 22 to bring relevant matters to UN bodies from reports sub-mitted under ICESCR, "which may assist such bodies in deciding . . . on the advisability of international measures likely to contribute to the ef-fective progressive implementation of the . . . Covenant." For example, in its general comment on the right to adequate food, contained in ICE-SCR article 11, the CESCR stated that "the international financial insti-tutions, notably the IMF and the World Bank, should pay greater atten-tion to the protection of the right to food in their lending policies and credit agreements and in international measures to deal with the debt cri-sis."[38] The CESCR made similar statements in its general comments on the implementation of other rights, for example, education[39] and health.[40]

In a general statement on globalization and human rights made on 1 May 1998, the CESCR called upon the World Bank, IMF, and WTO to "pay enhanced attention in their activities to respect for economic, so-cial and cultural rights."[41] This call has been echoed by ECOSOC's Subcommission on Prevention of Discrimination and Protection of Mi-norities in August 1998.[42]

Perhaps due to increasing criticism coming from the UN human rights elements, the IMF and World Bank are moving away "from micro-management in their conditionalities to emphasize country ownership and to invoke a more participatory approach."[43] This is reflected in the IMF's development of contingent credit lines that enable it to preemptively make loans to prevent a crisis. The focus seems to have reverted somewhat to financial stability rather than potentially destabilizing reforms of members' economic systems.

This approach is supplemented by the development of international codes of conduct (some of which have been drawn up by private international organizations such as the International Federation of Accountants and the International Association of Insurance Supervisors). These codes cover, for example, fiscal transparency, transparency of monetary and financial policies, accounting and auditing, banking supervision, insurance regulation, securities market regulation, bankruptcy, corporate governance, and the dissemination of financial data. However, the IMF still pierces the veil of the state by its system for assessing members' progress in observing internationally recognized standards and codes.[44] The approach is one of developing international standards before trying to ensure members are complying, rather than intruding into members' economies without standards much beyond notions of good governance. This is more acceptable as long as the international standards being pushed are compatible with overarching UN values, including economic, social, and cultural human rights. Examples would include labor and environmental standards and, perhaps above all, freedom from poverty.

Freedom from poverty is a basic human right deriving from article 25 of the UDHR of 1948. It provides that "everyone has the right to a standard of living adequate for the health and well-being of himself and of his family, including food, clothing, housing and medical care and necessary social services." The Bretton Woods institutions are concerned that management of the international financial system should reduce poverty while maintaining stability. Globalization, or "the increasing integration of economies around the world, particularly through trade and financial flows," has the potential to increase poverty in developing countries as well as countries in transition from planned to market economies through volatile capital movements, or to decrease poverty by enabling rapid economic growth.[45] To achieve the latter requires a greater degree of management, as well as a greater focus on poverty reduction, by promoting economic stability, domestic productivity, capital flows to developing countries, and external debt management, combining debt relief with aid where necessary.

A recognition that international stability necessitates an inclusionary vision, whereby developing states are helped to achieve integration and prosperity, is now prevalent in IMF and World Bank initiatives and policy statements. "Given the challenges facing the global economy, the work of the Fund and the Bank has become even more essential in helping to promote financial stability, sustainable growth and poverty reduction."[46] The challenge is immense, with more than 1 billion people living on less that a dollar per day.

The Bretton Woods institutions undertook two initiatives in the late 1990s—the HIPC and the Poverty Reduction and Growth Facility. The former aims to relieve the debt burden of qualifying countries (more than forty), whereas the latter focuses on poverty reduction based on low-interest loans within strategies devised by eligible member states (about eighty); both operate within the Comprehensive Development Framework.[47] This greater emphasis on poverty reduction and debt relief—combined with a less centralized and straightjacketed approach that allows developing states to devise home-grown strategies to improve economic performance while safeguarding basic human rights—is to be welcomed.

The IMF's increasing management of the world's financial stability is reflected in the declaration of the Interim Committee of the IMF board of governors on 29 September 1996.[48] This expanded the committee's Madrid declaration of 1994. The mid-1990s marked the start of a period of world financial instability, but the principles are still adhered to by the organization. The declaration stresses sound monetary, fiscal, and structural policies; avoidance of large imbalances; conditions for private savings; reduction in inflation; trade liberalization; careful progress to allow increased capital movements; budget balance; transparency of fiscal policies; reduction of unproductive spending while ensuring adequate investment in infrastructure; improvement of education and training; reform of public pension and health systems; alleviation of poverty; provision of well-targeted and affordable social safety nets; labor and product market reforms; promotion of good governance; ensuring the rule of law; improving the efficiency of the public sector; tackling corruption; and sound banking systems.

The exhortation to member states to follow these strictures is reinforced by the managing director's reminder that IMF missions "visit virtually every one of your countries at least once a year—and often more frequently than that. On a typical day, the Fund has missions in about 30 of your countries, discussing in depth your countries' policies and performance, their medium term prospects, and their longer term problems." The findings are reported back to the IMF executive board, which "transmit[s] conclusions back to all of [the] authorities" and, twice a year, brings matters of global significance to the interim committee. It then formulates guidelines premised on the fact that national decisions within one country can have significant influence and effects on other countries, not regionally but globally.

The implications are clear. Member states must adhere to the IMF's strictures if they expect IMF financial and technical assistance, not to mention international acceptance and financial viability in a globalized world. Such structures are based on the notion of globalization and liberalization of national and international economies. Free trade of goods (promoted by the WTO) is combined with a free flow of capital and services. These two freedoms are not matched by a third—the free flow of workers or, more broadly, all people—as found, for example, within the European Union. An adverse report from an IMF mission can itself produce financial consequences, even instability, and so is to be avoided at all costs. Thus the IMF has tremendous influence on states' financial policies, as well as domestic decisions that affect financial matters. An IMF executive director from a developing country states:

> The role of the Bretton Woods Institutions is to establish a code of conduct with regard to international monetary movements, trade movements etc, and to ensure that all countries adhere to such a code. Clearly, in the case of a small country that needs resources from the Bank and the Fund, the code of conduct has teeth. The country can only use the Institutions if it aligns its policies with the spirit of the law of these Institutions. The question arises when industrialized countries do not comply. The power of enforcement is then less clear. The only thing that the Fund can do then is to exert peer pressure.[49]

It is questionable whether the IMF has been the primary shaper of the liberal global financial system; in a way it has simply reacted to technological and ideological phenomena. However, its alignment with (and, in a loose sense, enforcement of) such a system means that the IMF creed has become a matter of UN law, not policy. But in so doing the IMF is under an obligation to ensure that its development of global financial laws and norms is in accordance with the fundamental principles governing the UN system, most especially human rights norms.

The World Bank Group, Development, and Human Rights

The IBRD (World Bank) and its affiliated institutions—the International Finance Corporation and the International Development Association—

together make up the World Bank Group. At its inception the World Bank was designed to be operational more than a standard-setter. In essence it was "created to promote the economic development of its member countries by providing loans and technical assistance for specific projects and for programs of economic reform in developing countries."[50] As stated in the IBRD Articles of Agreement, the Bank's main purpose is to "assist in reconstruction and development of territories of members by facilitating the investment of capital for productive purposes."[51]

Historically, the Bank's primary function was financing reconstruction after World War II; only later did it turn to development. Indeed, its significance was overshadowed by its partner institution, the IMF (the IBRD Articles of Agreement copied those of the IMF). Initially, the Bank was not authorized to collect information from member states. It could only request information from states when granting loans "just as any other bank requiring information to ensure loan security." This illustrated the "limited focus on project-specific lending that the Bank was originally designed for."[52] It was not designed, like the IMF, to be a regulatory agency. The Bank was restricted to making decisions only on the basis of economic considerations, but distinguishing between economic and political considerations was difficult as soon as conditions were attached to loans.[53]

In the period 1944–1948, the Bank concentrated on postwar reconstruction. Its biggest-ever loan in real terms was made in 1947 to France ($250 million). By the end of the 1950s, the Bank had become the fourth largest financier of international development projects. However, it was conservative, lending only to creditworthy countries (including Japan). It limited itself to financing projects where no other finance was available on reasonable terms; it made specific-purpose loans, not general-purpose loans, always on the basis of secured repayment. It financed many infrastructure projects during the first two decades— power plants, railways, roads, and so on. It disregarded so-called social overhead issues such as sanitation, education, and health.[54]

Within these narrow confines the Bank was successful. This helps explain why in the early 1960s markets permitted the IBRD's shift to developing countries, and a softer development orientation, through the creation of the International Development Agency. The IDA was created as "the soft-loan arm of the IBRD, a creature that Wall Street and conservative U.S. policy-makers advised strongly against only five years earlier."[55] The World Bank needed to do this, as postwar reconstruction projects were long gone. The Bank needed to transform itself from a "private international bank towards what was to become more and more of a development agency."[56]

In this phase, loans went to large-scale infrastructure projects and agriculture, with the IDA providing the latter through very-low-interest loans. In addition, it developed other activities beyond lending, including technical assistance, feasibility studies, and institution-building. Under the technical assistance program, the Bank became involved with social overhead issues such as education as early as 1962 in relation to Tunisia. In the 1970s, the focus was on poverty reduction. The debt crisis of the early 1980s (starting with Mexico's default) left multilateral aid institutions as the main source of development finance. This caused the Bank to impose greater conditions on loans that were required to save poor countries from unmanageable debt burdens. Yet the Bank's success rate (measured by the achievement of its major objectives) fell from nearly 90 percent in the 1970s to about 65 percent in the 1980s.[57] The Bank thus faced a choice of reverting to the narrow traditional conception of lending or evolving into a development agency. "But is the World Bank, which still is, basically, a bank, the right place to start when the task in question is poverty reduction on a global scale?"[58]

The constitutions of the IBRD and IDA do not define "development":

> The Bank does not disagree with the international community's conception of development as a comprehensive process incorporating economic, social, cultural, political and spiritual dimensions. Nevertheless, the IBRD and IDA contend that as specialized economic organizations they have a limited mandate. This restricts their permissible activities to the economic aspects of the development process.[59]

This tends to fit in with the ICJ's approach to the UN's specialized agencies in the *WHO Opinion* of 1996.[60] However, the inaccuracy of the Bank's own view (as well as that of the court) is seen in the current practice of the Bank (though selective and unequal among countries) and suggests that the bottom line is that "all issues are economic and that, as a result, there is no issue that is excluded from the scope of the Bank's jurisdiction."[61]

Although operating as a reconstruction bank in the early years, the Bank could respect borrowers' sovereignty. "It appeared to leave to the Borrowing State all the difficult political judgments, such as which potential projects should be given highest priority, who should benefit from the project, and how the costs associated with the project should be shared among the citizens of the Borrowing State."[62] Its move to a development bank and its concern with the alleviation of poverty

> has expanded the range of activities now funded by the Bank (in addition to its traditional infrastructure projects) to include: reform of the civil service; reform of the management of public sector enterprises; legal and judicial reform; family planning; improving the quality of education and the equity of access to primary education; reform of universities; development of the private sector; land titling and registration reform; and programs to ensure that vulnerable groups such as women, children, indigenous people, and other minorities get access to health, education, and other Bank-funded programs. In addition, during the past two years [1993–1995], the Bank has actively promoted public participation in its operations.[63]

The net result of these massively widened activities is that the Bank has an effect on many human rights, both civil and political (due process, free association, free expression, right to participate in government); economic, social, and cultural rights (right to work, health care, education, food, housing); as well as thematic human rights issues (rights of children, women, and indigenous peoples).[64] The challenge is to ensure that the Bank promotes these rights in an even-handed way and ensures that its programs do not lead to a violation of such rights. The Bank is under a duty to respect the UN Charter, international law, and the UN-sponsored human rights conventions. Even though it is not a party to these conventions, it should "ensure that its operations do not undermine the country's efforts to abide by the conventions."[65]

In its report *Development and Human Rights: The Role of the World Bank* (published in 1998 on the fiftieth anniversary of the UDHR), the World Bank reviewed its activities from a human rights perspective.[66] This was a partial recognition of past failures and an attempt to redress those failures by making human rights concerns central to its lending policies. The report is introduced by words of hope— that we can "look forward with realistic hope to lifting a large number of the world's poorest people from absolute poverty, to ending harmful child labor, to ensuring that every family in every city has safe drinking water and adequate nutrition, and to building a world in which we are truly neighbours." The Bank establishes its position at the center—"by placing the dignity of every human being—especially the poorest—at the very foundation of its approach to development, the

Bank helps people in every part of the world build lives of purpose and hope."

The argument is that without development there can be no proper realization of human rights. Bank development policies should support education, health, sanitation, and housing as well as strengthen judicial institutions and financial sectors. The Bank argues that it is creating the structures and minimal wealth needed for the development of human rights.[67]

In a sense this reflects the oft-repeated philosophical debate as to what political and economic system individuals would choose, all else being equal.[68] Would they choose a system in which basic needs are met regardless of one's position in society, or would they risk a society based on greater freedoms that would enable them to acquire and maintain wealth? Either choice (and realistically it would likely be a blend of the two) involves human rights—whether economic and social rights or civil and political rights. Thus it is disingenuous for the Bank to claim that its activities are a prequel to the realization of human rights. All choices concerning the development of a society are choices about human rights.

The Bank's poverty alleviation efforts reflect the human rights choices that have been made. The concern with alleviating poverty is reflected in the introduction of poverty assessments for states in 1988 to enable the Bank to understand the causes and effects. The Bank then developed poverty reduction strategies designed to increase productivity among the poor through investments in health and education. For example, during the period 1993–1998 Bank lending for education was $1.7 billion annually. The strategy will include support for improved economic policies (based on openness of trade and investment, stable exchange rates, low inflation, sound fiscal policies, and high technology; funding rural and agricultural economic development programs; and debt relief through HIPC).

The Bank is also determined to build better governance, arguing there is an indisputable connection between good economic performance and accountable governance based on openness and transparency. "Governments of whatever form work best when the policies they pursue are decided openly and implemented uniformly, with the ongoing participation of individual citizens and civil society."[69] The Bank encourages states to open access (for individuals and companies) to credit, to justice (e.g., judicial reform and judicial institution-building, as in Russia), and to property rights. The Bank also promotes the protection of vulnerable people—women, children, and victims of war.

Increasingly as well, the Bank's country assistance strategies include participation from NGOs and civil society, which inform development and lending programs.

During the 1990s the Bank moved toward becoming a development agency, with a continued concern for social issues, including the environment (dwarfing UNEP in this regard). In order to achieve so much, the Bank will have to enter into "expanded partnerships with the UN system, other regional development banks, NGOs and civil society and the private sector."[70] The Bank thus has widened its concern to include more than purely economic matters, as stated in its original mandate.

In the words of Ibrahim Shihata, "Conditionality [of loans] has thus evolved from macroeconomic measures to detailed reforms affecting the public administration [of a state] itself."[71] Often these conditions have nothing to do with the loan itself; they are essentially "non-financial conditions" derived "from assumptions about the normative and economic task of development."[72] "Today, there is hardly a slogan in the international development debate that is not a World Bank concern, whether it is the environment, gender, health, children, corruption or good governance," which "is a world apart from financing airlines and ports."[73]

The World Bank has set itself much harder tasks and is less likely to achieve great success, at least in purely banking terms. Its effectiveness and achievements must therefore be measured in development terms: greater transparency, decentralization to regional offices, the recruitment of larger numbers of noneconomists—all reflect the Bank's structural change and reflect its new focus.[74] Yet there is need for caution, as "the Bank will not succeed in riding . . . two horses at the same time. It will have to make a choice, either to be a good development institution or be a good bank."[75]

The issue thus becomes one of compatibility, that is, between its new expanded focus and its development of intrusive conditions subject to article 4(10) of the IBRD Articles of Agreement, which states:

> The Bank and its officers shall not interfere in the political affairs of any member; nor shall they be influenced in their decisions by the political character of the member or members concerned. Only economic considerations shall be relevant to their decisions, and these considerations shall be weighed impartially in order to achieve the purposes stated in Article 1.

Despite this provision, the World Bank "now asserts that the quality of 'governance' by developing country governments is within its jurisdiction."[76] The Bank points out that if it is to be an effective development bank under article 1 it must pay attention to wider (i.e., noneconomic) factors. This is an attempt to interpret "economic considerations" very broadly and is a recognition that the line between political and economic matters is blurry. "The Bank holds that so long as governance issues are related to economic development, the Bank may impose conditions on development."[77] However, this does not mean that the content of article 4(10) has been abandoned; some decisions by the Bank may be characterized as purely political and therefore, according to article 4(10), ultra vires.

Shihata attempts to reconcile the Bank's growing concern with governance issues and the constitutional prohibition against political matters. "The Bank's Executive Directors have the power to decide on any question of interpretation of the provisions of the Articles of Agreement subject to possible review by the Board of Governors at the request of any member."[78] The subsequent practice of the Bank has been to interpret the constitution widely "to ensure the borrowing countries' implementation capacity." Thus "conditionality has concentrated on institutional changes in macro-economic and financial management, sectoral restructuring and policy reforms, enhancement of public sector efficiency and constraints in public sector management."

Institutional reforms have included the organization of the civil service, the size of public administration, and the size and structure of the public sector.[79] Thus not all issues relating to the governance exercised by the authorities within a state, especially the political character of the government, are within the Bank's mandate. Only if political factors "lead to direct and obvious economic results relevant to the Bank's work, the Bank may properly take such results into account as economic considerations which only happened to have political causes or origins." In general this means that the Bank has a legitimate concern for "the governments' processes of establishing well functioning *rules* and *institutions* for the efficient management of the countries' resources—a process which should go hand in hand with the investment of capital for productive purposes." This creates the ability to address reform of the civil service as well as legal reform within a state, as the concern is to establish a system of economic management based on rules.[80] According to this view, then, World Bank practice is compatible with the constitution.

Although the Bank has become concerned with the rule of law and governments within states, it tackles only those aspects that directly relate to economic matters. Still, the Bank has moved a long way from making loans irrespective of the government of the borrowing country. Structural-adjustment lending by the Bank—as opposed to loans for specific projects—can further be justified under the constitution, according to Shihata. He refers to article 3(4)(vii), which states that "loans made or guaranteed by the Bank shall, except in *special circumstances*, be for the purpose of specific projects of reconstruction or development."[81]

There is leeway in the constitution for such development by practice. Indeed, Bank practice on governance issues can be seen to fit in with the UN's increasing promotion of democracy. Care must be taken, though, to assess the Bank's practice, not only in light of its own constitution but also with regard to UN law (including emerging law on democracy as well as established human rights principles). However, nonintervention is still the norm under UN law, and despite a half-century of UN practice it remains a core principle that should not be violated. Thus "the World Bank must carefully walk the fine line between illegally intervening in a member's internal affairs, and correctly identifying and requiring governance standards that will affect the economy of the member country as permitted by reasonable interpretations of its Articles of Agreement."[82]

Similar debates can be had in relation to the IMF's development of conditionality. Article 4(3)(b) of the IMF constitution states that in adopting principles for the guidance of all members such principles "shall respect the domestic social and political policies of members." Although expressed somewhat differently to reflect the IMF's greater lawmaking capacity, the principle of nonintervention has been whittled away much like it has in the Bank's practice.

There can be no doubt that the World Bank (and the IMF) have attempted to make their policies and activities compatible with human rights and environmental concerns. The World Bank posited two minimum conditions in assessing the social impact of its loans and conditions. First, it operates under a no-harm principle, meaning that nobody should be made worse off by its actions. Second, it ensures that vulnerable people share in the project's benefits.[83] Although not formulated as the positive achievement of human rights, especially the most relevant economic and social rights, the aim is to ensure that the Bank's policies do not *worsen* human rights in trying to improve the situation. This is a reasonable approach given that the Bank is an operational institution charged with development. Development activities should be compatible with human rights values but do not have to be aimed at furthering them, except insofar as development is itself seen as a right. The problem is that even in fulfilling minimum conditions the Bank sometimes falls short, and this the Bank needs to improve.[84]

The overall success and failure of the Bretton Woods institutions is intensely debated. The IMF and IBRD have been accused of causing the impoverishment of hundreds of millions of people through their macroeconomic stabilization and structural adjustment programs. Cuts in welfare programs, as well as state spending on health and education, under conditions attached to loans and credits are the root cause of these problems.[85] The Bretton Woods institutions seem to have attempted to redress this by ensuring that their policies and actions do not directly violate human rights standards. Thus we can see a conscious move away from the tunnel-vision focus on producing financial stability in borrowing states in the short term. The desire to achieve stability above all else may well have violated fundamental UN standards relating to the alleviation of poverty. The current concern of the international financial institutions is to attempt to shape a longer-term policy in which development and human rights are not disregarded. This is a much more ambitious project, but it is in line with UN values.

The World Bank's Inspection Panel raises another issue: whether a parallel institution should be developed in the IMF. The Inspection Panel does seem to be a first step in recognizing that the Bank is accountable to individuals for its actions, although not yet in a full human rights sense.

The panel is a three-member body created in 1993 by the board of executive directors to "receive requests for inspection presented to it by an affected party in the territory of the borrower which is not a single individual (i.e., a community of persons such as an organization, association, society or other grouping of individuals)."

> The affected party must demonstrate that its rights or interests have been or are likely to be affected by an act or omission of the Bank as a result of the failure of the Bank to follow its operational policies and procedures with respect to the design, appraisal and/or implementation of a project financed by the Bank (including situations where the Bank is alleged to have failed in its follow-up on the borrower's obligations under loan agreements with respect to such policies or procedures) provided in all cases that such a failure has had, or threatens to have, a material adverse effect.[86]

The Inspection Panel is a radical development in the UN system. It could be said that the panel provides "an independent forum to private citizens who believe that they or their interests have been or could be directly harmed by a project directly financed by the World Bank."[87] International law in general, as well as the UN system, lacks means for individuals to register complaints. The human rights system allows, with state consent, individuals to register complaints against states, and the World Bank system allows groups of individuals to register complaints against the Bank itself. Only twelve requests were filed in the period 1994–2000. Procedures are carefully restricted so as not to inundate the panel "with an accumulated fifty years of complaints about the role of the World Bank in developing countries."[88]

Thus only groups of individuals can complain, and some matters (e.g., complaints against procurement decisions by Bank borrowers from suppliers) are not within the jurisdiction of the panel. Above all, then, the Bank's activities are to be assessed by the panel only in light of the Bank's own policies and procedures rather than fundamental principles of the UN system.

Furthermore, even within that framework of policies and procedures reference should be made to IBRD constitution article 4(10), which prohibits political noneconomic activity by the Bank. This provision has been narrowed through practice, and given the recent spate of intrusive *nonfinancial* conditions to loans, a claim could be made that the Bank is directly violating its own constitution.

Nevertheless, if a request is within the panel's jurisdiction, it will receive evidence and forward its findings to the Bank's management and the board of executive directors; the former has six weeks to respond to the panel's findings, and the board has the ultimate authority on implementation. This in itself presents a problem given the "Board's dual role as directors of the Bank as well as final decision makers in an independent inspection process."[89] In the first panel decision in 1994, the complaint was over the Bank's financing of the Arun III Hydroelectric Project in Nepal, in that the project design violated Bank policies on environmental assessment, involuntary resettlement, and indigenous peoples. The panel's report upheld most of these complaints; management reassessed the project and decided to withdraw its financial support.[90]

Other UN Actors: Loans or Aid?

Many UN actors are involved in issues of development and economic welfare; I address some here. Some of the specialized agencies address industrial development in developing countries. UNIDO is a central player, but its impact is limited, mainly due to lack of finances. UNIDO is restricted mainly to technical assistance in the form of consultancies, conferences, and fellowships.[91] Other agencies, such as WIPO, have a greater impact on development even though they appear to be much more narrow in their competence. WIPO was created in 1967 "to promote the protection of intellectual property rights throughout the world." However, "basic notions of intellectual property have been challenged by developing countries as incompatible with an equitable international economic order."[92]

Subsidiary UN organs have a much greater impact. UNDP has a network of offices in 134 countries to ensure efficient application of assistance and resources by the UN system, and not only UNDP-funded projects (e.g., commercial fairs).[93] UNDP has been described as "the world's most important source of technical assistance to developing countries." This assistance is mostly nonmonetary, in the form of experts, equipment, and fellowships.

Cooperation is growing within the UN system, as well as between the Bretton Woods institutions and the UN political bodies (e.g., the UNDP helps the World Bank design development projects).[94] However, their differing philosophies has meant that cooperation and compatibility have been hard to achieve, though that is less so today. UNCTAD, for instance, created in 1964 to focus on least developed countries (LDCs), is concerned now with integrating LDCs into the rapidly globalizing and liberalizing world economy. UNCTAD implements more that two dozen technical cooperation projects in eighteen LDCs.[95]

This reflects a change in UNCTAD's approach, from changing the world economic order in the 1970s to ensuring that developing countries survive globalization. Thus it no longer sets itself up as a rival to the UN's financial institutions, instead studying and discussing economic issues of importance to developing countries and by having an "*indirect* influence on the creation and amendment of treaties dealing with international economic law."[96] For instance, "UNCTAD has been instrumental in forcing changes in the GATT to recognize that the GATT rules should reflect the needs of developing countries, even to the extent of 'violating' the most-favoured-nation principle by allowing preferential treatment for developing country trade."[97]

This move from confrontation to integration reflects the attitude of developing states, the majority in many UN forums. In the 1970s, UNCTAD initiated the UN's drive toward promulgating the New International

Economic Order. The General Assembly adopted resolutions on the establishment of the NIEO,[98] as well as the Charter of Economic Rights and Duties of States.[99] The NIEO was "more important for its expressions of dissatisfaction with the Bretton Woods regime than for the legal effects, direct or indirect, that the NIEO has created."[100] However, earlier General Assembly resolutions have become part of customary international law.[101]

Despite the general move to accept the economic order championed by the Bretton Woods institutions and the WTO, there is the need for a minimal safety net in the form of aid, not loans. The main entity for achieving this is the World Food Programme. Created in 1963, the WFP is the world's largest international food aid organization. The executive board is split between FAO and ECOSOC members. Under article 6(1) of the general regulations of the WFP, the executive board's actions are to be in accordance with the overall policy guidance of the UN General Assembly, the FAO, and ECOSOC. It is funded voluntarily by states, IGOs, corporations, and individuals. In 1998 the WFP delivered 2.8 million metric tons of food aid to nearly 75 million people in emergencies and long-term refugee operations (in conjunction with UNHCR), as well as development projects.[102]

The WFP is not generally included in analyses of the economic and development activities of the UN system because it provides food in emergency situations without any system of repayment. It can thus be seen as acting in contradistinction to the Bretton Woods/WTO ethos, which works on the basis of free trade supported by a loans system for countries in crisis. The WFP may even discourage development because it does not encourage countries to cope with the rigors of the international economic system. But any economic system should have a welfare element to support the weakest members; otherwise they will be condemned to increasing poverty and worse.

The WFP attempts to provide a safety net for countries and individuals, without which development would be impossible. It represents a limited attempt at redistribution from rich to poor. Its mandate is to save lives (food-for-life), help vulnerable people (food-for-growth), and help the hungry poor to become self-reliant (food-for-work). In the latter case, the WFP pays local workers with food to build roads, ports, and irrigation channels or to plant forests. According to the WFP, "The vision of the WFP is a world in which every man, woman and child has access at all times to the food needed for an active and healthy life. Without food, there can be no sustainable peace, no democracy and no development."[103]

The WFP states that it will endeavor "to avoid negative effects on local food production, consumption patterns and dependency on food aid."[104]

The WFP recognizes that food aid is a valuable political tool in civil conflicts. Problems include intimidation of WFP staff, looting, and lack of cooperation in targeting the most needy. Recent examples include the former Yugoslavia and Sudan.[105] Despite these problems, the value of WFP activities is revealed by its emergency reports. The April 2000 report on the Horn of Africa stated that about 1 million metric tons of food assistance was required for drought-affected people during 2000. By the end of March, the WFP had acquired pledges from donors of 225,000 tons.[106] Despite abuse and logistical problems in distribution, there is no doubt that the WFP performs an essential function within the UN system. It tries, with some success, to save lives.

Conclusion

It has been stated that "the international economic system is ill-served by a UN system in which a multiplicity of agencies operate in uncoordinated fashion to deal separately with economic issues that are interrelated" despite attempts at coordination.[107] However, concrete attempts at coordination are growing, with entities generally sharing a vision on development and the alleviation of poverty. There is an integrated framework for trade-related assistance to LDCs, with an interagency group consisting of the IMF, ITC, UNCTAD, UNDP, World Bank, and WTO generally coordinating trade assistance.[108] But cooperation also occurs at a very detailed level. For example, UNDP and the World Bank have been cooperating with the European Commission to promote accountancy reform in economies in transition. This recognizes the fact that accounting is the language of business, and in an international economy it is essential that internationally accepted accounting principles are used. Although there is financial and political pressure on states to accept these standards, everything is based on consent, as it is throughout the UN's economic legal order.[109]

The exceptions to consent[110] are seen in the IMF's balance-of-payments operations: if a member does not comply with performance criteria, it does not receive any more money. The World Bank will withhold funds from members that seriously deviate from the Bank's criteria. In extreme cases, the IMF will declare that a member is no longer entitled to use the fund and may even expel that member. Finally, there is the GATT/WTO dispute resolution mechanism, a method of self-regulation by state parties using panels of experts. The winning complainant can then adopt self-help remedies, principally retaliatory measures by suspending the application to the offending party of such concessions or obligations under the GATT/WTO agreement.[111]

Enforcement, at least in a direct sense, is rudimentary. Consent and cooperation are the norm. UNCTAD and the WTO, which is formally outside the UN system, cooperate through the International Trade Centre (ITC, a joint UN-WTO subsidiary organ) on technical issues in developing countries and trade promotion. The ITC also implements UNDP-financed projects for trade promotion in developing countries. An example is a series of projects aimed at developing internationally competitive products and ensuring that enterprises in developing countries have the facilities to export and import effectively. The ITC also coordinates its work with the FAO and UNIDO.[112] In its report on its activities in 1999, the ITC had helped government and private-sector individuals in developing countries through training programs, but this sort of approach will reap benefits only in the long run. The ITC identifies the long-term desire to eradicate poverty, stating that the aim of the ITC is to "create new job and income opportunities, develop a basis for the accumulation of capital, technology and skills, and provide the foundation for fostering other dimensions of economic and social development within those communities."[113]

UNCTAD provides technical assistance in debt management to developing countries and economies in transition. A component of this assistance is the Debt Management and Financial Analysis System, which operates in fifty countries, enabling them to record and monitor their external debt. This constitutes part of UNCTAD's cooperation with the World Bank and the IMF and their HIPC.[114]

The UN system, especially the Bretton Woods institutions and the WTO, has ensured that the world community moved away from raw economic power dictating international economic relations to a more rule-oriented approach, which means that powerful players are restrained.[115] However, the influence of the powerful states means that any rules are supportive of the economic system desired by those states. It has been stated that "the United Nations and its related agencies have sought to improve international economic relations by developing legal and quasi-legal processes to help resolve conflicts and promote world economic growth." Still, the complexity and change in the international economic order, combined with the relative weaknesses of the processes, has led to an imperfect system.[116]

Some sort of managed trading system does not prevail, whereby development money is seen as a fundamental obligation in light of the inequity of the current system (as opposed to merely voluntary aid to the needy, the system that prevails now). Free trade thus remains the bedrock of the system, embodied in article 1 of the GATT. There, the most-favored-nation principle applies, under which concessions given to one trading partner are to be given to all.[117]

It may be that the political elements of the UN system will develop principles of UN law that relate "to a general notion of an emerging obligation to provide development aid."[118] These principles can be outlined in several ways: as an obligation on wealthy states to contribute to development based on capability; as an international entitlement for poor states to aid; as a human right to development; or as an obligation for affluent countries to assist poor nations. It is argued by many in the UN system that this should take a specific form (e.g., 0.7 percent of each member state's GNP).[119] However, the fact remains that contributions are viewed by donor states as purely voluntary.[120] The United Kingdom has struggled to achieve 0.31 percent of GNP in 2000. Only a few small rich nations achieve the target, with Denmark at 1 percent and Norway at 0.9 percent representing the best of a sorry effort by the international community.[121]

Notes

1. Zamora, "Economic Relations and Development," 537–538.
2. Ibid., 514.
3. Art. 1(3) of the agreement between the IMF and the United Nations, 1947; Art. 1(2) of the agreement between the United Nations and the IBRD, 1947.
4. Ibid., Art. III, IV(2), IMF Agreement/IBRD Agreement.
5. Ibid., Art. VI, IMF Agreement/IBRD Agreement.
6. IMF B/G Res. Nos. 6–8, 13 Sept. 1951; IBRD B/G Res. No. 64, 1951.
7. Agreement between the IMF and the WTO, 9 Dec. 1996; IMF doc. EBD96/85, para. 2.
8. IMF Annual Report, 2000, 151–152.
9. D. D. Driscoll, "What Is the International Monetary Fund?" <http://www.imf.org/external/pubs/ft/exrp/what.htm>, 1.
10. <http://www.imf.org/external/np/ta/2000/index.htm>.
11. <http://www.imf.org/external/np/exr/facts/tech>.

12. Zamora, "Economic Relations," 520.

13. Edwards, *International Monetary,* 506.

14. Zamora, "Economic Relations," 521–523.

15. Bradlow, "The World Bank," 67–68.

16. Ibid., 69.

17. Ibid., 70.

18. Ibid.

19. Driscoll, "What Is," 1.

20. Bergesen and Lunde, *Dinosaurs,* 100.

21. IMF Agreement, Art. XII(5)(c).

22. WTO Agreement, Art. IX(1); IBRD Art. V(3)(b).

23. Schermers and Blokker, *Institutional Law,* 507.

24. Kirgis, *International Organizations,* 222.

25. But see Bichsel, "The World Bank," 147–150.

26. IMF Articles of Agreement, Arts. IV and VIII.

27. IMF Articles of Agreement, Art. IV(3). See also the surveillance under the World Economic Outlook—Communiqué of the International Monetary and Financial Committee of the Board of Governors of the International Monetary Fund, 24 Sept. 2000 <http://www.imf.org/external/np/cm/2000/092400.htm>.

28. Driscoll, "What Is," 7.

29. Ibid., 8.

30. Ibid., 15.

31. Ibid., 9.

32. Ibid., 11.

33. UN doc. E/C.12/1/Add.5, 28 May 1996, para. 9 (report on Guinea); UN doc. E/C.12/1993/6, 3 June 1993, para. 6 (report on Kenya); UN doc. E/C.12/1994/9, 31 May 1994, para. 9 (report on Gambia). See also UN doc. E/C.12/1/Add.33, 14 May 1999, para. 28 (report on the Solomon Islands).

34. UN doc. E/C.12/1/Add.40, 8 Dec. 1999, para. 10 (report on Cameroon).

35. UN doc. E/C.12/2000/SR.11, 8 May 2000, para. 16.

36. UN doc. E/C.12/1/Add.44, 23 May 2000, para. 28.

37. UN doc. E/C.12/1/Add.43, 23 May 2000, para. 20.

38. UN doc. E/C.12/1995/5, CESCR General Comment No. 12, 12 May 1999, para. 40.

39. UN doc. E/C.12/1999/4, CESCR General Comment No. 11, 10 May 1999, para. 11; UN doc. E/C.12/1999/10 CESCR General Comment No. 13, 8 Dec. 1999, para. 60.

40. UN doc. E/C.12/2000/4, CESCR General Comment No. 14, 4 July 2000, para. 39.

41. Cited in UN doc. E/C.12/1999/9, 26 Nov. 1999, para. 2.

42. UN doc. E/CN.4/SUB.2/RES/1998/12, 20 Aug. 1998, para. 2.

43. Intergovernmental Group of Twenty-Four on International Monetary Affairs, Communiqué, 23 Sept. 2000 <http://www.imf.org/external/np/cm/2000/092300.htm>.

44. IMF and World Bank, "Reports on Observance of Standards and Codes," 30 March 2000 <http://www.imf.org/external/np/rosc/2000/stand.htm>.

45. "Globalization: Threat or Opportunity?" IMF Brief, 12 April 2000 <http://imf.org/external/np/exr/ib/2000/041200.htm>.

46. Joint Statement by Heads of the Bretton Woods Institutions, 5 Sept. 2000 <http://www.imf.org/external/np/omd/2000/pArt. htm>.

47. IMF/IBRD Development Committee doc. DC/2000-17, 7 Sept. 2000.

48. <http://www.imf.org/external/np/sec/pr/1996/PR9649.HTM>.

49. Bishel, "The World Bank," 143.

50. Zamora, "Economic Relations," 525.

51. IBRD Articles of Agreement, Art. I(I).

52. Bergesen and Lunde, *Dinosaurs,* 102.

53. IBRD Articles of Agreement, Art. IV(10).

54. Bergesen and Lunde, *Dinosaurs,* 111.

55. Ibid., 116.

56. Ibid., 117.

57. Ibid., 132–133. But see Cahn, "Challenging," 160.

58. Bergesen and Lunde, *Dinosaurs,* 95.

59. Bradlow, "The World Bank," 53–54.

60. ICJ Rep. 1996, 76.

61. Bradlow, "The World Bank," 62.

62. Ibid., 55.

63. Ibid., 58–59.

64. Ibid., 59.

65. Ibid., 63.

66. World Bank, 1998.

67. Ibid., 1–3.

68. Rawls, *Theory of Justice,* 17–22.

69. World Bank Report, 1998, 12.

70. Bergesen and Lunde, *Dinosaurs*, 146.

71. Shihata, "The World Bank," 59.

72. Cahn, "Challenging," 160.

73. Bergesen and Lunde, *Dinosaurs,* 156.

74. Ibid., 158–159.

75. Ibid., 161.

76. Cahn, "Challenging," 163.

77. Ibid., 164.

78. Shihata, "The World Bank," 67; IBRD Arts of Agreement, Art. IX.

79. Shihata, "The World Bank," 59.

80. Ibid., 93–95.

81. Ibid., 60–61, 64 (emphasis added).

82. Wadrzyk, "Is It Appropriate," 555.

83. Jerve, "Social Consequences," 37.

84. Ibid., 65.

85. Chossudovsky, *Globalisation,* 33–34.

86. Res. No. IBRD 93–10, 22 Sept. 1993.

87. <http://wbln0018worldbank.org/ipn/ipnweb.nsf/Woverview>.

88. Bissell, "Recent Practice," 741.

89. Bradlow, "The World Bank," 294.

90. Bissell, "Recent Practice," 741–742. See also Bradlow, "A Test Case."

91. Zamora, "Economic Relations," 527.

92. Ibid., 528–529.

93. <http://www.idcs.org/undp.htm>.

94. Zamora, "Economic Relations," 527.

95. <http://www.idcs.org/unctad.htm>.

96. Zamora, "Economic Relations," 518.

97. Ibid., 519.

98. GA Res. 3201, 4 May 1974.

99. GA Res. 3281, 12 Dec. 1974.

100. Zamora, "Economic Relations," 535.

101. GA Res. 1803, 14 Dec. 1962. Declaration on Permanent Sovereignty Over Natural Resources—which recognizes the right to expropriate for public purposes subject to the payment of appropriate compensation.

102. <http://www.wfp.org/info/intro/Info.html>.

103. Ibid.

104. <http://www.wfp.org/info/POLICY/Mission.html>.

105. UN doc. WFP/EB.A/2000/4-C, 13 April 2000, 6.

106. <http://www.wfp.org/report/2000/00407b.htm>.

107. Zamora, "Economic Relations," 539.

108. <http://www.idcs.org>.

109. <http://www.unctad.org/en/techcop/finc0104.htm>.

110. Outlined in Zamora, "Economic Relations," 565–569.

111. Ibid., 567; Mavroidis, "Remedies."

112. <http://www.intracen.org/itcinfo/itc.htm>.

113. UN doc. ITC/AG (XXXIII)/180, 10 Feb. 2000, 24.

114. <http://www.imf.org/external/np/ta/2000/index.htm>.

115. Jackson, *World Trading,* 86. Zamora, "Economic Relations," 564.

116. Zamora, "Economic Relations," 569.

117. Ibid., 572.

118. Ibid., 549.

119. Ibid.

120. Schachter, "Principles of International Social Justice," 251.

121. L. Elliott, "British Aid Less Than Half Its UN Target," *Guardian Weekly,* 5–11 April 2001, 14.

12

Summary and Conclusion

It is inaccurate to view the United Nations as a series of conferences or meeting places no different than the great nineteenth-century diplomatic conferences, such as the Congress of Vienna. That fails to account for the numerous rules and principles adopted within UN organs, output that is intended to regulate the behavior of states, something that is not always a feature of conference gatherings. Although the United Nations occasionally sponsors conferences that produce treaties (e.g., the Rio Earth Summit of 1992), this is just one method of lawmaking within the UN system. The G7 or G8 is a better modern example of the conference model producing communiqués that are intended to have political impact. The simple view also ignores the sheer number of entities operating under the UN umbrella. States would not create so many costly bodies if all they wished to achieve were a formalization of the political balance of power within different contexts.

It has been shown throughout this book that the so-called UN family of organizations, organs, committees, funds, programs, and individuals is large and sometimes fractious. There are squabbles, divorces, members stop talking to each other, and they fight over territory, property, and possessions. Of course the term "UN family" suggests that the entities operating under it are part of a complex whole regardless of the problems. Such is the case, despite problems in coordinating such an unwieldy system. Primarily, the United Nations constitutes a system because the entities within it understand that they are part of a larger system. Furthermore, organizations, states, and other entities outside the United Nations view it as a whole system.

Coordination occurs within functional areas: the UN human rights system, the UN collective security system, the UN criminal justice system, and so on. Combined with a sense of identity within area, there are discrete, robust UN systems. The UN system as a whole is weaker because it is kept together primarily by a profound belief in the system. It is a belief that the United Nations is pursuing values fundamental to the international community, values that must be protected and enhanced by the organization. Values and goals can conflict in particular situations, necessitating prioritization by the United Nations, but this does not undermine the integrity of the system.

To argue that the United Nations is the natural embodiment of the international community is not without controversy, especially after the events in Kosovo. However, the United Nations has shaped the values of the international community and developed its institutional structure in an attempt to implement those values. Furthermore, there are mechanisms for coordinating the diverse activities of the system. The prime example is the ACC, previously consisting only of the heads of the specialized agencies under the chair of the UN Secretary-General; it now includes the heads of the other UN funds and programs, plus the heads of the IAEA and the WTO.

Despite manifest weakness in the past, there is increasing evidence that the elements of the system are operating in a fashion that is more than rudimentary.[1] Under the direction of the current Secretary-General, Kofi Annan, who was elected in 1997, mechanisms such as the ACC are starting to be a focal point tapping the resources of the system to find combinations of agencies and programs to address global problems like HIV/AIDS.[2] Furthermore, there is increasing evidence that the system is receiving more policy direction from ECOSOC and the General Assembly, the UN organs that have ultimate responsibility for managing the UN specialized agencies, funds, and programs.[3]

The conclusion that there is a UN system should not be dismissed as a futile exercise in idealism. The conclusion is not that there is a world government—which has not been achieved—but that the United Nations is a system that has elements of global governance in it that may or may not evolve into a form of government. Although the system may be evolving and developing toward further and further governance, there is no inevitability in this process. It could be reversed, but it would take a persistent effort on the part of powerful states to denigrate the United Nations, to starve it of funds, and eventually to reject it.

The main explanation for the widening and deepening of the UN system and the legal order it produces is the increasing desire to ensure that laws and mechanisms are put in place to uphold the UN's values, which reflect the basic concerns of humanity. There has been an increasing desire within the United Nations to make those values much more than mere political aspirations. During the Cold War the United Nations was mostly restricted to legalizing those values, but the end of the 1980s saw the start of an upward trend toward enforcement, though a great deal remains to be achieved.

The values are found in the preambles and opening articles of the system's principal treaties. However, these core values have been elaborated upon by the practice of the various bodies in the UN system. Many of these values—peace, human rights, self-determination—marked new departures for the international community in 1945. These values provide both the goals to which the system aspires and also the benchmarks against which the success or failure of the system can be measured. Added to these are other values (protecting the environment and promoting democracy), reflecting the ability of the United Nations to change and take on board other threats to humanity.[4] The prevention of terrorism may become entrenched as another value of the United Nations in the light of the organization's reactions over the past decade to acts of terrorism, culminating in its response to the terrorist attacks on the United States of 11 September 2001.[5] Care must be taken, however, to balance this development with proper respect for other UN values, especially human rights.

The ICJ in the *Expenses* case examined the purposes of the United Nations and stated that the maintenance of international peace and security had "primary place."[6] Although the court explained the primacy given to peace as a prerequisite to the fulfillment of the other UN purposes, this is an unproven assumption. Indeed, the assumption that peace must be established before other values are protected is potentially dangerous, placing the need to assert order above justice and other positive aspects of peace.

The hierarchy debate is misunderstood. Peace is no longer the absence of war but includes the entrenchment of "positive peace": promoting justice, human rights, democracy, and economic and social well-being. In other words, peace in this wider sense is an overarching value that encompasses all others. This is reflected in the constitutions of most of the specialized agencies, which link their purposes (whether developing civil aviation, preventing epidemics, or protecting workers) to the promotion of peace. This is not unique to the United Nations; other organizations have been founded on the desire to prevent further hostilities. The origins of the European Union in the 1950s can be traced to a common desire to prevent European conflict, even though the major achievements of the organization since then have been quite different.

Even though peace has an overarching character, it might not be the ultimate UN value. Law (or, less prosaically, justice) is the underlying value. All the other values and the mechanisms are based on the legal foundation of the UN Charter and the constitutions of the specialized agencies. However, it has been argued by some international lawyers that the Security Council, the most powerful UN organ, is not always limited by international law regarding protecting peace.[7] Clearly, the Security Council has latitude to take coercive action under chapter VII of the UN Charter, but this does not mean that it can ignore basic principles of international or charter law.

Furthermore, notions of law and justice infuse all other values, for it is possible to see most of the core values as human rights and therefore legal rights belonging to people either individually or collectively—the right to peace, the right to a clean environment, the right to health, the right to democracy, and so on. There is strong evidence that the orientation of the core values is toward individuals and away from states, though this has been more marked in some areas than others. The UN systems for peace and security and the environment are still of an interstate character.

Although peace in a positive sense is the primary aim of the United Nations, law underpins the system. It is not useful to debate whether law or peace is the primary value, because they serve different purposes. Peace can be achieved through pragmatic ends, but the United Nations seeks to achieve positive peace through law. Law in the United Nations has not fully taken the form of human rights law. And though it is possible to see all the core values as human rights, protecting the individual has developed much further in some areas than in others. Whereas it is feasible to speak of the right to democracy and freedom from poverty, it is not possible to convincingly deploy the same terminology for peace (in the negative sense) and the environment. Thus law, but primarily of an interstate nature, governs these areas.

In addition, human rights standards are applicable to the United Nations in all its activities. The jurisprudence of the two bodies created under the international covenants—the HRC and the CESCR—is a sober reminder that UN actions in upholding security, development, democracy, and justice are subject to the overriding concern not to violate fundamental human rights. For instance, a UN sanctions regime should not violate an individual's right to food; conditions attached to loans or aid should not violate the right to education by insisting on cuts in public spending; democracy assistance should not depart from the basic law contained in article 25 of the ICCPR.

Whether the United Nations can be held accountable or even legally responsible for actions (or inactions) that violate fundamental human rights is a woefully underdeveloped area. There have been mechanisms of political accountability for UN failures, with, for example, an internal inquiry by the Secretary-General into the failure of UN peacekeepers to prevent the fall of Srebrenica and consequent massacre of Muslims in Bosnia in 1995,[8] and an independent inquiry into the actions of the United Nations during the 1994 genocide in Rwanda.[9] In the latter inquiry, for instance, the commission found "responsibility" at various levels in the UN system—poor planning in the Secretariat in regard to the United Nations Assistance Mission in Rwanda (UNAMIR), as well as the lack of political will in the Security Council to mandate a robust force and to stop the killing. The report also points out that member states were equally responsible for their lack of commitment to UNAMIR. What is clear is that the report is not apportioning legal responsibility among member states and the United Nations for these acts. There is no question of the commission acting as a legal body, determining guilt.

The legal responsibility of the United Nations—and the question of concurrent responsibility with member states—represents an underdeveloped area of the law.[10] It is essential that it develops as a necessary method for ensuring that the United Nations is judged by its own standards. The rule of law dictates that the governed and the governor are subject to the law. However, the ICJ, the natural forum for issues of legal accountability, is an interstate forum and is reluctant to review UN actions, though developments in that direction are not out of the question. Other underdeveloped mechanisms of accountability within the UN system include the World Bank's Inspection Panel.

The United Nations is not an elaborate conference model but a system founded upon law, and its character is worthy of reconsideration here. Attempts have been made, mainly since the Covenant of the League of Nations in 1919, to suggest a considerable distinction between ordinary, "contractual" bilateral or multilateral treaties and "constitutional" multilateral treaties. This was a radical departure from the view that international law was in essence private law between consenting states acting as equals rather than any form of public law.[11] The fine balance can be seen as far back as 1919, when Max Huber stated that the legal character of the covenant was "neither contractual nor constitutional."[12] Huber was of the view that the covenant had a different legal character to the mainly contractual exchanges and agreements that occurred previously. Yet IGOs existed before the League (the International Telegraphic Union was created in 1865, the Universal Postal Union in 1874). Indeed, the treaty that established the UPU was called a "constitution." The UPU and ITU formed a union of services rather than the mere formalization of existing cooperation, again suggesting that the legal regime created by the member states of these organizations was something more than contractual.[13]

A. McNair, writing in 1930, was less cautious about the constitutional nature of the covenant, stating that "the society of states has not yet got a complete Constitution, but it has a great deal of Constitutional Law," including not only the covenant but also other foundational treaties. He concluded: "It seems to me that these constitutional treaties . . . create a kind of public law transcending in kind and not merely in degree the ordinary agreements between states."[14] Although the meaning of a bilateral or multilateral contractual arrangement, whereby all the "contracting parties concur in the purpose of creating identical rules binding upon all of them" is clear, what exactly is meant by a "constitution" or "constitutional law" is much more complicated.[15] McNair alludes to the verticalization of international law, which suggests a move away from the purely horizontal consensual system epitomized by the contract.

If we move from the post-1919 world order to the post-1945 order, societal values are shaping, informing, and regulating the operation of a complex set of institutions within a system framed by legal instruments of foundational significance. The UN system is not only governed by a series of treaties; it is governed by a complex constitution, with the UN Charter at its heart. O. Schachter's characterization of the charter in 1951 is relevant here: "The Charter is surely not to be construed as a lease of land or an insurance policy, it is a constitutional instrument whose broad phrases were designed to meet changing circumstances for an undefined future."[16]

It is arguable that in 1945 the UN Charter was constructed as a constitutional document and not as an international treaty, a fact indicated by the opening words of the UN Charter: "We the Peoples of the United Nations." The charter has become a constitution, indeed is the foundational constitutional document in the UN system. Again this is not to be viewed as an argument for world government, for a constitution at a basic level is not necessarily an instrument or reflection of government. A constitution basically aims at "the establishment and preservation of an international order in which basic rights and interests . . . are acknowledged and conflicting claims settled peacefully."[17] This does not lead automatically to government but rather to governance, whereby laws are made and applied and legal claims adjudicated.[18]

Law is at the heart of the UN system—not only the law that frames the system and embeds its values but also the law produced by the system, the purpose of which is to uphold, implement, and enforce those basic values. Rules governing safety in civil aviation and nuclear plants, rules aiming at the prevention of diseases, and rules governing the use of orbital slots for the placement of telecommunications satellites are just some examples of the regulatory frameworks being created at the global level; but they are applied at varying levels and in various areas, from the doctor's operating room to outer space.

Without a developed judicial structure, the elements of a legal system cannot be said to be present. However, there can be no doubt that there is a UN legal *order*.[19] Although the promulgation and application of UN laws proceed apace and are now an accepted part of the system, the third aspect of the UN's legal order—enforcement and compliance—is improving slowly despite horrendous lapses, as in Rwanda.[20] However, the UN's enforcement techniques remain inadequate by and large. Compliance mechanisms and common procedures include *reporting* and *supervision*, used widely in the human rights field and in many of the technical areas governed by the specialized agencies. States are obligated to report on their compliance efforts; often these reports are subject to critical scrutiny by a UN body.

This "naming-and-shaming" technique is sometimes supplemented in the human rights field with *individual complaints procedures;* under an optional protocol, and with states' consent, individuals within their jurisdictions can bring allegations of state abuse before a UN body. However, these methods might not affect persistent offenders, and so intrusive procedures are being debated to reduce the most flagrant human rights violations such as torture. These include an inspection regime of detention facilities, as well as developing effective mechanisms for discovering the whereabouts of disappeared individuals.[21] This is in addition to the *inspection regimes* utilized by some of the agencies (e.g., the ICAO and the IMF as well as the IAEA).

Armed *peacekeeping forces* help to ensure compliance with UN law. This can be a straightforward affirmation of a negative peace in the form of a cease-fire, or it can be a positive peace in the form of election monitoring teams that judge whether a process is free and fair. UN peacekeeping has become multifunctional and includes human rights and development components as well as the blue helmets (UN forces). The events in Sierra Leone show that UN peacekeeping is in need of reform; indeed the Brahimi Report of August 2000 confirms this.[22] But this should not detract from the successes of UN peacekeeping operations in Namibia, Nicaragua, Mozambique, and elsewhere. Furthermore, the United Nations is currently engaged in even more ambitious nation-building projects in East Timor and Kosovo.

More coercive techniques employed by the United Nations include *conditionality* of development aid and loans upon respect for UN basic laws, as well as *penalization* of a lawbreaking state by expulsion or suspension from the United Nations or, more commonly, through the denial of credentials to a government. *Nonmilitary* enforcement action by the Security Council acting under article 41 of the charter, normally in the form of economic sanctions imposed on the delinquent state, has increased during the post–Cold War era, as has *military enforcement* by the Security Council to reverse aggressions or address threats to the peace. The Security Council has authorized the use of armed force on numerous occasions since 1989; the Persian Gulf, Somalia, Albania, Bosnia, Haiti, East Timor, and Kosovo (in June 1999 after the NATO bombing campaign) are the main instances. The failure of the Security Council to authorize the use of force against the FRY in March 1999 may lead to an improvement in the UN system, with negotiations taking place for agreed principles upon which UN-authorized humanitarian intervention can take place.[23]

Again the major weakness is the judicial sphere. *Judicial enforcement* by the ICJ is weak, though once states have consented to jurisdiction its decisions are binding on the parties. The creation of the independent International Criminal Court is imminent following the agreement in Rome in June 1998. This represents a major step forward in establishing the legal responsibility of individuals for breaches of fundamental norms prohibiting genocide, war crimes, and crimes against humanity, as well as for punishing those individuals. Furthermore, the development of the International Criminal Court will overcome the problems of selectivity inherent in the current ad hoc approach to international criminal tribunals taken by the Security Council.

However, such developments should not mask the limited judicial inroads into state sovereignty. The conceptual problems that exist in bringing states, traditionally the supreme actors in the international field, before a judicial body have been obscured by the UN focus on judicial enforcement against individuals. Individuals must account for atrocities, but it is an open question whether this is the most effective way to ensure respect for values.

The organizations and bodies in the UN family form a complex political system that has a legal order. The legal norms produced by the system flow from the basic principles contained in the complex constitution governing the system. This body of law is recognized by states as governing international relations, despite breaches of it. The significance is that the UN system has a constitution in a strong sense. The UN system is far more significant than a collection of IGOs. Neither an elaborate international conference nor a contract-based entity, the UN system is an instrument of world governance. Of course, the system is imperfect and manifestly weak in many areas—but then what political system is perfect?

Improvements and reform are necessary in all of the organs and organizations. There is an overwhelming need to expand the Security Council and limit the use of the veto, perhaps the greatest flaw in the UN's constitutional edifice.[24] Other essential reforms include greater access for NGOs and other aspects of civil society to UN organs; a proper judicial system armed with the power of judicial review; the development of mechanisms of political accountability and for determining legal responsibility; a greater separation of powers; and a rationalization and coordination of bodies having overlapping competence.[25]

In addition to the slow process of institutional reform, there is the need to close the gap between the dictates of UN law and the practice of member states. Although there is always going to be a gap between law and reality, the United Nations needs to develop more and more intrusive mechanisms to close that gap.[26] In the Millennium Declaration of the General Assembly, agreed on 8 September 2000, heads of state and government resolved, inter alia, to halve the world's population whose income is less than a dollar per day; to halve the number of people without access to safe drinking water; to ensure that all children complete a full course of primary education; to reduce by three-quarters maternal mortality; to cut under-five mortality by two-thirds; and to halt and reverse the spread of HIV/AIDS, malaria, and other major diseases. These targets are to be met by 2015. In addition, members resolved to improve the lives of at least 100 million slum-dwellers by 2020.[27]

Although less specific targets were set in relation to the promotion and protection of other key values such as security and the environment, targets like this are to be welcomed. It not only puts the UN's effectiveness to the test; it is also a fundamental challenge to ensure that UN laws are observed. Let us hope that the United Nations and its member states meet this fundamental challenge and that the United Nations goes on to develop and achieve clear targets aimed at protecting other values and rights.

Notes

1. Idris and Bartolo, *A Better United Nations,* 91–138.
2. UN doc. ACC/2000/4.
3. ECOSOC Res. 1999/66, 16 Dec. 1999; GA Res. 53/192, 15 Dec. 1998.
4. For the latest statement of UN values, see the United Nations Millennium Declaration, GA Res. 55/2, 8 Sept. 2000.
5. SC Res. 1373, 28 Sept. 2001. See also GA Res. 56/1, 12 Sept. 2001.
6. ICJ Rep. 1962, 167.
7. Kelsen, *Law of the United Nations,* 727.
8. UN doc. A/54/549, 15 Nov. 1999.
9. <http://www.un.org/News/ossg/rwanda_report.htm>, 15 Dec. 1999.
10. See Dupuy, *A Handbook,* 886–896.
11. Lauterpacht, *Private Law Sources,* 53, 300.
12. Cited in Zimmern, *The League of Nations,* 290–291.
13. Crawford, "The Charter of the United Nations," 6.
14. McNair, "The Function," 112. See also Abromeit and Hitzel-Cassagnes, "Constitutional Change," 25, 30–31; Macdonald, "The United Nations Charter," 889.
15. McNair, "The Function," 105.
16. Schachter, "Review of Kelsen," 189.
17. Fassbender, "The United Nations Charter," 555.
18. Ibid., 574. See Abromeit and Hitzel-Cassagnes, "Constitutional Change," 28–30.
19. Schachter, "The UN Legal Order," 1.
20. Ibid., 16–23. Schachter's list of techniques is largely replicated here.
21. UN docs. E/CN.4/1999/50 + Add.1; E/CN.4/Sub.2/1998/19.
22. Report of the Panel on United Nations Peacekeeping Operation, UN doc. A/55/305, S/2000/809.
23. GA Fourth Committee debate, 12th mtg., 20 Oct. 1999 (Russia).
24. Brierly, "The Covenant," 92–93. Fassbender, *UN Security Council Reform.*
25. Millennium Report of the Secretary General 2000, "We the Peoples," <http://www.un.org/millennium/sg/report>, para. 46.
26. Kelsen, *Principles,* 561.
27. GA Res. 55/2, 5 Sept. 2000.

Acronyms
and Abbreviations

ACC	Administrative Committee on Coordination
ATS	Antarctic Treaty System
CAT	Committee Against Torture
CERD	Committee on the Elimination of All Forms of Racial Discrimination
CESCR	Committee on Economic, Social, and Cultural Rights
doc.	document
EAD	Electoral Assistance Division
ECA	Economic Commission for Africa
ECOSOC	Economic and Social Council
ECOWAS	Economic Community of West African States
FAO	Food and Agriculture Organization
FRY	Federal Republic of Yugoslavia
G7 (G8)	Group of Seven industrialized states (plus Russia)
GA	United Nations General Assembly
GAOR	General Assembly Official Records
GATT	General Agreement on Tariffs and Trade
GAVI	Global Alliance for Vaccines and Immunization
GEF	Global Environmental Facility
GNP	gross national product
HIPC	Heavily Indebted Poor Countries Initiative
HRC	Human Rights Committee
IAEA	International Atomic Energy Agency
IBRD	International Bank for Reconstruction and Development
ICAO	International Civil Aviation Organization
ICC	International Criminal Court
ICCPR	International Covenant on Civil and Political Rights

ICESCR	International Covenant on Economic, Social and Cultural Rights
ICJ	International Court of Justice
ICTR	International Criminal Tribunal for Rwanda
ICTY	International Criminal Tribunal for the Former Yugoslavia
IDA	International Development Association
IFAD	International Fund for Agricultural Development
IFC	International Finance Corporation
IFOR	Implementation Force
IGO	intergovernmental organization
IHRR	International Human Rights Reports
ILC	International Law Commission
ILM	International Legal Materials
ILO	International Labour Organization
ILR	International Law Reports
IMF	International Monetary Fund
IMO	International Maritime Organization
ITC	International Trade Centre
ITU	International Telecommunications Union
JIU	Joint Inspection Unit
KFOR	Kosovo Force
LDCs	least developed countries
LNTS	League of Nations Treaty Series
MINURSO	United Nations Mission for the Referendum in Western Sahara
MSC	Military Staff Committee
NATO	North Atlantic Treaty Organization
NGO	nongovernmental organization
NIEO	New International Economic Order
ONUC	United Nations Operation in the Congo
ONUMOZ	United Nations Operation in Mozambique
P5	permanent members of the UN Security Council
PCIJ	Permanent Court of International Justice
PLO	Palestine Liberation Organization
Prepcom	Preparatory Committee for the Establishment of the Court
Res.	resolution
SC	United Nations Security Council

SCOR	Security Council Official Records
SDRs	Special Drawing Rights
UDHR	Universal Declaration on Human Rights
UN	United Nations
UNAIDS	United Nations Programme on Human Immunodeficiency Virus/Acquired Immunodeficiency Syndrome
UNAMET	United Nations Assistance Mission in East Timor
UNAMIR	United Nations Assistance Mission in Rwanda
UNAVEM	United Nations Angola Verification Mission
UNCTAD	United Nations Conference on Trade and Development
UNDP	United Nations Development Programme
UNEF	United Nations Emergency Force
UNEP	United Nations Environment Programme
UNESCO	United Nations Educational, Scientific, and Cultural Organization
UNFPA	United Nations Fund for Population Activities
UNHCR	United Nations High Commissioner for Refugees
UNICEF	United Nations Children's Fund
UNIDO	United Nations Industrial Development Organization
UNITA	National Union for the Total Independence of Angola
UNITAF	Unified Task Force
UNITAR	United Nations Institute for Training and Research
UNMIK	United Nations Interim Administration Mission in Kosovo
UNMOGIP	United Nations Military Observer Group in India and Pakistan
UNOMIL	United Nations Observer Mission in Liberia
UNOSOM	United Nations Operation in Somalia
UNRWA	United Nations Relief and Works Agency for Palestine Refugees
UNSCOM	United Nations Special Commission
UNTAC	United Nations Transition Assistance Authority in Cambodia
UNTAET	United Nations Transitional Administration in East Timor
UNTAG	United Nations Transition Assistance Group
UNTS	United Nations Treaty Series
UNTSO	United Nations Truce Supervision Organization
UPU	Universal Postal Union

WFP	World Food Programme
WHO	World Health Organization
WIPO	World Intellectual Property Organization
WMO	World Meteorological Organization
WTO	World Trade Organization

Bibliography

Books

Abi-Saab, G., ed. *The Concept of International Organization*. Paris: UNESCO, 1981.

Allott, P. *Eunomia: New Order for a New World*. Oxford, UK: Oxford University Press, 1990.

Alston, P., ed. *The United Nations and Human Rights: A Critical Appraisal*. Oxford, UK: Clarendon, 1992.

Amerasinghe, C. F. *Principles of the Institutional Law of International Organizations*. Cambridge, UK: Cambridge University Press, 1996.

Bailey, S. D., and S. Daws. *The Procedure of the UN Security Council*. 3rd ed. Oxford, UK: Clarendon, 1998.

Beck, R. J., A. C. Arend, and R. D. Vander Lugt, eds. *International Rules: Approaches from International Law and International Relations*. Oxford, UK: Oxford University Press, 1996.

Beigbeder, Y. *Le Role International des Organizations Non Gouvernmentales* (The Role of Nongovernmental Organizations). Brussels: Bruyant, 1992.

―――. *International Monitoring of Plebiscites, Referenda, and National Elections*. Dordrecht, Netherlands: Martinus Nijhoff, 1994.

Bekker, P. H. F. *The Legal Position of Intergovernmental Organizations*. Dordrecht, Netherlands: Martinus Nijhoff, 1994.

Bennett, A. LeRoy. *International Organizations: Principles and Issues*. 6th ed. London: Prentice Hall, 1995.

Bergesen, H. O., and L. Lunde. *Dinosaurs or Dynamos? The United Nations and the World Bank at the Turn of the Century*. London: Earthscan, 1999.

Bertrand, M. *The Third Generation World Organization*. Dordrecht, Netherlands: Martinus Nijhoff, 1989.

―――. *The United Nations: Past, Present, and Future*. The Hague: Kluwer, 1997.

Bethlehem, D., ed. *The Kuwait Crisis: Sanctions and Their Economic Consequences*. Cambridge, UK: Grotius, 1991.

Birnie, P. W., and A. E. Boyle. *International Law and the Environment.* Oxford, UK: Clarendon, 1992.

Blokker, N. M., and H. G. Schermers, eds. *Proliferation of International Organizations: Legal Issues.* The Hague: Kluwer, 2001.

Blum, Y. Z. *Eroding the United Nations Charter.* Dordrecht, Netherlands: Martinus Nijhoff, 1993.

Boerefijn, I. *The Reporting Procedure Under the Covenant on Civil and Political Rights.* Antwerp: Intersentia, 1999.

Bourantonis, D., and M. Evriviades, eds. *A United Nations for the Twenty-First Century: Peace, Security, and Development.* The Hague: Kluwer, 1996.

Bowett, D. W. *United Nations Forces.* London: Stevens, 1964.

————. *The Law of International Institutions.* 4th ed. London: Stevens, 1982.

Boyle, A. E., and M. R. Anderson, eds. *Human Rights Approaches to Environmental Protection.* Oxford, UK: Clarendon, 1998.

Bradley, A. W., and K. D. Ewing, *Constitutional and Administrative Law.* 12th ed. London: Longman, 1997.

Brown, N. J., and P. Quiblier, eds. *Ethics and Agenda 21.* New York: UNEP, 1994.

Brownlie, I. *Principles of Public International Law.* 5th ed. Oxford, UK: Oxford University Press, 1998.

Bull, H., B. Kingsbury, and A. Roberts, eds. *Hugo Grotius and International Relations.* Oxford, UK: Clarendon, 1992.

Cameron, J., and K. Campbell, eds. *Dispute Resolution in the World Trade Organization.* London: Cameron May, 1998.

Cassese, A. *UN Law/Fundamental Rights: Two Topics in International Law.* Alphen aan den Rijn, Netherlands: Sijthoff and Noordhoff, 1979.

Chossudovsky, M. *The Globalisation of Poverty: Impact of IMF and World Bank Reforms.* London: Zed Books, 1998.

Ciobanu, D. *Preliminary Objections to the Jurisdiction of the United Nations Political Organs.* The Hague: Martinus Nijhoff, 1975.

Claude, I. L. *Power and International Relations.* New York: Random House, 1962.

Cosgrove, C. A., and K. J. Twitchett, eds. *The New International Actors: The United Nations and the European Economic Community.* London: Macmillan, 1970.

Craven, M. C. R. *The International Covenant on Economic, Social, and Cultural Rights: A Perspective on Its Development.* Oxford, UK: Clarendon, 1995.

Crawford, J. *The Rights of Peoples.* Oxford, UK: Clarendon, 1988.

Curtin, D., and D. O'Keefe, eds. *Constitutional Adjudication in European and National Law.* Dublin: Butterworths, 1992.

Damrosch, L., ed. *The International Court at a Crossroads.* Dobbs Ferry, NY: Transnational, 1987.

Davidson, S. *Human Rights.* Buckingham, UK: Open University Press, 1993.

De Smith, S., and R. Brazier. *Constitutional and Administrative Law.* 8th ed. London: Penguin, 1998.

Downs, G. W., ed. *Collective Security Beyond the Cold War.* Ann Arbor: University of Michigan Press, 1995.

Dupuy, R. J., ed. *A Handbook on International Organizations.* 2nd ed. Dordrecht, Netherlands: Martinus Nijhoff, 1998.

Dworkin, R. M. *Taking Rights Seriously.* London: Duckworth, 1977.

———. *Law's Empire.* London: Fontana, 1986.

Edwards, R. W. *International Monetary Collaboration.* New York: Transnational, 1984.

Eide, A., and B. Hagtvet, eds. *Human Rights in Perspective.* Oxford, UK: Blackwell, 1992.

Eide, A., et al. *The Universal Declaration of Human Rights.* Oslo: Scandinavian University Press, 1992.

Falk, R., S. S. Kim, and S. H. Mendlovitz, eds. *The United Nations and a Just World Order.* Boulder: Westview, 1991.

Farrar-Hockley, A. *The British Part in the Korean War, Volume 1: A Distant Obligation.* London: HMSO, 1990.

Fassbender, B. *UN Security Council Reform and the Right of Veto: A Constitutional Perspective.* The Hague: Kluwer, 1998.

Forsythe, D. *The Internationalization of Human Rights.* Lexington, MA: Lexington Books, 1991.

Fox, G. H., and B. R. Roth, eds. *Democratic Governance and International Law.* Cambridge, UK: Cambridge University Press, 2000.

Fox, H., ed. *The Changing Constitution of the United Nations.* London: British Institute of International and Comparative Law, 1997.

Franck, T. M. *Fairness in International Law and Institutions.* Oxford, UK: Clarendon, 1995.

Gibson, J. S. *International Organizations, Constitutional Law, and Human Rights.* New York: Praeger, 1991.

Goodwin-Gill, G. S. *The Refugee in International Law.* Oxford, UK: Oxford University Press, 1983.

Goodwin-Gill, G. S., and S. Talmon, eds. *The Reality of International Law: Essays in Honour of Ian Brownlie.* Oxford, UK: Clarendon, 1999.

Gregg, R. W., and M. Barkun, eds. *The United Nations System and Its Functions.* Princeton, NJ: Van Nostrand, 1968.

Gwynn, W. B. *The Meaning of the Separation of Powers.* The Hague: Martinus Nijhoff, 1965.

Haas, P. M., R. O. Keohane, and M. A. Levy, eds. *Institutions for the Earth: Sources of International Environmental Protection.* Cambridge: MIT Press, 1993.

Haraszti, G. *Some Fundamental Problems of the Law of Treaties.* Budapest: Akademia Kiado, 1973.

Harris, D. J. *Cases and Materials on International Law.* 5th ed. London: Sweet and Maxwell, 1998.

Harrod, J., and N. Schrijver, eds. *The UN Under Attack.* Aldershot, UK: Ashgate, 1988.

Hart, H. L. A. *The Concept of Law.* Oxford, UK: Clarendon, 1961.

Henkin, L. *The Age of Rights.* New York: Columbia University Press, 1990.

————, ed. *The International Bill of Rights: The Covenant on Civil and Political Rights.* New York: Columbia University Press, 1981.

Higgins, R. *The Development of International Law Through the Political Organs of the United Nations.* London: Oxford University Press, 1963.

————. *The Administration of United Kingdom Foreign Policy Through the United Nations.* Syracuse: Maxwell, 1966.

————. *United Nations Peacekeeping: Documents and Commentary, Volume 1: Middle East, 1946–1967.* Oxford, UK: Oxford University Press, 1969.

————. *Problems and Process: International Law and How We Use It.* Oxford, UK: Clarendon, 1994.

Idris, K., and M. Bartolo. *A Better United Nations for the New Millennium.* The Hague: Kluwer, 2000.

Lie, T. *In the Cause of Peace.* London: Macmillan, 1954.

Jackson, J. *The World Trading System.* Cambridge: MIT Press, 1989.

Jacobson, H. K., and C. Ku, eds. *Democratic Accountability and International Institutions: Using Military Forces.* Cambridge, UK: Cambridge University Press, 2001.

Kant, I. *Perpetual Peace and Other Essays on History and Morals.* Trans. T. Humphrey. Indianapolis, IN: Hackett, 1983.

Kelsen, H. *Principles of International Law.* 2nd ed. London: Stevens, 1967.

————. *The Law of the United Nations.* London: Stevens, 1951.

Kirgis, F. L. *International Organizations in Their Legal Setting.* 2nd ed. St Paul: West, 1993.

Kiss, A. C., and D. Shelton, *International Environmental Law.* London: Graham and Trotman, 1991.

Koskenniemi, M., ed. *International Law.* Aldershot, UK: Dartmouth, 1992.

Kreuger, A. O., ed. *The WTO as an International Organization.* Chicago: University of Chicago Press, 1998.

Ku, C., and P. F. Diehl, eds. *International Law: Classic and Contemporary Readings.* Boulder: Lynne Rienner, 1998.

Lauterpacht, E. *Aspects of the Administration of International Justice.* Cambridge, UK: Grotius, 1991.

————, ed. *The Kuwait Crisis: Basic Documents.* Cambridge, UK: Grotius, 1991.

Lauterpacht, H. *Private Law Sources and Analogies of International Law.* London: Archon Books, 1970.

Lester, Lord, and D. Oliver, eds. *Constitutional Law and Human Rights.* London: Butterworths, 1997.

Lister, F. K. *The European Union, the United Nations, and the Revival of Confederal Governance.* Westport, CT: Greenwood, 1996.

Loveland, I. *Constitutional Law: A Critical Introduction.* London: Butterworths, 1996.

Lowe, V., and M. Fitzmaurice, eds. *Fifty Years of the International Court of Justice.* Cambridge, UK: Cambridge University Press, 1996.

Luard, E. *The United Nations.* London: Macmillan, 1979.

————, ed. *The Evolution of International Organizations.* New York: Praeger, 1966.

Macdonald, R. J. *Essays in Honour of Wang Tieya*. Dordrecht, Netherlands: Martinus Nijhoff, 1993.

Macdonald, R. J., and D. M. Johnston, eds. *Structure and Processes of International Law*. Dordrecht, Netherlands: Martinus Nijhoff, 1983.

Makarczyk, J., ed. *Theory of International Law at the Threshold of the 21st Century: Essays in Honour of Krzysztof Skubiszewski*. The Hague: Kluwer, 1996.

Malanczuk, P. *Akehurst's Modern Introduction to International Law*. 7th ed. London: Routledge, 1997.

Marks, S. *The Riddle of All Constitutions*. Oxford, UK: Oxford University Press, 2000.

McDougal, M. S., H. D. Laswell, and J. C. Miller. *The Interpretation of International Agreements and World Public Order*. New Haven: New Haven Press, 1994.

McDougal, M. S., and W. M. Reisman, eds. *Power and Policy in Quest of Law*. Dordrecht, Netherlands: Martinus Nijhoff, 1985.

McGoldrick, D. *The Human Rights Committee*. Oxford, UK: Oxford University Press, 1991.

McNair, Lord. *Law of Treaties*. Oxford, UK: Clarendon, 1961.

Merrills, J. G. *International Dispute Settlement*. 3rd ed. Cambridge, UK: Cambridge University Press, 1998.

Mitrany, D. *A Working Peace System: An Argument for the Functional Development of International Organization*. London: Royal Institute of International Affairs, 1943.

Muller, A. S., D. Raic, and J. M. Thuranszky, eds. *The International Court of Justice: Its Future Role After Fifty Years*. The Hague: Martinus Nijhoff, 1997.

Nicholas, H. G. *The United Nations as a Political Institution*. 5th ed. Oxford, UK: Oxford University Press, 1975.

Peck, C., and R. Lee, eds. *Increasing the Effectiveness of the International Court of Justice*. The Hague: Martinus Nijhoff, 1997.

Ratner, S. R., and J. S. Abrams. *Accountability for Human Rights Atrocities in International Law: Beyond the Nuremberg Legacy*. Oxford, UK: Clarendon, 1997.

Rawls, J. *A Theory of Justice*. London: Oxford University Press, 1972.

Raz, J. *The Concept of a Legal System: An Introduction to the Theory of a Legal System*. Oxford, UK: Clarendon, 1980.

Report of the Commission on Global Governance. *Our Global Neighbourhood*. Oxford, UK: Oxford University Press, 1995.

Righter, R. *Utopia Lost: The United Nations and World Order*. New York: The Twentieth Century Fund, 1995.

Rittberger, V., ed. *Regime Theory and International Relations*. Oxford, UK: Oxford University Press, 1993.

Rosas, A., and J. Helgesen, eds. *Human Rights in a Changing East-West Perspective*. London: Pinter, 1990.

Rosenne, S. *Developments in the Law of Treaties*. Cambridge, UK: Cambridge University Press, 1989.

————. *The World Court: What It Is and How It Works.* 5th ed. Dordrecht, Netherlands: Martinus Nijhoff, 1989.

Russell, R. B., and J. M. Muther. *A History of the United Nations Charter.* Washington, DC: Brookings Institution, 1958.

Saksena, K. P. *The United Nations and Collective Security.* New Delhi: DK Publishing, 1974.

Sands, P., ed. *Greening International Law.* London: Earthscan, 1993.

Sarooshi, D. *The United Nations and the Development of Collective Security.* Oxford, UK: Clarendon, 1999.

Sato, T. *Evolving Constitutions of International Organizations.* The Hague: Kluwer, 1996.

Schachter, O., and C. C. Joyner, eds. *United Nations Legal Order.* Cambridge, UK: Cambridge University Press, 1996.

Schermers, H. G., and N. M. Blokker. *International Institutional Law.* 3rd ed. The Hague: Martinus Nijhoff, 1995.

Schwebel, S., ed. *The Effectiveness of International Decisions.* Leiden, Netherlands: Sijthoff, 1971.

Seyersted, F. *United Nations Forces.* Leiden, Netherlands: Sijthoff, 1966.

Shaw, M. N. *International Law.* 4th ed. Cambridge, UK: Cambridge University Press, 1997.

Shihata, I. F. I. *The World Bank in a Changing World.* Dordrecht, Netherlands: Kluwer, 1991.

Sieghart, P. *The International Law of Human Rights.* Oxford, UK: Oxford University Press, 1983.

Simma, B., ed. *The Charter of the United Nations: A Commentary.* Oxford, UK: Oxford University Press, 1994.

Sinclair, I. M. *The Vienna Convention on the Law of Treaties.* 2nd ed. Manchester, UK: Manchester University Press, 1984.

Steiner, H. J., and P. Alston. *International Human Rights in Context.* 2nd ed. Oxford, UK: Oxford University Press, 2000.

Stone, J. *Legal Controls of International Conflict.* London: Stevens, 1954.

Taylor, P. *International Organizations in the Modern World.* London: Pinter, 1993.

Taylor, P., and A. J. R. Groom, eds. *Global Issues in the United Nations' Framework.* London: Macmillan, 1989.

Tolley, H. *The UN Commission on Human Rights.* Boulder: Westview, 1987.

Tomuschat, C., ed. *The United Nations at Age Fifty: A Legal Perspective.* The Hague: Kluwer, 1995.

Turpin, C. *British Government and the Constitution.* 4th ed. London: Butterworths, 1999.

Van Dijck, P., and G. Faber, eds. *Challenges to the New World Trade Organization.* The Hague: Kluwer, 1998.

Waltz, K. N. *Theory of International Politics.* Reading, MA: Addison-Wesley, 1979.

Werksman, J., ed. *Greening International Institutions.* London: Earthscan, 1996.

White, N. D. *The Law of International Organisations.* Manchester, UK: Manchester University Press, 1996.

———. *Keeping the Peace: The United Nations and the Maintenance of International Peace and Security.* 2nd ed. Manchester, UK: Manchester University Press, 1997.

Williams, D. *The Specialized Agencies and the United Nations: The System in Crisis.* London: Hurst, 1987.

Wilner, G., ed. *Essays in Tribute to Wolfgang Friedmann.* The Hague: Martinus Nijhoff, 1979.

Zimmern, A. *The League of Nations and the Rule of Law, 1918–1935.* 2nd ed. New York: Russell and Russell, 1969.

Articles and Essays

A-Khavari, A., and D. Rothwell. "The ICJ and the *Danube Dam Case:* A Missed Opportunity for International Environment Law?" *Melbourne University Law Review* 22 (1998): 507.

Abi-Saab, G. "The International Court as a World Court." In V. Lowe and M. Fitzmaurice, eds., *Fifty Years of the International Court of Justice.* Cambridge, UK: Cambridge University Press, 1996, 3.

Abromeit, A., and T. Hitzel-Cassagnes. "Constitutional Change and Contractual Revision: Principles and Procedures." *European Law Journal* 5 (1999): 23.

Adede, A. O. "International Protection of the Environment." In C. Tomuschat, ed., *The United Nations at Age Fifty.* The Hague: Kluwer, 1995, 197.

Akande, D. "The Role of the International Court of Justice in the Maintenance of International Peace." *African Journal of International and Comparative Law* 8 (1996): 592.

———. "The Competence of International Organizations and the Advisory Jurisdiction of the International Court of Justice." *European Journal of International Law* 9 (1998): 437.

Alston, P. "U.S. Ratification of the Covenant on Economic, Social and Cultural Rights: The Need for an Entirely Different Strategy." *American Journal of International Law* 84 (1990): 365.

———. "Appraising the United Nations Human Rights Regime." In P. Alston, ed., *The United Nations and Human Rights: A Critical Appraisal.* Oxford, UK: Oxford University Press, 1992, 1.

———. "Neither Fish nor Fowl: The Quest to Define the Role of the UN High Commissioner for Human Rights." *European Journal of International Law* 8 (1997): 321.

———. "The UN's Human Rights Record: From San Francisco to Vienna and Beyond." In C. Ku and P. F. Diehl, eds., *International Law: Classic and Contemporary Readings.* Boulder: Lynne Rienner, 1998, 355.

Alvarez, J. E. "Rush to Closure: Lessons of the Tadic Judgment." *Michigan Law Review* 96 (1998): 2031.

Anderson, H. E. "The Benchmark Draft of the Earth Charter: International Environmental Law at the Grassroots." *Tulane International Environmental Law Journal* 11 (1997): 109.

Arangio-Ruiz, G. "The 'Federal Analogy' and UN Charter Interpretation: A Crucial Issue." *European Journal of International Law* 8 (1997): 1.

Arend, A. C. "The United Nations and the New World Order." *Georgetown Law Journal* 81 (1993): 491.

Bederman, D. J. "The Souls of International Organizations: Legal Personality and the Lighthouse at Cape Spartel." *Virginia Journal of International Law* 36 (1996): 275.

Birnie, P. "Environmental Protection and Development." *Melbourne University Law Review* 20 (1995): 66.

Bishel, A. "The World Bank and the International Monetary Fund from the Perspective of the Executive Directors from Developing Countries." *Journal of World Trade Law* 28 (1994): 141.

Bissell, R. E. "Recent Practice of the Inspection Panel of the World Bank." *American Journal of International Law* 91 (1997): 741.

Bloch, F. "Global Environment Facility." *Yearbook of International Environmental Law* (1998): 550.

Blokker, N. M. "Proliferation of International Organizations: An Exploratory Introduction." In N. M. Blokker and H. G. Schermers, eds., *Proliferation of International Organizations: Legal Issues*. The Hague: Kluwer, 2001, 1.

Blum, Y. H. "UN Membership of the 'New' Yugoslavia: Continuity or Break?" *American Journal of International Law* 86 (1992): 830.

Boer, B. "The Globalisation of Environmental Law." *Melbourne University Law Review* 20 (1995): 101.

Boister, N. "The Exclusion of Treaty Crimes from the Jurisdiction of the Proposed International Criminal Court: Law, Pragmatism, and Politics." *Journal of Armed Conflict Law* 3 (1998): 27.

Boutros-Ghali, Boutros. "Human Rights: The Common Language of Humanity." In United Nations, *World Conference on Human Rights: The Vienna Declaration and Programme of Action*. New York: UN, 1993.

Bowett, D. W. "The Council's Role in Relation to International Organizations." In V. Lowe and M. Fitzmaurice, eds., *Fifty Years of the International Court of Justice*. Cambridge, UK: Cambridge University Press, 1996, 181.

Boyle, A. E. "The Role of International Human Rights in the Protection of the Environment." In A. E. Boyle and M. E. Anderson, eds., *Human Rights Approaches to Environmental Protection*. Oxford, UK: Clarendon, 1998, 43.

Bradlow, D. D. "A Test Case for the World Bank." *American University Journal of International Law and Policy* 11 (1996): 247.

———. "The World Bank, the IMF, and Human Rights." *Transnational Law and Contemporary Problems* 6 (1996): 47.

Breidenich, C., D. Magraw, A. Rowley, and J. W. Rubin. "The Kyoto Protocol to the United Nations Framework Convention on Climate Change." *American Journal of International Law* 92 (1998): 315.

Brierly, J. L. "The Covenant and the Charter." *British Yearbook of International Law* 23 (1946): 83.

Brownlie, I. "The Powers of Political Organs of the United Nations and the Rule of Law." In R. J. MacDonald, ed., *Essays in Honour of Wang Tieya*. Dordrecht, Netherlands: Martinus Nijhoff, 1993, 91.

Bull, H. "The Importance of Grotius in the Study of International Relations." In H. Bull, B. Kingsbury, and A. Roberts, eds., *Hugo Grotius and International Relations*. Oxford, UK: Clarendon, 1992, 71.

Burchill, R. "The ICJ Decision in the Case Concerning East Timor: The Illegal Use of Force Validated." *Journal of Armed Conflict Law* 2 (1997): 1.

Cahn, J. "Challenging the New Imperial Authority: The World Bank and the Democratization of Development." *Harvard Human Rights Journal* 6 (1993): 159.

Cameron, J. "The GATT and the Environment." In P. Sands, ed., *Greening International Law*. London: Earthscan, 1993, 100.

Cassese, A. "Political Self-Determination—Old Concepts and New Developments." In A. Cassese, ed., *UN Law/Fundamental Rights: Two Topics in International Law*. Alphen aan den Rijn, Netherlands: Sijthoff and Noordhoff, 1979, 160.

———. "Ex Inuria Ius Oritur: Are We Moving Towards International Legitimation of Forcible Humanitarian Countermeasures in the World Community?" *European Journal of International Law* 10 (1999): 23.

Charney, J. I. "Anticipatory Humanitarian Action in Kosovo." *American Journal of International Law* 93 (1999): 834.

Crawford, J. "Democracy and International Law." *British Yearbook of International Law* 64 (1993): 113.

———. "The ILC's Draft Statute for an International Criminal Tribunal." *American Journal of International Law* 88 (1994): 140.

———. "The ILC Adopts a Statute for an International Criminal Court." *American Journal of International Law* 89 (1995): 404.

———. "The Charter of the UN as Constitution." In H. Fox, ed., *The Changing Constitution of the United Nations*. London: British Institute of International and Comparative Law, 1997, 1.

Cryer, R. "The Security Council and Article 39: A Threat to Coherence?" *Journal of Armed Conflict Law* 1 (1996): 161.

———. "A Commentary on the Rome Statute for an International Criminal Court: A Cadenza for the Song of Those Who Died in Vain." *Journal of Armed Conflict Law* 3 (1998): 273.

D'Amato, A. "Peace Versus Accountability in Bosnia." *American Journal of International Law* 88 (1994): 500.

D'Zurilla, W. T. "Individual Responsibility for Torture Under International Law." *Tulane Law Review* 56 (1981): 186.

Damrosch, L. "The Interface of National Constitutional Systems with International Law and International Institutions." In C. Ku and H. Jacobson, eds., *Democratic Accountability and International Institutions: Using Military Forces*. Cambridge, UK: Cambridge University Press, 2002.

Detter de Lupis, I. "The Human Environment: Stockholm and Its Follow Up." In P. Taylor and A.J.R. Groom, eds., *Global Issues in the United Nations Framework*. London: Macmillan, 1989, 205.

Di Leva, C. E. "International Environmental Law and Development." *Georgetown International Environmental Law Review* 10 (1998): 501.

Dommen, C. "Claiming Environmental Rights: Some Possibilities Offered by the United Nations Human Rights Mechanisms." *Georgetown International Environmental Law Review* 11 (1998): 1.

Donnelly, J. "International Human Rights: A Regime Analysis." *International Organization* 40 (1986): 599.

Drezner, D. W. "Bargaining, Enforcement, and Multilateral Sanctions: When Is Economic Cooperation Counterproductive?" *International Organization* 54 (2000): 73.

Due, O. "A Constitutional Court for the European Communities." In D. Curtin and D. O'Keefe, eds., *Constitutional Adjudication in European and National Law*. Dublin: Butterworths, 1992, 8.

Dupuy, P-M. "The Constitutional Dimension of the Charter of the United Nations Revisited." *Max Planck Yearbook of United Nations Law* 1 (1997): 20.

Ebersole, J. N. "The United Nations' Response to Requests for Assistance in Electoral Matters." *Virginia Journal of International Law* 33 (1992): 91.

Emders, A. "The Role of the WTO in Minimum Standards." In P. Van Dijck and G. Faber, eds., *Challenges to the New World Trade Organization*. The Hague: Kluwer, 1998, 61.

Emmeriji, L. "The International Labour Organization as a Development Agency." In J. Harrod and N. Schrijver, eds., *The UN Under Attack*. Aldershot, UK: Ashgate, 1988, 111.

Farer, T. J. "Collectively Defending Democracy in a World of Sovereign States: The Western Hemisphere's Prospect." *Human Rights Quarterly* 15 (1993): 716.

Fassbender, B. "The United Nations Charter as Constitution of the International Community." *Columbia Journal of Transnational Law* 36 (1998): 529.

Ferencz, B. B. "An International Criminal Code and Court: Where They Stand and Where They're Going." *Columbia Journal of Transnational Law* 30 (1992): 375.

Figa-Talamanca, N. "The Role of NATO in the Peace Agreement for Bosnia Herzegovina." *European Journal of International Law* 7 (1996): 174.

Fitzmaurice, G. "The Law and Procedure of the International Court of Justice: Treaty Interpretation and Certain Other Treaty Points." *British Yearbook of International Law* 28 (1951): 1.

———. "The Law and Procedure of the International Court of Justice." *British Yearbook of International Law* 33 (1957): 223.

Fitzpatrick, D. "The United Nations General Assembly and the Security Council." In J. Werksman, ed., *Greening International Institutions*. London: Earthscan, 1996, 11.

Fox, G. H. "The Right to Political Participation in International Law." *Proceedings of the American Society of International Law* 86 (1992): 252.

Franck, T. M. "The Emerging Right of Democratic Governance." *American Journal of International Law* 86 (1992): 46.

———. "The 'Powers of Appreciation': Who Is the Ultimate Guardian of UN Legality?" *American Journal of International Law* 86 (1992): 519.

———. "The *Bona Fides* of Power: Security Council and Threats to the Peace." *Recueil des Cours Académie de Droit International* 240 (1993 III): 189.

———. "The United Nations as Guarantor of International Peace and Security." In C. Tomuschat, ed., *The United Nations at Age Fifty: A Legal Perspective*. The Hague: Kluwer, 1995, 25.

———. "Lessons of Kosovo." *American Journal of International Law* 93 (1999): 857.

French, D. "1997 Kyoto Protocol to the 1992 UN Convention on Climate Change." *Journal of Environmental Law* 10 (1998): 227.

Frulli, M. "The Special Court for Sierra Leone: Some Preliminary Comments." *European Journal of International Law* 11 (2000): 857.

Garvey, J. I. "United Nations Peacekeeping and Host State Consent." *American Journal of International Law* 64 (1970): 241.

Gassama, I. J. "Safeguarding the Democratic Entitlement: A Proposal for United Nations Involvement in National Politics." *Cornell International Law Journal* 30 (1997): 287.

Gill, T. D. "Legal and Some Political Limitation on the Power of the UN Security Council to Exercise Its Enforcement Powers Under Chapter VII of the UN Charter." *Netherlands Yearbook of International Law* 26 (1995): 61.

Goodwin, G. L. "World Institutions and World Order." In C. A. Cosgrove and K. J. Twitchett, eds., *The New International Actors: The United Nations and the European Economic Community*. London: Macmillan, 1970, 55.

Gordon, R. "United Nations Intervention in Internal Conflicts: Iraq, Somalia, and Beyond." *Michigan Journal of International Law* 15 (1994): 519.

Gowlland-Debbas, V. "Security Council Enforcement Action and Issues of State Responsibility." *International and Comparative Law Quarterly* 43 (1994): 55.

———. "Judicial Insights into Fundamental Values and Interests of the International Community." In A. S. Muller, D. Raic, and J. M. Thuransky, eds., *The International Court of Justice: Its Future Role After Fifty Years*. The Hague: Martinus Nijhoff, 1997, 327.

———. "The Relationship Between the Security Council and the Projected International Criminal Court." *Journal of Armed Conflict Law* 3 (1998): 97.

Gray, C. "After the Cease-Fire: Iraq, the Security Council, and the Use of Force." *British Yearbook of International Law* 68 (1994): 135.

Greenwood, C. "The Development of International Humanitarian Law by the International Criminal Tribunal for the Former Yugoslavia." *Max Planck Yearbook of United Nations Law* 2 (1998): 97.

Grieco, J. M. "Anarchy and the Limits of Cooperation: A Realist Critique of the Newest Liberal Internationalism." *International Organization* 42 (1988): 485.

Guyett, S. C. "Environment and Lending: Lessons of the World Bank—Hope for the European Bank for Reconstruction and Development." *New York University Journal of International Law and Politics* 24 (1992): 889.

Harris, D. J. "Progess and Problems in Establishing an International Criminal Court." *Journal of Armed Conflict Law* 3 (1998): 1.

Harrod, J. "United Nations Specialized Agencies: From Functionalist Intervention to International Co-operation." In J. Harrod, and N. Schrijver, eds., *The UN Under Attack*. Aldershot, UK: Ashgate, 1988, 5.

Heyvaert, V. "Regulation of Chemicals." *Yearbook of Environmental Law* (1997): 239.

Higgins, R. "Western Interpretation of International Organizations as Reflected in Scholarly Writings." In G. Abi-Saab, ed., *The Concept of International Organization*. Paris: UNESCO, 1981, 194.

Highet, K. "The Peace Palace Heats Up: The World Court in Business Again?" *Commonwealth Law Bulletin* (1992): 755.

Hill, M. "The Administrative Committee on Coordination." In E. Luard, ed., *The Evolution of International Organizations*. New York: Praeger, 1966, 104.

Hurrell, A. "International Society and the Study of Regimes: A Reflective Approach." In V. Rittberger. ed., *Regime Theory and International Relations*. Oxford, UK: Oxford University Press, 1993, 49.

Jacobs, F. G. "Varieties of Approach to Treaty Interpretation: With Special Reference to the Draft Convention on the Law of Treaties Before the Vienna Diplomatic Conference." *International and Comparative Law Quarterly* 18 (1969): 318.

Jerve, A. M. "Social Consequences of Development in a Human Rights Perspective: Lessons from the World Bank." *Rights in Development Yearbook, 1998: Global Perspectives and Local Issues* (1998): 37.

Joyner, C. C. "The United Nations and Democracy." *Global Governance* 5 (1999): 340.

Kartashkin, V. "The Marxist-Leninist Approach: The Theory of Class Struggle and Contemporary International Law." In R. J. Macdonald and D. M. Johnston, eds., *The Structure and Processes of International Law*. Dordrecht, Netherlands: Martinus Nijhoff, 1983, 84.

Kennedy, D. "The Move to Institutions." *Cardozo Law Review* 8 (1987): 841.

Keohane, R. O. "International Institutions: Two Approaches." *International Studies Quarterly* 32 (1988): 379.

Kim, S. S. "Global Rights and World Order." In R. Falk, S. S. Kim, and S. H. Mendlovitz, eds., *The United Nations and a Just World Order*. Boulder: Westview, 1991, 356.

Kirgis, F. L. "Specialized Law-Making Processes." In O. Schachter and C. C. Joyner, eds., *United Nations Legal Order*. Cambridge, UK: Cambridge University Press, 1996, 109.

Kiss, A. C. "La nation de patrimonie commun de l'humanité." *Recueil des Cours Académie de Droit International* 175 (1982): 99.

Krasner, S. "Structural Causes and Regime Consequences: Regimes as Intervening Variables." *International Organization* 36 (1982): 184.

Krisch, N. "Unilateral Enforcement of the Collective Will: Kosovo, Iraq, and the Security Council." *Max Planck Yearbook of United Nations Law* 3 (1999): 59.

Kritsiotis, D. "Security Council Resolution 1101 (1997) and the Multi-national Protection Force of Operation Alba in Albania." *Leiden Journal of International Law* 12 (1999): 511.

Kupchan, C. A. "The Case for Collective Security." In G. W. Downs, ed., *Collective Security Following the Cold War.* Ann Arbor: University of Michigan Press, 1995, 42.

Lamb, S. "Legal Limits to the United Nations Security Council Powers." In G. Goodwin-Gill and S. Talmon, eds., *The Reality of International Law: Essays in Honour of Ian Brownlie.* Oxford, UK: Clarendon, 1999, 361.

Lauterpacht, E. "The Development of the Law of International Organization by the Decisions of International Tribunals." *Recueil des Cours Académie de Droit International* 152 (1976): 460.

Lavalle, R. "The Inherent Powers of the UN Secretary General in the Political Sphere: A Legal Analysis." *Netherlands International Law Review* 37 (1990): 22.

———. "The Law of the United Nations and the Use of Force Under the Relevant Security Council Resolutions of 1990 and 1991 to Resolve the Persian Gulf Crisis." *Netherlands Yearbook of International Law* 23 (1992): 3.

Lee, J. "The Underlying Legal Theory to Support a Well-Defined Human Right to a Healthy Environment as a Principle of Customary International Law." *Columbia Journal of Environmental Law* 25 (2000): 283.

Lee, R. S. "The Rwandan Tribunal." *Leiden Journal of International Law* 9 (1996): 37.

Lipschutz, R. "Wasn't the Future Wonderful? Resources, Environment, and the Emerging Myth of Sustainable Development." *Columbia Journal of International Law and Policy* 2 (1991): 35.

Lobel, J., and M. Ratner. "Bypassing the Security Council: Ambiguous Authorizations to Use Force, Cease-fires, and the Iraqi Inspection Regime." *American Journal of International Law* 93 (1999): 124.

Lyall, F. "Posts and Telecommunications." In O. Schachter and C. C. Joyner, eds., *United Nations Legal Order.* Cambridge, UK: Cambridge University Press, 1996, 789.

Macdonald, R. St. J. "The United Nations Charter: Constitution or Contract." In R. St. J. Macdonald and R. M. Johnston, eds., *Structure and Processes of International Law.* Dordrecht, Netherlands: Martinus Nijhoff, 1983, 889.

Mak, T. D. "The Case Against an International War Crimes Tribunal for the Former Yugoslavia." *International Peacekeeping* 4 (1997): 536.

Marks, S. "International Law, Democracy, and the End of History." In G. H. Fox and B. R. Roth, eds., *Democratic Governance and International Law.* Cambridge, UK: Cambridge University Press, 2000, 352.

Marks, S. P. "Education, Science, Culture, and Information." In O. Schachter and C. C. Joyner, eds., *United Nations Legal Order.* Cambridge, UK: Cambridge University Press, 1996, 577.

Marotta, M. "Regional Seas." *Yearbook of Environmental Law* (1996): 141.

Mavroidis, P. C. "Remedies in the WTO System: Between a Rock and a Hard Place." *European Journal of International Law* 11 (2000): 763.

McCluney, R. "Sustainable Values." In N. J. Brown and P. Quiblier, eds., *Ethics and Agenda 21*. New York: UNEP, 1994, 16.

McCoubrey, H. "Kosovo, NATO, and International Law." *International Relations* 14, no. 5 (1999): 32.

McDougal, M. S. "The International Law Commission's Draft Articles Upon Interpretation: Textuality *Redivivus*." *American Journal of International Law* 61 (1967): 992.

McDougal, M. S., W. M. Reisman, and A. R. Willard. "The World Processes of Effective Power: The Global War System." In M. S. McDougal and W. M. Reisman, eds., *Power and Politics in Quest of Law*. Dordrecht, Netherlands: Martinus Nijhoff, 1985, 357.

McNair, A. D. "The Function and Different Character of Treaties." *British Yearbook of International Law* 11 (1930): 100.

Morozov, G. "The Socialist Conception of International Organization." In G. Abi-Saab, ed., *The Concept of International Organization*. Paris: UNESCO, 1981, 179.

Mourik, M. "UNESCO: Structural Origins of Crisis and Needed Reforms." In J. Harrod and N. Schrijver, eds., *The UN Under Attack*. Aldershot, UK: Ashgate, 1988, 123.

Mowbray, A. "The Role of the European Court of Human Rights in the Promotion of Democracy." *Public Law* (1999): 703.

Munch, W. "The Joint Inspection Unit of the United Nations and the Specialized Agencies." *Max Planck Yearbook of United Nations Law* 2 (1998): 287.

Murphy, J. F. "International Crimes." In O. Schachter and C. C. Joyner, eds., *United Nations Legal Order*. Cambridge, UK: Cambridge University Press, 1996, 993.

Mutua, M. W. "The Ideology of Human Rights." *Virginia Journal of International Law* 36 (1996): 589.

Nanda, V. P. "Environment." In O. Schachter and C. C. Joyner, eds., *United Nations Legal Order*. Cambridge, UK: Cambridge University Press, 1996, 631.

Ndiaye, B. "International Co-operation to Promote Democracy and Human Rights: Principles and Programmes." *Review of the International Commission of Jurists* 49 (1992): 23.

Nsereko, D. D. "The International Court, Impartiality, and Judges *Ad Hoc*." *Indian Journal of International Law* 13 (1973): 207.

O'Brian, J. C. "The International Tribunal for Violations of International Humanitarian Law in the Former Yugoslavia." *American Journal of International Law* 87 (1993): 639.

Ofuatey-Kodjoe, W. "Self-Determination." In O. Schachter and C. C. Joyner, eds., *United Nations Legal Order*. Cambridge, UK: Cambridge University Press, 1996, 349.

Ortega, M. C. "The ILC Adopts the Draft Code of Crimes Against the Peace and Security of Mankind." *Max Planck Yearbook of United Nations Law* 1 (1997): 283.

Ott, H. E. "Global Climate." *Yearbook of Environmental Law* (1997): 174.

Pallemaerts, M. "International Environmental Law from Stockholm to Rio: Back to the Future?" In P. Sands, ed., *Greening International Law.* London: Earthscan, 1993, 1.

Partch, K. J. "Freedom of Conscience and Expression and Political Freedoms." In L. Henkin, ed., *The International Bill of Rights: The Covenant on Civil and Political Rights.* New York: Columbia University Press, 1981, 240.

Petersmann, E-U. "How to Promote the International Rule of Law? Contributions by the WTO Appellate Review System." In J. Cameron and K. Campbell, eds., *Dispute Resolution in the World Trade Organization.* London: Cameron May, 1998, 75.

Pierce, J. C. "The Haitian Crisis and the Future of Collective Enforcement of Democratic Governance." *Law and Policy in International Business* 27 (1996): 477.

Pollux. "The Interpretation of the Charter." *British Yearbook of International Law* 23 (1946): 54.

Quigley, J. "Security Council Fact Finding: A Prerequisite for the Prevention of War." *Florida Journal of International Law* 7 (1992): 191.

———. "The United States and the United Nations in the Persian Gulf War: New Order or Disorder?" *Cornell Journal of International Law* 25 (1992): 1.

Quintana, J. J. "The International Court and the Formulation of General International Law: The Law of Maritime Delimitation as an Example." In A. S. Muller, D. Raic, and J. M. Thuransky, eds., *The International Court of Justice: Its Future Role After Fifty Years.* The Hague: Martinus Nijhoff, 1997, 367.

Rama-Montaldo, M. "International Legal Personality and the Implied Powers of International Organizations." *British Yearbook of International Law* (1970): 111.

Reisman, W. M., and D. L. Stevick. "The Applicability of International Law Standards to United Nations Economic Sanctions Programmes." *European Journal of International Law* 9 (1998): 86.

Roberts, L. D. "United Nations Security Council Resolution 687 and Its Aftermath: The Implications for Domestic Authority and the Need for Legitimacy." *New York University Journal of International Law and Politics* (1993): 593.

Rosas, A. "Democracy and Human Rights." In A. Rosas and J. Helgesen, eds., *Human Rights in a Changing East-West Perspective.* London: Pinter, 1990, 22.

Rosenne, S. "State Responsibility and International Crimes: Further Reflections on Article 19 of the Draft Articles on State Responsibility." *New York University Journal of International Law and Politics* 30 (1997–1998): 145.

Rostow, E.V. "Until What? Enforcement Action or Collective Self-Defense?" *American Journal of International Law* 85 (1991): 506.

Schachter, O. "Review of Kelsen: *Law of the United Nations.*" *Yale Law Journal* 61 (1951): 189.
———. "Principles of International Social Justice." In G. Wilner, ed., *Essays in Tribute to Wolfgang Friedman.* The Hague: Martinus Nijhoff, 1979, 251.
———. "United Nations Law in the Gulf Conflict." *American Journal of International Law* 85 (1991): 452.
———. "United Nations Legal Order: An Overview." In O. Schachter and C. C. Joyner, eds., *United Nations Legal Order.* Cambridge, UK: Cambridge University Press, 1996, 1.
Schermers, H. G. "The International Court of Justice in Relation to Other Courts." In A. S. Muller, D. Raic, and J. M. Thuransky, eds., *The International Court of Justice: Its Future Role After Fifty Years.* The Hague: Martinus Nijhoff, 1997, 261.
———. "We the Peoples of the United Nations." *Max Planck Yearbook of United Nations Law* 1 (1997): 117.
Schlemmer-Schulte, S. "The World Bank Inspection Panel: A Model for Other International Organizations." In N. M. Blokker and H. G. Schermers, eds., *Proliferation of International Organizations: Legal Issues.* The Hague: Kluwer, 2001, 483.
Schreuer, C. H. "Recommendations and the Traditional Sources of International Law." *German Yearbook of International Law* 20 (1977): 103.
Schuett, O. "The International War Crimes Tribunal for the Former Yugoslavia: Peace Versus Justice." *International Peacekeeping* 4 (1997): 91.
Schwarzenberger, G. "The Problem of an International Criminal Law." *Current Legal Problems* 3 (1950): 263.
Sen, G. "UNCTAD and International Economic Reform." In P. Taylor and A. J. R. Groom, eds., *Global Issues in the United Nations' Framework.* London: Macmillan, 1989, 245.
Seyersted, F. "International Personality of Intergovernmental Organizations." *Indian Journal of International Law* 4 (1964): 1.
———. "Basic Distinctions in the Law of International Organizations: Practice Versus Legal Doctrine." In J. Makarczyk, ed., *Theory of International Law at the Threshold of the Twenty-First Century.* The Hague: Kluwer, 1996, 691.
Seymour-Ure, C. "War Cabinets in Limited Wars: Korea, Suez, and the Falklands." *Public Administration* 62 (1984): 181.
Shahabuddeen, M. "The World Court at the Turn of the Century." In A. S. Muller, D. Raic, and J. M. Thuransky, eds., *The International Court of Justice: Its Future Role After Fifty Years.* The Hague: Martinus Nijhoff, 1997, 3.
Shaw, M. N. "The Security Council and the International Court of Justice: Judicial Drift and Judicial Function." In A. S. Muller, D. Raic, and J. M. Thuransky, eds., *The International Court of Justice: Its Future Role After Fifty Years.* The Hague: Martinus Nijhoff, 1997, 219.
Shihata, I. F. I. "The World Bank and 'Governance' Issues in Its Borrowing Members." In I. F. I. Shihata, *The World Bank in a Changing World.* The Hague: Kluwer, 1991, 53.

————. "Implementation, Enforcement, and Compliance with International Environmental Agreements: Practical Suggestions in Light of the World Bank's Experience." *Georgetown International Environmental Law Review* 9 (1996): 37.

Simma, B. "NATO, the UN, and the Use of Force: Legal Aspects." *European Journal of International Law* 10 (1999): 16.

Sohn, L. B. "The Stockholm Declaration and the Human Environment." *Harvard International Law Journal* 14 (1973): 423.

Stoelting, D. "The Challenge of UN Monitored Elections in Independent Nations." *Stanford Journal of International Law* 28 (1992): 371.

Suy, E. "Democracy in International Relations: The Necessity of Checks and Balances." *Israel Yearbook of Human Rights* 26 (1996): 128.

Szasz, P. "General Law Making Processes." In O. Schachter and C. C. Joyner, eds., *United Nations Legal Order.* Cambridge, UK: Cambridge University Press, 1996, 37.

Tomuschat, C. "Obligations Arising from States Without or Against Their Will." *Receuil des Cours Académie de Droit International* 241 (1993): 195.

————. "International Law." In C. Tomuschat, ed., *The United Nations at Age Fifty.* The Hague: Kluwer, 1995, 281.

Tsakaloyannis, P. "International Society at a Crossroads: The Problem of Conceptualization." In D. Bourantonis and M. Evriviades, eds., *A United Nations for the Twenty-First Century.* The Hague: Kluwer, 1996, 19.

Tunkin, G. I. "The Legal Nature of the United Nations." *Recueil des Cours Académie de Droit International* 119 (1966): 7.

Valticos, N. "The International Labour Organization." In S. Schwebel, ed., *The Effectiveness of International Decisions.* Leiden, Netherlands: Sijthoff, 1971, 134.

Van Boven, T. "Political and Legal Control Mechanisms: Their Competition and Coexistence." In A. Eide and B. Hagvet, eds., *Human Rights in Perspective.* Oxford, UK: Blackwell, 1992, 36.

Vines, D. "The WTO in Relation to the Fund and the Bank: Competencies, Agendas, and Linkages." In A. O. Kreuger, ed., *The WTO as an International Organization.* Chicago: University of Chicago Press, 1998, 59.

Vu, N. T. "The Holding of Free and Fair Elections in Cambodia: The Achievement of the United Nations' Impossible Mission." *Michigan Journal of International Law* 16 (1995): 1177.

Wadrzyk, M. E. "Is It Appropriate for the World Bank to Promote Democratic Standards in a Borrower Country?" *Wisconsin International Law Journal* 17 (1997): 553.

Walter, C. "Security Council Control Over Regional Action." *Max Planck Yearbook of United Nations Law* 1 (1997): 129.

Warbrick, C. "The United Nations System: A Place for Criminal Courts?" *Transnational Law and Contemporary Problems* 5 (1995): 237.

————. "International Criminal Courts and Fair Trial." *Journal of Armed Conflict Law* 3 (1998): 45.

Watson, R. "Constitutionalism, Judicial Review, and the World Court." *Harvard Journal of International Law* 34 (1993): 1.

Weiss, E. B. "Judicial Independence and Impartiality: A Preliminary Inquiry." In L. Damrosch, ed., *The International Court at a Crossroads.* Dobbs Ferry, NY: Transnational, 1987, 123.

Werksman, J. D. "Greening Bretton Woods." In P. Sands, ed., *Greening International Law.* London: Earthscan, 1993, 65.

White, N. D. "Commentary on the Protection of the Kurdish Safe-Haven: Operation Desert Strike." *Journal of Armed Conflict Law* 1 (1996): 197.

———. "To Review or Not to Review: The Lockerbie Cases Before the World Court." *Leiden Journal of International Law* 12 (1999): 401.

———. "The Legality of Bombing in the Name of Humanity." *Journal of Conflict and Security Law* 5 (2000): 27.

———. "The World Court, the WHO, and the UN System." In N. M. Blokker and H. G. Schermers, eds., *Proliferation of International Organizations: Legal Issues.* The Hague: Kluwer, 2001, 85.

———. "The UK: Increasing International Commitment Requires Greater Parliamentary Involvement." In C. Ku and H. Jacobson, eds., *Democratic Accountability and International Institutions: Using Military Forces.* Cambridge, UK: Cambridge University Press, 2002, 410.

White, N. D., and R. Cryer. "Unilateral Enforcement of Resolution 687: A Threat Too Far?" *California Western International Law Journal* 29 (1999): 243.

White, N. D., and O. Ulgen. "The Security Council and the Decentralized Military Option: Constitutionality and Function." *Netherlands International Law Review* 44 (1997): 378.

Williams, M. P. Silveira. "UN Commission on Sustainable Development." *Yearbook of International Environmental Law* (1996): 374.

———. "United Nations Commission on Sustainable Development." *Yearbook of International Environmental Law* (1997): 464.

Winkelman, I. "Bringing the Security Council into a New Era." *Max Planck Yearbook of United Nations Law* 1 (1997): 35.

Winter, R. L. "Reconciling the GATT and WTO with Multilateral Environmental Agreements: Can We Have Our Cake and Eat It?" *Columbia Journal of Environmental Law and Policy* 11 (2000): 223.

Wofford, C. "A Greener Future at the WTO: The Refinement of WTO Jurisprudence on Environmental Exceptions to GATT." *Harvard Environmental Law Review* 24 (2000): 563.

Wright, Q. "Recognition and Self-Determination." *Proceedings of the American Society of International Law* 48 (1954): 29.

Zamora, S. "Economic Relations and Development." In O. Schachter and C. C. Joyner, eds., *United Nations Legal Order.* Cambridge, UK: Cambridge University Press, 1996, 503.

Zimmermann, A. "The Creation of a Permanent International Criminal Court." *Max Planck Yearbook of United Nations Law* (1998): 169.

Zoller, E. "The Corporate Will of the United Nations and the Rights of the Minority." *American Journal of International Law* 81 (1987): 610.

Index

About the Book

To what extent does the United Nations system work? This comprehensive survey of the world's most important family of international organizations examines the structure and powers of the United Nations and considers whether it is achieving what it set out to do.

Focusing on legal rather than political issues, White first examines the objectives of the United Nations, not only as defined in the original charter and the constituent documents of its various agencies but also in terms of how its goals and values have been implemented. He then explores its institutional structure, explaining legal powers and relationships; he also evaluates the various bodies in terms of democratic accountability and transparency. In the core of the book—a wide-ranging review of UN activities—he assesses whether the organization has sufficient powers to implement its goals in the key areas of security, justice, human rights, the environment, and economic development.

Nigel D. White is professor of international organizations at the University of Nottingham. His many publications include *Keeping the Peace: The United Nations and the Maintenance of International Peace and Security* and *The Law of International Organizations*. He is also editor of the *Journal of Conflict and Security Law*.